James Lorenzo Bowen

History of the Thirty-Seventh Regiment

James Lorenzo Bowen

History of the Thirty-Seventh Regiment

ISBN/EAN: 9783337412265

Printed in Europe, USA, Canada, Australia, Japan

Cover: Foto ©ninafisch / pixelio.de

More available books at **www.hansebooks.com**

HISTORY

OF THE

Thirty-Seventh Regiment

MASS. VOLUNTEERS,

IN THE

CIVIL WAR OF 1861-1865,

WITH A COMPREHENSIVE SKETCH OF THE DOINGS OF MASSACHUSETTS
AS A STATE, AND OF THE PRINCIPAL CAMPAIGNS
OF THE WAR.

By JAMES L. BOWEN.

CLARK W BRYAN & COMPANY, PUBLISHERS,
HOLYOKE, MASS., AND NEW YORK CITY.
1884.

COPYRIGHT, 1884,
BY JAMES L. BOWEN.

CLARK W. BRYAN & CO., PRINTERS, HOLYOKE, MASS.
111 BROADWAY, NEW YORK.

TO
THE MEMORY
OF
THOSE BRAVE MEN
WHOSE NAMES FORM OUR
ROLL OF HONOR
THIS RECORD OF THEIR SACRIFICE
AT DUTY'S CALL
IS REVERENTLY DEDICATED
BY
THEIR COMRADE
The Author

OUR ILLUSTRATIONS.

It is believed that no illustration which could be presented as a frontispiece would be more universally pleasing to members of the Thirty-seventh regiment than a faithful portraiture of the colors which for nearly three years they faithfully followed. The tattered standards were therefore carefully taken from their resting place in the State House, at Boston, photographed by E. F. Smith of that city in several different positions, and from the most satisfactory production the accompanying picture was made.

The excellent view of "Camp Edwards," directly after its occupation by the regiment, before the later decorations were added, is reproduced from the larger lithograph drawn by Hospital Steward W. A. Champney. Both of the present lithographs are from the establishment of Milton Bradley Company of Springfield.

TO THE READER.

The first attempt at a historical sketch of the Thirty-seventh Massachusetts Regiment was a paper read by General Edwards at the reunion in Springfield, September 19, 1871. While the document thus presented was necessarily little more than an epitome of the service of the organization, it excited great interest and woke the demand for a more complete and detailed production. The following year, at the reunion at Pittsfield, September 24, the first appointment of a historian was made, E. P Bridgman being selected. Two years later, at the Bernardston gathering of 1874, Colonel Montague was appointed historian, and the following year the office passed to Lieutenant S. E. Nichols, the following vote being taken: "That Lieutenant Nichols be urgently requested to fill the office of historian of the regiment. In case of his refusal so to do the matter to be left in the hands of the Executive Committee."

At the Northampton reunion of September 8 and 9, 1876, " It was voted that Comrade W E. Lewis be appointed historian of the Association, that he be authorized to employ any assistance he deems necessary, and that this organization pledge itself to give him all details in their possession of interest to the companies or regiment, and that he shall have authority to draw upon the treasurer through the secretary for such disbursements for this purpose as in his judgment shall be deemed proper. Upon Comrade Lewis's acceptance of this office a vote of thanks was tendered him by the association."

At the Northampton reunion of 1877 Lieutenant Lewis was reelected historian, though no report was furnished regarding his work. At the meeting of 1878 at Westfield a communication was read from him stating that "the history would probably be ready for publication by the next annual reunion," and he was again elected to the position. The following year no definite action was taken regarding the history, but the records show that a letter was read from Comrade Lewis, containing, it would seem, no specific information. At the gathering of 1880 a letter was read from the historian "expressing expectation that the history of the regiment would be completed during the coming year." At the same time "the committee on the history was newly constituted to consist of the following members: W E. Lewis, S. E. Nichols and William Bliss." The record of the meeting of 1881 says: "It was voted that General Oliver Edwards, Colonel George L. Montague, Captain William Bliss, Colonel Thomas G. Colt, Lieutenant S. E. Nichols and Lieutenant William E. Lewis be a committee to have full charge of the revision and publication of the completed history of the Thirty-seventh Regiment."

At the meeting of the association at Westfield, September 19, 1882, a report of progress was made by the committee, of which Comrade James L. Bowen was elected a member. At a meeting of the committee held some three months later Comrade Bowen presented briefly his idea of the form which a regimental history should take and it was voted to instruct him to prepare a history of the regiment on such a plan. At the 1883 reunion Mr. Bowen made a report of progress, saying that it was hoped to have the book ready for delivery during the early part of the coming year. To fill the vacancy in the committee caused by the death of Colonel T G. Colt, Captain Walter B. Smith was appointed, and Captain H. M. Abbott was added to the number.

Somewhat longer time than was anticipated has necessarily been consumed in the preparation of the book, but it is hoped that the work may be found sufficiently satisfactory in character to compensate for the delay.   S. E. NICHOLS, *Secretary*.

BUFFALO, N. Y., AUGUST, 1884.

PREFACE.

In this age of book-making no apology is needed for presenting in permanent form the present narrative. As will be seen by the statement of the History Committee, the matter of preparing a history of the Thirty-seventh Massachusetts Regiment had been long discussed, and numerous steps taken looking to that end, when at a meeting of the Committee held at Pittsfield, December 15, 1882, I was asked to undertake the task. The invitation was accepted, not without serious misgivings. Arduous duties in connection with daily journalism promised very little leisure for the new undertaking; my retirement from wounds previous to the later campaigns of the regiment prevented that full personal knowledge of its movements so desirable; my position as a private soldier was not one to especially qualify for the historian's office; the records of the regiment were found to be missing or incomplete; its members were widely scattered, many of them with details of soldier life quite driven from mind by the stress of 20 years of active civil pursuits. For these reasons leniency is craved for any shortcomings which may appear in the following pages.

The book has been written with a sincere desire to do justice to a deserving organization; having no prejudice and no individual ends to serve, I have sought to record the work of the regiment faithfully and impartially. The scope of the volume has been broadened to include features which, while not directly connected with the story of the Thirty-seventh regiment, it seemed after this lapse of time desirable to present, that the doings of the regiment might be traced with an understanding of contemporaneous and relative events. The details of personal history have not been closely followed, and in most cases no attempt is made to trace the fortunes of individuals subsequent to the disbanding of the organization. It did not seem to me either desirable to undertake to do so in connection with the extended scope of the work or possible to make such a record if attempted in any way satisfactory or complete. At the same time I have striven to follow the regiment closely in its varying fortunes, and to reproduce its experiences on the march, in camp or on the field of action, with the unfolding of military life as it presented itself to the citizen-soldier.

I desire to express my sincere thanks to all comrades and others who have kindly assisted me in collecting material for the volume. Necessarily I have been obliged to make many demands on the time and patience of others. In this direction I have met only kindness and encouragement. I feel under especial obligation to General Charles Devens, General H. S. Briggs, Mrs. E. J Morse and Rev. J. W Lane ; and among members of the regiment to Lieutenant Colonel Hopkins, Sergeant A. G. Taylor and George C. Clapp, in addition to the History Committee, all of whom have responded promptly to all demands made upon them. I must especially mention the tireless and invaluable services of the Secretary, Lieutenant S. E. Nichols.

In the hope that to the survivors of the regiment and the friends of the fallen the book may prove an acceptable record of their deeds in the day of supreme trial, it is sent forth.   J. L. B.

SPRINGFIELD, MASS., SEPTEMBER, 1884.

CONTENTS BY CHAPTERS.

I.—FROM SECESSION TO ANTIETAM.   17
The Election of Lincoln.
Revolt of the Southern States.
Opening of the War.
The Operations of the Army of the Potomac.

II.—MASSACHUSETTS IN THE WAR.   42
The Record of the Commonwealth.
Its Public Men.
Its Soldiers.
Its Citizens.

III.—THE THIRTY-SEVENTH REGIMENT.   58
The Gathering at Camp Briggs.
Character of the Command.
The Original Roster of Officers.
Personal Notes and Incidents.

IV.—FROM PITTSFIELD TO DOWNSVILLE.   68
The Journey to Washington.
Life at Camp Chase.
Via Frederick and South Mountain to the Army of the Potomac.

V.—THE ADVANCE TO FALMOUTH.   82
The Expedition to Hancock and Cherry Run.
Into the Land of Secession.
A Change of Commanders.
Incidents by the Way.
White Plains and "Camp Misery."

VI.—ON THE RAPPAHANNOCK.   104
   The Battle of Fredericksburg.
   In Winter Quarters.
   The Mud March.
   Camp Edwards.

VII.—THE ARMY UNDER HOOKER.   127
   Events in the West.
   Chancellorsville, Marye's Hights and Salem Church.

VIII.—TO GETTYSBURG. .   153
   After the Defeat.
   The Skirmish with A. P. Hill.
   The Northward Movement.
   Exit Hooker, Enter Meade.
   The March to the Battle-field.

IX.—THE TURN OF THE TIDE.   175
   The Battle of Gettysburg.
   The Thirty-seventh Tried by Fire.
   The Pursuit of Lee.
   Climbing the Mountains.
   Once More in Virginia.

X.—THE REGIMENT IN NEW YORK.   202
   The Union Victories.
   Northern Treachery and Disloyalty.
   The Riot in New York.
   The Thirty-seventh sent to the City.
   Its Creditable Service There.

XI.—AGAIN AT THE FRONT.   223
   The Return Trip.
   The Fortunes of the Army.
   The Victory at Rappahannock Station.
   The Dismal Expedition to Mine Run.
   Changes and Promotions.

XII.—WINTER ON THE RAPIDAN. 245
The Closing Year.
Progress of the War.
The Winter Camp and the Life in it.
A Futile Expedition.

XIII.—NINE DAYS OF CARNAGE. 267
The Reorganization of the Army.
The Grapple in the Wilderness.
By the Left Flank to Spottsylvania.
Death of Sedgwick.
"The Angle."

XIV.—A GLANCE TO THE REAR. 299
The Wounded and Dying.
Hospital Scenes and Incidents.
The Christian and Sanitary Commissions.

XV.—SPADES AND BULLETS. 313
The Closing Struggles at Spottsylvania.
"By the Left Flank."
Crossing Swords at North Anna.
The Death Harvest at Cold Harbor.

XVI.—GOING TO MEET EARLY. 337
In Front of Petersburg.
At Reams Station.
Early in Maryland.
Fort Stevens.
The Spencer Rifle.

XVII.—THE CAMPAIGN UNDER SHERIDAN. 357
The Wagon Trains.
Seeking Early by March and Countermarch.
Sheridan at the Helm.
The Fight at Charlestown.
The Battle of Opequan.

XVIII.—THE SERVICE AT WINCHESTER.   382
On Provost Duty.
Changes and Promotions.
Battle of Cedar Creek.
Sherman's Campaign.

XIX —THE PETERSBURG CAMPAIGN.   396
Again in the Trenches.
Days of Siege.
At Hatcher's Run.
Preparing to Strike.
Fall of Petersburg.

XX.—ONE COUNTRY AND ONE FLAG.   413
Lee's Flight and the Pursuit.
The Grapple at Sailor's Creek.
The Surrender at Appomattox.
In Search of Johnston.

XXI.—THE CLOSING SCENES.   425
Facing Northward.
Reviews at Richmond and Washington.
The Final Roster.
Mustered Out.
The Welcome Home.

CHAPTER I.

FROM SECESSION TO ANTIETAM.

THE ELECTION OF LINCOLN.—REVOLT OF THE SOUTHERN STATES.—OPENING OF THE WAR.—THE OPERATIONS OF THE ARMY OF THE POTOMAC.

THE election of Abraham Lincoln of Illinois and Hannibal Hamlin of Maine, the Republican candidates for President and Vice-President of the United States, November 6, 1860, furnished the pretext for an attempt on the part of the Southern states for a division of the Union. In this movement South Carolina had been a leader, and its Legislature was the first to adopt an ordinance of secession, which was done on the 20th of December. Mississippi, Florida and Alabama followed her example on the 9th, 10th and 11th of January, 1861, Georgia on the 19th, Louisiana on the 26th and Texas the 1st of February. The action of these seven states, in declaring themselves no longer a part of the Federal Union, was thus taken long before the inauguration of Mr. Lincoln, and while the national government remained in the hands of their political friends. President Buchanan, undoubtedly loyal at heart, sat in his high office, dazed and helpless before the sweep of the tempest. Uncertain as to his duty, he met the most conflicting opinions from those to whom he turned for advice. Questions had arisen on which the Constitution shed no light—the situation was one which had not been provided for in the formation of the nation. But had his duty been never so clear, the President had no power with which to oppose the revolution. He sat in the midst of disloyalty. The cabinet, Congress, the departments, the army and navy were swarming with secessionists, and it was impossible to determine who was true and who false to the country he professed to serve. Men were daily resigning high positions of trust and hastening to join the councils of the conspirators. In the mean time the government property throughout the southern states and along the coast was being taken possession of in the name of the various states, and so well had affairs been manipulated in the interests of treason that at very few points was it possible for any resistance to be made. Forts, arsenals, naval vessels, navy-yards, custom-houses and the branch mint at New Orleans shared a common fate. Three forts on the Florida coast held out,—Pickens, Jefferson and Taylor,—and Fortress Monroe at Old Point Comfort, Va., was also saved to the Union; with these exceptions the entire governmental possessions were seized throughout the sea-board states south of the Potomac.

A convention of delegates from the seceded states met at Montgomery, Ala., on the 4th of February, and five days later the "Confederate States of America" were proclaimed a nation, Jefferson Davis of Mississippi being elected president, and A. H. Stephens of Georgia vice-president. On the 18th they were inaugurated, amid the most enthusiastic demonstrations throughout the Confederacy. Blinded and deluded, the Southern people indulged the wildest visions of a speedy and bloodless success, and the demagogues who were luring them to ruin were hailed as the heroes of a glorious cause.

A very different feeling prevailed at Washington and through the loyal states. The magnitude of the conspiracy and the threatening attitude of the insurgents, who were organizing in every part of the South, excited fears of some desperate attempt to prevent the inauguration of Mr. Lincoln; but the prompt measures of General Winfield Scott, in command of the available fragments of the United States army, prevented any hostile demonstration, and the ceremony transpired March 4 in the presence of an immense gathering of people without disturbing incident. The inaugural address of President Lincoln was conciliatory, almost to weakness, and its tenor was revoiced in the closing sentences: "We are not enemies, but friends. We must not be enemies. Though passion may have strained it must not break our bonds of affection. The mystic chords of memory, stretching from every battle-field and patriot grave to every living heart and hearthstone all over this broad land, will yet swell the chorus of the Union, when again touched, as they surely will be, by the better angels of our nature."

But words of reason and kindness had no power over ears split by the din of demagogues, and the inevitable conflict drew near. The initial clash was to come at Charleston, S. C., where Major Anderson, whom the opening of the troubles found in command of the fortifications of the harbor, had with a few men been for months practically besieged in Fort Sumter. As early as January an attempt had been made by President Buchanan to send provisions to the garrison, but the unarmed steamer carrying the supplies had been fired upon at the entrance to the harbor and returned to New York. On the 6th of February President Buchanan refused a demand made by Isaac W. Hayne for the surrender of the fort to South Carolina, and rapid preparations were made for its reduction. General P T. G. Beauregard was assigned to the command of the rebel forces early in March, and as Major Anderson refused to surrender his trust without explicit orders from his government, fire was opened on the fort April 12, and the following day terms of evacuation were agreed on.

The fall of Sumter marked the end of hesitation and banished all hopes of conciliation. The most important events followed rapidly. On the 15th President Lincoln called for 75,000 militia to serve for three months and ordered Congress to assemble in special session July 4. On the 17th President Davis of the Confederacy authorized privateering, and on the same day Virginia, which had been dallying over the question, finally decided upon secession. This precipitated like action in North Carolina, which was taken May 20, while Arkansas had also seceded on the 6th. The situation now became intensely critical. On the 19th of April the President proclaimed a blockade of the Southern ports, but it was at first only a paper blockade, for the government had no navy worthy the name, though the rapidity with which one was created was little short of marvelous. At the same time the first of the troops called from the loyal states began to arrive, the Sixth Massachusetts regiment fighting its way through a mob in the streets of Baltimore ; reaching the Capital that evening, but leaving the route behind it closed and Washington cut off from communication with the loyal portion of the country till General Butler with the Eighth Massachusetts regiment and some other forces opened a new route by way of Annapolis. Fort Pickens had been strengthened on the very day that the attack opened on Sumter. Fortress Monroe was saved from the designs of the Virginia forces under Magruder by the arrival of the Third and Fourth Massachusetts regiments, followed by others ; Baltimore was garrisoned and brought to its senses, though unwillingly ; and the Capital was soon safe from immediate danger ; the whole galaxy of the Free states rose to the support of the Union ;—but on the other hand many of the ablest officers of the army, including Hood, Lee and the Johnstons, had resigned their commissions to enter the Confederate service ; the fragments of the United States army in Texas were captured in detail ; the sturdy efforts of Governor Houston to hold that state loyal to the Union were overcome and himself finally swept from his loyalty by the current ; the border states of Kentucky, Tennessee and Missouri were strongly urged to secession, and it was a question whether or not they could be saved for the Union. Tennessee, in fact, voted secession in June, though the people of East Tennessee, like those of West Virginia, remained loyal and fought bitterly and bravely for their principles.

No sooner had the ordinance of secession passed in Virginia than active military operations were begun by a night expedition for the capture of the government armory and arsenal at Harper's Ferry. The loyal soldiers in charge of the post amounted to some 40 men under Lieutenant Roger Jones, and while the insurgents were preparing to march upon the place three companies of Virginia militia stationed there voted to disband. On the night of the 18th of April, learning that a large force was within a mile of the place, Lieutenant Jones fired the shops and arsenal and retreated with his little command into Pennsylvania. Thwarted in their attempt to capture the arms and buildings, the Confederates held and fortified the adjacent hights and gathered there a considerable force, threatening Washington and cutting off communication in that direction.

The situation had become most perplexing. Scores of regiments were ready to set out for Washington, but the way was blocked and they had no weapons. The arsenals in the loyal states had been depleted to put their contents within reach of the plotters, and the President, Secretary of War, and General Scott were hemmed in at the Capital. Fortunately General John E. Wool, in command of the Eastern Military District, comprising the region east of the Mississippi, was at New York, and feeling that the occasion demanded prompt action, he at once ordered the troops supplied with whatever arms could be obtained, and in securing transportation and forwarding soldiers he rendered a service that won the admiration of the people. Invaluable as was this service, it provoked so much official jealousy that General Wool was rebuked for taking such responsible steps without orders and sent to his home at Troy; but the popular indignation at the injustice was so strong and so vigorously expressed that he was in a short time given command of the district of Southeastern Virginia, with head-quarters at Fortress Monroe.

But the severest blow to the government was the loss of the Gosport or Norfolk navy-yard, which was evacuated and burned on the night of April 21, it being deemed impracticable to hold it longer. Here was a vast amount of naval property, heavy cannon to the number of 2,000, and 11 of the most valuable war vessels of the United States navy, though none of the latter were in a sea-going condition. A few were got away, and the rest with the buildings and stores were set on fire and abandoned; but the work of destruction was by no means thoroughly done, and the Confederates under General Taliaferro rescued millions of dollars worth of property, including the partially burned Merrimac, which was afterward to become so famous.

Thus far the government had struck no offensive blows, and

those which it had dealt in defense of its possessions had been pitiably weak. With the management of affairs so largely in the hands of Southern men and sympathizers with rebellion, the way had been skillfully paved for the humiliation of the nation during the last months of Buchanan's administration. The arsenals at the North had on some pretext been nearly stripped of arms and munitions of war to supply those in the disaffected states, and the first care of the conspirators had been to secure these sinews of war for their own use. This work being completed, the Confederate Congress on the 6th of May formally declared war against the United States.

In the mean time the situation at Baltimore was becoming unbearable. Following the assault upon the Sixth Massachusetts regiment and the destruction of the railroad bridges near the city, cutting off rail communication with New York and the East, the spirit of secession for a time ran wild and the city became an active rebel stronghold. Armed men poured in from all points, troops were organized and cannon maneuvered in the streets, while the display of the Stars and Stripes for 30 days was forbidden, on the ground that it would be dangerous to the peace. On the 5th of May General Butler, who had remained at Annapolis and gathered a considerable force there, finding that there was much latent Unionism in Baltimore and through the state, resolved to give it such encouragement as would if possible make it the controlling power and save the shedding of blood. For this purpose he moved a part of his forces to the Relay House, nine miles from the city, and established headquarters there. The effect was at once noticeable in the encouragement of loyalty, and plans were matured for the occupation of the city itself.

Before Butler's plans were perfected, General Patterson, commanding the department of Pennsylvania, decided to attempt a passage of loyal troops through Baltimore, and on the 9th of May some 1,200 infantry and artillery under Colonel F. E. Patterson, a son of the general, landed near Fort McHenry and marched through the city, not only unopposed but receiving many words of encouragement as they went. During the evening of the 13th General Butler with about 1,000 men and two field-pieces entered the city by train, the Sixth Massachusetts forming a part of the column. A heavy thunder storm was prevailing and few in the city knew of the presence of Federal soldiers till the morning papers printed a proclamation from the commander, dated at his head-quarters on Federal Hill, where the troops were encamped. The effect of the movement was all that had been counted upon. Considerable quantities of arms intended for the rebels were seized, the state wisely gave its voice for the Union, and General Butler, appointed by the President a major-general, was given command of a district embracing Eastern Virginia and the Carolinas, with head-quarters at Fortress Monroe.

It was early apparent that the Federal government was now in the hands of those who would protect the interests which had been confided to them. A week after the fall of Sumter the original telegrams for a year previous, on file in the principal telegraph offices, were seized by the United States marshals, and evidence damaging to many prominent sympathizers with treason was obtained. A few of the more active were arrested and committed to military prisons, the keepers of which refused to recognize the writs of habeas corpus which were obtained by their friends. This measure, like many another which the exigencies of the struggle necessitated, evoked sharp discussion in the papers and elsewhere, but its lesson was not lost upon the disloyal, while encouraging the loyal.

Already it had become evident that the 75,000 militia which had been called into service for three months would not prove sufficient for the purpose of restoring peace, and on the 3d of May President Lincoln called for 42,000 volunteers for three years, 18,-000 sailors for the manning of the fast increasing navy, and some 23,000 recruits for the regular army. This call was responded to with alacrity, for the loyal states were full of volunteer organizations anxious to be taken into the service of the nation.

The Capital was swarming with military life; the public buildings had become vast barracks, and the work of training and disciplining a large army went steadily forward. On the 23d of May, learning that the Confederates contemplated the occupation and fortification of the hights on the Virginia side of the Potomac which commanded the city, some Union troops were ordered across the river to take possession of Alexandria and guard the approaches to the city. The movement was unopposed by the insurgents, who were gathering in force at Manassas Junction, 30 miles from Washington, a point giving them direct railroad communication with the Shenandoah valley, Richmond and the entire Confederate states. But a sad loss was sustained by the Union army in the assassination of Colonel E. E. Ellsworth of the New York Fire Zouaves at Alexandria on the morning of the 24th, by which the country was deprived of the services of one of its most promising young officers.

This loss was speedily followed by another of like nature and even more mortifying in character. General Butler, in command at Fortress Monroe, learning that the rebel Colonel Magruder was in a threatening attitude at the Bethel churches, sent a night expedition of two columns, June 9, to surprise and destroy the force. The result was a series of disasters. The two columns fired into each other in the darkness, alarming the enemy, who had concentrated in a strong position at Big Bethel, where they were attacked without plan or concert, the result being a defeat of the Union troops with a loss of 50 killed and wounded. Among the former were Major Winthrop, of General Butler's staff and his military secretary, and Lieutenant Greble of the artillery,—both very gallant and promising young officers.

A month passed without serious demonstrations on either side, when the loyal heart was gladdened by the sharp and very successful campaign of General McClellan in Western Virginia. Thirty-nine of the Northwestern counties of Virginia had refused to follow the rest of the state in seceding from the Union, and a considerable force of Confederate soldiers was scattered through the region to manufacture public sentiment favorable to the Southern cause. Under McClellan's vigorous attack the rebel commander, General Garnett, was killed at Carrick's Ford, his forces captured or dispersed, and the people temporarily freed from the presence of the foe.

Mean time the terms of enlistment of the three-months' militia were about expiring, and it became necessary, not only from that fact but to appease the clamor of the impatient people of the loyal states, that a blow should be struck against the Confederate force threatening Washington. On the 1st of June General Beauregard, flushed with his conquest of Sumter, arrived at Richmond and took command of what was styled the Department of Alexandria. His main force was gathered near Manassas Junction, with fortified outposts advanced to Centreville and Fairfax Court House.

General McDowell, in command of the Union army, advanced slowly, the enemy readily abandoning their outposts, till on the 18th of July General Tyler's command encountered a force under General Longstreet strongly posted at Blackburn's Ford, and a sharp skirmish convinced the Federal commander that a direct assault was impracticable. It was decided, therefore, to throw the main body of the army well to the right, so as to strike the Confederates on the left flank and gain their rear; but being obliged to wait for supplies it was not till the night of the 20th that McDowell was ready to move. By a strange coincidence Beauregard also issued orders on the same day for the advance of his army on the following morning, and he in turn planned to strike his enemy on the left flank. After the issuance of this order General J. E. Johnston arrived on the ground from Winchester, where he had been facing the Union force under General Patterson, bringing a portion of his army with more following. Being the senior officer he took command, approved the plans of Beauregard, and prepared to advance next day.

The attack by McDowell, intended to be delivered at daylight, was several hours late, but it anticipated the Confederate movement and served to put Johnston on the defensive. With varying fortunes, but generally favorable to the Union arms, the conflict raged till near 4 o'clock, when the coming of their fresh troops from the Shenandoah valley, with reinforcements from other points, enabled the Confederates to throw a heavy force on the Federal right flank, which broke in some disorder—the panic spread rapidly, and soon the day was irreparably lost. The retreat was well covered by the troops that stood firm, and the wreck of the army gathered unmolested within the strong defenses in front of the Capital.

On the following day General McClellan was summoned to Washington and given the command of the Army of the Potomac, his recent success in Western Virginia having brought him into deserved prominence. He assumed command on the 27th, and at the same time many other changes took place. General Scott, who up to this time had been general-in-chief, was on account of age and infirmity relieved from active duty: General Patterson, whose term of service had expired, was succeeded by General Banks in the department of the Shenandoah; General John A. Dix took command at Baltimore in place of Banks, and General Rosecrans succeeded to McClellan's former command.

The new commander devoted his wonderful powers as an organizer to the constructing of a new army, the perfecting of the defenses about the seat of government, and bringing order out of chaos generally. The magnitude of the undertaking was now more justly realized, and to the work of preparation the remainder of the summer, the succeeding autumn and winter were given. Gradually an impregnable line of works containing more than 50 forts grew up around the Capital, and within them gathered an army fine in material, admirable in discipline, perfect in equipment and formidable in numbers.

About the middle of October a portion of the Federal army advanced into Virginia as far as Fairfax Court House, the enemy retiring to Centreville, and a few days later a small force without support or means of retreat was thrown across the Potomac near Leesburg, and the result was the terrible disaster of Ball's Bluff, which sent a chill to every loyal heart. The fight was opened by Colonel Devens with the Fifteenth Massachusetts regiment, which had been sent forward on reconnaissance, and Colonel E. D. Baker, United States senator from California, who commanded the brigade, decided to reinforce him and make a stand. In the struggle which followed Colonel Baker lost his life, his troops were driven back to and into the river with sad loss, many were captured, and Colonel Devens only escaped by swimming his horse across the Potomac. With the exception of some insignificant skirmishes,—in one of which near Drainsville General Ord's brigade quite severely punished the command of the Southern cavalry leader Stuart,—nothing more was done by the Army of the Potomac till the following spring, and in a short time the main force was drawn snugly within its intrenchments about Washington.

The close of 1861 brought mingled hope and fear to the Union heart. Along the entire frontier from Virginia to Missouri rival forces were almost daily coming into conflict, and the Federal arms seemed, on the whole, to be making progress. On the 7th of November was achieved the first great naval success—the capture of Forts Walker and Beauregard, at Hilton Head, on the South Carolina coast, and on the same day General Grant, by his attack upon the intrenched camp of the Confederates at Belmont, which he occupied and destroyed, successfully cutting his way through an overwhelming force which closed in about his small command, laid the foundation for those great military successes that followed at Forts Henry and Donelson, to be crowned at the decisive, though critical, battle of Shiloh the following April. Of the operations in the great western field it is sufficient for the purposes of this sketch to say that the Union cause steadily advanced, with few defeats and no disasters.

When winter came it found the nation greatly disturbed over the "Trent affair." The Southern commissioners to England and France, Mason and Slidell, had been taken from the British mail steamer Trent, by Captain Wilkes of the United States navy; an act which at once aroused the ire of the offended Britons, and the demand for the return of the captives to the protection of the English flag was accompanied by the most vigorous preparations for war on the part of her majesty's government. As this was a distinct avowal of the "American principle" on which the war of 1812 had been fought, and a complete change of the British base, the moral victory was considered satisfactory compensation for the loss of the prisoners, and they were at once surrendered.

Edwin M. Stanton succeeded Simon Cameron as Secretary of War, January 13, 1862, and early in the following month, while General Grant was in the midst of his successful campaign, General Burnside's expedition, which had sailed nearly a month previous, relieved the popular anxiety by the capture of Roanoke Island, whence a month later his forces moved to victory at Newbern. The close of February also saw General Butler's expedition against New Orleans well on its way to one of the most substantial victories of the war. Thus far the navy, in its operations both at sea and on the rivers, had been remarkably successful; but a sad disaster was now in store for it. On the 8th of March the rebel iron-clad Merrimac, constructed from the Federal steam-frigate of that name, which had been captured with the Gosport navy-yard and repaired, came down upon the Union fleet in Hampton Roads, destroying the frigates Cumberland and Congress, and retiring to her lair at night intending to finish the fleet next day. But when in the early morning she came steaming down to the encounter a new antagonist met her—the original Monitor, then on its trial trip. A desperate encounter followed, in which the Merrimac, though not disabled, was so much damaged that she steamed away toward Norfolk, and never again ventured forth.

With the opening of spring came the long-looked-for movement of General McClellan's Army of the Potomac. It had been decided to adopt the plan favored by the commander of moving against Richmond by way of Fortress Monroe and the Yorktown peninsula with the main force, leaving in the defenses about the Capital a sufficient force to defend the place from any assault by the Confederates, whose main body still held Manassas and Centreville. On the 8th of March, however, General Johnston evacuated these points and retired toward Richmond. The Union army crossed the Potomac next day, and the cavalry followed the enemy as far as the Rappahannock, but there was no other pursuit, and on the 17th the embarkation of the army at Alexandria began. The force under McClellan's immediate command consisted of something over 200,000 men, and had been divided by the President into five army corps, commanded respectively by Generals McDowell, Sumner, Heintzelman, Keyes and Banks—the latter operating with his Fifth Corps in the Shenandoah valley and one division of Sumner's Second Corps being sent to Fremont in the mountain department. The 1st of April found Sumner's two remaining divisions and the Third and Fourth Corps safely landed, though the troops on the transports had nervously looked for the re-appearance of the dreaded Merrimac. McClellan came the next day, and on the 3d the army moved toward Yorktown, 24 miles distant. Magruder still held the rebel command on the peninsula, and he had made his position as strong as possible with the small force available. At Yorktown his principal line of works was encountered, running entirely across the peninsula along the line of Warwick Creek. The advance thus far had been through swamps and mud over corduroy roads, and before the apparently formidable intrenchments the 100,000 men halted. A siege of Yorktown, which lasted a month, ensued. In the mean time Franklin's division of McDowell's First Corps arrived on transports, but the remainder of the corps, which McClellan expected, was retained for the defense of the Capital. This retention disconcerted the commander's plans for a flank movement on the enemy's position by water, and the siege went on. On the 16th of April an attempt was made to pierce the line of defense, and a part of the Vermont Brigade was thrown across the creek at Lee's Mills, making a lodgment in the works, but the brave fellows were not supported and were obliged to retire with serious loss.

The preparations for opening fire were all completed, when on the 4th of May it was discovered that the works were deserted, and the Confederates in full retreat up the peninsula. Pursuit was at once ordered, and Stoneman's cavalry, in the advance, came upon the enemy toward night, in strong force behind intrenchments near Williamsburg. Next day the battle of Williamsburg was fought, principally by Hooker's division, which maintained a desperate struggle all through the day, being hard pressed till Hancock's brigade brought them relief by a skillful movement across a narrow dam and a vigorous attack upon the Confederate flank. Late in the afternoon McClellan came up, and preparations were at once made for a decisive battle on the morrow, but when the morning of the 6th dawned it revealed only abandoned earthworks in front of the Union army.

The skillful tactics of the Southern chieftain, General Joseph E. Johnston, had thus delayed the Federal advance till his own army could be concentrated at its chosen position in front of Richmond, to which all the troops available were summoned. Huger was withdrawn from Norfolk and the dreaded Merrimac blown up, allowing that post to fall into the hands of General Wool's troops, advancing from Fortress Monroe, and the Union gunboats ascended the James river till checked by Fort Darling at Drewry's Bluff, 12 miles below Richmond; the force in front of Burnside in North Carolina was mostly recalled to the threatened Capital, and every preparation made for a desperate defense. McClellan's advance over the miserable roads was slow, so that two weeks were occupied in traversing the 50 miles from Williamsburg to the front of Johnston's lines on the Chickahominy.

Something of a reorganization of the Federal army had meantime been made. General Porter was made commander of a new corps, called the Fifth, composed of his own division of the Third Corps with those of McCall and Sykes; while the Sixth Corps, composed of the divisions of Smith of the Third Corps and Franklin of the First, was commanded by the latter. The army on the peninsula thus consisted of five corps, generally of two divisions each, and the men present for duty at the time of encountering the enemy seem to have been something over 115,000. The base of supplies was at White House, the head of navigation of the York river, up the right bank of which the army had thus far moved. Between McClellan and Richmond flowed the Chickahominy river, a sluggish, swampy stream, and as the army swung into position, Heintzelman and Keyes with their corps were thrown across that water course at Bottom's Bridge, about the 20th of May, the other corps remaining on the left or northern bank.

General McDowell with some 30,000 men had meantime been sent forward in support of the peninsular movement as far as Fredericksburg on the Rappahannock, his left being then at Bowling

Green. To establish connection with him, General Porter was instructed to surprise the Confederates at Hanover Court House under General Branch, which he did on the 27th, after a night's march in a heavy rain, thoroughly dispersing the Southern troops. But the defeat of General Banks by "Stonewall" Jackson in the Shenandoah valley recalled McDowell toward Washington, and McClellan was, for the second time, deprived of the assistance expected from him.

General Johnston, anticipating the junction of McDowell with McClellan, prepared to strike the latter with all his force before the conjunction occurred, and the result was the battle of Fair Oaks, which opened on the 31st of May. Changing the original programme somewhat, Johnston threw the bulk of his army upon the two Federal corps south of the Chickahominy; Casey's division, which received the first blow, was scattered, and although the Union soldiers fought desperately, the assailants steadily gained ground till late in the afternoon. At that time General Sumner, who had succeeded in getting a bridge across the river, brought forward Sedgwick's division of his corps, which met a flanking movement of the Confederates with a sharp attack, when the struggle ceased for the night. Beyond a terrible artillery fire, it was not seriously renewed the following day. Both sides had lost heavily, General Johnston being among the severely wounded, his command being taken by General Robert E. Lee, who was thenceforward to lead the Confederate Army of Northern Virginia to the close of its career at Appomattox, almost three years later. Each army re-possessed its former lines, and almost a month of inaction succeeded.

Finally McClellan seemed ready for the forward movement, and on the 25th of June Hooker's division, supported by other troops, was advanced a mile on the Richmond road, meeting slight resistance and holding the ground covered. Simultaneously with this success, the Union commander learned that Jackson had left the Shenandoah valley and was rapidly moving to strike his exposed right flank and cut him off from his base of supplies at White House. Immediate preparations were made for a change of base to the James river, hastened by the prompt and ponderous blows which attested the energy with which the Confederate plan was to be carried out. Porter's corps alone now held the north bank of the Chickahominy, and the brunt of the battle of Mechanicsville, on the 26th, fell upon McCall's division. These troops, the Pennsylvania Reserves, which did good service on many a hard-fought field, received a resolute attack by D. H. Hill's and Longstreet's forces, which was repulsed with heavy loss to the assailants. But no sooner had night fallen than the victors began to retreat from the field, and the next morning found the corps in a new position at Gaines's Mills, near the crossing of the river. There, on the following day, was fought one of the most stubborn contests of the campaign. The Southern troops under Hill, Longstreet and Jackson, impetuously and repeatedly attacked less than half their number, and the lone Fifth Corps as often held its ground in triumph. Near night the left gave way before the persistent hammering, and had been pressed back for some distance, when the arrival of reinforcements saved the corps from utter rout.

Daylight of the 28th found Porter's command across the river and the bridges destroyed behind it, when the enemy turned their attention to the supplies at White House. To their annoyance, most of the stores had been removed and the rest were fired at their approach. Divining now the real purpose of the Federal commander, they bent every energy toward cutting off or overwhelming his retreating columns. A succession of desperate struggles ensued. Magruder in direct pursuit came upon Sumner, who was protecting the rear at Savage's Station, on the 29th. Magruder attacked, only to be repulsed, and during the night Sumner followed the retreating army, though obliged to abandon his sick and wounded in hospitals. Desperate conflicts marked the 30th at White Oak Swamp and at Glendale. On the former field Franklin held Jackson at bay through the afternoon; at the latter, McCall's division contested manfully the desperate onsets of Longstreet, McCall himself being made prisoner, and his Pennsylvania Reserves suffering sadly, but gaining the necessary time. During the night the entire Union army went into position at Malvern Hills, where, in a position of immense natural strength, the inevitable afternoon attack was received next day. With comparatively slight loss to the defenders, the assaulting columns were bloodily repulsed as often as they advanced, an when the hopeless nature of the struggle was realized, General Lee withdrew his shattered legions toward Richmond, while McClellan retired his army to Harrison's Landing, and the peninsular campaign was at an end. The incubus of defeat rested upon the Union arms, and the President called for 300,000 additional men to serve for three years.

Scarcely had the thunders of battle ceased on the peninsula when they broke forth between the two capitals. The need of unity in the direction of the minor Federal forces scattered through the northern portion of Virginia induced the Washington authorities to summon General John Pope from the West, to command the forces of Fremont, Banks and McDowell. The former, displeased at the promotion of a junior in rank, resigned his command, and was succeeded by General Sigel. Pope had won signal success in his former field, especially at New Madrid and Island Number Ten, and much was hoped from him in the new position, but it seems unquestionable that his transfer created great jealousy in many of the officers with whom he now came in contact. He took command of the Army of Virginia on the 28th of June, and two weeks later General Halleck was summoned to Washington to assume direction of all the National armies—a position which he retained till early in 1864, when General Grant was made lieutenant-general, thus superseding him.

General Pope was directed to pivot his left upon the Rappahannock near Fredericksburg, withdraw his force to the east of the Blue Ridge and swing his right forward, sweeping the country in the direction of Gordonsville. Jackson, having accomplished his purpose against the Army of the Potomac, was again sent northward to operate against him. The two forces confronted each other on the 19th of July, at which time Pope's advance had passed Orange Court House and was moving toward Gordonsville, when Jackson reached the latter place before him. Preparations for a struggle at once began, Pope concentrating his army near Culpeper, midway between the Rappahannock and the Rapidan, while Jackson, feeling that his strength was insufficient, waited at Gordonsville for reinforcements.

Jackson was across the Rapidan with his whole strength on the 8th of August and Banks's corps was thrown forward to meet him. In the afternoon of the following day the Confederates were found strongly posted on the slopes of Cedar Mountain, and Banks at once delivered a skillful and vigorous attack which broke the enemy's lines, and for a time it almost seemed that a complete rout would follow. But Jackson had heavy reserves at hand, which were promptly brought into action, checking the Federal pursuit of the broken battalions, and though Gordon's brigade, the only Union reserve, was thrown in and suffered severely, it was unable to withstand the overwhelming masses which bore down upon it, and Banks's whole force retired behind Cedar Run. There they were reinforced by Sigel and Ricketts, and when the Confederate troops attempted a pursuit, the reception they received was so warm that the purpose was immediately relinquished.

Two days later Jackson withdrew to the south bank of the Rapidan, across which stream the pickets of the two armies watched each other for a week, when Pope, finding that Lee's entire army, set free by the withdrawal of McClellan's forces from the peninsula, was in his front, fell back behind the Rappahannock. Skirmishing continued till the 25th, when Jackson's corps, starting from Jefferson and marching by way of White Plains and Thoroughfare Gap, descended upon the railroad at Bristoe Station, in the rear of Pope, which point was reached on the evening of the 26th. From the Station to Manassas Junction large captures of stores and prisoners were made, after which the daring corps drew back toward Groveton to await the inevitable attack. Pope, thus assailed in the rear, faced his army about and strove to crush Jackson before the other Confederate corps under Longstreet could join forces with him. On the 29th began the battle of Manassas, or the Second Bull Run, and the result of the first day's fighting, while indecisive, was at least equally favorable to the Union arms. The main engagement had been prefaced by two sharp passages at arms, each of which may properly enough claim the dignity of an independent battle. Near evening of the 27th General Hooker's division came upon the Confederate rear guard at Bristoe Station, under General Ewell, and drove them speedily in the direction of Manassas Junction in search of the main body. McDowell's corps had been thrown across the line of Jackson's retreat at Gainesville, and on the afternoon of the 28th, as King's division moved toward Centreville, two of its brigades were savagely struck in the flank by the divisions of Ewell and Taliaferro. In the plucky fight which ensued, known as the battle of Gainesville, both the Southern division commanders were wounded, Ewell losing a leg, and their repeated assaults were repelled with heavy loss on both sides.

During the battle of the two succeeding days, General Pope had under his command, in addition to his original force, six divisions from the Army of the Potomac—two each under Heintzelman, Porter and Reno. The fight of the 29th is generally spoken of as the battle of Groveton, especially by Southern writers, and was opened by the troops of Sigel and Reynolds, who had succeeded in locating the wily Jackson, and when sharp encounters had shown that the latter was not, as Pope had supposed, anxiously seeking a way of escape, there was a pause while the necessary troops for a decisive engagement were thrown into position. Before noon Heintzelman and Reno came up, but Porter was some hours later. Near the close of the afternoon, brilliant attacks upon the Confederate position were made by the divisions of Hooker and Kearney, that of the former, led by Grover's brigade, cutting through the opposing lines like a knife, while Kearney's blow was at least equally powerful and effective. But the attacks were not supported as they should have been, an expected advance by Porter against the enemy's right was not made, for Longstreet was already on the field and had joined forces with Jackson, so that night fell with the two armies in substantially the positions of the early afternoon. The morning of the 30th brought a renewal of the battle, but it was hopeless on the Union side from the outset. The men were exhausted and dispirited, out of food, and many of the best divisions without an adequate supply of ammunition. But the men fought bravely—even desperately—under all these disadvantages. Porter's corps, especially, strove tenaciously to dislodge Longstreet from his strong position, and from every assault it recoiled in torn fragments. Night found the Federal army in full retreat upon Centreville, the few available brigades scarcely equal to the covering of the retreating columns.

The corps of Franklin and Sumner had been pushed forward from Alexandria, by direction of General McClellan, as far as Centreville, and under the protection of their firm battalions the broken army rested the following day, thence falling back to the vicinity of Fairfax Court House and Germantown. A drenching storm had set in, but even this did not dampen the ardor of the Confederate victors. Again Jackson resorted to his favorite strategy of a long detour by his left flank to fall suddenly upon the Federal right, and on the evening of September 1 he joined battle at Ox Hill, near Germantown, fighting what is known as the battle of Chantilly. The action was brief, the use of ammunition next to impossible, owing to the storm, and the repulse was made complete by a fine bayonet charge of Birney's brigade of Reno's corps; but the Union army counted among its lost two noble officers in Generals Stevens and Kearney. The former was shot dead while leading a charge of his division, and the latter met a similar fate by riding into the enemy's lines in the storm and darkness.

On the following day the army, by direction of General Halleck, retired within the Washington defenses, where it was secure from further attack in its exhausted condition. General Pope on the same day resigned his command, the Army of Virginia was merged with that of the Potomac, and General McClellan was given command of the united forces. In the reorganization and reinspiriting of the remains of the two armies the wonderful genius of McClellan found ample field, and the hand of the master was at once apparent. In a remarkably short time the shattered corps emerged upon the soil of Maryland, marching with confident step in pursuit of Lee's invading army.

The Confederate general had good cause for congratulation. In three months from the time of taking command, he had driven McClellan's magnificent army of investment from in front of the Confederate capital into the shelter of the Federal gun-boats, whence it had withdrawn to the strong defenses at Alexandria, from which it originally came forth full of bright anticipations of victory; then turning upon a second army, equal to his own in numbers, he had sent that in turn broken and disorganized before his triumphant legions. It was natural for him to feel that there was little to fear for the present from this supposed fugitive crowd, though the strength of the Washington fortifications and the extent of his own losses precluded the idea of a direct attack upon the Federal capital.

General Lee, therefore, resolved upon the invasion of Maryland. He moved promptly, the 7th of September finding the Southern army all on Maryland soil, and the following day, from his headquarters at Frederick, General Lee issued a proclamation to the people of the state, in which he assumed the tone of a liberator, and invited them to espouse the cause of the South. The response was not encouraging. The bulk of the fighting Maryland secessionists had already joined the army in Virginia, while the people of the state at large, even had their sympathy been greater, had no ambition to see their fair fields devastated by the tramp of opposing armies. Nor was there much time for the development of results. No sooner was the purpose of Lee manifested than McClellan put the Army of the Potomac in motion to meet the invaders. Crossing to the Maryland side and proceeding with the reorganization of the army on the march, he pushed sturdily forward toward Frederick, covering all the available roads.

The Confederates meantime were not idle. On crossing the river they had seized the railroad at Point of Rocks, cutting off the garrison of some 12,000 men at and about Harper's Ferry from communication with Washington. Finding that the position was not abandoned, Lee sent Jackson with a large force to cross the Potomac in front of Sharpsburg and invest the place from the Virginia side, while McLaws co-operated from the Maryland side. The move was a complete success, and resulted in the surrender of the entire force with little show of resistance, as their position was capable of no effective defense against the batteries on the surrounding hights, which opened fire on the morning of the 15th. Colonel Miles, in command of the garrison, was mortally wounded, and his second in command, General White, speedily gave up the contest.

Lee, meantime, finding that McClellan was advised as to his plans, withdrew the bulk of his army to the vicinity of Sharpsburg, in order not only that his forces might be reunited as soon as possible after the accomplishment of Jackson's enterprise, but that he might be able to retreat by way of the Shenandoah valley into Virginia, in case retreat became necessary. To check McClellan's advance as much as possible, General D. H. Hill was posted at Turner's Gap of the South Mountain, with his own division reinforced by two of Longstreet's divisions, while at Crampton's Gap, near Burkittsville, was stationed a portion of McLaws's force. General Franklin moved against the latter force with the Sixth Corps on the afternoon of the 14th, and after some three hours of sharp, though not heavy fighting, the pass was carried. At Turner's Gap, six miles to the northward, where the principal struggle in the battle of South Mountain occurred, the task was much more serious and the force on each side much greater. The assault was made by the right wing of the army, under General Burnside, composed of Reno's corps, the Ninth, and Hooker's, the First. From early morning, till darkness put an end to further operations, there was a sharp struggle on the part of the Federal forces to gain possession of the rocky fastnesses, and a stubborn resistance on the part of the defenders. The Confederate General Garland, whose brigade received Reno's first attack, was killed, and the crest held by his forces was wrested from them, but here the Union advance was checked till Hooker's corps, which came upon the field in the afternoon, climbed the mountain sides in the face of strong opposition and secured a position to the north of the Confederates which commanded the pass proper. At that time, when the Union forces were in a position to secure the fruits of their persistent efforts, night came on, and in the morning their antagonists had withdrawn. Hill had gained for his chief a day's time, though at a heavy cost in casualties and prisoners ; while the Federals, in addition to the delay, had to mourn the death of General Reno, a brave and valuable officer, who fell about sunset, almost in the moment of triumph, as the Stars and Stripes waved from the conquered hights.

Pursuit was made next morning, as soon as it was found that the defenders were in retreat, and there was skirmishing during the day as the Federals pressed the Confederate rear guard, but there was no serious engagement, and the close of the afternoon displayed the bulk of Lee's army drawn up in a strong position on the right or Sharpsburg bank of Antietam Creek. In the mean time, McLaws, driven from Crampton's Gap by the Sixth Corps, was cut off from Lee's main body, and his safety seriously complicated. He, however, formed a strong line of battle across Pleasant Valley, covering Harper's Ferry, where the beleaguered Union troops were on the point of surrendering, and when that event occurred McLaws hastily retreated across the Potomac, by way of the Ferry, into Virginia, whence recrossing at Shepardstown, he rejoined his superior at Sharpsburg. Jackson, having received General White's capitulation, very hastily paroled his captives and flew to the support of the imperiled Southern chieftain, on the banks of the Antietam, with whom he formed a junction during the night of the 16th.

As the two armies faced each other on the morning of the 16th of September, Lee had in his front the Antietam Creek, while the Potomac protected each flank, rendering a direct attack necessary. The creek was spanned by four stone bridges, three of which were strongly defended by the Confederates, but to the left of their position there was another which was unprotected, and across this, when the preparations were completed, which was not till late in the afternoon, the right wing of the Federal army was ordered to pass to assault the Confederate left flank. Hooker with his own corps led the way, as so often before he had done, his crossing being unopposed, and his lines were established, pushing back his opponents for a considerable distance. With a plan of battle developed and thus much of initial action taken, the operations of the day ceased. McClellan's programme was to cross Sumner with his own Second Corps and the Twelfth under General Mansfield, to the support of Hooker, delivering a heavy attack against the Confederate left, and when the action was well under way to throw General Burnside with the Ninth Corps across a bridge in his front to engage the forces of Longstreet, on the opposite flank. Porter's Fifth Corps formed the Union center, while the Sixth, under Franklin, were still in Pleasant Valley, with one division posted at Maryland Hights, opposite Harper's Ferry.

It cannot be said that McClellan's programme was efficiently carried out. With the early morning Hooker advanced vigorously, and was as vigorously met. The enemy was pushed back, with heavy loss on each side. Finally the attack lost its momentum, Hooker was severely wounded, his corps broken, and the fight at a stand-still till reinforcements came up on both sides. Sumner and Mansfield came upon the scene, but the latter was killed, General Richardson, commanding one of Sumner's divisions, mortally wounded, and both corps were sadly shattered. Sedgwick's division had reached an advanced position, whence with adequate support it would seem that it might have attained decisive results. But the support was not at hand, the division was forced back, and Sedgwick, twice wounded, was carried from the field. In this piecemeal attack of single regiments, brigades and divisions, a murderous loss had been inflicted on both sides, but no advantage gained. Meanwhile it was not till afternoon, when the action on the Federal right had ceased, that Burnside succeeded in getting across the creek. The crossing was difficult, and a small force had sufficed to hold his corps at bay till it was too late for them to carry out their part of the programme. They did, indeed, drive back the troops in their front for some distance when once across the stream, but were themselves in turn pushed down to the shelter of the bluff, near the crossing.

Here the battle ended. Franklin's two available divisions had come up, and had been put in position on the right, where the struggle had been so terrible, and Porter's corps had not yet been engaged; but McClellan shrank from a renewal of the fight on the morning of the 18th, and the day was devoted to burying the dead and caring for the wounded, the Union loss having been upward of 12,000, and that of the Confederates nearly as great. If it was McClellan's intention to resume the battle on the 19th, he was doomed to disappointment, for the coming of that day found the Army of Northern Virginia once more on the "Sacred Soil," and no pursuit was attempted. For a few days, more or less skirmishing across the Potomac occurred, and small forces from each army crossed the river to annoy their antagonists, only to return speedily to their own side. Lee, with the remnants of his army, moved up the Shenandoah valley to the vicinity of Winchester, while the Union troops remained in Maryland, so distributed as to guard against possible incursions from marauding parties of the enemy

Both armies were sadly in need of rest and supplies of various kinds. According to their own reports, the invaders had been in a terribly ragged and destitute condition for a long time, while the Army of the Potomac was far from being well supplied after its summer's campaign. Recruits were sent forward from Washington to strengthen the various commands, among the new regiments of three-years' troops permanently attached to the army being the Thirty-seventh Massachusetts. The history of this organization becomes from that time identified with that of the larger body. Let us now sketch the work of Massachu: setts as a loyal member of the national Union, before taking up the especial story of her Thirty-seventh Regiment.

CHAPTER II.

MASSACHUSETTS IN THE WAR.

THE RECORD OF THE COMMONWEALTH.—ITS PUBLIC MEN.—
ITS SOLDIERS.—ITS CITIZENS.

The record of Massachusetts in the war for the Union was one of which all who love its good name may justly be proud. In the field and in the legislative halls, in conflict on land and sea as in the council chambers, the sons of the Old Bay State led the advance ; while in the blessed offices of mercy which sought to alleviate the sufferings of those dreadful years and as far as possible to rob war of its horrors, in whatever way the purpose might be advanced, the whole people, irrespective of age, sex or social condition, joined with an exemplary energy. Yet in the group of all who did such valiant, faithful service one figure must ever stand gloriously above all the rest—the central figure of the stout-hearted, clear-headed war governor, John A. Andrew. Born in Maine in 1818, a graduate of Bowdoin College in 1837 and admitted to the Suffolk bar in 1840, Mr. Andrew in 1860 undoubtedly stood at the head of the legal profession in the state. Never in the narrow sense a politician, his experience in public place had been confined to a single term in the state Legislature and the chairmanship of the Massachusetts delegation in the National Republican Convention at Chicago which nominated Lincoln for the presidency. Yet to the mighty task to which he was called, Governor Andrew brought a statesmanship, a power of resource and an unwavering purpose which won the admiration of the country.

Mr. Andrew was elected to his first term on the day of Mr. Lincoln's election to the presidency—November 6, 1860,—by a vote of 104,527 and a clear majority over his three competitors, representing the three factions of the Democratic party, of 39,445 —the largest vote up to that time ever cast in the Commonwealth. The state delegation in Congress, the Executive Council and nearly the entire Legislature were Republican in politics and therefore in general accord with the new administration. Nor was the support of Governor Andrew by any means confined to the party which elected him to office. The vast majority of the democratic party of the state were faithful to the cause of union, and the soldiers in the field represented all shades of political belief subordinated to national loyalty.

Before the inauguration of Governor Andrew, January 5, 1861, the war cloud grew threatening, and thoughtful men began to despair of averting an appeal to arms. Yet so dreadful seemed that alternative that, while nerving themselves for the struggle should it come, the people of the state neglected no opportunity to urge conciliation and concession, and late in the month a petition bearing 15,000 prominent names was sent to the Massachusetts delegation in Congress, urging conciliatory measures. The people were ready to sanction any reasonable sacrifice for the sake of peace, but they were not ready to see the nation, in the building of which their fathers had borne so honorable a part, fall in ruins about them. If that were to be the alternative, they would prove that the sons were ready to sacrifice for the preservation as much as their ancestors for the creation. In his inaugural the new governor spoke for the whole state when he said: "The people will forever stand by the country." There was no more comprehensive expression of the popular feeling than that given by Adjutant-General William Schouler when, responding to a toast in honor to Major Anderson, then besieged in Fort Sumter, he said: "We have no boasts to make. History tells what the men of Massachusetts have done, and they will never disgrace that history." These were the calm utterances of earnest men, typical of the invincible purposes of loyal men everywhere; they put into words that earnest determination which led the soldiers of the old Commonwealth, hopeful and unshrinking, through every disaster and discouragement to final consummation. Quite the reverse of of this, in speech and action, found favor among the demagogues who were plotting the destruction of the nation. Calm utterance following earnest thought could never have served their purpose, and we find instead fiery bluster and impetuous, passionate acts, in the field as on the forum. While the latter were anxious only that the national Union should be destroyed, Governor Andrew had no greater ambition than to know and faithfully do his duty under the general government for its preservation. In his message of the following year, when the issue had been joined and the fearful magnitude of the struggle began to be realized, he uses these noble words:—

Let him lead to whom the people have assigned the authority and the power. One great duty of absorbing, royal patriotism, which is the public duty of the occasion, demands us all to follow. Placed in no situation where it becomes me to discuss his policy, I do not stop even to consider it. The only question that I can entertain is what *to do*, and, when that question is answered, the other is what next to do, in the sphere of activity where is given me to stand; for by deeds, and not by words, are this people to accomplish their salvation. Let ours be the duty in this great emergency to furnish, in unstinted measure, the men and the money required of us for the common defense. Let Massachusetts ideas and Massachusetts principles go forth, with the industrious, sturdy sons of the Commonwealth to propagate and intensify, in every camp and upon every battle-field, that love of equal liberty, and those rights of universal humanity, which are the basis of our institutions; but let none of us who remain at home presume to direct the pilot or to seize the helm. To the civil head of the national state, to the military head of the national army, our fidelity, our confidence, our constant, devoted, unwavering support, rendered in the spirit of intelligent freemen, of large-minded citizens, conscious of the difficulties of government, the responsibilities of power, the perils of distrust and division, are due without measure and without reservation.

To this magnificent expression of loyal devotion Governor Andrew remained intensely faithful to the end. At the conference of loyal governors at Altoona, Pa., in September of the same year, when the peninsular fiasco, the defeat of Pope and the doubtful result at Antietam might well have cast a gloom over the most ardent, his was the voice of unfaltering courage, and his the hand which wrote the petition to the President asking for another levy of 300,000 men for the strengthening of the Union armies. But with this intense earnestness of purpose Governor Andrew mingled no vindictive feeling, and when the end was reached, when the test of arms had decided that the Union was to live, stronger, grander, purified and redeemed by its awful baptism of blood, he could say, after pronouncing a touching eulogy on the martyred President Lincoln:—

> Order, law, freedom, and true civilization, must rise into life all over the territory blasted by despotism, barbarism and treason. The schemes of sentimental politicians, who neither learn nor forget, whose ideas of constructive statesmanship are only imitative as are the mechanical ideas of the bee or the beaver, the plans of men who would rebuild on the sand, for the sake of adhering to a precedent,—must be utterly, promptly and forever rejected. Let the government and the people resolve to be brave, faithful, impartial and just. With the blessing of God, let us determine to have a country the home of liberty and civilization. Let us deserve success and we shall surmount every obstacle, we shall survive delays, we shall conquer defeat, we shall win a peaceful victory for the great ages of the future; and, for the cause of humanity, we shall requite these years of toil and war. The blood of all this noble army of martyrs, from the soldiers of Massachusetts who fell in Baltimore to Abraham Lincoln, the President, who has mingled his own with theirs,—the blood of this noble army of martyrs shall be, as of old, the seed of the Church.

In the national councils the state was well represented. In the Senate it had Charles Sumner and Henry Wilson, the former holding the chairmanship of the Committee on Foreign Affairs. When the delicate condition of our foreign relations during the whole time of the war is borne in mind, it scarcely needs to be said that in this field the magnificent intellect of Mr. Sumner found an ample task. This position naturally brought him in very close relations to the President, and on the last week of Mr. Lincoln's life he said to Mr. Sumner, during a very cordial interview: "There is no person with whom I have oftener advised throughout my administration than with yourself."

If it be just to give to Senator Sumner the prouder place as a national statesman, it will be equally just to give Senator Wilson a place closer to the warm heart of the loyal people, especially those of his own state. During the war he was chairman of the Committee on Military Affairs and of the Committee on the Militia—no man did more faithful service than he, none had a keener comprehension of the national situation. No sketch, however brief, of the part taken by Massachusetts in the conflict would be complete without an appreciative reference to the great work of Mr. Wilson. He had already served upon the Military Committee for four years, under the chairmanship of Jefferson Davis, and with no power to prevent had seen the naturally feeble military power of the government manipulated in accordance with the purposes of the conspirators and made still more feeble for the government's protection. When Fort Sumter fell Mr. Wilson urged the President to call for 300,000 men instead of the 75,000 actually asked for, but the magnitude of the numbers was staggering, and the advice was not heeded. When the call was issued he prevailed upon the Secretary of War to double the quota of Massachusetts, and then hastened home to consult with the state authorities. From that hour his duties were multitudinous and unceasing. Returning to Washington, he devoted much of his time to caring for the soldiers, especially those in the hospitals; yet on the assembling of Congress in extra session, July 4, 1861, he was ready with the important military bills demanded by the condition of affairs. At the adjournment of the special session he returned to Massachusetts to give his personal influence to the promotion of enlistments, and raised by his own efforts, among other troops, the Twenty-second regiment, of which he was commissioned colonel. This commission, however, was soon resigned, and Mr. Wilson, the better to familiarize himself with the service in all its branches and its needs, became a volunteer aide on General McClellan's staff, which position he held till January, 1862, when duty again called him to active work in the Senate.

His position had now become one of immense responsibility. All the important legislation required in connection with the enormous military service of the ensuing four years was either originated or passed upon by the committee of which Mr. Wilson was the head and the heart. In the single matter of commissioned officers, 11,000 nominations of all grades from second lieutenant to lieutenant-general were referred to them for investigation and report; interested parties naturally flocked to the committee with requests and complaints, and even the common soldiers felt at liberty to seek out Senator Wilson, "The Soldier's Friend,"—the man in whose great heart there was a warm corner for the humblest human being. Among the multitude of bills prepared by Mr. Wilson in person were those for bettering the pay and condition of the soldiers, and all of those relating to the military service of the blacks, freeing the families of colored soldiers, as well as the men themselves, and abolishing slavery in the District of Columbia; for Mr. Wilson never forgot that the rebellion was built upon slavery as a corner-stone; and he wrought unceasingly for its destruction and for the constitutional equality of the negro race—a work in which he was the efficient co-laborer of Mr. Sumner, having from his position an influence and an opportunity second to none in the country.

In the Thirty-seventh Congress, which began its labors with the special session of 1861, Massachusetts was represented in the House by Thomas D. Eliot, James Buffinton, Benjamin F. Thomas, Alexander H. Rice, Samuel Hooper, John B. Alley, Daniel W Gooch, Charles R. Train, Goldsmith F. Bailey, Charles Delano and Henry L. Dawes. Two years later Mr. Buffinton was succeeded by Oakes Ames, Mr. Train by George S. Boutwell, Mr. Bailey by James D. Baldwin, and Mr. Delano by William B. Washburn. The faithful service of these men can only be hinted at in this brief sketch. Mr. Rice was chairman of the Committee on Naval Affairs, Mr. Hooper on that of Ways and Means, Mr. Dawes served on the Committee on Elections, Mr. Alley on Post-offices and Post Roads, Mr. Gooch on the Conduct of the War, and Mr. Eliot on the Committee on Confiscation and that on Emancipation.

Among the representatives of the United States at foreign courts, the Commonwealth furnished Charles Francis Adams, who at London had the most delicate, difficult and important position in the entire foreign service, J. Lothrop Motley, minister to Austria, and Anson Burlingame to China, the latter doing a work of world-wide importance, though remotely related to the great struggle at home, in opening that country to the commerce of the world.

The first official act of Governor Andrew after his inauguration was to dispatch trusty messengers to each of the governors of the New England states urging preparation for the worst and a hearty support of the government at Washington. The results of this movement were of the most satisfactory nature. The next measure, and indeed the only one which was in order in the absence of actual hostilities, was thorough preparation for the expected event. In this, as in all the military measures which ensued, the strong right arm of the Governor was Adjutant-General William Schouler, who had been appointed to office by Governor Banks, and whose indefatigable and well-judged labors did so much for the success of the plans of his chief. The organized militia of the state at this time consisted of about 5,600 men, divided into nine regiments, seven battalions and thirteen unattached companies. January 16, a general order was issued requiring every company to be put in efficient condition for active service if called upon. Those who from age, physical defect or other cause were unable or unwilling to serve were to be honorably mustered out, the companies recruited to their maximum and held subject to the orders of the Governor. To show the spirit of the officers and men it may be stated that within a week from the issuance of the order Colonel Jones of the Sixth regiment tendered his command for immediate service if required. In the mean time the Legislature had passed a resolution pledging to the general government "her entire means, civil and military," that the President might "execute the laws of the United States, defend the Union and protect national property," which it was declared the universal sentiment of the people of the state that we should do. Legislation and preparation for the demands likely to be made upon the military forces of the Commonwealth went on with zeal, but it was not till the Stars and Stripes were humiliated at Sumter that the call came.

The 15th of April brought the expected message, the first dispatch being from Senator Wilson asking for twenty companies, but later in the day the Secretary of War sent a formal requisition for two full regiments. Orders were at once issued to Colonel Wardrop of the Third, Colonel Packard of the Fourth, Colonel Jones of the Sixth and Colonel Monroe of the Eighth to report at Boston with their commands, and on the morning of the following day the companies began to arrive, the first to reach the city being the three Marblehead companies of the Eighth regiment. The enthusiasm was something wonderful for steady-going Massachusetts. Money and service were offered from every hand in unstinted measure; everywhere the eye rested on the national colors in many a patriotic device.

While the hum of preparation was at its hight on the 16th word came from Senator Wilson that the state was to furnish four regiments under the command of a brigadier-general. General B. F. Butler was assigned to the latter position, and orders were forwarded to Colonel Lawrence of the Fifth to report at Boston with his command, the Massachusetts regiments not having the number of companies required for the United States service. On the afternoon of the 17th the Third and Fourth regiments set out for Fortress Monroe, the former by steamer direct, the latter from Fall River by way of New York. The Sixth regiment also left Boston on the evening of the 17th, going by rail to Washington direct. The story of the brutal attack of a Baltimore mob on the 19th, in which Massachusetts gave the first blood and the first lives in the great sacrifice, has given this regiment a fame that will never die. That story needs no rehearsal here.

The Eighth regiment, accompanied by General Butler, left Boston on the afternoon of the 18th, intending to follow the Sixth. At Springfield they were joined by Captain Henry S. Briggs of Pittsfield with the Allen Guards, completing the organization. Philadelphia was reached on the afternoon of the 19th when news came to them of the assault upon the Sixth in Baltimore. A night of intense anxiety followed, during which General Butler decided upon a plan for reaching Washington, by "flanking" the hostile city; but Colonel Lefferts of the Seventh New York, whose command had reached Philadelphia, declined to accompany the Massachusetts soldiers, though following a few hours later. The ensuing afternoon cars were taken for Perryville, where the regiment was transferred to the large ferry-boat Maryland, which was placed at General Butler's service by President Samuel M. Felton of the Philadelphia and Baltimore railroad, who seems to have suggested the course which was adopted. As soon as the regiment and its property were aboard the Maryland steamed away for Annapolis, where it anchored the following morning near the famous frigate Constitution, then used as a school ship, and for the safety of which fears were felt. Two companies of the Eighth were at once put on board, and the historic craft was in due time taken to New York for safety. From Annapolis to the Junction, 22 miles, the regiment repaired the Annapolis and Elk Ridge railroad, which had been destroyed, put the engines and cars in running order, built bridges and opened railway communication between the Capital and the North. On the 26th they reached Washington, much worn by their arduous duties, but having performed a service winning for them imperishable renown.

In the mean time the news of the situation reached Boston and produced the most thrilling excitement, not only in official circles but among the people of every class. The Fifth regiment was rapidly put in readiness and sent forward on the 20th to the support of the Eighth, and on the same day Major Asa F. Cook's battery of light artillery and the Third battalion of riflemen, three companies under Major Charles Devens, Jr., started for the front, joining the Fifth at New York, whence the entire force went by water to Annapolis. Major Devens with his command was soon sent to Fort McHenry, while the Fifth and the battery accompanied the Eighth to Washington.

Thus was met the first call upon the patriotism of Massachusetts. It came to a people who knew not war, whose lives had been lives of peace and luxury. Within five days after the call was received the state had sent forward five full regiments of infantry a battery of artillery and three companies of riflemen, —a fourth following a few days later and proceeding up the Potomac to Washington. Wherever they went these troops were

THE THREE-YEARS' VOLUNTEERS. 51

the pioneers; the arrival of the Third and Fourth regiments at Fortress Monroe secured to the government the possession of that important stronghold, on which the conspirators were looking with eager eyes, while the Sixth, quartered in the Senate chamber on their arrival after the deadly struggle through the streets of Baltimore, gave the first positive assurance of the safety of the national Capital.

On the 3d of May, fearing that the return home of the 75,000 who had been summoned for three months would leave the government with an inadequate military force, President Lincoln called for some 40,000 volunteers for three years' service, and Massachusetts was instructed to furnish six regiments. "It is important to reduce rather than enlarge this number, and in no event to exceed it   and if more are already called for, to reduce the number by discharge," was the language of Secretary of War Simon Cameron in transmitting the requisition. Thus cautious and groping were the steps taken by the national government in the early days of the struggle. Even this permission to send troops to the defense of the country was not received at Boston till the 22d, 19 days after the call.

On the 25th the Second regiment, Colonel George H. Gordon, was mustered into the United States service, being the first New England regiment accepted for three years. The other regiments of the quota were mustered during the month of June in this order: Ninth, Colonel Thomas Cass, June 11; Eleventh, Colonel George Clark, Jr., June 13; First, Colonel Robert Cowdin, and Seventh, Colonel D. N. Couch, the 15th; and the Tenth, Colonel Henry S. Briggs, the 21st. The First left the state June 15, marched through Baltimore on the 17th, and was the first three-years' regiment to reach Washington.

Extremely dissatisfied at the meager force called for, Governor Andrew, in common with many prominent men through the country, urged the acceptance of more troops, and a vigorous prosecution of the war—for that there was to be a bitter and cruel war, could no longer be doubted. It was with much satisfaction, therefore, that on the 17th of June permission was received to forward ten additional regiments. Colonel Fletcher

Webster, the heroic son of the great orator, had his Twelfth regiment already organized, and it was mustered June 26. Then during the months of July and August, followed, in order of their acceptance, the Fifteenth, Colonel Charles Devens, Jr.; Thirteenth, Colonel Samuel H. Leonard; Seventeeth, Colonel T. J. C. Amory; Nineteenth, Colonel Edward W Hinks: Sixteenth, Colonel P F Wyman, Twenty-first, Colonel Augustus Morse; Eighteenth, Colonel James Barnes; Twentieth, Colonel W R. Lee, and Fourteenth or First Heavy Artillery, Colonel W B. Greene.

The state Legislature, meantime, had been called to meet in extra session, May 14, and no more important session of that body was ever held. The multitude of new and pressing questions which had to be met, the rapidly increasing magnitude of the struggle, the raising, equipping and sending forward of vast levies of men, the provisions for their comfort and for the care of those dependents whom they left behind,—all joined in demanding the best intelligence and the most unswerving patriotism on the part of the legislators. How faithfully those duties were performed history records, but the details cannot be given in a single general chapter. In addition to other sources of anxiety, it was necessary to send an agent abroad to procure arms; a mission which was promptly directed by the Governor as soon as it became apparent that the national government could not arms its defenders.

Boston, too, was open to the mercy of any nautical foe, the forts erected for its protection being garrisonless and in a sad condition of neglect. Pressing representations to the general government of this fact brought no response, and finally, as a matter of self-defense, the state was obliged to take the responsibility of ordering details of its soldiery to occupy the works and put them in as defensible a condition as possible—a work for which the Washington authorities have yet made but partial acknowledgment and compensation.

Thus in ceaseless activity the first year of the war rolled away. Before the close of 1861, the Twenty-ninth regiment had been mustered into service, and the new year saw the Thirtieth,

Thirty-first and Thirty-second nearly ready to follow. The anniversary of the first call found 27 infantry regiments from Massachusetts in the field, for three years, in addition to the cavalry and artillery which had gone forward in proportionate numbers. The spring and early summer of 1862 brought a short respite from the work of enlistment and organization. The eyes of the people were upon General McClellan's army on the peninsula, hoping to see a fatal blow given to the rebellion. That hope vanished, as the shattered army recoiled before the fierce onsets of Johnston and Lee.

An order was received from the President, May 28, 1862, calling for two new regiments—the Thirty-third and Thirty-fourth—and the four companies required to complete the Thirty-second, already in service, as well as six companies to garrison Fort Warren, in Boston harbor. These were being filled when the President called a levy of 300,000 men, to serve for three years, and on the 7th of July Governor Andrew officially asked for the quota from Massachusetts. Every effort was put forth by the state, city and town authorities, and in two months the last man called for had been mustered into service. In addition to the 4,000 men sent to the old regiments, in the field, seven new regiments, in numerical order, from the Thirty-fifth to the Forty-first, inclusive, went in response to this demand.

Following the call for the three-years' men, and only a month later, a draft was ordered for 300,000 more to serve for nine months, and the quota of Massachusetts under this demand was fixed at 19,080. There was no hesitation, no delay. The five militia regiments which had responded so promptly to the first call for three months' service the previous year were about going into camp for the annual state muster. Their ranks were filled, and they again went forward to serve their country. In addition, 12 new regiments, from the Forty-second to the Fifty-third, inclusive, were organized and sent. This ended the work of 1862, so far as the sending out of regiments was concerned.

With the opening of 1863, the Emancipation Proclamation took effect, and toward the close of January the long-desired permission was given for Massachusetts to raise a colored regiment. Before the middle of May the regiment was filled, and on the 28th it left Boston by steamer, for South Carolina. It was ably commanded by Colonel Robert G. Shaw, who fell at its head in the terrible night attack on Fort Wagner, July 18 following. This was the Fifty-fourth, and on the 21st of July the Fifty-fifth, also composed of colored men, under Colonel N. P. Hallowell, left for the same destination. The Fifth Cavalry was also a colored regiment. Regarding the part taken by these soldiers, it is simple justice to say, in a word, that wherever they were placed, they performed faithfully every duty which came to them.

With the appointment of General Hooker to the command of the Army of the Potomac, came his recommendation that recruits should be sent to fill the regiments already in the field, rather than that new organizations should be formed, and that, with few exceptions, was the course thenceforward pursued in Massachusetts. In the winter and early spring of 1864, four regiments of "veterans" were organized, and went at once into the Wilderness campaign, where they suffered frightful losses. These were the Fifty-sixth, Fifty-seventh, Fifty-eighth and Fifty-ninth. In July of that year five regiments were sent out for 100 days' garrison duty, to allow veteran troops to go to the front—the Fifth, Sixth, Eighth, Forty-second and Sixtieth. Nine unattached companies were also formed for garrison duty on the Massachusetts coast. For these forces the state received no credit from the general government. The Sixty-first, for one year, was raised and sent forward by detachments the ensuing fall and winter, and the Sixty-second was being recruited when the collapse of the rebellion ended the long sacrifice.

In addition to the infantry regiments, the state had in the service 16 batteries of light artillery, three regiments of heavy artillery, numerous unattached companies of the latter and of sharpshooters, and two regiments of cavalry, besides the infantry afterward reorganized as such.

The total of men furnished by Massachusetts for all terms of service reached 159,254—a surplus over all calls of 13,492. Of this number 31,165 served in the navy, 6,039 were colored, and only 907 were non-resident "foreigners." The last-given figures are answer sufficient to the imputation sometimes heard that the ranks of our volunteer regiments were filled with foreign hirelings. To offset the few aliens thus employed, it may be stated that, in the early period of the war, more than 3,000 men from the state enlisted in other states, for which no credit could be received by Massachusetts. Of the officers and men, 3,543 were killed in action, 1,986 died of wounds, 5,672 of disease, 1,843 in rebel prisons, and 1,026 were missing and never accounted for.

In this connection it is worthy of note that the men of Massachusetts received from all quarters the highest commendation for the manliness, courage and intelligence, with which they bore the sufferings incidental to soldier life, especially in hospital; the cheerfulness and strong rallying power manifested, their prompt return to duty on recovery, and Christian heroism in meeting death when that became the sad alternative. Of those who returned to their homes, it is equally gratifying to know that their after lives gave no indication of general demoralization from the associations met during their soldier days. Where the early life gave good promise, it was generally broadened and strengthened by the experience, and if there were exceptions to the rule, so there were unquestionably genuine reformations of character.

The total expense incurred by the state in raising and equipping troops reached $27,705,109, and that of the cities and towns as such was nearly as much more, making $50,000,000 in round numbers as the money cost to the state.

Properly a part of the record of Massachusetts, as the work was performed by her mechanics under the direction of the general government, may be counted the production at the Springfield armory, in the five years succeeding July 1, 1860, of 805,636 muskets, with extra parts and repairs equal to 120,845 more. The rifled musket, as there produced, was the standard weapon of the service, and undoubtedly the best muzzle-loader ever manufactured.

The draft riots of the summer of 1863, which in New York were so disgraceful, found a slight echo in Boston, and for a time there was ground for alarm. But the action of the Governor was prompt and efficient. Troops were hastily assembled, and every important point protected. In but a single instance did the mob, which gathered in considerable numbers, venture on violence. The armory of the Eleventh Battery on Cooper street, which contained the only available artillery in the city, with a quantity of ammunition, was assaulted on the evening of July 14 by a mob of several thousand. Major Stephen Cabot was in command inside the armory, and when the mob ventured upon an assault on the doors, the order to fire was given. One volley, which killed several of the rioters and wounded many, ended the trouble in Massachusetts, though the precautions were continued in Boston and other cities till all indications of a riotous purpose had disappeared.

While the outline thus given exhibits a devotion, patriotism and heroism, of which any commonwealth might well be proud, no record of these troublous times would be complete that failed to acknowledge the equal consecration of the daughters of the Old Bay State. No women bore a more faithful part, whether we consider the devotion of those who, as nurses, went into the hospitals, the labors in the great fields of the Sanitary Commission and the Christian Commission, or the Soldiers' Aid Societies, which, in all the towns and cities, labored indefatigably for the comfort of the sick and wounded soldiers, and the welfare, spiritual and physical, of those in the field. No less patriotic in purpose and commendable in spirit was the action of those who, like the teachers in the schools of Boston and elsewhere, voluntarily sacrificed a large percentage of their salaries, in order to lighten the burdens of the state and city. Even the inmates of the state prison volunteered to perform extra labor in the cause. The first act in aid of the families of volunteers was that passed by the Massachusetts Legislature, May 23, 1861. The first president of the United States Christian Commission was Rev. A. Rolin Neale, D. D., of Boston; Massachusetts had more delegates in the service than any other state, and furnished the four field agents. In providing for the navy, in this direction, the first and principal work was done by Massachusetts.

Following the great battles, contributions of money were made at Boston for the relief of the wounded—after Gettysburg, $35,000 was received in small amounts; for the Wilderness, over $60,000; at the taking of Richmond, $30,000. The 1864 Thanksgiving dinner for 17,000 soldiers, in the Washington hospitals, was furnished by Massachusetts friends.

In labor for the welfare of the soldiers all classes and ages joined. Among the contributions of socks, were 191 pairs made by Mrs. Abner Bartlett of Medford, aged 85; several pairs by Mrs. S. A. Frazer of Duxbury, who was 92 at the opening of the war, and a pair knit by a Conway woman of 97.

Hospitals were opened on Pemberton Square, Boston, at Readville and Worcester; the first home for discharged soldiers in the country was at Boston, followed soon after by another at Weston. In November, 1864, the National Sailors' Fair, to secure a sailors' home, was held in Boston, netting $282,370. For the relief of Savannah in 1865, Boston joined with New York and Philadelphia, and $100,000 was raised, and so the list might be continued.

Governor Andrew had served faithfully throughout the entire war, and when peace came, he declined further service in the position he had filled with such honor. Alexander H. Bullock was chosen his successor, and entered upon the office, January 6, 1866. In his inaugural address referring to the soldiers, and the deposit of the regimental colors at the State House, he said:

In storm and sunshine, in success and repulse, they carried those banners through 12 hostile states. In the hour of utmost need they, before all others, had planted them on the National Capitol, staining on the way with the life-blood of some the pavement of a city in rebellion. They had carried them with Hooker to the summit of Lookout Mountain, and had fixed them, with Strong and Shaw, on the ramparts of Wagner. With Burnside, they had crossed the mountains of Tennessee, and had sheltered the hearthstone of Andrew Johnson. With Butler, they had forced the channel of the Mississippi and proclaimed law and order in the city of the Cresent. In all the campaigns of the East, in Sherman's grand march, with Banks at Port Hudson, with Grant at Vicksburg—whenever and wherever there was hazard to be encountered, or laurels to be won, they had carried the battle-flags of Massachusetts with unyielding devotion and national renown.

CHAPTER III.

THE THIRTY-SEVENTH REGIMENT

THE GATHERING AT CAMP BRIGGS.—CHARACTER OF THE COMMAND.—THE ORIGINAL ROSTER OF OFFICERS.—PERSONAL NOTES AND INCIDENTS.

The progress of General McClellan's campaign on the peninsula early demonstrated to careful observers that the Union forces, thus far mustered into the service, were far from adequate to the task of suppressing the armed rebellion, and on the 28th of June, while the two armies were still in their desperate grapple in front of Richmond, the governors of 16 of the loyal states, with representatives of Tennessee and Kentucky, strongly advised President Lincoln to call for 300,000 more volunteers. Such advice, at a time when the need of more men was becoming severely felt was not to be disregarded, and on the 1st of July, 1862, the call was made. The energies of Massachusetts were at once directed to furnishing the quota of the Bay State. In his proclamation announcing the call, after urging the people of the state to every exertion in behalf of the national cause, Governor Andrew said: "Massachusetts, which has never slumbered or slept, must now arise to still higher efforts, and pledge to all the duties of patriotism, with renewed devotion, the individual efforts, the united hearts, heads and hands, of all her people."

Throughout the Commonwealth the echo of this sentiment was everywhere heard. Public meetings were held, the press came nobly to the support of the government, municipalities and towns bent their best energies to the filling of the quotas severally required of them. The most complete arrangements were made for the care of the volunteer's family during his absence,

THE RENDEZVOUS AT PITTSFIELD. 59

and considerable bounties were offered, payable on the muster in of the recruit.

At this time Massachusetts had three incomplete regiments in process of being filled—the Thirty-second, some companies of which were already in the service, the Thirty-third and the Thirty-fourth in camp, the latter at Camp John E. Wool, at Worcester. A considerable portion of the recruits under the call were mustered for the regiments already in the field, and pushed forward to their destinations in squads, in connection with which the work of filling up the new regiments, just mentioned, was carried on. In pursuance of this purpose, the delegations from the western portion of the state all gathered at Worcester, and after the selection of the companies constituting the Thirty-fourth regiment, there remained a large number of skeleton companies or squads, mostly under the temporary command of men who expected or hoped for commissions. The organization of the Thirty-fourth being reasonably complete, a division was made of the remaining fragments of companies; those from Worcester county remained on the ground to occupy the camp when vacated and become the Thirty-sixth regiment, while the representatives of the four western counties—Berkshire, Hampden, Hampshire and Franklin—repaired to the rendezvous at Pittsfield, where a new camp had been formed.

Camp Briggs was so named from General Henry S. Briggs of Pittsfield, the original colonel of the Tenth regiment, who had just received a promotion well earned by bravery on the field, and who was at that time at his home recovering from a severe wound received at the battle of Fair Oaks. It was located on what is now (1884) the Pleasure Park, on the Washington road, something over a mile eastward from the village, and was in every way a desirable site. The location in itself was favorable, the ground having a very slight southerly slope, dry and airy, well supplied with good water, surrounded by the beautiful mountain scenery which makes the county a favorite resort for the lovers of nature from all portions of the country.

To this delightful spot, in the early days of August, came the advance guard of what was to be the Thirty-seventh regiment of

Massachusetts Volunteer Infantry. It was a peculiarly fitting scene amidst which to teach the first lessons of a noble soldier life. The breath of the eternal hills whispered to the enthusiastic campers of strength, of patriotism, of freedom. The earnest, manly life of the sturdy sons of New England had no better representatives than those who had grown to early manhood amid such environments, and who now left the shop and the farm to consecrate themselves to the demands of their common country. To breathe such air, and to gaze upon such scenes of natural beauty, was to grow yet stronger in patriotic devotion.

The camp was for a time in charge of Lieutenant Alonzo E. Goodrich of the Allen Guard, Pittsfield, who, in providing for the arriving recruits, was assisted by Quartermaster Daniel J. Dodge of the same town, both of whom were identified with the early history of the regiment. As the number in camp increased, however, Colonel William Raymond Lee, of the Twentieth regiment, was placed in command of the post, and continued in that duty for a few days, till the arrival of Major Oliver Edwards, about the 12th of August. At that time there were the skeletons of 11 companies on the ground, and the different commands grew daily in numbers and in military education.

With characteristic energy, Major Edwards brought his soldierly qualities to the work of organization. Company and battalion drills at once began and were continued with vigor, while great care was manifested to preserve a healthful and an orderly camp. If some of the regulations and requirements at the time seemed unduly stringent and exacting to men coming from the utter freedom of rural life and without military experience, or any adequate conception of the requirements of the service, the result showed their wisdom, and with most of the recruits they were cheerfully accepted from the first. The commander and his command were well adapted to each other. While the former was especially qualified to create an efficient and well-disciplined regiment, the material which came to his hand was admirably adapted to the purposes of such a creation. Almost without exception the men had enlisted from the most patriotic motives, and each was anxious that his service should be of honor to himself, as well as of benefit to his country. While the great majority had never seen military experience, even of the simplest sort, not to speak of the battle-field, there were a few who had gone out in the earlier regiments, from which they had been discharged for wounds or other cause. These men, wherever they might be during the abundant leisure of the camp, formed centers of interested groups. Their words had a charm which no civilian voice could equal, for the speakers had personal knowledge of the sphere of life for which the listeners were training, and he who bore the marks of recent wounds was, to a most gratifying extent, the hero of his mess.

Let it not be supposed that the life upon which the men had entered was an idle or a wearisome one. Every day brought fresh accessions to the companies, there were many acquaintances to develop, the closeness and importance of which none could estimate in advance; the duties of the camp, the rapid succession of new developments, the preparations for a long, and perhaps a final adieu to home and friends;—all these combined to fill the waking hours of the citizen-soldier with thought and labor. Nor was amusement of a healthful nature wanting. In the intervals of the busy day, groups would be visible here and there, keenly enjoying some athletic sport, or laughing heartily at the whimsical oddities of those whose best work in the camp, it may be, was to lighten the spirits of their comrades. Especially was the early evening given to this species of enjoyment. Who that remembers his experience in those stirring scenes does not recall with especial interest the uncouth elephants composed of soldiers covered by their army blankets, that in the dimming twilight roamed about the grounds indulging in such laughter-moving pranks as no bona fide elephant could ever have perpetrated; the vigorous tossing in a blanket by a half-dozen stalwarts of some willing or unwilling victim, whose evolutions were more rapid and varied than graceful; the bounding foot-ball, propelled by hundreds of vigorous feet; the thousand and one kindred means of diversion and companionship?

The 15th of August found Companies C, F and B filled, and within a week, Companies D, G and H were also completed.

These six companies were mustered into the United States service on the 30th, and the remaining four were ready for the services of the mustering officer, Captain Thomas of the United States Army, on the 2d of September, with the exception of Company K, which was not filled till the 4th, the term of the regiment consequently counting from the latter date. This company was the result of a consolidation, attempts having been made to raise two exclusively Irish companies for the regiment,— one by Peter Dooley of Cheshire, and the other by John B. Mulloy of Springfield. As neither could be filled in time, it was decided to unite them. At the final examinations a few men were rejected, much to their mortification and disappointment, but, as a whole, the command was highly complimented by competent judges, among others by General Briggs, who was often on the grounds and watched the formation of the regiment with much interest.

Meantime preparations were actively pushed for the departure of the Thirty-seventh for active service, the anxiety of the government for additional troops increasing with the unfortunate developments that crowded fast upon each other from the Virginia fields. The men, having been uniformed, were given furloughs of three or four days each, going out in squads, and almost without exception returning promptly on time. The officers' commissions were issued August 27, and were as follows:

Colonel, Oliver Edwards of Springfield; lieutenant-colonel, Alonzo E. Goodrich of Pittsfield; major, George L. Montague of South Hadley; surgeon, Charles P Crehore of Boston; assistant-surgeons, Thomas C. Lawton of Sheffield, Joshua J. Ellis of Marshfield; adjutant, First Lieutenant Thomas G. Colt of Pittsfield; quartermaster, First Lieutenant Daniel J. Dodge of Pittsfield; chaplain, Rev. Frank C. Morse of Blandford.

Non-commissioned staff—Sergeant-major, Robert A. Gray of Springfield; quartermaster's sergeant, Thomas Porter, Jr., of Chesterfield; commissary sergeant, James C. Chalmers of Pittsfield; hospital stewards, W A. Champney of Hatfield, Richard E. Morgan of Pittsfield; principal musician, John L. Gaffney of Chicopee.

Company A—Captain Jarvis P. Kelley, First Lieutenant Eli T. Blackmer, Second Lieutenant Carlos C. Wellman, all of Chicopee.

Company B—Captain Franklin W Pease of Lee; First Lieutenant Thomas F. Plunkett, Jr., of Pittsfield; Second Lieutenant P. Woodbridge Morgan of Lee.

Company C—Captain Edwin Hurlburt of Great Barrington; First Lieutenant John C. Robinson of Adams; Second Lieutenant Rufus P. Lincoln of Amherst.

Company D—Captain Algernon S. Flagg of Wilbraham; First Lieutenant Charles L. Edwards of Southampton; Second Lieutenant George H. Hyde of Lee.

Company E—Captain Archibald Hopkins of Williamstown; First Lieutenant Jonas A. Champney of Adams; Second Lieutenant Walter B. Smith of Pittsfield.

Company F—Captain Eugene A. Allen of Springfield; First Lieutenant Mason W Tyler of Amherst; Second Lieutenant Elihu R. Rockwood of Greenfield.

Company G—Captain Marcus T. Moody, First Lieutenant William Bliss, Second Lieutenant Edward Bridgman, all of Northampton.

Company H—Captain Joseph L. Hayden of Williamsburg; First Lieutenant Joshua A. Loomis of Northampton; Second Lieutenant Andrew L. Bush of Westfield.

Company I—Captain Hugh Donnelly, First Lieutenant J. Milton Fuller, Second Lieutenant Charles Phelps, all of Springfield.

Company K—Captain Peter Dooley of Cheshire; First Lieutenant John B. Mulloy of Springfield; Second Lieutenant George B. Chandley of Springfield.

It is but simple justice to say that few volunteer regiments left Massachusetts with a more capable complement of officers than those just named. While it would have been too much to expect that every selection should prove the best possible for the position to be filled, the few weaknesses were more than offset by the general strength of the roster, and the Thirty-seventh may properly claim ever to have been a well-officered regiment.

A fair proportion had already seen active service. Colonel Edwards, going to the front a year previous as the adjutant of the Tenth regiment, was serving as senior aide on the staff of General D. N. Couch when he was directed by Governor Andrew to proceed to Pittsfield to organize a regiment under the new call. Lieutenant-Colonel Goodrich had served with the Eighth regiment the previous year as first sergeant and second lieutenant. Quartermaster Dodge having been a sergeant in the same company—the Allen Guards of Pittsfield. Major Montague had abandoned his teacher's desk at the firing on Sumter, and entered the service as a first lieutenant in the Sixth Wisconsin, serving till autumn of 1861, when he took a position on the military staff of the governor of that state, engaged in recruiting service till that official lost his life by an unfortunate accident at Pittsburg Landing in the spring of 1862, when Mr. Montague came east to offer his services to his native state. Adjutant Colt was also a graduate of the Tenth, as were Captain Moody and Lieutenants Loomis and Smith. Captain Allen, in addition to service in the same school, had long been connected with the Springfield militia, while the sturdy Drummajor Gaffney, also formerly identified with the Tenth, had taken his youthful lessons in the British service. Lieutenant Edwards had found his early military excitement in the days of the "Border Ruffian" troubles in Kansas, and others had received knowledge from the state militia and other sources.

One of the number, at least, Lieutenant Smith of Company E, had good personal reasons for lifting the sword against the fanatic horde who were bent on the destruction of the Union. The fall of Fort Sumter found Mr. Smith engaged in mining on the Yahula river, near Dahlonega, Ga., where he was superintending works in which he had a considerable financial interest. Obliged to abandon everything and escape as best he could, he made his way with much difficulty to Richmond, where he succeeded in obtaining a pass through the rebel lines and finally reached Washington and the shelter of the Stars and Stripes, having had many narrow escapes. Passing through Philadelphia on his way to join the Tenth regiment in camp at Washington, he was severely wounded in the leg by a shot fired from a window, but on recovery was mustered into the service in time to receive a wound in the shoulder at Fair Oaks. Lieutenant Smith was not with the regiment at Pittsfield, however, joining it subsequent to the arrival at Washington.

Soon after taking command Major Edwards had announced, as an incentive for men and officers to strive for excellence, that the company standing best in drill and discipline should be made the color company, while the second best should be given the right of the line. The first position was won by Company F, then under the command of Captain George L. Montague, while Captain Moody's Company G took the right.

At the organization of the regiment Sergeant Charles S. Bardwell of Whately and Company F was appointed color sergeant, and all who saw him in that position will remember how every inch a soldier he looked as he bore the national flag in that capacity. In reply to a friend who expressed regret at his appointment to so dangerous a position he said: "This is the proudest day of my life. To this work I have devoted myself, and if I fall it is for my country and my God!"

The men borne on the regimental rolls were principally from the four western counties of the state, Berkshire furnishing 384, Hampshire 332, Hampden 259 and Franklin 87. It has already been remarked that in every respect they were a fine body of men. To an especial degree they embodied the best New England patriotic devotion. Largely they represented the thrifty, native-born element, with home ties and material interests centering about them. There was no longer hope or expectation that the war was to be else than long and bloody. They were called to no holiday scenes, but to face in the field a desperate and at that time dangerously victorious enemy. The money compensation for the service, while liberal from the military stand-point, was no consideration as offset by the comfortable homes which they were leaving, the pain of parting from the dearest friends and all the sad uncertainties of the camp and the field. Under these circumstances the claim to the pure patriotism so worthily voiced by Sergeant Bardwell will readily be allowed for the great majority of his comrades, who on many a desperate field were to prove that claim but just.

The closing days of the regiment in Camp Briggs were full of touching interest. Daily the streets and grounds were thronged by visitors, a few from motives of mere curiosity, no doubt, but the great majority bearing thoughtful offerings for the comfort of the soldiers in that strange life to which they were going forth, or seeking for a few brief hours that communion with dear friends which they might never more enjoy. They manifested the liveliest interest in all the military movements of the command, but especially in the dress parade of the afternoon, when the rear of the parade ground was invariably lined by a sea of proud and interested faces.

The usual gifts were bestowed upon the departing soldiers by the citizens, including Bibles or Testaments, with which each was provided, and many of the officers had special tokens of regard either from their commands or from friends. A fine sword was presented to Captain Moody by his company, their Springfield friends remembered Captain Donnelly with a complete uniform and Lieutenant Mulloy with a full sword equipment, and the day before camp was broken a splendid sword was given to Colonel Edwards. Chaplain Morse, who had left his pastorate of the Methodist Episcopal church at Blandford and enlisted as a private in Company A from a pure and conscientious desire to serve his country, was presented with a horse by his friends in the regiment, and there were other pleasant tokens of like character bestowed.

The Springfield muskets with which the regiment was equipped were issued on the 3d of September, and were received by the men with delight. Not only were they without doubt the most efficient muzzle-loading military rifles ever made, and the most satisfactory in form and construction, but there was a patriotic aversion to the foreign-made weapons with which some of the troops were armed. At dress parade on the 6th a fine silk flag was presented to Colonel Edwards by Mrs. J. R. Morewood of Pittsfield, and was accepted with an appropriate response. The body of the flag had been made by the young ladies of

Pittsfield under the direction of Mrs. Morewood, and it was affixed to a staff made from wood cut on Mount Greylock. On the staff was a silver plate thus engraved: "Presented to Colonel Edwards, 37th Mass. Vols., by his friend, Mrs. M." This flag was never borne in battle by the regiment, but was used to mark the head-quarters of Colonel Edwards, was sometimes under fire and received some bullet holes, was inscribed with the names of the battles in which the regiment participated, and still remains in the possession of General Edwards, a treasured memento of the ladies of Pittsfield who in all stages of the great conflict did so noble a part in caring for the needy, wounded or suffering soldiers and in helping to maintain the honor and unity of the nation.

At the same dress parade the first marching orders of the regiment were read, announcing departure on the morrow for Washington.

CHAPTER IV
FROM PITTSFIELD TO DOWNSVILLE.

THE JOURNEY TO WASHINGTON.—LIFE AT CAMP CHASE.—VIA FREDERICK AND SOUTH MOUNTAIN TO THE ARMY OF THE POTOMAC.

A busy scene was witnessed at Camp Briggs on Sunday, September 7, 1862. Great numbers of visitors were present—friends who came from distant towns, it might be, to speak a parting word with dear ones on the day of departure; patriotic citizens, with a just pride in the regiment composed of their friends and acquaintances; the curious and the indifferent who came to view the scene and to indulge in gossip and speculation. There were final gifts of trinkets and keepsakes to swell the already plethoric knapsacks, and as the forenoon waned the last articles were packed, and with impatient weariness the soldiers waited the word of command that was to be their farewell to the spot. The tents only were left, for a draft had been ordered early in August for 300,000 militia for nine months' service, and the Berkshire regiment under that call was to occupy the camp, and the advance squads were already on the ground—the nucleus of the Forty-ninth regiment.

At noon the line was formed, with every man for the first time in his place, and a proud line it was that stretched entirely across the camp and bent to the front on each flank. Never again was that line to be so long and strong and handsome as on that calm Sabbath day! They thought not of that, be sure, nor did they imagine that almost three long years would pass before their work should be done, and through the sacrifice of so many of their noblest and bravest the integrity of their country at last be assured.

The march to the Pittsfield depot, where cars were to be taken for Hudson, N. Y., though very wearisome to the men from the weight of their heavily-laden knapsacks and the heat of the day, was a continuous ovation. Not the village only, but the entire neighboring country, seemed to have gathered to witness the departure of the "boys." The streets were packed with men, women and children, the national colors freely displayed, not only from buildings and flag-staffs, but worn, especially by the young of both sexes, in rosettes and ribbons, knots and bows of every description. It was a gala day, yet over all there spread a touch of sadness, and painful to all witnesses were the partings of many dear friends, as the last farewells were spoken.

At the public square, in the center of the village, the regiment halted and formed, and brief services were held, prayer fervent and eloquent being offered by the venerable Rev. John Todd, D. D. The ride to Hudson was uneventful, and that city was reached just as the shades of evening were falling. The popular greeting there seemed every whit as earnest, though the passing regiment came from another state. The streets were filled to overflowing with a cheering throng, and amid great enthusiasm the Thirty-seventh marched through the place to the steamer Oregon, the procession headed by the Hudson firemen, accompanied by their mayor and a deputation of prominent citizens. A collation was served by the people of the city, and everywhere the most earnest well-wishes were manifested.

After the boat was well under way down the river it was made known that considerable quantities of bad liquor had been smuggled aboard by some who had not the best good of the command at heart, and much to the grief, and possibly the anger, of the possessors it was relentlessly poured into the Hudson. With that exception the trip down the river was markedly delightful. The night was pleasant and many of the men, finding sleep out of the question amid their novel surroundings, gazed in silence on the matchless beauty of the Highlands and the Palisades as the sturdy boat steamed steadily past them. Quite a party of friends from Pittsfield accompanied the regiment as far as New York, as did Superintendent Henry Gray of the Western railroad from Springfield, two of whose sons were members of the regiment.

Early morning of the 8th found the Thirty-seventh landing at the wharf in Jersey City, and stacking arms on a street in the immediate vicinity they waited till noon for further transportation. Still the same lively interest in the welfare of the soldiers was manifested. A very acceptable luncheon was furnished by the citizens, and those not already supplied with Bibles or Testaments were sought out and given a copy; one little girl engaged in this work especially winning kindly remembrance for her charming, earnest manner. Cars were finally taken for Philadelphia, and that place was reached about dusk.

The blessings of all the soldiers who passed through the City of Brotherly Love rest upon the heads of its devoted and patriotic inhabitants. While all the loyal cities, and all the towns as well, did noble service in the way of care for the volunteer soldiers, by common consent the palm of excellence must be awarded to the Pennsylvania metropolis. In health, in disease, or suffering from wounds, the Union soldier who came within its confines was sure of the most thoughtful provision for his comfort, the most kindly ministrations for his welfare. The greeting received by the Thirty-seventh was no exception to the rule. On leaving the cars the command marched to the Cooper Shop refreshment saloon, where a bountiful repast was in waiting, seasoned with many a kind word from those in attendance. Afterward the regiment rested on one of the public squares in the vicinity till near midnight, when it marched toward the depot. Late as was the hour, the streets were packed the entire distance with men and women, who pressed close to the marching column to utter words of encouragement and to clasp the soldiers' hands.

A train, principally composed of freight cars, was found in waiting, into which the men stowed themselves as well as they could in the darkness, and most of them were soon asleep, while the train rushed away toward Baltimore. A few miles only had been passed, when there came a crash, a sharp shock, and the train stopped so suddenly that the occupants were piled in heaps in the front ends of the cars. It was found that some detached cars from a preceding train had been run into by the train bearing the Thirty-seventh and terribly wrecked. They were principally loaded with Pennsylvania troops on their way to defend the ferries at Elkton and Havre de Grace against the threatening Confederate cavalry, then in Maryland, and many of the unfortunate men were killed or wounded. The engine and forward cars of the colliding train were badly broken, but no member of the Thirty-seventh was seriously hurt, and as they could only wait for the coming of a relief train, the men presently composed themselves to sleep till such time as the journey could be renewed. They were awakened by a roar, another crash and shock, to find that the relief train had come down upon the same track and driven its engine into the rear of the already disabled train, completing its wreck and further blockading the road. Fortunately, and almost miraculously, no serious harm had come to the Thirty-seventh, even then. The baggage cars of the regiment were in the rear, and had saved the lives of the men, though only a single car in the center of the train had escaped more or less breakage.

It was nearly noon before another engine and cars were in readiness to take the impatient command from the scene of the double disaster, and when they were once more ready to proceed Colonel Edwards placed Captain Hayden, an experienced engineer, in charge of the locomotive. Wilmington was soon reached, and there much enthusiasm was shown by the populace, who provided generous refreshment, though the soldiers did not leave the cars. Not till evening did they arrive at Baltimore, and the streets were nearly deserted and almost ominously quiet. But a bountiful supper had been provided near by, and after that was disposed of the line of march to the Washington depot was taken up. To the men this was a most impressive event. They did not forget that but a little more than a year previous their brother soldiers of the Old Bay State had been murdered in Baltimore streets by a frenzied mob, and there had been many earnest speculations as to the spirit that would be awakened in the city by the victories of General Lee and the presence of his hosts in Maryland. That speculation was in no way answered, for the streets were utterly deserted, and darkness and gloom covered the city like a pall. On the evening before leaving Pittsfield ten rounds of ball cartridges had been drawn and afterward carefully treasured, "for the Baltimore mob" if wanted, but there was no occasion for their use.

The remainder of the night and the early part of the following day, September 10, were passed in the vicinity of the depot, waiting for transportation, which came at length in the shape of still less inviting freight cars, and about 5 o'clock that afternoon the national Capital was reached. High anticipations had been raised in regard to the reception which might be expected at Washington. Since all the other cities had been so enthusiastic in applauding and providing for the volunteer soldiers on their passage, it was, perhaps, natural to expect that on reaching their destination they should meet especial manifestations of welcome. All such anticipations faded rapidly. The first movement was to the "Soldiers' Relief" for supper, and this proved to be insufficient in quantity and abominable in quality. Citizens there seemed to be none, though wounded and convalescent soldiers were abundant, their sallow features and doleful words by no means calculated to create enthusiasm in the breasts of the Massachusetts listeners. The sanitary condition of the region, which was on the outskirts of the city, was anything but creditable. Goats and hogs were running at large, and the air was heavily laden with poisonous odors. The approach of darkness and a storm caused the command to seek shelter in huge barracks near by, and the men were soon well settled, in anticipation of an unbroken night's sleep, of which they felt the need. Scarcely were they comfortably disposed, when other regiments came pouring in, and narrower quarters were assigned, till the entire great building was wedged to its utmost capacity with troops. Through the uncomfortable night there may have been memories of the time, early in the struggle, when Massachusetts soldiers were luxuriously quartered in the Senate chamber, but there was little restful sleep, and the impressions of Washington in the autumn of 1862 were anything but agreeable.

Next morning another visit was made to the "Soldiers'

Relief," and the breakfast proved a measurable improvement on the supper. A long wait followed upon the street-side, during which venders of all manner of trifles, useful and otherwise, diligently improved their opportunities, and then the column moved away. Brave, indeed, was the heart that did not shrink before the doleful surroundings. Everywhere were wounded soldiers wearing slings and bandages, armless, legless, or the more wretched fever patients, creeping about like miserable ghosts of once robust men. Along the business streets, physicians, surgeons, undertakers, embalmers and kindred professions, seemed to have a monopoly, and to vie with each other in advertising their horrible specialties. Hearses and ambulances were abundant, with here and there an army wagon rearing its soiled canvas top to break the ghastly monopoly. A passing glance afforded ample food for reflection, and the column moved on, past the unfinished Washington monument and across Long Bridge, guarded by cannon, and then their feet, in most cases for the first time, pressed the "sacred soil of Virginia."

The march of some five miles to the designated camp was quite trying to the participants. The rain of the previous evening was supplemented by showers during the march, giving the weary men their first experience with Virginia mud, and, like all new soldiers, they had undertaken to carry so many apparently needful articles as to make a distressingly heavy load. They were quite ready when camp was reached to throw themselves upon the bare earth and defer the work of putting up tents till the morrow. The ground occupied had last seen service as a corn-field, and many of the men, wrapped in their blankets, went to sleep in the furrows. A sudden and furious shower in the night, which converted each hollow into a miniature canal, gave them a forcible lesson in the selection of a bivouac.

The Thirty-seventh had been assigned to General Henry S. Briggs's Brigade of Casey's Division of Reserves, forming a part of the defenders of Washington, while McClellan, with most of the veteran troops, was moving through Maryland in pursuit of the invading army under General Lee. General Briggs had taken command on the day before the arrival of the Thirty-seventh—September 10—other regiments in the brigade being the Thirty-ninth Massachusetts, Tenth Vermont, Eleventh New Hampshire and Twenty-first Connecticut. These were all fresh troops, containing the germs of excellent service, but requiring hardening and development. For this important work, they could have been in no better hands than those of General Briggs.

"Camp Chase," the new home, was delightfully located on the eastern slope of Arlington Hights, a little beyond Fort Albany, overlooking Washington, the Capitol and most of the public buildings clearly defined above the surrounding mass of the city, the whole forming a delightful panorama upon which the defenders never tired of gazing. There was much of the charm of soldier life in the few weeks spent there. The mellow warmth of early autumn was delicious, the duties light and interesting, on account of their novelty, while mail communication with home was prompt and uninterrupted. Besides, many of the men had acquaintances in neighboring regiments, and frequent visits were exchanged, not always strictly according to camp rules, on the part of the enlisted men. Not that there was at any time a wanton disposition to violate the restrictions imposed. Most of the men intuitively comprehended the need of thorough discipline, and were prepared to obey all regulations that might be necessary for their welfare and efficiency. But it was undoubtedly a weakness of the volunteer system that the man who wore the shoulder-straps and he who carried the musket came from the same walks of life, had perhaps associated together from boyhood, and hence did not at once drop into the perfect relations of military commander and subordinate. This feeling was naturally intensified in those cases where the officer failed to grasp the prestige of his new relation, and to win the confidence of his command. To feel that in the hour of supreme trial on the battle-field the officer could not "handle his men," was to sunder the one tie which made unquestioning obedience a pleasure as well a duty. But this digression is not intended as an apology for want of discipline. No such apology is needed, for the Thirty-seventh, from its organization to the close of the contest, bore the proud honor of being one of the very best disciplined volunteer regiments in the service, and the foundation of its subsequent efficiency in the most trying places was laid in these early days of its history, under the thorough yet salutary discipline enforced by Colonel Edwards and his associates.

The principal duties, apart from those of the camp and drill, consisted of work upon the inner lines of defense in the neighborhood of "Camp Chase," with an occasional brigade drill or division review, which were found extremely tedious at this stage of the soldiers' experience. But it was something of recompense to see the long lines of brightly uniformed troops, to note the great strength of the endless fortifications, and then in camp when the day's toil was over to listen to the music of many a band, softened and sweetened by the distance, playing one after another the familiar tunes which annihilated distance and carried the listener back to childhood, friends and home.

These pleasant scenes were not long to continue. The armies of the Union and of the Confederacy had met near Sharpsburg and the bloody battle of Antietam had been fought. To make the result substantially a victory, General McClellan needed immediate reinforcement, and on the 29th of September General Briggs was directed to report in command of the division and five additional regiments, with the Ninth Massachusetts battery, at the army head-quarters. The following day camp was broken, and the Thirty-seventh, with the remainder of the division, marched once more over the Long Bridge into Washington. They were to go by rail to Frederick, Md., but there were not cars enough to move so large bodies immediately, and that night was passed in the Capitol grounds, the sleep of the men watched over by the statues of Washington and the Goddess of Liberty beneath which they reposed. Before leaving "Camp Chase" the knapsacks belonging to the regiment had been sent to Washington, to be forwarded to the army at some future time, and the men were restricted to such possessions as could be wrapped in their blankets or provided for in haversacks or pockets. But with even these limited accommodations, nearly every man had managed to stow away somewhere a portfolio with writing materials, and during this tedious wait for transportation many were to be seen sitting along the street curbing penning or penciling letters to the friends at home to apprise them of each change of fortune or situation. The massive buildings of the government were near, and not a few visited them, finding in the Capitol, now doing duty as a hospital, not less than a thousand wounded from the recent battles.

In the early part of the afternoon of October 1 cars were taken for Frederick, and the train crept slowly away—so slowly, indeed, that next morning found it not more than a dozen miles beyond Relay House. The remainder of the ride was charming, for it was through one of the most lovely of countries, the neat dwellings and massive barns, surrounded by rich and far-reaching fields, everywhere speaking of prosperity and competence.

The afternoon was well advanced when Frederick was reached, and exciting as had been the recent scenes in that quiet city, with the passage of Lee's army, closely followed by that of McClellan, and all the annoyances inseparable from the presence of large bodies of armed men, the majority of the inhabitants manifested great pleasure at the sight of the fresh regiments, which, after a brief stop in the city, went into bivouac in a neighboring meadow. There the troops rested after their cramping ride in the cars till late the following afternoon, when they marched in the direction of Sharpsburg. In the mean time General Briggs's command had been dissolved and the individual regiments were assigned to the weakened brigades already in the field, losing sight of each other from that time forward, save as the fortunes of war might chance to throw them temporarily together.*

From Frederick the line of march led over the Catoctin Mountains, and on their pleasant slopes the regiment halted the first night, having made a few miles quite comfortably during the early evening. These easy stages were very pleasing to the men, many of whom were suffering from the effects of a changed

---
* General Briggs, with whom as an aide-de-camp went Captain Hopkins of Company E, of the Thirty-seventh, was assigned to the command of the Second Brigade, Third Division, Fifth Corps, composed of new Pennsylvania regiments. Before the movement of the Army of the Potomac in pursuit of Lee, however, his health again gave way, and he was obliged to further recruit his strength at home in Massachusetts, returning in the winter to take command of the department of Baltimore, extending from Annapolis to Frederick, forming a part of General Schenck's Eighth Corps, occupying the Middle Department.

climate, different water and new methods of life, bowel complaints being very prevalent. The medical staff did all in their power to preserve the health of the command, and the sufferers generally struggled along pluckily, frequently receiving assistance from their more robust comrades. It was the beginning of that long era of mutual helpfulness, by deed and word, which marked the entire experience of this organization, as of most in the army, which still survives in fraternal associations, and forms one of the brightest elements in the character of the American soldier. No sight was more common at the end of a long and fatiguing march than to see some stalwart private bending under the weight of two or three guns, another file jointly supporting an extra knapsack or blanket roll, that some exhausted comrade might be spared the discredit, or the danger, of falling from the ranks. All honor to the brave men whose heart-prompted kindnesses still live in many a grateful memory, or softened the rigors of many a patriot who finally yielded his life on the common altar.

The bivouac of the night was on the ground occupied by "Stonewall" Jackson's corps a few weeks before, from which they had set out on the expedition against Harper's Ferry, and this fact was an interesting one to the Massachusetts occupants. At 7 o'clock next morning the march was resumed, across the beautiful valley watered by the Catoctin creek and its tributaries, in the midst of which nestled the neat village of Middletown, surrounded by vast corn-fields in which the ripened grain had been gathered in shocks. Notwithstanding the passage of so many armed men, there were few evidences of wanton depredation, General Lee hoping by a politic course in this respect to win the inhabitants to his cause, and the Union troops, feeling that they were in the presence of friends, respecting the citizens as such.

Soon after leaving the Catoctin the towering sides of South Mountain were approached, and before noon the regiment was climbing the sharp ascent which had witnessed on the 14th of the previous month so desperate a struggle and the loss of the gallant Reno's life. As the mountain side was scaled the evidences of the battle were everywhere apparent, and to other senses than those of sight. The forest trees were torn and scarred by artillery fire, large branches were cut away, and occasionally a tree trunk, broken and splintered, lifted high in the air its testimony to the severity of the cannonade. Through the forest and over the fields bullet marks were visible on every side, and the sadly suggestive debris of the battle-field freely scattered about. The slain horses had been gathered in piles and partially burned, the fuel still smoldering in some places; but this process had been so imperfectly carried out that a terrible stench filled the air for a great distance.

At noon the summit was reached, and there the regiment halted till 5 o'clock. Both officers and men occupied much of the time in strolling over the historic ground in the vicinity, collecting such relics as came to hand, many of which were forwarded to friends at home as the first keepsakes from a recent battle-field. Here, too, General Briggs finally parted company with the Thirty-seventh, riding ahead with his staff to join his new command.

Resuming its march the regiment passed through the little village of Boonsboro, where much earnest Union sentiment was manifest, but where, as in most Maryland communities at that time, there was likewise a strong minority with exactly the opposite principles, which found so bitter expression between the factions that the children of tender years took up the exultant refrain as the presence of the Gray or the Blue gave pretext. "There now, Secesh, what do you think of Old Jackson coming back here again?" piped one youthful voice, animated by the steady sweep of the passing column; and immediately a brisk war of words rose on the dust-laden air, for "Secesh," like his corporate namesake, had no idea of acknowledging defeat short of "the last ditch."

A mile beyond the village the bivouac for the night was made and named "Camp Crehore," in compliment to the surgeon. It was in a fine forest grove, untouched by the hand of man, with great rocks distributed here and there at some time away back in the unknown, among which the now ancient trees had grown, flourished and faded. Here one had fallen and was slowly crumbling back to dust, while there the smoother trunk and pliant limbs showed how as in human life one generation gave way to another. A hundred camp-fires were soon blazing cheerily, the ruddy light bringing out in majestic relief the natural beauties of the scene. "This is grand!" remarked more than one weary soldier as he lay beside his camp-fire and gazed up into the leafy expanse till the visions of the present mingled with those of scenes far away, and sleep wrapped officer and private alike in its mantle. Later in the night a gentle rain fell, but those who awoke to find it beating in their faces merely drew their rubber blankets a little closer and slept on.

The morning of Sunday, the 5th of October, dawned clear and beautiful. The rain of the previous night had ceased, only that now and then a passing breeze threw down a few drops from the trees upon the busy host below. The fires were quickly crackling in every direction, the coffee cups nestled about each cheery blaze in wonderful number, and the simple breakfasts were soon prepared and disposed of. Battalion line was then formed and the men with uncovered heads listened reverently while Chaplain Morse offered prayer, and at the close all were invited to join in singing "Praise God from whom all blessings flow." The spirit of the occasion seemed to impress each one—the Sabbath day, the scene, the approach to the Army of the Potomac, with whose fortunes from that time the destinies of the regiment were to be blended; the nearness of the great battleground, on which so recently thousands of brave men had laid down their lives; all these thoughts with others combined to make the moment one never to be forgotten. Men who seldom sang joined their voices, and as the rich chorals of "Old Hundred" rose from hundreds of earnest voices and thrilled through the mighty forest arches the spot seemed indeed a temple of praise. The rich sunlight poured a flood of gold upon the treetops, while occasionally a yellow ray glinted through between leaf and branch and trunk to lighten a mossy rock or warm some youthful soldier.

These appropriate Sabbath morning exercises over, the march

was resumed, passing presently through Keedysville, where every available building was still filled with the wounded from the battle of the Antietam and with the sick who had been temporarily placed there. At this point the regiment turned to the right, crossing Antietam creek on the bridge used by General Hooker in reaching his position on the Confederate left, and passing near the battle-field proper. Chaplain Morse who, riding in advance of the regiment, mistook the route and went by way of Sharpsburg and the Hagerstown pike, wrote thus of his passage through the scene of conflict :

> The appearance from the road was such that I had no desire to go into the field on either side to examine particularly. I could count dead horses by the scores. There were graves and trenches almost innumerable in every direction. All the single graves appeared to have a board at the head with a name written on it. Some of the trenches had numerous boards adjoining each other. Some graves looked rough and carelessly filled, and others appeared rounded with care. Some had an inclosure around them of rails put together in the form of a cob-house. There were fragments of broken wagons and gun carriages lying about profusely. The fences that remained standing were completely perforated with bullets. The woods presented a strange appearance. Some trees as large as my body were completely cut off 20 feet high. Limbs were cut off and strewn upon the ground, and others were lopped and left hanging. The corn-field looked as if a large drove of cattle had foraged through it. All along the road for miles there were indications of a terrible carnage. If the appearance be such three weeks after an engagement I almost shrink from the thought of beholding the bodies of dead and dying men covering the ground and of witnessing the terrible carnage of battle.

Marching leisurely a distance of some ten miles, the command observed indications of the presence of large bodies of troops. Through the trees glimpses of tents could be seen, and curious-eyed knots of soldiers were assembled at intervals beside the road. Presently from the head of the column a strong, hearty cheer rang out, and traveled quickly from company to company, taken up by many who only guessed the cause. "It's the Tenth regiment!" ran from file to file, and the cheers were redoubled. The marching column halted and the two commands mingled. They were brothers, schoolmates, friends. The hills of Berkshire and the valley of the Connecticut were the homes of each. The older regiment had given some of its best material toward the formation of the new. Their fortunes were henceforth to be identified; their banners to go side by side into the supreme test of battle. Yet there was a marked contrast in the two bodies as they thus came into association. Exposure, disease, the march and battle had wasted the Tenth to a remnant of its original self; its banners and clothing gave unmistakable testimony to the arduous service through which it had passed. The Thirty-seventh, on the other hand, had full ranks, bright banners, fresh uniforms; but the hearts which beat along the different lines were filled with the same love of country, the same consecration to principle, the same devotion to "the old flag" as the emblem of national unity.

Turning to the left from the road on which they had come, the Thirty-seventh filed into a magnificent open grove of oak and walnut, in the midst of which their camp was made and christened "Camp Dodge," in behalf of the quartermaster. The spot was one of the most charming that could be imagined. The trees had many of them grown to giant proportions, but the ground beneath them was covered with a soft carpet of grass, quite unknown to New England forests, and overlooking this scene of beauty the tents of the "field and staff" were pitched upon a smooth, round eminence near by. The men were without tents, but the weather was warm and delightful, and very satisfactory shelters were speedily constructed from their rubber blankets. Thus pleasantly began the life of the regiment as a factor of the Army of the Potomac.

CHAPTER V

THE ADVANCE TO FALMOUTH.

THE EXPEDITION TO HANCOCK AND CHERRY RUN.—INTO THE
LAND OF SECESSION.—A CHANGE OF COMMANDERS.—INCI-
DENTS BY THE WAY.—WHITE PLAINS AND "CAMP MISERY."

The Army of the Potomac, at the time it was joined by the Thirty-seventh regiment, was undergoing something of a reconstruction; or, it might be more accurate to say that the reorganization attempted by General McClellan, and which had been partially accomplished with his army on the march in pursuit of Lee, was not yet completed. Changes were continually occurring in the make-up of brigades and divisions, especially in those corps which had suffered most severely at Antietam. In some instances the reinforcements of new regiments were organized into brigades by themselves, but more generally they were incorporated in those already formed and decimated in the field. The army was now composed of three principal divisions, designated as the right and left wings and the center, each under a commander. The right wing under Major-General Burnside consisted of the First Corps, Major-General Hooker, and the Ninth, Brigadier-General O. B. Willcox. Each of these corps comprised three divisions, those of the First commanded by Brigadier-Generals A. Doubleday, James B. Ricketts and George G. Meade; those of the Ninth by Brigadiers W W Burns, S. D. Sturgis and George W Getty. The center, under Major-General E. V Sumner, consisted of his own Second Corps, its divisions commanded by Brigadier W S. Hancock, Major-General John Sedgwick and Brigadier W H. French, and the Twelfth Corps, Brigadier-General A. S. Williams, with its two divisions (five brigades) under Brigadiers S. W Crawford and

George S. Greene. The left wing, under Major-General William B. Franklin, consisted of his own Sixth Corps and General Fitz John Porter's Fifth Corps, the two divisions of the latter led by Brigadiers George W Morell and George Sykes. The Sixth Corps proper at that time consisted of two divisions commanded respectively by Major-Generals H. W Slocum and William F. Smith, each of three brigades. Attached to the corps, and afterward consolidated with it, was Major-General Darius N Couch's division of the Fourth Corps, composed of the First Brigade, General Charles Devens, Second, General A. P Howe, and Third, General John Cochrane.

With General Devens's First Brigade the Thirty-seventh regiment was to be henceforth identified, and its fellow-regiments were found to be the Second Rhode Island, Colonel Frank Wheaton; Seventh Massachusetts, Colonel David A. Russell; Tenth Massachusetts, Colonel H. L. Eustis; and Thirty-sixth New York, Colonel W H. Browne—a regiment enlisted for two years. This brigade had already made a record highly creditable to both officers and men. The Second, the senior regiment, began its service on the bloody field of Bull Run, where it lost more than a hundred men, among the killed being Colonel Slocum and Major Ballou, and faithfully from that time onward it had responded to every call for service. The Seventh had early given its first colonel, Darius N. Couch, to a broader field, and the Tenth had yielded to higher claims its loved and gallant Colonel Briggs, who so bravely led it in its first baptism of fire at Fair Oaks. These officers in accepting promotions had left their commands in able hands—Wheaton, Russell, Browne, Eustis and Edwards—what brigade could boast an abler list of regimental commanders? And the men whom they commanded were worthy of such leadership.

Six weeks of inactivity followed the exhausting contest on the Antietam, General Lee's army resting in the Shenandoah valley near Winchester. The Fifth Corps had made an effort directly after the Confederate retreat to pursue across the Potomac, but the reception met with was so warm as to discourage the Federal commander from a more vigorous movement. After a month of recuperation, finding he was not likely to be disturbed, Lee ventured to send his daring cavalry leader, General J. E. B. Stuart, on one of his characteristic raids. The latter, crossing the river at the fords above Williamsport with something less than 2,000 men, dashed across Maryland and penetrated Pennsylvania as far as Chambersburg. Some 300 sick and wounded Union soldiers in hospital there were captured and paroled, and considerable public stores destroyed. Thence the slender column swept swiftly around in the rear of McClellan's army, and recrossed the Potomac into Virginia at White's Ford, below the Monocacy, without the loss of a man. Stuart was closely pursued all the way by a body of Pleasonton's cavalry, but though the latter rode nearly 80 miles in 24 hours, they were unable to come up with the raiders.

This raid by Stuart, though not of great importance from a national stand-point, proved of especial interest to the Thirty-seventh, as one result thereof was their first experience in active campaigning. As early as the 10th of October, marching orders were promulgated, and it was known that there was intense anxiety at Washington and through the country that the army should move against the enemy while the weather and roads were favorable. But nothing came of these orders, and on the 15th they were repeated, followed the next day by considerable cannonading in the direction of Harper's Ferry, to which the newer troops listened with much interest. These orders having been countermanded almost as soon as promulgated, the enlisted men, especially, had come to look upon them as a part of the school of the soldier, and were quite surprised when late in the afternoon of the 18th the call came for an immediate departure. It afterward appeared that at the first summons, on the 10th, Howe's brigade had marched up the Potomac in the hope of intercepting Stuart on his return, but that wily commander, as already noted, had moved in quite a different direction. Now a fresh alarm came from the same direction and the balance of Couch's division was hurried that way with all possible celerity.

With whatever they chanced to have in the way of rations and blankets the command hastily formed, and at 5 o'clock the march began. It was soon dark, but the column pressed resolutely forward, through Williamsport, across Conococheague Creek to Clear Spring, which was reached after midnight, some 13 miles from the starting point. The men, unused to such "forced marches," were sadly exhausted before the bivouac was reached, but the novelty of the event gave them inspiration, and the regimental pride, which was in many a trying place to bring them credit and renown, was already pleasantly manifest. Scarcely a straggler fell from the ranks, in pleasing contrast to the experience of some, if not most, of the older regiments in the column.

A laughable incident occurred near the close of the night's jaunt. The regiment was plodding wearily along its way, unable to see through the darkness what was before it, when suddenly there came a swashing, rustling, indefinable sound from a point just in advance, and extending some distance away. At once the suggestion was offered that the leading regiments were fording the Potomac, and apparently the sound was recognized as coming from the splashing of shallow water through which men and horses were passing. There were no signs of a halt to prepare for the crossing, and immediately the roadside was lined with soldiers stripping off their shoes and stockings and rolling up their pants. Meantime the rustling became each moment nearer and louder as the column advanced, what appeared to be the smooth, shining surface of the stream could be dimly seen, and the officers were already riding into—not the Potomac, but an immense corn-field, in which the bivouac was to be made! The troops in advance, on halting, had begun to pull down the great shocks of harvested corn to serve them for bedding, causing the sound which had been so ludicrously misinterpreted. As the bare-footed stragglers came tenderly picking their way and looking for the "ford," they learned the truth at the cost of many a hearty jest.

Morning found the command lame and weary, and not in the best of humor, for the night had been quite too chilly for comfort. A hasty breakfast of hard bread was swallowed, and at an early hour the march was resumed. Some two miles beyond Clear Spring was Fair View Inn, a humble hostelry beside the highway, and "fair" indeed was the view which opened before the gaze of the delighted soldiers, as they paused for a moment to feast upon its beauties. The stand-point was the summit of North Mountain range, which there breaks and slopes on either shore toward the Potomac. The river was but a few miles away, and it seemed even nearer in constrast with the magnificent expanse of the Shenandoah valley, which stretched far to the southward, mountain-bound on every side. A continuation of the range upon which he stood, but seeming to the beholder an independent conformation. Little North Mountain swept away toward the southwest, boldest and clearest defined of all the wide panorama, because the nearest. Far in the dim blue to the southward Massannutten Mountain bounded the view, while to the left the far-reaching Blue Ridge, softened by the distance, stood in everlasting grandeur. What a magnificent prospect! what historic ground was embraced in that outlook! With many an exclamation of appreciation, the sturdy New Englanders feasted their eyes upon the scene, and forgot for a time their weariness.

Some 20 miles still remained between the division and its destination, and it was not till about sunset that the weary force halted near Hancock village. A picket line was established along the river, between it and the canal, to which unpleasant position Company F was assigned. An uncomfortable night followed, as a cold wind swept down the river, chilling the men to the bone, whether on outpost, crowded around the insufficient fires, or wrapped in their blankets to sleep. The day following, October 21, was eventless till midnight, when orders were received to change the location of the brigade to Cherry Run Ford, some ten miles down the Potomac. Colonel Edwards at once issued the necessary directions for the moving of his command, and by the time Company E, which had relieved F on the picket line, could hurry into camp the column was formed and at once moved away.

Steadily through the night the brigade plodded along, and at daybreak met its supply trains—a very welcome meeting, since the rations taken from Downsville were wholly exhausted, and not a few had gone supperless to sleep the previous evening. With the wagons had also come a mail, and in the shelter of a noble forest the men gathered about the cheerful camp-fires to enjoy the warmth, prepare a hearty meal and read over and over the news and words of cheer from friends and home.

From this point it was only some half a mile to the river, in the vicinity of which the brigade went into temporary camp. Across the Potomac were commanding hights from which an aggressive enemy might have made the position very uncomfortable, and there were unquestionably fears among both officers and men that the first night would be broken by the rude howling of solid shot or shell; but nothing of the kind occurred, and a cavalry force, supported by the Second Rhode Island, was pushed across to look for signs of the foe.

Early on the morning of the 23d the regiment was roused with the announcement of marching orders, and at sunrise the road was taken. Less than a mile had been made when the brigade halted in the forest, and after waiting there till well into the afternoon returned to the camp just vacated. One or two sad incidents which occurred about this time deeply touched the members of the Thirty-seventh, for they had not yet become familiar with death in its more appalling forms. On the way to Cherry Run, at the foot of a sharp hill they passed the remains of a broken wagon, with a dead man lying beside the ruins. In the darkness the wagon had left the road and rolled down the steep bank, carrying down and killing a sick soldier who was riding in it, and it was no discredit to the soldierly qualities of the men that in looking upon the spectacle they gave utterance to many a word of sorrow for his sad fate. But the interest in this event was not so close as in the death of a member of the Tenth regiment during the halt beside the highway on that 23d of October. He had but just returned to duty after an illness, complained of exhaustion when the halt was made, and died in a few minutes, to be buried in that lone spot with the last honors of his comrades in arms.

Four days more were passed at Cherry Run, and they were days of discomfort, a cold rain-storm setting in and continuing most of the time. The officers were far from comfortably provided for, while the men were without tents, and not a few without woolen blankets, though nearly all had rubber blankets, and these were forced to do duty as tents, for outside protection for those on guard, and in many another way. Of course a single rubber was wholly inadequate to so many uses at the same time, and as a consequence every man was soaked early in the storm. But with an occasional exception the spirits of the soldiers seemed to rise in proportion as the external circumstances were disheartening; the unpleasant situation was cheerfully accepted, exhibitions of selfishness were rare, and everywhere was manifested the utmost consideration for the welfare of the ill and the less robust.

On Monday morning, the 27th, definite orders came to march, and night found the command at Williamsport, where it bivouacked. The storm had just ceased, the ground was still soaked, and everything about the soldiers wet, heavy to carry upon the march and uncomfortable. But in knots of from one to four, according to circumstances, the weary men spread their rubbers upon the damp earth, drew the wet woolen blankets over them, and slept soundly, despite the sharp cold which followed the storm. In the morning many of the damp blankets were so stiffly frozen that they could be lifted by a corner, but blazing fires were soon aglow in every direction, before which they were thawed and dried and everything put in the best possible condition for the continuance of the march.

No movement was made during the 28th, however, though there was a bustle of preparation going on throughout the Sixth Corps, the removal of all the sick to permanent hospitals having been ordered, with other measures indicating an important movement. In fact, General McClellan had already begun his long-expected crossing into Virginia, the advance of the army having passed over the ponton bridges at Berlin on the 26th. On the afternoon of the 29th the brigade returned to the old camp at Downsville, and the ensuing forenoon was devoted to a thorough inspection, followed by fresh marching orders for the next day.

Very early in the morning of the 31st the regiment stood in line beside the road waiting to take its place in the long column which moved past in ceaseless procession, and finally the word was spoken that bade farewell to the pleasant camp and its surroundings. The line of march led back along the route followed by the Thirty-seventh in going to Downsville, across the Antietam and through Keedysville, turning thence more toward the south and reaching the end of the day's journey near Rohrersville. But no stop was to be made there, and before the coming of light next morning the camp was astir. The scene was an impressive one to all who looked upon it in the darkness of that fading night. Here and there the ruddy gleam of a camp-fire could be seen, and every moment the number increased. One after another was added as the awakening soldiers began to stir, and then more rapidly they flashed up adown the valley, along the slopes of the hills and far up to the summit, where they seemed to mingle with the fading stars. Here a bright flame would shoot up clear and radiant like a beacon light, revealing the merry group beside to the casual gaze of those far away; close by a heavy, uncertain column of smoke would indicate the unsuccessful efforts of some less fortunate squad, forced by circumstances to use inferior fuel, or perchance wanting in the experience and tact necessary to win the best results. Finally the light of day came in its full splendor, the camp-light faded, the pillars of smoke died away; from behind the hills, out of forest recesses, almost from the bosom of the earth, it seemed, came the long columns of men in blue, moving steadily away to the southward till lost among the hills and swells of the South Mountain range.

The journey of that day was very wearying, as the route led over hills and mountains, not in gradual ascent but with much climbing and descending, and all concerned were heartily glad to reach the shore of the Potomac near the village of Berlin a little after noon, with the prospect of a few days' rest and a supply of clothing which the increasing severity of the weather and the wear and tear of the march had made necessary.

The regiment encamped somewhat below Berlin, on low

ground between the railroad and the Chesapeake and Ohio canal, and there the following day, Sunday, November 2, was passed. It was a day of thoughtful rest. Far off over the Virginia hills could be heard the constant booming of cannon; troops were continually moving; the head-quarters of the commander-in-chief were in the little village just above; the massive stone piers of what had been a great bridge rose in desolate blackness at intervals across the river, all showing the grim presence of dread war in a manner to impress the Massachusetts soldiery to whom, generally speaking, these sights were new and interesting. Everywhere the pen was busy, officers and men alike embracing what might be the last opportunity for a long time to respond to the missives which had just come to hand; for that great bond of union between home and camp, the mail, followed the army wherever it went—on the march or into the battle.

The 3d of November was a memorable one to the Thirty-seventh. From early in the morning a ceaseless procession had been moving across the long ponton bridge, but it was not till about noon that Colonel Edwards led his command into its place in the column and across the historic river on to the "sacred soil." Anticipation and a mild excitement filled every frame with an unwonted thrill. The impatient demands for a forward movement of the army were answered at last, and every development was followed by the keen-eyed men of New England with the utmost interest. The ponton bridge itself came in for no little share of admiration—the heavy boats anchored upon the bosom of the river, supporting the timbers upon which the planks were laid and firmly held in place by binders across the ends—the whole so simple and meeting the requirements so perfectly. Then as they gained some commanding hight, what a view it was to look back and behold the long lines still moving toward the river, while on the other hand they stretched away farther than the eye could reach, one unbroken thread of blue winding through the brown and gold of the landscape, the afternoon sun glancing back from tens of thousands of shining muskets and polished breastplates. It was indeed a sight to fill the patriotic heart with pride and hope. It could not be that such a magnificent army could be marching but to victory! Alas, the subordinate knew but little how much jealousy and incompetence in high places were doing to make of that magnificent army a weakling!

It was at once evident that the country through which the army marched was not pervaded by love for the old Union. In Maryland the people met with had been mostly friendly to the soldiers, and were glad to show them little favors as opportunity presented. That disposition was no longer manifest, but everywhere secession was freely talked and defended; the able-bodied men were almost without exception absent with the Confederate armies, or at home recovering from sickness or wounds resulting from their service in such armies; any application for food was curtly dismissed; and in not a few cases the buckets were taken from the wells and hidden, that the Union soldiers might not obtain water as they passed. From only a single class was there ever kindness and frankness—the numerous blacks, of all ages and both sexes, who swarmed about the more well-to-do places, were ever ready to aid the soldiers, and to convey such limited knowledge as they might possess. And the passing Yankees, to whom the institution of slavery and its belongings was a new spectacle, were never weary of listening to the droll fancies and rude conceptions of the colored people whom they encountered. "Where is your master?" was asked of one aged man whose life had been worn out in unpaid servitude. "He is in de Southern army, sah." "Do you suppose he would like to have you talking with the Northern soldiers?" "No, sah, I don't think he would like dat!" "Perhaps he may whip you when he learns of it." The bent form straightened with the assertion of a manhood that felt the day of its redemption at hand. "No, sah; he *neber* did that, and he don't dare try it now." Not always was the purport of a question framed from a New England stand-point comprehended by the dusky chattel of a different civilization. "What town is this?" asked a file-closer, for the twentieth time, on a long march, as a group of slaves appeared at the roadside. "Dis?" was the response, with a nod toward the great "master's house," standing a few rods back; "dis is no *town*, dis is a private house!" The honest fellow had no knowledge of the Massachusetts institution which forms the unit of local government and gives its name to the foundation-stone of democracy, the town-meeting, but supposed the mansion to be mistaken for some characteristic Virginia "city."

On the afternoon of that 3d of November, a march of some 13 miles was made after crossing the river, and the following day 15 miles were added, bringing the command to the vicinity of Union—a name decidedly out of keeping with the spirit manifested by the few inhabitants that were to be seen. The weather, which had been cool and comfortable, now became sharp and threatening, and though only about five miles were covered on the 5th, the soldiers were glad to reach their stopping-place. Nor were they sorry to leave it on the following morning, for the bivouac had been made on a hill where the chilling wind swept with penetrating force, and even tolerable comfort was out of the question. But this was only the beginning of discomfort. The march of the 6th covered some 18 miles, to White Plains, and was very trying, the cold wind being so keen that in crossing the hills the men could scarcely hold their guns in their benumbed hands.

Camp was reached just before dusk, and bright fires were built, but there remained one serious want. The supply of rations had given out, and the disheartening word came from the rear that the wagons were impeded by the bad condition of the roads, and could not come up for a day or two. What were men to do with a mild form of starvation staring them in the face? They were not in a friendly country where appeal could be made to the inhabitants for help—of that fact they had had many a forcible reminder. Their logic was sharp and decisive; secessionists were not entitled to protection in property while Union soldiers suffered with hunger, and they would help themselves. Very early in the evening, there was a general strolling out by the men from the immediate scene of the bivouac, and shortly thereafter smells of suspicious savoriness began to permeate the air. It transpired later that a large flock of sheep had been discovered in a pasture near the camp, and when the naturally incensed owner went out the following morning to inspect his herd, he found some 300 pelts and fragments of carcasses awaiting collection.

Of course, this wholesale foraging met with official disapproval as soon as it was known, but before guards could be posted and in control of the situation, there were few hungry men in the brigade. This incident was the more noteworthy, as it was probably the only occasion in his experience as a regimental commander when Colonel Edwards allowed himself an official jest, but on this occasion an order for regimental inspection the following day was accompanied with the request that the muskets should be "well greased with mutton tallow!" But the 7th witnessed a severe snow-storm, following the rain of the previous evening, and the proposed inspection did not take place. Great discomfort was suffered as a result of the storm. Several inches of snow had fallen, but no sooner was it on the ground than the temperature rose and it began to melt. During the 8th it quite disappeared, leaving a sea of mud, through which the unfortunate men floundered, and in the midst of which they existed as best they could.

On the morning of the 9th, the regiment was again on the road—still without rations—and during the day marched as far as New Baltimore, where at last the wagon trains were found and food supplied. This journey, though not long, was very tedious and difficult. The roads were in execrable condition from the recent storm, and the men in poor condition from their exposure and want of food. But there was a feeling that their condition could not well be worse than it had been at White Plains, and they made the best of their way through the mud and over the difficult roads. Those who were unable to keep in the ranks found assistance from their comrades, and many an officer lent a hand to the help of some member of his command. On all such marches, Chaplain Morse gave the best possible exposition of the spirit of the Master by his compassion for the suffering. Nothing was more common than to see him walking beside his faithful horse "Billy," carrying a gun or two, while the saddle was piled with the blanket bundles of men who were in need of help. In extreme cases, the soldier himself would be assisted to mount, but usually the lightening of the load would enable the man to recover his place in the ranks and finish the march with his fellows.

The encampment of the Thirty-seventh at New Baltimore was on a hillside some four or five miles northwest of Warrenton, beside the turnpike leading from the latter place by the way of Gainesville, Centerville and Fairfax Court House to Alexandria. Northward rose the Bull Run Mountains, with no break till Thoroughfare Gap was reached; but toward the other points of the compass the view was far-reaching, embracing many populous camps, with columns of soldiers and trains of all kinds constantly passing by day, and the whole vast area lighted up with hundreds of fires at night. At the foot of the slope flowed an unnamed creek, which presently joined a twin stream from the Gap above, and then made its tortuous way to Occaquan Creek, which it joined near Brentville, passing Bristoe Station on its way. The position was admirably adapted to a temporary camp, and under the influence of good rations and rest the morale of the troops rapidly improved.

In the mean time, an event of great importance to the entire army had transpired. On the night of November 7, while General McClellan was sitting in his tent at Rectortown in the rear of the storm-bound Sixth Corps at White Plains, a messenger from Washington entered and handed him General Orders, No. 182, which read as follows:—

> WAR DEPARTMENT, ADJUTANT-GENERAL'S OFFICE,
> WASHINGTON, November 5, 1862.
>
> By direction of the President of the United States, it is ordered that Major-General McClellan be relieved from the command of the Army of the Potomac, and that Major-General Burnside take the command of that army.
>
> By order of the Secretary of War.
>
> E. D. TOWNSEND,
> Assistant Adjutant-General.

It is not within the scope of this record, which aims simply to tell the story of a single regiment, to criticise men or measures. The President, long dissatisfied with the slowness of

McClellan's movements, had at last decided upon his removal. The history of the army was almost identical with the history of the deposed commander. Under his direction it had grown into existence, and under his command it had met the foe on a dozen bloody fields. That his was a great and just pride in the creation of his organizing genius, was entirely natural, and in a wonderful degree he had won the enthusiastic admiration of the men of his command—a degree which no subsequent commander ever approached. With a reorganized army, inspirited by the success at Antietam, stronger in spirit and in military experience than ever before, and already moving against the foe with a definite plan of campaign, the transfer of the command to another at that time was a serious blow both to the young commander and the men who loved him. Many an indignant discussion and denunciation might have been heard in the various camps when the fact became generally known. "The army will never fight so well under any other commander as it has under him," said many men of sound judgment; but the mistake of all such predictions was convincingly shown within a few weeks at Fredericksburg, where the intrepid bravery of the Army of the Potomac, under its new commander, fighting a battle almost hopeless from the first, won the admiration even of those fought against.

To General Burnside the order was far from welcome. His success in North Carolina had given him great popularity through the country, and made him many friends in military circles. Twice before had the command of the army been offered him and declined, his own feeling, which he did not hesitate freely to express, being that he was incapable of the proper handling of so great a force.

The Confederate army at this time was considerably divided, about half of it having been sent forward to Culpeper, to check McClellan's advance, while the remainder was still held on the west side of the Blue Ridge, in a scattered condition. The plan of the retiring general had been to move sharply from Warrenton to the southwest, interpose between the divided wings of the Southern army and attempt their defeat in detail. This plan

General Burnside did not choose to follow out, but decided to move by way of Fredericksburg in the direction of Richmond, though his plan seems never to have been defined farther than to seize the hights beyond Fredericksburg—a change of purpose to which the authorities at Washington assented.

On Monday, November 10, McClellan took formal leave of his late command. Riding slowly with bared head past the long lines, he received an ovation of which any commander might well carry proud memories through all his remaining life. He was accompanied by his successor, whom many saw for the first time, and when the procession had passed the soldiers returned to their camps, as true in their loyalty to the new as they had been to the old, even if less enthusiastic.

The week of rest which followed the arrival at New Baltimore, whatever the effect on the military fortunes of the army may have been, was very grateful to the weary soldiers. They were now well supplied with rations, the sanitary conditions were good, and health and spirits rapidly improved. On the march at all times, and often in the more temporary camps, each man was his own cook. Receiving his rations of hard bread, raw meat and tea or coffee and sugar, with such variable minor articles as were furnished, he cooked and ate at such times and in such manner as his fancy and appetite prompted His "kit" was not an extensive one. In addition to the canteen and haversack, for holding water and solid food, respectively, each man had generally a tin cup holding about a quart, a plate of the same material, a knife, fork and spoon—the three latter in some instances combining into a single article adapted to the pocket. Here and there a mess were the joint owners of a frying-pan, which they took turns in carrying upon short marches, but when the journey became tedious it was usually cast aside, to be replaced by purchase or some happy find in the future. Usually the office of the frying-pan was delegated to the tin plate, to which a split stick had been affixed by way of handle, and many and laughable were the mishaps which resulted from the burning away of the improvised handle, a momentary inattention, or the want of skill in fitting. The frying accomplished and the handle removed, the plate returned to its normal duties, and not infrequently many an undreamed of use fell to its share. The cup, in addition to its legitimate functions, served for the boiling of coffee, potatoes, beans or meat, for heating water, and, in case of necessity, for an intrenching tool. In fact, it was wonderful to how many uses and how efficiently these two articles could be applied.

It was fascinating to watch the preparation of a hasty meal when bivouac was reached at the close of a march, or when a halt was made for the purpose. Naturally the men were divided into squads of two to five—usually four—who tented together, and in other ways felt a community of interests. No sooner were the ranks broken than a scramble ensued for fuel. If happily a "Virginia rail fence" could be espied, how rapidly it disappeared, and how quickly the bright blaze shot into the air from myriad points. Unless the canteens had been filled at some spring or creek on the way, in anticipation, a part of the squad bounded off in search of water, while the remainder prepared the fire. By the time the first clear jet of flame leaped into view it was hidden beneath a cluster of cups; some with a bit of wire serving for a bail were suspended from sticks, others placed in some convenient position on the blazing wood and closely watched, while if the facilities were limited, and many obliged to utilize the same fire, still others might be supported by the fingers in a manner to be "warming," till there should be opportunity to secure more favorable quarters. As the coffee boiled and was withdrawn, it would be replaced by meat broiling on the end of a sharpened stick, or frying on a swaying plate, to be followed by whatever variety of cookery the culinary skill, the fancy or the resources of the soldier might decide; and truer zest never flavored the repast of epicure than seasoned many of those simple meals eaten beside the dying embers of the disused camp-fire.

The routine of camp life gave promise of becoming monotonous, and on Saturday, November 15, drill was resumed by the Thirty-seventh, only to be followed the same evening by marching orders for the morrow. In accordance with the programme, camp was broken next morning, and three days of continuous tramping followed, of the most wearisome sort. The route lay through one of the most desolate portions of Virginia. The inhabitants were few and, as a rule, wretchedly poor and ignorant. The roads, or it were more proper to say the ways, were barely tracks through brush and trees, narrow, muddy and difficult, especially when torn to pieces by the passage of wagons and artillery. Again there was a scarcity of food, and this time it is but just to say that the severest want was felt by some of the officers. Accustomed to depend largely upon the inhabitants for their supplies, and in that way faring almost sumptuously while in a loyal region, it proved quite different now that the boundary had been crossed. The few people to be met with had very little to spare, and what they had was zealously conserved. Their blind devotion to the Confederacy would not allow them to feed its enemies, if it could be avoided, and as for the worthless greenbacks issued by the Lincoln administration, they would not think of receiving them for anything. Coin or Confederate scrip only was acceptable, and it is to be feared that some of the latter which changed hands in this way saw its origin no farther south than Philadelphia or New York, though in the end it proved just as valuable as the issues made at Richmond.

No feature was more noticeable to the New England men than the entire absence of school-houses in the region through which they were marching. At home no by-ways could have been found so obscure that they would not have passed every few miles structures devoted to the free education of every child resident in the community. Here nothing of the sort was to be seen in hundreds of miles of travel, and the absence did not go unremarked. It was easier to realize now how the common people of the South had been swayed by the will of a few reckless demagogues. Naturally chivalrous and patriotic, these people had lived in a narrow world, and knew little of the great national government of which they had formed a part. With common schools and general information among the mass of the Southern people, the slave-holders' rebellion would have been an impossibility. Thank God! out from the ruins of that wicked structure the enduring twin temples of universal freedom and universal education have now arisen!

On the 18th of November, after a wearying march as "wagon guard," the Thirty-seventh reached temporary camp near Stafford Court House, and on the following day, changing location somewhat, they proceeded to make themselves as comfortable as possible till further orders. The degree of comfort attained was not great. The weather had now become disagreeable, with frequent rain and cold, the location of the encampment was in a low region illy adapted for the purpose, and the only tents for the enlisted men were, as previously, such as they could construct from their rubber blankets. "I hope you uns don't have to stop here this winter," said a native with a showing of humanity, as time passed and there were no indications of a further movement of the army. "I have often seen this whole region where your camp is flowed over and frozen into one sheet of ice—it is a very bad place for a camp." But Thanksgiving came and passed, and the same ground was occupied.

The great New England holiday was not allowed to go by without observance, and as it was the first occasion of the kind in the history of the regiment, it had an unusual interest. By strenuous exertions many of the boxes of home comforts sent for the purpose by friends of the soldiers reached camp, accompanied by Mr. William Birnie of Springfield, and at 10 o'clock the especial exercises began. The command formed into a hollow square, inclosing the field and staff officers mounted, who dismounted and all uncovered while the chaplain offered prayer. Colonel Edwards then read the Thanksgiving proclamation of Governor Andrew, after which a detail from each company superintended the distribution of the boxes, from the contents of which the fortunate recipients prepared a dinner appropriate to the anniversary; the only drawback to the general enjoyment being the realization, as attested by here and there sad faces, that *all* had not received the kindly bounty, and even while the pleasant exercises were taking place, a detail were engaged in the construction of a more roomy regimental hospital to accommodate the increasing number of victims who came under the care of the medical staff. As though to round out the features of the day, the long-delayed knapsacks which the men had parted with on leaving Washington two months before were, through the efforts of Quartermaster Dodge, received and distributed, and the supplies of extra clothing and comforts which they contained proved very acceptable at that time. Two days later the pleasing intelligence went forth that the paymaster had arrived, and no detail ever went to its work more cheerfully than those who were allotted to prepare a tent for his use. On Sunday, the last day of November, the first payment of the regiment in the field was made, and the money then received enabled many of the men to procure gloves and other articles much needed for comfort during the cold weather and disagreeable storms that had become prevalent. Yet, in most instances, a large percentage of the amount received was sent home to assist the dependent ones there, if arrangements had not previously been made assigning a part of the soldier's pay to be deducted and appropriated for this purpose direct. In yet other cases the funds received formed a capital for speculative purposes, and not a few enterprising individuals might have been seen stealing far out into the country in search of anything which could be made merchandise of and sold to their associates at a profit. Doubtless every regiment had such enterprising members, and the make-shifts to which they resorted, and the often ludicrous termination of apparently promising ventures, will be recalled by every one;—such as one unfortunate speculator from the Thirty-seventh experienced when, after pursuing a bovine for several miles in the expectation of obtaining a supply of milk, he discovered at last that the animal was of the wrong gender, and returned to the marching column to endure the endless chaffing of his comrades.

At length, as the army finally moved into position along the Rappahannock, the Sixth Corps was ordered to take position on the extreme left and front, and on the 4th of December, after the men had received a fresh supply of clothing, the command marched leisurely to Belle Plain, where a halt was made for the night. At an early hour next morning the movement was resumed, the column proceeding slowly and halting before noon, with every indication of a permanent stop. The threatening look of the morning had already changed to a cold, drizzling rain, and the men hastened to put up their customary blanket tents and prepare dinner. The location was in a pleasant wood, in favorable contrast with the disagreeable camp at Stafford, and many an exclamation of satisfaction was indulged. But the enjoyment was short-lived. By some mistake a wrong position had been reached, and the command to "Pack up and fall in!" destroyed in a moment the pleasant bivouac. It was obeyed, and the column crept slowly forth through the chilling storm and the resultant mud, moving a little distance and then halting, so that the march of a mile occupied not less than two hours.

Finally, the regiment paused at the foot of a considerable hill, covered with a growth of small pines, so dense that it was necessary for the pioneers to cut a way by which the column could enter the thicket. Crowding and climbing for a short distance through the dripping, uninviting tangle, up the rocky, slippery hill-side, the command halted and the men were invited to make themselves comfortable! A more cheerless bivouac it would be hard to imagine. The rain had now changed to snow, which loaded the tree-tops and dripped dismally upon everything below. The ground was like a soaked sponge, and not a splinter of wood was to be had save from the standing green pines. The men were wet through long before, and chilled to the marrow; while the officers were even more uncomfortable, as the wagons containing their tents were somewhere in the rear and did not arrive till long after dark, so that they were forced to stand about such fires as could be maintained with the heavy storm beating upon them. With plenty of fuel the situation might have been made in some sort tolerable; but the only supply was to be obtained by felling one of the larger of the small pine trees, cutting out a portion of the heart, and in the most sheltered nook to be found seeking to coax it into flame. As only two or three dull axes to a company could be obtained, supplemented with an occasional light hatchet, the procuring of anything like an adequate supply was out of the question. Fortunate indeed were the squad who could develop combustion enough to boil a few cups of coffee, for the most strenuous efforts could do no more. All through the night the storm continued, and dismal enough were the long hours, with sleep, in most cases, out of the question, and the constant storm wrapping everything in its disheartening chill. Men who up to that moment would never have confessed to a thought of homesickness, could not quite repress their feelings as the night wore away, while the more impulsive were loud and emphatic in their expressions of disgust. To add to the general gloom, intelligence was received that a member of Company K, J. Elliot Bliss of Longmeadow, who had been obliged to fall from the ranks during the march of the morning, had been found later in the day by the wayside fatally wounded and robbed by some unknown assassin.

The following day proved cold and stormy, and as the location occupied by the Thirty-seventh could by no possibility be made endurable, they moved a few rods, over rocks and fallen trees, to a somewhat more favorable position on the summit of the hill, where in the midst of the snow which had fallen to a depth of some inches the officers' tents were pitched and the men improvised such shelters as they could from their blankets. Whatever the official name bestowed upon that encampment, it will live in the memory of all who suffered its discomforts as "Camp Misery on Smoky Hill." The large fires necessary to be made from the green pine wood filled the atmosphere with an acrid smoke terribly irritating to the eyes and lungs of the men, and a great many were obliged to sit in their apologies for tents with handkerchiefs wrapped about their heads, utterly unable to bear the light of day. In a day or two more the weather moderated somewhat, the snow disappeared, a limited supply of hard wood was found at a considerable distance from camp, which the men were only too glad to bring in on their shoulders, and when on the 9th of December marching orders were received for the following morning—to be countermanded later and repeated for the 11th—they found the command once more in tolerable physical condition.

With such experiences it scarcely needs be said that the health of the regiment suffered severely. The report of October showed but 15 men in hospital—that for November gave 43, while those who remained in their quarters or under medical treatment outside the hospital had increased in even larger proportion. In many cases no doubt greater pains in the enforcement of sanitary measures might have prevented illness and saved valuable lives; but at the same time it must be remembered how new and strange to the participants was camp life, and under how many disadvantages the regiment had been placed in its experiences thus far—disadvantages which it had shared in common with others and which were no fault of its officers or those in immediate command. On the day of the opening of the battle at Fredericksburg, December 11, the deaths from disease had reached eight, of which five were from typhoid fever, with one each from brain fever, diphtheria and congestion of the liver. Thus early and sadly was the truth being demonstrated that disease was more to be feared than the bullets of the enemy.

Already a few changes had taken place in the roster of officers. Captain Hurlburt of Company C resigned October 14, and dating from the following day Second Lieutenant Rufus P. Lincoln of the same company was promoted to fill the vacancy, his place in turn being filled by the promotion of Erastus W Harris of Company G, who had been serving for a time as orderly sergeant of Company E. First Lieutenant Eli T. Blackmer of Company A resigned November 17, and three days later Second Lieutenant Wellman of the same company was promoted to the vacancy and Commissary Sergeant James C. Chalmers succeeded to the vacant second lieutenantship. The vacancy thus created in the Commissary Department was admirably filled by the appointment of Dwight H. Parsons of Company D as commissary sergeant,—a position which he retained to the closed of the regiment's service with the highest credit to himself and satisfaction to all who were interested in the efficiency of his important department.

CHAPTER VI.

ON THE RAPPAHANNOCK.

THE BATTLE OF FREDERICKSBURG.—IN WINTER QUARTERS.—
THE MUD MARCH.—CAMP EDWARDS.

While waiting at Warrenton for the authorities at Washington to approve his plan for a movement on Fredericksburg, General Burnside carried out a reorganization of the Army of the Potomac into three grand divisions—the right under General Sumner being composed of the Second Corps, General Couch commanding, and the Ninth, General Willcox; the center under General Hooker had the Third Corps, General Stoneman, and the Fifth, General Butterfield; General Franklin had the left, comprising the First Corps, General Reynolds, and the Sixth, General W F. Smith. General Couch being assigned to the command of the Second Corps, General John Newton succeeded him as commander of the Third Division, Sixth Corps, General A. P. Howe taking the Second Division, as General Smith's successor.

Consent having been given to General Burnside's plan for an advance by the way of Fredericksburg, Sumner pushed forward rapidly, and on the 17th of November reached the hights opposite the city. A regiment of cavalry, four companies of infantry and a light battery, seem to have constituted the Confederate force in that immediate vicinity at that time, and Sumner was anxious to ford the river at once and establish his lines on the opposite hights. To this the commander did not assent. He wished a base of supplies established at Aquia Creek, before proceeding further, and did not wish to throw a portion of his force across the Rappahannock until his ponton trains should arrive from Washington, as in the event of a rise in the river—

very liable to occur at that season—they would be hopelessly cut off from the main body. By some oversight, the boats were long delayed ; those that finally came to Belle Plain were unaccompanied by wagons and could not be moved. Before it was possible to construct bridges for the crossing of an efficient force, as the fords at the best were impracticable for artillery, Longstreet's wing of Lee's army was planted directly in the path of the proposed advance, and the remainder under Jackson was within supporting distance.

It was not until the 10th of December that everything was in readiness for a forward movement, and the final orders were issued. Now that the boats were provided, it seemed that there could be no great difficulty in constructing the bridges and passing the river. On each side of the Rappahannock ran a well-defined range of hills, and these were occupied by the rival armies. On the Falmouth or Stafford side they approached within a short distance of the bank of the river, but on the other shore a plain from half a mile to a mile and a half in width extended for five or six miles along the stream. Some little distance above Fredericksburg the course of the river carries it between the hills, shutting off the plain, and at the lower extremity it is terminated by Massaponax Creek and the hills below. Southward along this plain, near the foot of the hills, ran the Richmond Railroad, and parallel to it, but about half way to the river, was the old stage road to Richmond via Bowling Green, from which a mile and a half above Massaponax Creek a newer road ran to the southwest, passing the railroad at what was called Hamilton's Crossing. The hill where crossed by this road was much less elevated than nearer the city, and the plan of General Burnside seems to have been to make a strong movement at this point against the flank and endangering the rear of Lee's army. How the plan was carried out will be seen presently. The other roads leading over the hights were the Orange plank road, running almost directly over Marye's hill, in the rear of Fredericksburg, diverging from which was the Telegraph road, cut into the hill-side and running toward the southwest. Such in general features was the environment of Fredericksburg, henceforth and forever to be crowned with a sacred fame.

During the night of December 10 the ponton trains were moved down to the river bank, and the engineers set vigorously to work constructing bridges at two points—opposite the city, where it was intended that Sumner's grand division should cross, and some three miles below for the passage of Franklin's troops. Along the Stafford hights were ranged 29 batteries of Federal artillery, a total of 147 guns, trained upon the town, the hights beyond, sweeping the plain,—to cover and protect the crossing. In the darkness of the waning night, intensified by a heavy fog which hung over the river, it was hoped that the bridges might be completed without serious opposition; but that hope was speedily crushed. Scarcely had the work begun to take form when the engineers opposite the city were assailed by sharp volleys of musketry, so well aimed as to prevent all further progress on the part of the unarmed artisans. A force of Mississippi riflemen had found shelter behind the stone-walls and in the cellars and low houses next the river, savagely determined to prevent as long as possible the laying of the bridges. At the same time that their volleys rippled forth, two heavy cannon-shots in rapid succession roared out from the hights above, signaling to the various Confederate camps that the anticipated attack was about to be made, and rapidly the defenders hurried to their designated places to meet the assault.

For many hours all attempts to dislodge the murderous marksmen failed. Two regiments from Zook's brigade of the Second Corps opposed them with the musket, with no other effect than to lose from their own ranks 150 men. With a bravery worthy of immortal renown the engineers went forth again and again upon their hopeless mission, but every effort ended in disaster and the death of brave men. At 10 o'clock Burnside gave the order to dislodge the sharp-shooters with artillery, and for an hour shot and shell crashed and tore through the devoted city, firing the buildings, wrecking and destroying everything within reach. But the riflemen crouching close to the river bank were protected from the cannonade, and when in the heat of the bombardment the bridge men attempted to finish their work they met the same deadly reception as before.

Every weapon had failed save one—the bayonet—and it was at last decided to resort to that, sending men across the river in the ponton boats to dislodge the Confederate sharp-shooters from their positions. It was a deadly mission, but Hall's entire brigade, consisting of the Seventh Michigan, Nineteenth and Twentieth Massachusetts and some other troops, volunteered for the service. A selection was made, as there were not enough boats for all, the forlorn hope landed on the other bank and the Mississippians were driven from their shelter with a heavy loss of prisoners. The engineers sprang to their work, the bridge was finished in an incredibly short space of time, the rest of the brigade rushed across to secure the vantage, followed in a short time by the whole of Howard's division of Couch's corps, which occupied the town after some fighting in the upper streets.

Long before light that morning the troops had been roused from their bivouacs, the Thirty-seventh with the others, extra cartridges had been furnished, and the march over the frozen ground began. The distance to be covered was not long, for the army had been already concentrated as much as possible in anticipation of the battle, and early in the forenoon the Thirty-seventh filed over the Stafford hills and moved down upon the narrow plain next the river. The scene was an inspiriting one. A considerable portion of the left grand division was already there, massed along the brown plain between the river bank and the Riverside road which ran near the foot of the hills; while an incessant column still flowed down the hill-side as though from some hidden reservoir. Brigade followed brigade, one division succeeded another; the banners of a score of states, each in support of the national emblem, dotted the vast sea of blue. Officers in bright uniforms and with rich swords swinging at their sides rode about to exchange views with their fellow-officers, while others, more thoughtful in manner and sober in dress, gazed earnestly at the frowning range of hills in the distance, as though dreading, while never shrinking from the ordeal to come. As the hours wore away the men strolled about somewhat, mingling with those of neighboring commands, occasionally a few sticks were gathered and a little fire built over which numberless cups of coffee would be made, and not a few slept upon the warming earth while shot and shell from the opposing batteries howled through the air over their heads.

The short winter's day was almost gone when the intelligence came of the completion of the bridges opposite the city. Early in the day those intended for the use of the left had been finished, the numerous Federal batteries on the river bank commanding the position rendering any serious opposition impossible, and during the struggle above the signal for crossing had been suspended. At last it was given, and Devens's brigade alone of the great mass covering the plain rose to its feet, moving quickly down toward the river bank. Its heroic commander had volunteered to perform the perilous task,—full of honor, though no one could say what might be the reception on the other shore. Cheered on by their comrades the brigade moved down the slippery roadway leading to the bridges. The pickets on the opposite bank fired a volley or two, and bullets dropped suggestively near to many a man, but nobody was hurt and not a second thought given to them. A part of the Second Rhode Island regiment was to deploy as skirmishers, and that regiment led the way over one of the two bridges in waiting. The Thirty-seventh, General Devens riding at its head beside Colonel Edwards, was first on the other bridge, and at a double-quick the two commands, followed by the rest of the brigade, rush across, while the batteries on the bluff send rapid discharges of shot and shell over their heads. How the long bridges of boats pulsate and throb, sway and bound, beneath the hurrying streams of humanity that pour across them! The footing is difficult, and there is danger that the outermost men will be thrown into the water, but they join hands with the inner files or clutch them bodily, and the crossing is made without casualty.

The skirmishers at once deployed, drove the Mississippians from their hiding places and established a line well in advance, while the thin line of battle, hastily formed, pushed up the bluff to the plain above and halted in a position to protect the bridge head. By that time it was dusk, for the days were at their shortest, and no more could be done. The remainder of the division had followed the brigade across the bridges, to give the impression of a crossing in force, but presently returned to the Falmouth shore where they remained through the night, leaving only the indomitable brigade, like a short thread of blue on that vast plain through the long night. For some hours there was almost momentary anticipation of an attack, and the novelty of the position warmed the men with its gentle excitement; but as the night deepened and all remained quiet the monotony and disagreeableness of the situation made themselves felt. Midnight came and passed, and no sound from the front broke the silence. The sharp chill of the winter air benumbed the men, and when permission was at length given for a part of them to lie down and rest on their arms sleep was wholly out of the question, for the ground was covered with a white frost that gleamed in the dim starlight like snow, and one could as well have slept in an ice pack. Finally muskets were stuck in the ground at each flank of the company fronts and in Indian file an endless circle of men went around on a trot to start the half-congealed blood into fresh circulation. Now and then one would slip and fall upon the frosty grass, and half a dozen might tumble over him before the momentum of those in the rear could be checked; but the exercise dispelled the numb drowsiness which could not be relieved by sleep and warmed the chilled limbs, and so the night wore away.

With the coming of dawn the lonely vigil ended, for soon after the troops of the left grand division began to cross in force, filing away past the weary brigade and taking position to the left. As the location of the little command became visible to the Confederate gunners on the hights in front a battery was directed upon it, which presently succeeded in dropping some shots uncomfortably close to the officers' horses and servants, gathered about a haystack just in the rear of the line, and a lively scamper to the rear ensued, while the soldiers moved forward a short distance to the shelter of a slight swell of ground. There the day was passed with little of especial moment, yet there was much to hold the attention of the Thirty-seventh, for it was their first experience on the battle-field. With what interest they watched the various commands as they filed past—now a squad of cavalry hurrying out to the front to return presently with a few saddles emptied; the long columns of infantry broken at intervals by batteries and occasionally dotted by regiments still wearing the gay Zouave costumes which had been so popular at the outbreak of the war. At the bridges opposite the city the scene was similar, the day being thus consumed in getting the Federal army into position. Yet amid all the excitement of these preparations the communion of the soldiers with friends at home was not neglected, and twice during their occupancy of the field the Thirty-seventh were cheered by the distribution of a mail. What other army ever presented a like spectacle? Here in the pauses of a great battle were the men in the ranks encouraged by love-freighted messages from home, or snatching the opportunity of a few hours' respite to assure anxious ones of their safety thus far or to send early tidings of those who had fallen!

The outline of the terrible battle of the 13th of December may be briefly given. The initiative was taken by General Franklin, who was ordered to attack in the direction of Hamilton's Crossing, but so vague was the order that to the present day it is impossible to decide as to Burnside's exact purpose. It seems probable, however, that he expected Franklin to reach and hold the military road which General Lee had constructed from that point to the left of the Confederate line, thus threatening the hights in the rear and forcing their evacuation; but whatever the purpose or expectation it was not clearly embodied in the orders issued and was not to be realized in action.

At about 10 o'clock the First Corps moved to the attack, General Meade's division in advance, General Gibbon's in support and General Doubleday's protecting the left flank, which was threatened by Stuart's cavalry. General Meade's attack was directed against Jackson's corps of Lee's army, formed in three lines; A. P Hill's division in front, supported by those of Early and Taliaferro, while D. H. Hill's division was posted in reserve

THE BATTLE OF FREDERICKSBURG. 111

between the Richmond road and Massaponax Creek. The first Confederate line was broken by Meade's assault and the second was reached, but there the attacking column lost its force, wavered and broke. General Gibbon of the supporting line was wounded, his command also became disorganized and fell back, inviting a counter charge by the Confederates, which was met and checked by Birney's brigade of the Third Corps thrown upon their exposed flank. The troops engaged had suffered severely, but they had also smitten the enemy heavily. Now, however, the battle paused and on the left it was not again seriously renewed. Preparations were indeed made for another attack, but they were not completed till dusk, and it was then too late.

In the mean time terrible and unavailing fighting had been in progress all the afternoon in the rear of Fredericksburg. The Second Corps occupied the town, and about noon was ordered to assault the rebel position on Marye's hights. The ground was especially unfavorable to the maneuvering of troops, as they were obliged to cross the canal on narrow bridges, deploy almost in the face of the enemy and advance over broken and difficult ground. The whole distance from the streets of the city to the foot of the hill was swept by a terrible cross-fire of artillery, and at the latter point a Confederate line of infantry was posted behind a stone-wall.

French's division went first, supported by Hancock's, and one after the other was torn to pieces before the wall was reached. The Ninth Corps advanced on the left of the Second, and made one assault after another, but nothing could be gained save a worthless advanced position in the open field. General Hooker's command was then ordered across the river and directed to renew the attack. Its indomitable commander reconnoitered the field and protested against the waste of life, then hurled Humphreys's division with empty muskets and fixed bayonets against the impregnable wall of fire. Like those which had gone before, it drifted back in fragments with nothing accomplished. The commander-in-chief, grown desperate, formed the Ninth Corps in column of regiments and prepared to lead it in person against the enemy's lines. They were his North Carolina victors, devoted to him, and would follow him to the gates of death without shrinking. Personally he had ever been very popular with his troops, for well they knew his kindness of heart, his bravery and integrity. But his lieutenants protested against the mad attempt, there was no coöperative movement on the left, the men lay on their arms through the night and the assault was never made.

While the battle raged with such fury to both right and left, the Thirty-seventh remained in nearly the position it had occupied since the crossing, exposed frequently to artillery fire, from which it found a partial shelter by lying close to the ground in rear of a slight swell which there ran across the field. But it was while thus lying that its first member was killed in action—Stephen G. Warner of Company H, from Williamsburg, being struck in the head by a fragment of shell, while David B. Dwight of the same company was wounded. Toward evening, when the preparations were made for renewing the conflict, the brigade was hurried to the left, through a scattering artillery fire, and formed in a large corn-field, where it lay for a considerable time under the hot fire of Stuart's horse artillery in its front, the regiment being finally advanced to the shelter of a ridge a little nearer the hostile guns. This position was maintained for some time after dark, no noise being allowed, and the men looked for a night encounter, but at length the order to move to the rear was received and the regiment returned nearly to its original position, where the night was passed. Sunday morning, the 14th, it moved nearer the river, a little below the bridges, where rations and a mail were distributed, and the day passed very quietly along the entire field. It was seen on the Federal side that further attack would be madness, and the Confederates did not think best to leave their vantage ground. Jackson, who commanded Lee's right wing, seems after the failure of Meade's advance to have contemplated the aggressive, and about sunset sent word to Stuart to push forward his batteries and help to drive the Yankees into the Rappahannock. But the greeting received from the Union artillery as the first of

Jackson's lines came into view, convinced that warrior of the unwisdom of his proposed attempt, and it was abandoned.

The Thirty-seventh moved to the front again Monday morning, taking position on the Richmond road in support of a New Jersey battery, which occupied a favorable location just beyond the road. The high embankments formed an admirable shelter for the infantry, which lay behind them regardless of the sharp artillery dueling which from time to time broke out. Thus keeping up a strong front through the day, no sooner had darkness settled over the scene than the batteries and their supports were quietly withdrawn and moved swiftly back toward the bridges. There a fresh honor was in waiting for the Thirty-seventh and its fellow-regiments of the brigade. They had been the first to cross at the lower bridges, and they were to be the last to retreat. Knowing the character of the men composing his command, General Devens, at an evening consultation of general officers at Franklin's head-quarters, when the proposed withdrawal was announced, volunteered to cover the crossing.

"As you led the advance," was the reply, "your brigade will not be entitled to that honor should any other be volunteered." But no other was volunteered—it was not a duty for which even brave men aspired; and to General Devens, assisted by Colonel Torbert and his New Jersey brigade, from the First Division of the Sixth Corps, was assigned the delicate task. Forming in line of battle near the spot on which they had stood through that first night, the undaunted handful faced to the rear during the long hours, while artillery and infantry in ceaseless throngs poured past them and wound back over the Stafford hills, the strong south wind bearing away from the enemy every sound which might betray the movement.

Finally the procession became scattering, and the pickets in squads and singly hurried anxiously toward the bridges, fearing lest they might be too late. They were assured by the firm line of the two brigades standing there to ensure the safe delivery of every man from what might so appropriately be called a death-trap. When the last straggler had passed, Torbert's regiments followed, and, last of all, Devens and his heroic band. The engineers were standing at their posts, ready to cast the bridges loose, and in a very few moments the unspanned river flowed once more between the two armies.

The night was far advanced when the Thirty-seventh, sadly wearied by its four days and five nights on the battle-field, climbed the Stafford hights, and after a short march turned into the forest for a bivouac. Before the ranks were broken, the ringing voice of Colonel Edwards was heard in the more than welcome order, "Captains will see that their men build as large fires as they please, and make themselves as comfortable as possible!" No second bidding was needed; a score of great fires lighted up the forest as by magic, but the weary men did not long enjoy their luxury, and in a few minutes nearly every one was soundly sleeping, unmindful of the driving rain-storm which had set in. That was little to be regarded in comparison with the storm of battle to which they had so long listened.

The battle of Fredericksburg was over, and its purpose had sadly failed. The Union army had suffered a loss of 12,300 and their enemies of but 5,300, while the prestige of victory remained with the latter. The Army of the Potomac had fought with its accustomed bravery, winning even from its antagonists the most unqualified admiration; and the recrossing of the river during the night of December 15 by 100,000 men, without the knowledge of the enemy and without the loss of a gun or a straggler, challenges admiration, as one of the military feats of modern times. A critical analysis of the battle would have no place in this work, yet there are facts which the general reader will not overlook, and first of all, he will admire the manly frankness with which General Burnside accepted the responsibility for the failure. Taking the command with an oft-repeated disavowal of his ability properly to fill the high place, the prompt carrying out of the plans which had been decided on thwarted by delays for which he was in no sense responsible, with rankling and undisguised jealousy among his subordinate commanders and a questionable conduct of some portions of the battle, General Burnside could still utter these worthy sentences: "To the brave officers and soldiers who accomplished the feat of recrossing the river in the face of the enemy I owe everything. For the failure in the attack I am responsible, as the extreme gallantry, courage and endurance shown by them was never exceeded and would have carried the points had it been possible. To the families and friends of the dead I can only offer my heartfelt sympathies; but for the wounded I can offer my earnest prayers for their comfort and final recovery." How far these facts and this utterance shall go to disarm criticism, each must decide for himself.

On the morning of December 18 the now familiar order to "Pack up and fall in!" was again heard, and this time there was no murmuring. Earlier in the autumn, when the long marches were wearing upon the men, they had often expressed a wish that instead they might go into battle. Now that they had seen something of the horrors of the field of strife, a different disposition prevailed. They were ready to endure the severest march and to accept it as a luxury in contrast with the screaming of shells, the hissing of bullets and the sight of dead or mangled comrades. Marching some two miles by the narrow roads, which seemed to run in every direction, the Thirty-seventh came to a halt beside a pine grove which might as properly have been called a thicket, moved by the right of companies to the rear, and was on the site of what was to prove the long talked of "winter quarters." The location was some three miles due east from the village of Falmouth, and was officially known as "Camp near White Oak Church"—the name coming from a small, plain wooden building still further to the eastward bearing that designation.

The trials of the march and the field now gave place to the experiences of the winter camp. The men were at once set at work "policing" the site, the ground to be occupied by the company streets being cleared of the undergrowth and comfortable houses roofed with their rubber blankets built by the men from saplings and the mortar-like earth. The quarters of the company officers were at the rear of their respective commands, while the field and staff occupied a gentle elevation at the left of the line, sheltered by a knot of pines of moderate size. Here also the hospital was located, and it filled rapidly, for the exposure of the past two months, combined with other unfavorable influences, continued to make sad havoc with the health of the regiment. During the weeks which followed, death came often to claim its victims, and it seemed that the more robust fell rather than men of feebler physique. This cause, in combination with others, made the winter anything but a cheerful one to the majority of the army. There was another cause of disquiet, not previously referred to, which should not escape mention. The time was approaching when the Emancipation Proclamation of President Lincoln was to take effect, and hand-bills were posted throughout the army calling attention to the fact. With the new year, the shackles of the bond man were to fall. While generally this act was hailed as one of justice too long delayed, and a wise and important military step, such was not the unanimous verdict. By a noisy minority the proclamation was derided, the war was declared to have changed into an abolition crusade, and there can be no doubt that many of the desertions from that class may be properly set down to this cause. Others who remained faithful to the flag saw in it a factor of gloomy import, felt that it was a mistake and an unnecessary complication, and lost courage. Yet, while despondency and desertion seemed epidemic through the army, the former was by no means serious and the latter was almost unknown in the Thirty-seventh. From the time of joining the Army of the Potomac to the close of Burnside's command, but four desertions occurred from the regiment.

Gradually the weeks wore away. When the weather would permit the day was largely occupied with drilling and the duties of the camp and of guard, with an occasional tour to the outposts for picket service, usually for three days at a time, and it was there that the new year of 1863 found the regiment. The 2d of January was marked by the occurrence of what proved to be a false alarm. The main body of the regiment, forming the reserve, were comfortably settled to sleep in such quarters as they had been able to improvise, when word came back from the river-side that the Confederates were laying ponton bridges to cross the stream. In a very few moments the men had been roused, formed in column and were hurrying at the double-quick toward the river, a mile away. The incident was a memorable one. The night was clear and the air sharply cold, the ground being slightly frozen, so that the cadence of the foot-falls, uniform and perfect as on review, rang out with a sharp resonance. It was one of those sudden tests which mark the quality of the command, and riding beside their men the field officers of the Thirty-seventh had just cause for pride in the perfect response of the rank and file. However the alarm originated, it was carried back to the camps, the long roll broke the slumbers of the entire corps, the regiments were formed and stood for hours shivering in the cold, only to be told at last that nothing was the matter.

The following day the regiment returned to camp, and the enlisted men were much gratified to find a supply of shelter tents awaiting them. Up to that time they had been obliged to make their rubber blankets serve as such, and despite many an ingenious makeshift, the deficiency had been the cause of much unnecessary exposure and suffering.

The winter was not to pass without another effort on the part of General Burnside against the enemy. Within two weeks of the retreat from Fredericksburg he had decided upon another plan and began arrangements for carrying it into execution, when he was dissuaded by the President from making the attempt on account, it would seem, of the disapproval of many of the subordinate officers. This plan contemplated the crossing the Rappahannock several miles below Fredericksburg and a movement against the Confederate right flank, while the Union cavalry were to operate in the rear of the enemy and, if possible, destroy his lines of communication. The cavalry was, in fact, on its way when the disapproval of President Lincoln necessitated its recall. General Burnside being thus made more fully than before aware of the distrust in the minds of his subordinates, felt the necessity of such immediate action as would restore his waning prestige, and finally decided to once more cross the river and offer battle, intending to cross at one of the upper fords, move to the rear of the Fredericksburg hights, and strike Lee's army on the flank. Banks Ford was decided on as the point of crossing, but to deceive the enemy as to the real intention, demonstrations were made at every other possible crossing, above and below, batteries were planted, roads prepared, and the bustle of preparation filled all the camps.

The Thirty-seventh were on picket when, on the morning of January 20, 1863, orders were received to repair to camp and prepare to march immediately, and at noon camp was broken. Many of the soldiers, thinking that they were in permanent winter quarters, had sent to their homes for various comforts and luxuries, and a quantity of express boxes containing them had just been received. How most of them were disposed of it would be difficult to say. What the possessor could not eat, wear or carry, he divided with others or abandoned on the spot, superfluous clothing and camp conveniences were discarded, the log huts were dismantled, and in some cases burned. After the regiment was well under way it halted to hear the reading of a general order from the commander-in-chief, announcing in the usual hopeful terms that the army was again to meet the foe. With the rank and file there was a mingling of doubt and hope. The weather was fine, the army strong in numbers and well appointed; but on the other hand there was the memory of Fredericksburg and the known want of confidence in the ability of Burnside to cope with the Southern commander.

It would be useless to speculate on what might have been. The weather—the factor apparently most favorable to the Federal cause—was yet the one from which the disaster was to come. A good distance was easily covered during the afternoon, but just as the troops went into bivouac for the night the weather suddenly changed, and a gentle rain began falling. It continued all night with increasing intensity, and when the march was resumed in the morning the extent of the mischief became apparent. The clayey road-beds, indifferent at the best, were soaked to the extent that every passing regiment, every wagon, even, stirred the slippery depths and made them more treacherous. As far as possible, the roads were given over to the pontons and artillery, the infantry making their way through fields and across untraveled regions, partly that the men might have better footing, but principally because it was impossible for them to go in any other way. The rain still poured down and the ground everywhere became a bottomless sea of mud. Soldiers carefully picking their way slipped and fell into the tenacious mass, carrying comrades with them, their ridiculous plight when extricated affording about the only relief from the somber gloom of the scene.

Every road was blocked. The immense weight of the artillery, ammunition wagons and pontons, sunk them hopelessly in the mire. In vain the efforts of the drivers, profanity included. Their animals sank bodily from sight in the sloughs or dropped dead in their places. Long ropes were rigged, and great details of men put to the task of assisting them. Sixteen horses and 50 soldiers pulled a 10-pounder Parrott gun along only by spasmodic jerks. A regiment with 50 horses could not move one of the boats. Humanity can do no more; flesh and blood have been struggling with the elements and their struggle proves vain. Burnside has wrestled with fate for many long hours since all hope of success had gone, and the unequal contest is finally given over. The infantry could possibly move, but nothing on wheels; the river is too deep to be forded; the intention of the Federal army has been penetrated, the opposite fields are being filled with entrenchments, and many a sarcastic jest is thrown across the stream by the exultant Confederates. A large board is erected on which has been rudely scrawled, "Burnside stuck in the mud!" "Come over, Yanks, as soon as you can," cries a picket with a loud voice; "Old Stonewall is right back here and wants to see you!" "Wait till to-morrow," suggests another, "and we uns will come over and help you bring up the bridges." Not a shot is fired by either side, for the men have no desire to indulge in wanton murder, and it would be no less than that to shoot each other under such circumstances.

It was about noon that the Thirty-seventh abandoned the attempt to proceed farther, and turned into the woods beside the road. A pitifully bedraggled and muddy lot of men they were, yet others who had floundered through vaster depths, manning the ropes and lifting the bemired carriages, had fared far worse than they. After a short respite for food, rest and a general cleaning up, the regiment moved a little distance to a steep hill-side, and the men were urged to make themselves "as comfortable as possible." Comfortable! The storm showed no sign of abatement, and all through the night it raged on, seeming each hour to increase in force. The slope was so steep that many of the men were obliged to sleep with their feet against logs or rocks to prevent slipping away with the rivulets that trickled down the hill-side in every direction, and not a few awoke in the night to find that the foothold had given way and they had rolled out into the pelting storm.

The following day the rain ceased, and a spark of comfort came to the miserable host from the realization that matters could become no worse, and that in their demoralized condition there was no possibility of their being forced into battle—which, under the circumstances, all felt would prove only a useless slaughter. They also realized as never before, from generals to privates, the madness of an overland winter campaign. To imagine the army many miles advanced and dependent upon wagon trains for its supplies, was to picture an ignominious retreat toward the base of supplies as an alternative to starvation. Even now that was almost the condition. The rations with which the men had started were nearly exhausted, and no wagon train could reach them.

That evening the wooded slopes occupied by the army presented a picturesque scene. The various organizations were compactly massed, and now that the rain had ceased a multitude of fires were ablaze, drying the garments and blankets and warming the chilled limbs of the men. Opposite to the slope occupied by the Thirty-seventh rose another, similar but less abrupt, and through the evening its surface was lighted up with hundreds of fires, ranged with almost mathematical accuracy, the red light of each disclosing groups of men in blue, and the whole forming a picture upon which hundreds of those across the ravine gazed with a sort of fascination, and from which they drew what seemed an inspiration of cheer and fresh courage.

THE DARK SIDE OF CAMP LIFE. 121

The return to the old camps took place on the next day, the 23d, and it is probably safe to say that the like march was never seen in the Army of the Potomac. The men were without food and in every way demoralized. Obliged to pick their way as best they could, it was not long till the regiments dwindled to skeletons of the most meager dimensions, and a mixed throng representing everything and nothing scrambled through fields and along the roadways as best it could. The old quarters were reached at length, the stragglers came in singly and in groups, the old huts were reoccupied, those that had been burned or destroyed were rebuilt, and the campaign under Burnside was at an end.

The regimental reports at this time, with one company on detached service, show a total present for duty in the regiment of 578. A few had been discharged for disability, 17 had died, 110 had been sent to general hospital, and as was inevitable, a fresh outbreak of sickness followed the experience just ended. The regimental hospital was soon filled, and the death-roll rapidly lengthened.

Thus far the weather had been moderate and comparatively comfortable, and the rigors of winter had not made themselves felt to a serious extent, but now a marked change was noticed. Storms were frequent, the ground was alternately a mass of tenacious mud and frozen. When in the latter condition, the cold winds which swept over it chilled the men through, rendering every outdoor duty of fatigue, guard or picket a severe tax. And there was no lack of such duty. Every fall of snow necessitated the clearing up of the company streets, and when thawing and freezing had produced a compound of snow, ice and frozen mud, the task was no slight one. Much labor was necessary, too, in providing the fuel essential to comfort. The hundreds of fires necessary in officers' quarters, cook-houses and the tents of the rank and file, rapidly exhausted the wood in the vicinity, and it became necessary to transport it long distances on the shoulders of the men. Every morning, regardless of cold or storm, squad after squad could be seen emerging from the quarters of the different companies, each group in possession of a single dull ax in the hands of the man best skilled in its use. Presently the procession would come staggering back, each individual bending under a stick of oak or walnut as large as he could carry, having learned by unpleasant experiences to discriminate against those soft, sappy varieties which nothing could coax into a flame. As the vast stretches of beautiful forest melted away before the incessant attacks of the axmen, many an exclamation of regret went up from sincere hearts over the necessary devastation. Not even Virginians themselves could have felt more keen regret than did the New Englanders at the unceasing destruction.

The picture of gloom which hung over the camps of the great army was not unbroken. Here and there were agencies and influences which brightened it all with a better and purer than earthly light. While such efforts were put forth for the physical well-being of the men as no similar army had ever before experienced, their spiritual care was not forgotten. Six stations were opened by the Christian Commission from which not only food for the sick suitable to their needs was distributed, but earnest endeavors were made to improve the moral condition of the well and to awaken a religious interest. Papers and tracts were distributed to the soldiers directly as well as through the chaplains of the regiments, prayer-meetings were established in many places through the assistance of the Christians in the ranks, and often the voice of supplication, the hymn of praise, and the avowal of consecration to a nobler life were heard above the camp jest and thoughtless song.

Such was the case in Captain Flagg's Company D, which had been detailed at the time of the advance into Virginia for guard duty at General Franklin's head-quarters. The use of a large tent had been procured for the holding of meetings, which were carried on by the devout members of the company, assisted and strengthened by an occasional visit from Chaplain Morse and others from the regiment, much good and great enjoyment resulting. "The praying captain and his company of Christians," was the remark of more than one as they returned to the regiment. From no lips did such words fall mockingly,

However lightly the speaker might himself regard religious matters, he could but respect a consistent Christian life in others, and nowhere was this respect more perfectly shown than in the regard of the men for their chaplain.

The duties of that officer, as he saw and interpreted them, were of no trifling nature. Serving as the postmaster of the regiment, much of his time was consumed in the duties of that place. To secure the mail for the Thirty-seventh as soon as it should arrive at brigade head-quarters, day or night, and see to its proper distribution to the several companies, had its counterpart in the reception of the letters written from the regiment, and the seizing of every opportunity to send them forward whenever a mail was to leave the army. The postal laws at that time required the prepayment of letter postage, but an exception was made in the case of soldiers in the field, whose letters were forwarded when certified, and as the soldiers were seldom provided with postage stamps, the familiar inscription was to be written, in cold or storm or darkness, hundreds of times daily, "Soldier's Letter. F. C. Morse, Chaplain 37th Reg't Mass. Vols." During the winter inactivity it was the custom of Mr. Morse to daily visit the hospital, reading the Scriptures, praying and conversing with the inmates, experiencing often most touching scenes, and in the evening to pay an informal visit to one of the companies, talking with the men, distributing tracts and papers, greeted everywhere with the most hearty welcome.

Despite all sanitary efforts in behalf of the army, the most painstaking medical care and attention to all camp details, the health of the regiment failed to improve, it rather grew worse; fevers prevailed, and they were not confined to the enlisted men; the officers began to fall victims, and as a last resort a change of camp was decided upon. The location selected was some half a mile southeast of the original site, and covered a well-drained plateau, sloping gently toward the south, from which the wood had recently been cut.

The regiment returned March 1 from three days' duty on the picket line, and the following day every able-bodied man save a camp guard was set to work in the preparation of the new quarters. Three axes were provided for each company, and the work was systematized and supervised so perfectly that on the 9th the old camp was quitted and the Thirty-seventh removed to what may properly be designated as the model regimental camp in the Army of the Potomac, named "Camp Edwards," in compliment to the colonel. The work had been carefully laid out in advance, and not only were the company streets uniform, but every hut was built to a common plan. There were 158 of them, each intended for four occupants, built of small pine logs, either whole or split according to size, interlocked at the corners, with a door-way in front, a fire-place and chimney at one side, and two bunks built of poles and covered with boughs, elevated a certain distance from the ground, at the rear. Each house was eight feet by twelve, five feet high at the eaves and nine at the ridge-pole, the roof being formed by four sections of shelter tent. The crevices were stopped and the chimneys lined by a liberal application of clay, a floor made of small poles, and thus a habitation was created quite as comfortable as the dwellings of the poorer classes of Virginians. After its occupation the camp was decorated with arches of evergreen across the company streets, and as uniformity was not required a brisk rivalry developed in this respect which had the effect of bringing forth a profusion of neat designs, the whole giving the camp a considerable fame throughout the army. But best of all, the good effect sought in a sanitary way was fully realized; there were few additional cases of sickness, the hospital patients generally improved, and from that time forward the Thirty-seventh may properly be spoken of as enjoying exceptionally good health. In front of the parade a small stream flowed, giving an abundance of pure water, and on the eminence beyond, opposite the right of the regiment, were the head-quarters of Colonel Edwards and his staff, with the hospital adjacent. From the little cluster of tents the officers could look out upon a beautiful and animated scene, and may well have indulged feelings of pride at the spectacle.

Important changes among the officers had taken place during the winter. The first following those noted at the close of the

CAMP EDWARDS, Near Falmouth, Va.

previous chapter was the resignation from December 29, 1862, of First Lieutenant J. Milton Fuller of Company I. The vacancy was filled by the promotion of Second Lieutenant Charles Phelps and of Orderly Sergeant F. Edward Gray of the same company to first and second lieutenants respectively. The resignation of Lieutenant-Colonel Alonzo E. Goodrich* took effect January 16, 1863, Major George L. Montague advancing and Captain Eugene A. Allen becoming major. First Lieutenant Mason W Tyler of Company F in turn became its captain, and in consequence Second Lieutenant George H. Hyde of Company D was promoted, but was assigned to Company B, taking the place of First Lieutenant Thomas F. Plunkett, Jr., who after having commanded Company E for a time was detailed as an aide on the staff of General Devens. First Sergeant George N. Jones of Company F was commissioned second lieutenant and filled the vacancy in Company D's roster. Quartermaster Daniel J. Dodge resigned January 28, and his place was filled by the promotion of Second Lieutenant Edward Bridgman of Company G; First Sergeant John S. Bradley of Company B becoming second lieutenant in Company G. First Lieutenant Joshua A. Loomis of Company H was on the 25th of February assigned to the command of Company E, which had thus far in its history been unfortunate in having a succession of temporary commanders in the absence of Captain Hopkins on staff duty. It may not be amiss to say that under the firm and skillful hand of Lieutenant Loomis the command improved rapidly in efficiency and morale. March 9 Captain Peter Dooley of Company K was discharged. Previous to this he had from November 20 been absent from the regiment on account of an injured ankle, though much of the time on duty in charge of convalescents reported to their regiments. In 15 trips between the hospitals and the front, often in charge of detachments numbering hundreds, he did not lose a man by desertion or

---

*Mr. Goodrich was a substantial and respected citizen of Pittsfield. In every relation of life he was enthusiastic, patriotic, loyal. To his native town, which was his life-long home, he gave liberally of his service and his counsel. Chosen selectman in 1869, he was annually re-elected to that position by an appreciative constituency as long as he lived, the last 12 years of his life being devoted to the service of the town. He died February 25, 1881, after a long illness, at the age of 66, deeply mourned by a wide circle of personal friends. Truthfully might it be said of him that he was "a faithful and zealous public servant, a true friend and an upright man."

otherwise. First Lieutenant Mulloy succeeded him as captain of Company K, Lieutenant Chandley was advanced in turn, and First Sergeant Michael Harrigan of the same company became its second lieutenant. Assistant Surgeon Joshua J. Ellis ceased to hold that position on the 27th of March, and was succeeded by Dr. Albert L. Mitchell of Boston. Dr. Ellis died at Newport, R. I., during the summer. In the non-commissioned staff John E. Banks of Company G succeeded Thomas Porter Jr., as quartermaster sergeant, January 1; but the latter remained in the department as clerk throughout, rendering valuable and appreciated service.

CHAPTER VII

THE ARMY UNDER HOOKER.

EVENTS IN THE WEST.—CHANCELLORSVILLE.—MARYE'S HIGHTS
AND SALEM CHURCH.

We must now glance very briefly at the progress of the great struggle on other parts of the vast arena. Over the disputed territory of Tennessee and the adjacent regions great armies were surging back and forth, the advantage shifting from one banner to the other, but generally favoring the Union arms whenever the test of decisive battle was reached. Following the battle of Pittsburg Landing, April 7, 1862, Beauregard with the remains of his army had fallen back to Corinth, Miss., which place he evacuated late in May on the approach of the Union army under General Halleck. During the following month General Pope, who had joined the combined armies operating against Beauregard, was summoned to Washington to take command of the Army of Virginia, and in July Halleck followed to assume direction from the national Capital of all the Federal armies. The armies at Corinth now separated, General Grant being assigned to the Department of West Tennessee while Buell with the Army of the Ohio operated against General Bragg, who had succeeded Beauregard in the command of the Confederate army. Tennessee and Kentucky were now free of any considerable bodies of Southern troops, and after arranging his army to protect Nashville, Buell contemplated the occupation of Chattanooga, an important strategic point near the Georgia boundary, when he found that Bragg, moving by way of northern Alabama, had already passed through the place and was pushing to the northward past the left flank of the Union army. Crossing the Cumberland at Carthage, the Confederates moved directly toward Louisville, Ky., while at the same time a smaller force under E. Kirby Smith had entered the state through Cumberland Gap, and on August 30 defeated General Nelson at Richmond. At Munfordsville, Bragg encountered a small but determined garrison commanded by Colonel John T. Wilder, which after three days' resistance was forced to surrender on the 17th of September; but the time gained had enabled Buell to overtake his antagonist, and for several days the two armies maneuvered and a battle was expected. Finally the Confederates withdrew to the eastward, Buell marched to Louisville and provisioned his troops, and on the 30th moved once more in search of Bragg. A severe battle ensued at Perryville, Ky., October 8, and during the night Bragg retired leaving his dead and wounded on the field, and retreated toward Cumberland Gap. Buell followed the retiring invaders without further engagement till he felt obliged to concentrate his army toward Nashville, and October 30 he was relieved of his command and succeeded by General Rosecrans.

On the departure of General Pope for Washington his western command had been given to General Rosecrans, and about the middle of September the latter was ordered by Grant to move with the Army of the Mississippi against the Southern General Sterling Price, who on the 10th had occupied Iuka, Miss., capturing considerable amounts of government property. Rosecrans moved vigorously and on the 19th fought the battle of Iuka. Price retired during the night, in season to escape the coöperating column of General Ord, who was moving to the assistance of Rosecrans, giving to the Federal forces the prestige of victory though the engagement itself had been indecisive. Rosecrans concentrated his forces at Corinth, where on the 3d of October he was attacked by the combined armies of Price and Van Dorn, under the command of the latter. From early morning till noon of the following day the assailants fought desperately. Corinth was the military key to Western Tennessee, and it contained vast quantities of stores and supplies, but though one assault followed another with destructive fury and at great cost to the Confederates, they achieved no permanent success, and by noon of the 4th were in full retreat. On the following day General Ord intercepted the fugitives at the Hatchee, and inflicted further loss upon them, being himself severely wounded, and Rosecrans pursued Van Dorn's flying columns for 60 miles, till recalled by General Grant.

With the prestige of these vigorous acts fresh in the public mind, Rosecrans succeeded to the command of Buell's army, much to the popular satisfaction, so impatient had the loyal people become of the delays of campaigns East and West. Henceforth this command was designated as the Army of the Cumberland, and it was at this time organized as the Fourteenth Corps, though on the 9th of January following it was divided into the Fourteenth, Twentieth and Twenty-first, under the command, respectively, of Generals Thomas, McCook and Crittenden. Following the battle of Perryville, Bragg concentrated his army at Murfreesboro, 30 miles from Nashville, threatening the latter city, and on the 7th of November General McCook reached the city with Rosecrans's right grand division just in time to prevent a threatened attack by General Forrest. The two armies watched each other till late in December, when Rosecrans, annoyed by the extensive cavalry raiding of Forrest in his rear, with Morgan operating in Kentucky, moved forward his entire force and on the last day of the year opened the terrible battle of Stone River or Murfreesboro. The opposing forces were in position the night before, and by one of the singular coincidences of war each commander decided to make a very vigorous attack in the morning with his left on the right wing of his antagonist. Bragg was the first to deliver battle, and while Rosecrans was moving his own forces to the assault he was astonished to find his entire right swept back by a resistless onslaught. His purpose of attack was at once abandoned, and every energy devoted to resistance of the Confederates, who still continued to sweep back McCook's right wing, though Sheridan's division fought bravely, repelling three desperate attacks and holding the enemy at bay for four hours, when with ammunition exhausted they were obliged at last to give way. As this last division of the right wing gave way the Confederate advance struck and seriously involved the center, where the iron courage of General Thomas and his command inspired some of the most obstinate fighting of modern times. At last the firm lines withstood the shock of the repeated rebel onsets, and the heroic Federal commander saw the attacking legions break and drift away in fragments, and knew that the impetuosity of their dash had spent itself. The Union loss had been severe, in some commands terrible, and included the commander of McCook's Second Division, General Sill, and Colonel Kirk commanding a brigade, as well as Gareschè, the chief of staff to Rosecrans, whose head was carried away by a shell that barely missed his commander. To the position thus tragically made vacant General Garfield was appointed a few weeks later. For two days Bragg sought in vain to pierce the Federal lines. In every case his demonstrations were met with such determination that he realized the hopelessness of his task. Toward the close of the 2d of January one more desperate effort was made to drive the Union forces from a position across the river threatening the Confederate right; but it only resulted in severe loss to the attacking party, which was forced back for a considerable distance and the whole position occupied by Bragg put in such peril that he gave the order for a general retreat on the night of the 3d. Concentrating and intrenching near Tullahoma, some 40 miles south of Murfreesboro, General Bragg placed his army in winter quarters, while General Rosecrans devoted his energies to the repair of his communications and to strengthening the weak spots in the organization of his army, in which the next few months were spent.

West of the Mississippi the situation had not greatly changed during the fall and winter. In Missouri General Blunt had operated vigorously, defeating the Confederates under Marmaduke at Boston Mountains, November 28, and following this victory by one over Hindman at Prairie Grove on the 7th of December, practically freeing the state from any organized rebel army. Texas, however, where so earnest a stand had been made against secession, seemed now utterly abandoned by the national government. Galveston had been occupied by three companies of the Forty-second Massachusetts regiment, supported by a fleet of gun-boats in the harbor, but on the first day of January, 1863, the fleet was dispersed by that of the Confederates and General Magruder easily captured the handful of infantry left unprotected in the streets. With the exception of an insignificant force at certain points on the Rio Grande, no Union soldiers were left in Texas.

All other interests in that region were now subordinated to the supreme object of opening the Mississippi. With that vast waterway under the national control, cutting off the great trans-Mississippi region whence enormous quantities of supplies were furnished the Confederates, a powerful blow would be struck against the cause of disunion. Already great progress had been made, so that at only two points—Vicksburg and Port Hudson— did the secessionists retain control. These posts, admirably adapted to the command of the river, had been strengthened by every device known to engineering skill. At Vicksburg the first battery on the Mississippi had been built, from which on the 18th of January, 1861, the steamer A. O. Tyler had been fired on. Here General Lovell had retreated with his army when the approach of General Butler drove him from New Orleans, and in May he was followed by Farragut's fleet, the batteries at Port Hudson not being completed. Fire was opened by Farragut, but the siege was not prosecuted, and toward the end of July, 1862, he returned to New Orleans. On the 7th of September the first fight with the batteries at Port Hudson occurred, and the Federal naval commander found the river practically closed to his vessels at that point.

Early in November General Grant began the concentration of his available forces for a vigorous campaign against Vicksburg, and was pressing forward with all speed when the capture of his depot of supplies at Holly Springs by Van Dorn obliged him to retire to Grand Junction till the loss could be repaired, and this respite gave General Pemberton time to concentrate his command for the defense of the threatened stronghold. At this time Grant divided his Army of the Tennessee into four corps— the Thirteenth, Fifteenth, Sixteenth and Seventeenth, commanded respectively by Generals McClernand, Sherman, Hurlbut and McPherson. On the 20th of December,—the day of Van Dorn's successful raid on Grant's supplies,—Sherman left Memphis, Admiral Porter's fleet transporting his troops down the Mississippi and up the Yazoo to the rear of Vicksburg, where they debarked on the 26th, and three days later unsuccessfully attacked the Confederates in a strong position at Chickasaw Bayou. This movement having thus proved a failure, the idea of a flank attack on Pemberton was abandoned. A week later McClernand joined forces with Sherman and took command, being the senior officer, and January 11, 1863, the land forces in conjunction with the fleet captured Fort Hindman, on the Arkansas river, with its garrison of some 5,500 men. The next notable attempt was to cut a canal across the long peninsula opposite Vicksburg, in the hope of diverting the river from its natural course; but after two months of incredible exertions in swamps, bayous and forests, the rise of the river compelled the abandonment of the scheme. On the 2d of February General Grant reached Young's Point and assumed personal command of the operations, and the following night the Queen of the West of Porter's fleet ran the batteries, destroyed four Confederate vessels below, and returned without serious damage. On a second passage this vessel was lost through the treachery of a pilot, and similar attempts followed, attended with more or less success, but it was demonstrated that the batteries could be passed, and Grant presently decided on one of the boldest movements known to military history. This was no less than to move his army on the west side of the river far below Vicksburg, cross the Mississippi by transports which Porter would undertake to run past the batteries, throw his force between the Confederate armies in Mississippi, defeat them in detail and capture Vicksburg. This plan, daring as it was, the indomitable genius of its originator carried out almost exactly.

Porter successfully passed Vicksburg with the vessels required, but at Grand Gulf, near the mouth of the Big Black river, he found other strong batteries which he ineffectually attacked on the 29th of April, but that night ran his transports past them and immediately moved the waiting army across the river. General McClernand's command encountered and defeated the Confederates under General John Bowen on the 1st of May, which defeat necessitated the abandonment of the works at Grand Gulf. On the 8th General Sherman, who had been operating against Haines Bluff with the gun-boats, joined Grant on the Big Black, and the march toward Jackson was promptly taken up. General J. E. Johnston, the ablest of the Southern chieftains in the West, was reported on his way to assume personal command of all the troops in that vicinity, but when he came he found only broken fragments. On the 12th McPherson's corps defeated General Gregg at Raymond, and two days later the Fifteenth and Seventeenth Corps defeated the Confederates at Jackson and captured the place. Finding that Pemberton was seeking to strike him in the rear, Grant now faced about, and on the 16th met and defeated his antagonist at Champion Hills. Pemberton fell back to a strong position on the Big Black, but on the following day he was attacked and driven with such vigor that he was unable to destroy the bridge over which his troops retreated, and on the 19th he found himself forced back upon Vicksburg by the victorious Federals. A combined and desperate assault upon the fortifications there was made on the 22d, but it was bloodily repulsed, when Grant, changing his base of supplies to the Yazoo, settled down to a siege of the place. Among the troops which came to his reinforcement at this time were two divisions of the Ninth Corps under General Parke, detached during the winter from the Army of the Potomac. The course of the siege cannot be followed here ; suffice it to say that it was pressed with desperate energy and valiantly resisted. On the 15th of June General McClernand, who had, in an order to his command, allowed some reflection on General Grant, was relieved from command of the Thirteenth Corps and succeeded by General E. O. C. Ord.

General Butler was relieved from the command of the Department of the Gulf, November 9, 1862, and a week later General N. P. Banks succeeded him, with head-quarters at New Orleans. A thorough campaign was at once planned, Baton Rouge being reoccupied by a force under General Grover, and during the succeeding months General Dick Taylor, the Southern commander, was driven from point to point till his army was effectually scattered. Crossing the Mississippi at Bayou Sara, Banks moved down from the north toward Port Hudson, while General Augur approached on the south, and on the 24th of May the investment was complete. Here, too, strong assaults were made, but stubbornly repulsed by the garrison under General Gardner, and the slower process of siege became necessary.

This, then, was the situation in the West and Southwest at the end of June, 1863: Burnside, relieved of the command of the Army of the Potomac, had been assigned to East Tennessee, where he was gathering a considerable army; Van Dorn's command—that officer having been killed in a personal quarrel by a Dr. Peters—had joined Bragg at Tullahoma, against whom Rosecrans was preparing to move; Grant was besieging Pemberton at Vicksburg, and Banks performing a like service for Gardner at Port Hudson.

Return we now to the Army of the Potomac, of which, on the 26th of January, 1863, General Joseph Hooker had taken command, Sumner and Franklin retiring at the same time. The former died soon after of disease while preparing to take a command in the West, and the latter had no further connection with the Army of the Potomac. The new commander at once bent his energies to the reorganization of his command, and as his accession followed close on the "mud march," there was abundant opportunity for the exercise of his genius. There was unmistakably much demoralization. Desertions had been frequent and the absentees from the army at this time, including all causes, amounted to nearly 85,000. Many of these were sick or wounded, or on furlough, but these causes did not by any means cover the entire number. Better food, better clothing and better sanitary regulations were at once ordered, and what seemed mountains of discouragement to former commanders were now made to give way. Vegetables in some form were issued with regularity, ovens were built for the baking of soft bread, rations lost or damaged when in the possession of the soldier were replaced, sinks and drainage received careful attention, and with these and many other evidences of a lively interest in the physical welfare of his command, General Hooker won the confidence and strengthened the morale of his men. At the opening of the Chancellorsville campaign the Army of the Potomac was undoubtedly in the finest physical condition known to its history. The desertions, which were reported as reaching 200 per day at the time Hooker took command, soon nearly ceased, and a judicious system of brief furloughs gave an added incentive to excellence in soldierly duties.

In the organization of the army many changes occurred. The system of grand divisions was abolished, and in the place of the Ninth Corps, which left the Army of the Potomac during the winter, the Eleventh had been added, General Sigel, its recent commander, being succeeded by General O. O. Howard, to the serious displeasure of its large German element. But two of the corps commanders at Fredericksburg remained—General Reynolds of the First and General Couch of the Second. The Third was under General Daniel E. Sickles. General George G. Meade advanced from the Third Division of the First Corps to command the Fifth Corps. General John Sedgwick left the Second Division of the Second Corps to command the Sixth Corps, succeeding General W F. Smith, assigned to duty in North Carolina. The Twelfth Corps was under General H. W Slocum, advanced from the command of the First Division, Sixth Corps.

The make-up of the Sixth Corps during the Chancellorsville campaign may be thus described: The First Division, under General Brooks, previously commander of the Vermont Brigade, was composed of the First or New Jersey Brigade, General Torbert, the Second, General Bartlett, and the Third, General David A. Russell, promoted November 29, 1862, from the colonelcy of the Seventh Massachusetts. General Howe's Second Division consisted of the Second or Vermont Brigade, Colonel L. A. Grant, and the Third, General Neill. The First Brigade of this division had been broken up, and a "Light Division" formed, under the command of Colonel Burnham, composed of the Fifth Wisconsin, Sixth Maine, Thirty-first and Forty-third

New York and Sixty-first Pennsylvania. The Third Division, now under General John Newton, one of the most thorough engineers in the army, saw many changes among its commanders. General Devens having been appointed to the command of a division in the Eleventh Corps, his brigade became the Second, and passed to the command of Colonel Browne of the Thirty-sixth New York, the senior regimental commander at the time, Colonel Wheaton having been commissioned a brigadier-general at the time of Colonel Russell's promotion, and assigned to the command of the Third Brigade. The First Brigade was commanded by General Alexander Shaler. Colonel Horatio Rogers succeeded Wheaton in the Second Rhode Island, and Colonel Thomas D. Johns was assigned to the Seventh.

Especial effort had been made by General Hooker to organize the cavalry of his command as an important arm of the service, which thus far it had never been. The entire available force of this arm was consolidated under General Stoneman, and at the opening of the campaign it comprised an efficient total of some 12,000 men. Including the cavalry, Hooker's army now numbered not far from 125,000, of which he might well say that it was "the finest army on this planet."

It was during this period of reconstruction that the system of corps badges was adopted by General Hooker's order for the instant identification of the different commands. The figures adopted for the seven corps of the Army of the Potomac were: First, a disk; Second, a trefoil; Third, a diamond; Fifth, a Maltese cross; Sixth, a Greek cross; Eleventh, a crescent; Twelfth, a star. The color for the first division of each corps was red, for the second white, and for the third blue—employing in regular order the three national colors. Small cloth badges of the proper figure and color were sewn upon the tops of the men's caps or on the left side of hats when worn, and the head-quarters flags of the divisions and brigades were thus distinguished: First division, a red figure on a white ground; second, a white figure on a blue ground; third, a blue figure on a white flag. The flags of divisions were rectangular, of brigades triangular. The brigade flags being of the same color as those of the division, with the corps badge in the center, the number of the brigade was thus designated: First, a plain flag; second, a stripe or border next the staff; third, the same on the three sides of the flag; fourth, a sector at each of the three corners. The color of these borders was that supplementing the body of the flag and the corps badge, the Second Brigade, Third Division, thus having a white flag with a blue cross in the center and a red bar next the staff. This excellent system, which was soon adopted by nearly every corps of the Union armies West and South, was the outgrowth of a device of General Kearney during the peninsular campaign to distinguish the officers of his division, who for a time were all obliged to dress in the uniforms of enlisted men. After the death of that gallant officer at Chantilly, those who had fought under him continued to wear the badge in his memory.

The Confederate force at this time opposed to Hooker consisted of something over 60,000 men, so disposed as to be easily concentrated at any point where they might be needed, while for 25 miles along their front, from United States Ford above Fredericksburg to Port Royal below, extended a system of intrenchment as perfect as military skill highly favored by the contour of the country could produce. Behind these defenses lay the four divisions of "Stonewall" Jackson's Second Corps, commanded respectively by Generals A. P Hill, D. H. Hill, Trimble and Early, with two divisions of Longstreet's First Corps, under Generals Anderson and McLaws, Longstreet in person with his other two divisions having been sent to the south of Richmond in February, to operate against General Peck.

The plan of attack which Hooker decided upon might be called an elaboration of Burnside's January attempt which had ended in the mud. Briefly stated, it was to throw the main body of his army far around the left of the Confederate position, while a demonstration in force was made at the old battle-ground near the city, to cover the real intention; meantime 10,000 cavalry under Stoneman were to raid as far and as vigorously as possible against the enemy's lines of communication.

The cavalry on both sides had already become active. On the 8th of March the guerrilla leader John S. Moseby dashed into the village of Fairfax Court House with a small force, captured several prisoners, among them Colonel Stoughton, the commander of the Vermont nine-months' brigade which was doing duty in that vicinity, and escaped without loss, the affair occurring at the dead of night and Colonel Stoughton being taken from his bed. At Kelly's Ford on the 17th occurred the first purely cavalry fight in the history of the Army of the Potomac, a force under General Averell encountering the brigade of Fitz Hugh Lee, with whom a sharp but not decisive engagement occurred.

Meantime the events transpiring in and about Camp Edwards convinced its occupants that they must soon expect again to meet the enemy. The early part of March, following the occupation of the new quarters, was especially stormy and disagreeable, but toward the close of the month the skies brightened and the mud gradually gave place to firm earth. Nearly every day was marked by the occurrence of inspection, review or brigade drill. On the 2d of April, which was Fast day in Massachusetts, the division was reviewed by General Sedgwick, and on the following day by General Hooker; the memorable review of the army by President Lincoln taking place on the 8th. The latter occasion was one of much interest to those who then for the first time saw the President. The Thirty-seventh regiment was on the right of the massive line, and the reviewing party rode down almost in front of its colors, Mr. Lincoln uncovering his head as its flags drooped low, the artillery thundered and the bands at the right began to play. Great was the contrast between that plain, modest man,—almost awkward in his movements, his naturally furrowed face more deeply worn by the load of care which he had so long borne,—and his magnificent escort of richly dressed officers, the embodiment of military pomp and splendor. Many a man in the ranks noted that contrast as the cavalcade moved down the line, and it is not too much to say that from that momentary glimpse many a heart beat more warmly and kindly toward "Honest Abe."

The division was called out again on the 11th for review by a visiting Swiss general, and on the 14th the expected marching orders came. The campaign had begun, a cavalry force being pushed across the Rappahannock at Kelly's Ford to feel the way for the infantry, but that night a severe rain-storm set in and the movement was postponed, the furious storm raising the river so rapidly that the cavalry with some difficulty recrossed to the northern side.

One sad experience was still in store for the brigade before it should again meet the enemy. General Devens had been assigned to the command of the First Division of the Eleventh Corps, and on the afternoon of April 21 a brigade dress parade was held at which the honored commander in affecting words took leave of his command. From the opening days of the peninsular campaign the present relation had existed, with but temporary interruption in the previous autumn when General Devens had commanded the division; and as the speaker referred to the faithful services of his command in whatever position it had been placed, and the sincere regret he felt in leaving them, with an expression of his confidence that in the future they would render equally faithful service to the cause of Union, those who heard felt that he spoke no perfunctory words.*

That evening the detachment of the Fiftieth New York regiment of Engineers which had been encamped just south of the Thirty-seventh in charge of a ponton train broke camp and disappeared in the direction of the river, and an invitation to fol-

---

*General Devens was severely wounded in the foot at Chancellorsville, May 2, and after the draft riots of the following July, not being able to return to active duty in the field, he was assigned to command the Massachusetts draft rendezvous in Boston harbor, where he remained till the following spring when he rejoined the army in the field, taking a command in the Eighteenth Corps at the special request of General W. F. Smith, its commander, having part in the engagements at Port Walthal, Arrowfield Church, etc., under General Butler, then operating from Bermuda Hundred. When, a little later, three divisions were sent under General Smith to join the Army of the Potomac, General Devens commanded one of them—a provisional division of three brigades from the Tenth Corps. With this he fought bravely at Cold Harbor, but was soon after prostrated by rheumatic fever, serving during convalescence as president of a military commission for the trial of various classes of offenders and when recovered was assigned by General Ord to the command of the First Division of the Eighteenth Corps. At the reorganization of the Army of the James he took command of the Third Division of the Twenty-fourth Corps, which was the first command to enter the city of Richmond. For gallantry and good conduct at this time he was at request of General Grant brevetted major-general, remaining in command of the division till the corps was mustered out of service. He was then appointed to the command of the Northeast military district of Virginia, and at the end of August was ordered to the command of the military district of Charleston, embracing the eastern section of South Carolina, where he remained till the spring of 1866, when he was mustered out, after almost five years of very honorable service. In April, 1867, he was appointed a judge of the superior court of Massachusetts, and promoted in October, 1873, to the bench of the supreme judicial court of the state. Resigning this position to serve as attorney-general of the United States in President Hayes's cabinet, he was on the expiration of his term re-appointed a judge of the supreme judicial court of Massachusetts, which position he holds at this writing (1884).

low them was hourly expected. That afternoon the regiment was sent on picket duty for three days, during which time it rained almost without cessation, so that on the return to camp no further changes had taken place. The paymaster made a welcome visit on the 25th, paying the regiment for four months' service to March 1, and on the 27th the brigade was drilled and had a dress parade under its new commander, Colonel W H. Browne. Final orders were received at the same time to be ready to move early in the morning.

It was not till 3 o'clock of the following afternoon, however, that the order to march was heard. Then, by a circuitous route, through a drizzling rain, a few miles were made and the regiment halted for the night on the north slope of the Stafford hills, out of sight of the Confederates across the stream but within easy distance of the Rappahannock. It was not quite comfortable for the men to lie down in their wet garments without the privilege of making fires to boil a cup of coffee, but every one submitted cheerfully and slept well till early morning, when rapid firing in the direction of the river brought every sleeper to his feet. Presently the brigade marched down to the vicinity of the river, halting very near the spot where in December they had waited for orders to cross. But this time a lodgment had already been made on the opposite bank. During the night ponton bridges had been quietly laid at Franklin's crossing of the previous battle and at Pollock's Mills, a mile below. Small parties had been pushed over in boats, capturing the enemy's pickets at each point and saving the engineers from the annoyance of their musketry. Bridges being hastily laid, Brooks's division of the Sixth Corps crossed at the upper and Wadsworth's division of the First at the lower, and established their lines on the Spottsylvania side. The enemy showing no disposition to dispute the occupancy of the historic plain, the Third Corps, which had been detached to support the movement, marched rapidly up the river to United States Ford, to cooperate in the main movement directed by Hooker in person. During that night and the following day everything remained quiet in Sedgwick's command, those of his troops on the left bank of the river pitching their shelter tents and experiencing no further excitement than an occasional artillery duel and the sounds of distant skirmishing as the detachments across the river felt the position of the enemy in their front. On the evening of the 30th the Thirty-seventh were detailed to accompany a ponton train up the river, some of the bridges having been taken up. The journey was made to the vicinity of Banks's Ford, and it was 8 o'clock next morning when the thoroughly weary regiment returned to its place in the brigade, and the men slept most of the day, falling in near night to march around the base of the hill and up over its crest, thence down to the plain, repeating the operation till darkness shut the performance from the sight of the enemy for whose benefit it was undertaken, to give the impression of a movement in force at that point. In fact the left was being weakened, for the First Corps was now ordered to the right to assist in Hooker's main attack, leaving Sedgwick with but his own corps and Gibbon's division of the Second. Let us now sketch the fortunes of the main army.

According to the programme, during the night of April 28, the Fifth, Eleventh and Twelfth Corps crossed the Rappahannock at Kelly's Ford, and the following night forded the Rapidan—the Fifth at Ely's Ford and the others at Germanna. The Second Corps moved by way of United States Ford, a short distance below the junction of the two rivers, and as soon as the Rapidan was passed above they also crossed and pushed forward, the four corps on the night of the 30th bivouacking at Chancellorsville, a point on the Orange turnpike ten miles southwest of Fredericksburg, marked by a single brick house, which Hooker made his head-quarters. The Third Corps now moved up from the left, crossed at United States Ford and hastened to the support of those in advance. The general commanding was greatly elated by the success which had thus far attended his movements. Although the operations of the cavalry had been delayed by high water, so that Stoneman failed to render the efficient service that had been counted on, the column was now on its way toward Richmond, while more than 50,000 infantry under the immediate command of their valiant chieftain had reached a position of his selection directly in rear of the Confederate intrenched line. There was a substantial foundation for the congratulatory order issued by Hooker and read to every regiment in his army, in which he said : "It is with heartfelt satisfaction that the commanding general announces to the army that the operations of the last three days have determined that our enemy must either ingloriously fly, or come out from behind his defenses and give us battle on our own ground, where certain destruction awaits him."

The enemy had no thought of flying, though even so able a general as Lee might well shrink from the peril of his position. His army was at once disposed to meet the changed situation. Leaving what seemed an adequate force under General Early to hold the hights in front of Sedgwick, Lee with all his available troops prepared to dispute the Federal advance. Hooker, finding the ground about Chancellorsville unfavorable to military operations, pushed forward his left, composed of the Fifth Corps, within view of Banks's Ford, while the Twelfth Corps advanced along the plank road till it encountered Stonewall Jackson's troops, when, after a brisk engagement, it was decided to concentrate and intrench near Chancellorsville and await the rebel attack, if one was intended. The position of the Union army on the 2d of May may be briefly stated. The First Corps had crossed the Rappahannock at United States Ford and was held in reserve near there; the left of Hooker's main line was formed by the Fifth Corps, which extended from the sharp bend in the Rappahannock where Mineral Spring Run empties into the parent stream. Its line of battle faced in a southeasterly direction and was joined and prolonged by the Second Corps. Then the line bent around so as to face due south in front of the Chancellor house, where the Twelfth Corps was posted, and on the right of this the Third Corps began to face to the southwest. The curve in this direction was still more pronounced at the extreme right, formed by the Eleventh Corps. This flank was the weak point in the Federal position, being "in the air"— that is, having no protection against the attack of an enemy on the flank or rear. True there seemed very slight probability of any such attack, as the weak flank might be considered safely swung around behind the main line,—but that proved exactly what the Confederates were to successfully attempt. A direct attack could hardly be thought of, and the shrewd Jackson proposed to execute his favorite movement, and passing entirely around the Federal army, strike one of his characteristic blows, swift and terrible, on the flank which from the position of the army could not but be weak.

It was impossible to entirely conceal the movement of his column, as it passed over an elevation some distance to the south of the Union lines, but its purpose was wholly mistaken, being construed by the enthusiastic Hooker into an attempt to retreat. General Sickles with his Third Corps moved forward to attack it, and achieved some success, but in doing so left a great gap between the threatened Eleventh and Twelfth Corps, which came near sacrificing the entire army. Gaining his coveted position with no suspicion on the Federal side of his destination, Jackson, late in the afternoon, hastily formed his lines and swept down upon the fated corps. Devens's division of two brigades, on the extreme right, was the first to receive the shock. The men with stacked arms were idling about or cooking their suppers when the Confederate lines came crashing through the thicket. Not more than a round or two could be fired before the great waves of gray swept over and around the slight defenses and through the camps which a moment before had seemed established in the midst of profound peace. Almost at the opening of the attack General Devens, while trying to rally and hold his command against the onset, was severely wounded, and every colonel and general in the division was either disabled or captured. The broken division rolled back upon that of Schurz, next to it, and the latter crumbled away almost without a blow, but Steinwehr's division, the Second, formed a line in the face of the triumphant foe and momentarily checked his progress. Yet the two brigades, strengthened by a few of the fugitives from the rest of the corps, could not long withstand the triumphant fury of the attack, and presently the entire Eleventh Corps was driven to the rear, a panic-stricken mass of fugitives. A scene of the most terrible excitement and confusion followed, during which, amidst the general rout, occurred some of the grandest instances of heroism known to history. A handful of men here and there opposed the relentless advance, laying their lives down with a smile in order that time might be gained for bringing fresh batteries into position and forming new lines in the rear.

By superhuman exertions a respectable opposition was at last made to the Confederate advance, and there came a lull in the storm of battle. Jackson's attack had thus far been made by the divisions of Rodes and Colston, and as these were much disorganized, the troops commanded by A. P. Hill were placed in front, and though it was now dark, Jackson contemplated a continuance of the fight. Before his arrangements were completed he was fired upon by his own men and received wounds from which he died a week later, depriving the Confederacy of one of its ablest chieftains. Hill received a disabling wound shortly after, and General J. E. B. Stuart, who took temporary command of Jackson's corps, decided not to fight any more that night. Morning witnessed a renewal of the struggle, and till noon it raged incessantly. General Hooker was stunned by a shell striking a pillar against which he was leaning, seriously compromising the safety of his entire army, the center of which was steadily pushed back, in spite of the most desperate fighting, till the divided wings of the Confederate army were reunited and orders were issued for a combined advance along the whole line to complete the victory. It was at this time that news came to the Southern commander of Sedgwick's movements, which caused him to pause, and the battle of the main armies was not again renewed with earnestness. Among the Federal officers killed on the 3d, were Generals Berry and Whipple, commanding the Second and Third Divisions of the Fifth Corps.

We come now to the part taken by the Sixth Corps and the Thirty-seventh regiment as an integral part thereof. During Saturday, the 2d of May, there was more or less of what seemed a purposeless activity. Several times the command was placed under arms, perhaps moved a short distance, after which the muskets would be stacked and a period of suspense follow. As night approached there were evidences of skirmishing across the river, and about 9 o'clock the regiment moved quietly across the bridges, took its position with the other troops whose long lines could be dimly seen stretching away in the darkness, and the command was whispered to "Load at will." Then another rest. About 11 o'clock the expected summons from Hooker came, ordering General Sedgwick to move at once by way of Fredericksburg, seize the hights, crush whatever force might oppose him, take the plank road and form a junction with Hooker by daybreak. It is not the purpose of this narrative to criticise; but it is surely not amiss to call attention to the magnitude of the task thus outlined. The distance to be covered was from 12 to 14 miles, or more than the corps could have accomplished by an unimpeded march during the time named. At the very outset were to be encountered the terrible hights against which in the former battle half the army had dashed in vain, and which the present commanding general had at that time pronounced impregnable to direct assault. During the winter, and especially in the few previous days, in anticipation of an immediate attack, the works had been strengthened, and were now held by six brigades of choice Confederate troops under Early, with artillery support, making a force equal in strength to that actually engaged on the Confederate side in the repulse of Burnside.

But the stout-hearted commander of the Sixth Corps, though ordered to undertake a prima facie impossibility, promptly obeyed the spirit, if he could not meet the letter, of his instructions. As rapidly as his skirmishers could push back those of the enemy the column moved toward Fredericksburg, and finally halted in the streets. A skirmisher who had fallen at the very entrance of the town and was dying from a terrible wound in the chest, faintly encouraged his comrades as they passed. "God bless you, boys," he said, "I believe you are going to capture Richmond now, and it is my only regret that I cannot go with you to the end." Brave in death as in life, he was a type of that vast army of martyrs who gave their lives willing sacrifices on the altar of their country.

To advance further in the darkness was out of the question, as a demonstration proved, and the men dropped upon the sidewalks, in the streets, anywhere, for a few moments' sleep. With the first light of day all were astir, and the men of the Thirty-seventh, who trod the streets of the famous city for the first time, were beginning to take note of their surroundings, when the artillery on the hights opened and the frightful crashing of the missiles through the buildings dissipated all emotions of mere curiosity. Moving rapidly out of the city toward the hights the regiment for a time took shelter in a railroad cut, where it was effectually protected from the enemy's fire. The position, though safe, was not one to induce reflections of a pleasing nature. The memory of that terrible 13th of December would intrude. There were the same hights which had then defied the Union army; at their base was the deadly stone-wall before which the charging lines had been swept away in ruin. That experiment was to be repeated—would the result be different? There was no alternative to a direct assault. With the first light Gibbon's division of the Second Corps had laid bridges from Falmouth and crossed the river, taking position on the Federal right, between the city and the river. Newton's division occupied the city front, and to the left, beyond Hazel Run, was Howe, with Brooks's First Division protecting the bridges at the crossing below. Gibbon, to whose assistance the Tenth Massachusetts and Second Rhode Island had been detached, felt for an opening in the Confederate left, but his advance was checked by the canal and a railroad cut. Howe on the left of Newton had advanced and been driven back. "We must depend upon the bayonet alone!" said Sedgwick, and proceeded to form a storming party to charge the entire crest. Somewhere the wedge must be driven through. Directly in front of Newton's division rose Marye's hill, with a fine brick mansion near the crest, distant about a thousand yards from the Federal lines. For two-thirds of the distance the ground slopes gently upward, then rises quite sharply till the summit is gained. From the principal street of the city, straight up and over the hill, runs the plank road which Sedgwick is ordered to take. At the foot of the hill proper is a toll-house and to the south of this along the base of the hill runs the sunken Telegraph road and the fatal stone-wall. Behind the wall lies Barksdale's brigade of Mississippians; in front of it, sheltered by a swell of the ground, Colonel Burnham holds four regiments of his Light Division. They have attacked and been repulsed, but await the moment for a more determined advance. On the plank road a column of four regiments was formed under Colonel Spear of the Sixty-first Pennsylvania, consisting of his own regiment and the Forty-third New York, supported by the Sixty-seventh New York and Eighty-second Pennsylvania. Between Spear's command and that of Burnham the Seventh Massachusetts and Thirty-sixth New York under the command of Colonel Johns of the Seventh are formed to move parallel to Spear's advance up the plank road, the men leaving knapsacks, haversacks—everything that can impede their movements. Beyond Burnham to the left Howe's division is also in waiting. It is 11 o'clock, and at length everything is ready. The Union batteries have been playing with dreadful energy upon the Confederate entrenchments, but the Washington artillery on the hights holds on defiantly. Suddenly Spear's column emerges on the plank road, moving straight forward at the double-quick with fixed bayonets. The two regiments from Browne's Brigade are beside it, also pushing forward by the right flank in column of fours. As they approach the toll-gate a terrible artillery fire tears through the head of each column, and Barksdale's men from behind the stone-wall send a hot musketry fire into their flank. The regiments in advance are sadly shattered. Colonel Spear is mortally and Colonel Johns seriously wounded, and the commands falter, but they hear the cheers of the sturdy lines on their left and press on once more. Barksdale had almost forgotten the line in his front in his anxiety to demolish the columns on his left, when Burnham's men spring forward with a bound, scatter the Mississippians with their bayonets, capture half the brigade and send the rest flying helter-skelter along the Telegraph road. Then on up the hill they go with a sweep, breaking through the intrenched line, the flag of the Sixth

Maine being the first to wave from the rebel stronghold. Howe's three brigades were pressing up the slope to the left, and Gibbon, although unable to reach the enemy, was holding his attention at the right. Lieutenant-Colonel Harlow of the Seventh is wounded but not disabled, and with a few files of his regiment cuts through the Confederates and effects a lodgment with a cool bravery never surpassed. The shattered residue of the regiment catch the spirit of their heroic commander and rally to his assistance, swarming over the works and driving the astounded chivalry before them. It had been asked if the Thirty-sixth New York would stand such desperate service, for in a few days more their term of enlistment would have expired. Never was doubt more bravely dissipated. Straight up to and over the hostile works goes their tall color-sergeant and his flag, which he plants proudly on a captured gun, while the shortened line springs over the breastworks and the men with clubbed muskets dash the panic-stricken defenders to the earth and receive their surrender with a cheer which is answered from the plains below as the reserve lines come rushing up to complete the occupation. The remnants of Spear's column nerve themselves for one more effort and they, too, make a lodgment in the fortifications. Howe has carried the hights in his front, and the broken Confederate line is crumbling away, hurrying squads here and there trying to reach the Telegraph road or fleeing over the plank road in advance of the pursuers.

As the Thirty-seventh charged up the slope in support of the advance regiments and reached the first line of fortifications, it paused for a moment to reform its line and change direction toward the left, where from a second series of defenses on still higher ground the flying Confederates were scampering forth and hurrying toward the Telegraph road, their forms outlined like dwarf silhouettes against the clear sky. Looking behind them the men saw the batteries which had thundered valiantly all the morning against the hights driving desperately up the plank road, the horses lashed to a gallop, the men and their beloved guns hidden from sight in the heavy clouds of dust. Here and there a blue line with the Stars and Stripes in the center swept steadily up the slope, while an occasional farewell shot from the flying foe came back like a note of defiance. All these were elements of satisfaction, but there was a sadder feature comprised within the picture. All that green slope was dotted over with little points of blue, and those who looked back upon them knew that each represented a comrade who had fallen by the way. Brilliant as had been the success won, it had been achieved at the cost of over a thousand men killed and wounded on the Union side. Already the stretcher-bearers were hurrying over the field in quest of their ghastly burdens, under a system so perfect that within an hour every wounded man was sheltered in the hospitals which had been organized in the town.

Moving some distance to the rear of the fortified line, the Thirty-seventh halted till the other regiments of the brigade came up. Then with eager haste messengers passed back and forth between the different commands, to learn the fate of friends or the general fortunes of the various organizations. There was a brief respite, during which General Sedwick was busy with preparations to follow up his advantage. Gibbon's division was left in charge of Fredericksburg, the red crosses of the First Division moved out in advance along the plank road, the other divisions followed, and the hights of Fredericksburg were left behind.

It was a beautiful Sabbath day, the sun shining clear and warm; Nature was in her most charming dress. Beside the road as the troops advanced were fields of grain waving with promise, and bird-songs trilled forth to fall unheeded on the ears of men whose thoughts and senses were not for scenes of beauty or notes of joy. Presently the boom of cannon in advance is heard, and a few solid shots go over and uncomfortably near the marching column; the speed slackens somewhat, but there is no halt, and the men think little of the familiar greeting—probably some retreating party is making a little stand somewhere to gain time.

Some miles have been passed and the afternoon is well advanced when a small stream, tributary far below to Hazel Run, is crossed. Here the brigade leaves the highway and halts upon the steep slope beside the streamlet in column by regiments, the

Thirty-seventh, on account of its fuller ranks, being formed in two lines, the left wing under Lieutenant-Colonel Montague in rear of the right. Very soon, one by one, the regiments rise, but instead of returning to the plank road they advance in line directly up the hill and disappear. Close on the heels of its predecessor the Thirty-seventh climbs to the plateau and the mystery is solved. Not far in front there is a terrific fire of musketry, and as the regiment moves steadily forward toward the scene it encounters a spectacle to chill the stoutest heart. The Federal lines have broken and the horrible fragments are pouring to the rear. Some of the fugitives are bleeding from sickening wounds, others unhurt are seeking panic stricken for some shelter from the bullets which are still hissing sharply around them.

What was the matter? That may be briefly told. Wilcox's Confederate brigade, posted near Banks's Ford, had been summoned to assist Early in defending the hights, but had not arrived in time. It at once planted itself in front of Sedgwick to delay his march as much as possible, while news of the disaster was sent to General Lee—the news which had caused the postponement of his intended attack on Hooker. Four brigades under General McLaws were at once hurried down to Salem Church, midway between Fredericksburg and Chancellorsville, to which point Wilcox fell back, and when Brooks's division reached that vicinity he found his advance checked. He attacked valiantly, won some success, but was driven back. As the Thirty-seventh gained the field it confronted the triumphant hosts of the foe pushing forward to flank the shattered Union lines. It was a moment of supreme importance. Colonel Browne had fallen with a severe wound, and the command of the brigade devolved upon Colonel Eustis of the Tenth. The command was scattered, the individual regiments being thrown in at the most important points. Williston's battery of brass guns comes up the road at a mad gallop, the captain riding on in advance. He shrinks from the prospect. "Captain, bring in your guns," exclaims Colonel Edwards in his most emphatic tones; "the Thirty-seventh is here!" The fierce gallop of the battery horses never ceases till the pieces are wheeled into position, and almost before the trails drop to the ground the gunners are sending storms of cannister into the faces of the enemy. Still the charging line overlaps and the left is threatened. General Brooks, rough as a lion and as brave, gallops to the spot. "Is there a regiment here that I can have?" he demands. "Take my left wing; it's as good as a whole regiment!" says Edwards. The right wing advances close to the battery and gives it a steadfast support, while the left wing, led by the soldierly lieutenant-colonel, moves by the left flank through a bushy ravine under a shower of bullets, and occupies a commanding position beyond. As it halts the stream of fire which bursts out along its line shows the flanking column of graycoats that they are beaten at their own game, and in a few moments they go drifting back toward the woods from which they came. It is an exciting moment, and Lieutenant Loomis observes that some members of his command are firing at random. His men are brought to a "shoulder arms," drilled in the manual for a few moments till calm self-possession is restored, and then direct their fire once more upon the retreating foe. Nightfall comes on, the sounds of battle cease,—only the sad refrain from the hundreds of agonized ones stretched helpless on the field, and the low bustle of preparation among men and officers for the expected renewal of the struggle on the morrow.

In the establishing of the Union lines the Thirty-seventh was reunited and moved forward a short distance to a commanding position, where with the Thirty-sixth New York it formed three sides of a square at the most advanced angle of Sedgwick's lines. From that point the Third Division with one brigade of the First extended in a long, weak line to the river above Banks's Ford, fronting to the west; the remainder of the First Division—little more than a picket line in strength—faced to the south and extended eastward till it joined Howe's Second Division, which was still in the rear of the Fredericksburg hights and facing them, its front being to the east. Thus disposed the Sixth Corps formed three sides of a vast, irregular quadrangle, with a total frontage of more than six miles.

Little sleep came to the men as they lay on their arms through the night. Early in the evening word was brought that the Thirty-sixth, who had thrown off knapsacks and haversacks to charge the hights in the morning, were still without food, and in a short time the well-filled haversacks of the Thirty-seventh had contributed a generous supply, and from the moment of that simple act the friendship between the two regiments was of the warmest nature. Directly in front, and some 500 yards distant, were the woods into which the Confederates had retired, pursued by the fire of the Federal batteries, and which had been set on fire by the bursting shells. The cries of the wounded could be plainly heard, and the feeling that they had been burned in the flames haunted many a brain long after the last flicker had died away.

The morning of the 4th found the situation unchanged, and not till afternoon were there serious demonstrations on either side. Occasionally a rebel skirmish line would show itself from the edge of the woods, but invariably received a sharp greeting from the Union pickets and artillery, and once or twice when a line of battle also appeared a wave of fire burst from the rifles of the Thirty-seventh, and the shelter of the forest was promptly resumed. General Sedgwick had repeatedly acquainted General Hooker with his situation, and asked coöperation from the main army; but the only response was in effect that the Sixth Corps must take care of itself, and the Federal guns at Chancellorsville remained dumb, while reinforcements poured back from Lee's army and enveloped the isolated corps, threatening each moment to crush in its frail sides. Early's scattered division had been collected and reinforced, and had taken possession again of the hights above the city from which it had been driven. A determined attempt to crush Howe's division and cut the corps off from the river followed, and Neill's brigade was broken, but the Vermont Brigade, with its accustomed bravery, saved the field.

As the day neared its close, the Thirty-seventh could hear the sullen mutterings of the battle-storm as it closed in around them, till they seemed to be surrounded by a vast circle of hostile fire. Beyond the woods in their front the arrival of reinforcements could be constantly heard; cheer answered cheer, and a brass-band played the favorite Southern airs with an energy which left no doubt of the Confederate elation over the situation. The rank and file of that exposed quadrangle realized well the danger of their situation, but there was no uneasiness, no despair. They were in the hands of officers whom they could trust—whom they did trust implicitly on the field of battle, and many a man in his own way expressed the unwavering conviction that General Sedgwick would take care of the corps, and Colonel Edwards would be sure to do the best possible for his beloved regiment.

Finally the crisis came. It was almost dusk, and it was known that the line was to be evacuated as soon as darkness would cover the movement from observation. The pressure in front had been growing stronger and was applied more frequently. Again the Confederate skirmishers came out from their woody covert, and again they were met by a sharp fire, but this time they did not retire. On they came through the growing dusk, and behind them came line after line of battle, showing the purpose of McLaws to strike a crushing blow. The time had come to move! Fortunately dusk had come with it, and the enemy, checked by the admirable fire of the skirmish line, composed of Companies D and F, advanced so slowly that an orderly retreat to the vicinity of the bridge near Banks's Ford was made without loss, where the corps was concentrated to await permission from Hooker to recross the river.

The safety of the Thirty-seventh evoked the most lively satisfaction at corps head-quarters, since from its peculiarly exposed position it had been feared that it must be cut off, but the most remarkable fact was that the skirmish line had been able to do so valiant work in delaying the advance of the enemy and still bring away every man. The admirable steadiness and efficiency of Company F had been closely watched and warmly praised by their comrades in the regimental line, but the position of Company D was not so favorable for observation. The latter, which had rejoined the regiment while waiting to cross the river three or four days before, had served at Sixth Corps head-quarters after Franklin's retirement, and had been much flattered by warm compliments bestowed by General Hooker on one of his visits to General Sedgwick. Captain Flagg had given especial attention to the skirmish drill, and in recognition of this fact his command was deployed to cover the angle to the left of Company F's line on the regiment's front and right. After the line was established it was supported by Company H and reinforced by four companies from other regiments.

No loss was suffered by the skirmishers in retreating, but as the first halt was made near the bridge a member of Company H,—Jonas H. Thayer of Belchertown,—died suddenly from exhaustion. His comrades, much affected, prepared as suitable a grave in the bed of a gully as circumstances permitted, loosening the earth with their bayonets and performing the last sad rites while the Confederate shells whistled savagely overhead and the moonlight struggled fitfully through the broken clouds.

Decidedly the most uncomfortable position of the entire campaign was that of waiting in the darkness for orders to recross the river. The enemy, not quite daring to press the retiring corps in earnest, amused themselves by keeping up an artillery fire directed at the bridge, but a providential ridge of ground saved the pontons from being struck, and finally, long after midnight, the disorganized column crept silently across to the Stafford side and the battle of Salem Church was ended.

In the matter of casualties, remarkably good fortune had attended the Thirty-seventh. Company K had lost Corporal Dennis Driscoll of Springfield and Private Michael Conway of Chelsea mortally wounded, besides which some 25 wounds, mostly slight, were reported.

CHAPTER VIII

TO GETTYSBURG.

AFTER THE DEFEAT.—THE SKIRMISH WITH A. P. HILL.—THE NORTHWARD MOVEMENT.—EXIT HOOKER, ENTER MEADE.— THE MARCH TO THE BATTLE-FIELD.

General Sedgwick, having safely crossed the Rappahannock, halted his corps near the river to await further developments—so near, in fact, that some of the men were wounded the following day by the scattering artillery fire from the other side. Rations and ammunition were supplied, mails were distributed and the usual quota of letters written to anxious friends at home, after which the soldiers shivered through a very uncomfortable storm for two days and blankly wondered "what next." The battle was not to be renewed. General Lee, having driven Sedgwick from the dangerous position in the Confederate rear, once more consolidated his army in front of Hooker and on the morning of the 6th of May his skirmishers pushed forward to develop the Federal position and renew the battle. They failed to find an active enemy—only the Union dead and wounded remained on that side the river. The swollen, discolored river once more rolled between the hostile armies, the Confederates reoccupied the old line of fortifications, and the loyal army was disposed practically as before.

The Thirty-seventh returned to Camp Edwards on the 8th, making a spiritless, wearisome march, though the distance was only some eight miles. The experiences of the ten days of ceaseless activity and battle, followed by the drenching storm, had not been productive of exuberant physical energy. Fortunately the camp was found intact, the men having merely removed the canvas coverings of their huts; when these were replaced, with such new dispositions as the casualties of the campaign had necessitated, the regiment immediately found itself very comfortably at home. The usual camp routine was at once resumed, the first battalion drill being varied by a short address from the colonel, warmly expressing his satisfaction with the conduct of his command during the recent experiences. Company D speedily provided itself with quarters the exact counterpart of the others, and evergreens were displayed in profusion in the different streets, though there was the ever-present likelihood that each day in the comfortable camp might be the last.

Severe as was the disappointment in the army over the outcome of the movement which had opened with so much of promise, there was nothing of demoralization manifest. Apart from the disaster to General Howard's command, the field had been bravely fought, and it was known that the victory had been won by the enemy at terrible cost. Naturally the Eleventh Corps received an unjust award of blame for their unfortunate defeat and dispersion. So intense was this feeling that for a time the mere sight of the crescent corps badge was hateful to the rest of the army. With the feeling that upon this one corps the onus of the defeat should be placed, and with especial pride in the work of the Sixth Corps in carrying the dreaded hights and making so gallant a fight in their effort to reach the main army, the soldiery settled down once more to the routine of camp life with their confidence in the final result unshaken. Chancellorsville had been a great improvement upon Fredericksburg—sooner or later the fortunes of war would bring the two armies together on equal ground, then should the true test of battle come. Thus feeling, the loyal army maintained its calm hopefulness.

On the Confederate side, while there was a sorrowful appreciation of the cost in the loss of Jackson—Lee's most efficient lieutenant—and the sacrifice of the very best troops of the Confederacy in numbers so vast that the official report was never given to the world, there was much to be hoped from the moral effect upon outside nations. Victory again wreathed the Confederate banners after a great battle, and the sympathy of the European governments for the Southern cause must be intensified. Already this had reached a point intensely dangerous to the United States. While only the Pope of Rome had officially recognized the Confederate government, every considerable power in Europe with the exception of Russia, while nominally neutral, was actually in sympathy with secession. While British ports were sending out Confederate cruisers to destroy American commerce and blockade runners to supply the waning resources of the insurgents, France, in the person of Maximilian, had planted the standard of monarchy on Mexican soil and was watering it with the blood of those who dared to oppose the propagation of despotism. Surely it could not be long till this half-covert coöperation must break forth in public recognition, in which the nations of the world should join, and the success of the rebellion be won at last. Thus hoped the people of the South—thus feared those loyal to the Federal government. So general was this feeling of hope on the Southern side that the pickets could not refrain from shouting it across the river, coupled often with taunting inquiries as to the purposes of the Federal commander. "Say, Yank, when is Old Joe Hooker coming over the river again?" would be shouted across to the northern bank. "He isn't coming over next time," might be the quizzical reply; "he's only going to send Uncle John Sedgwick over with two companies of the Sixth Corps while the rest of us watch him clean you fellers out!" Not a little such badinage occurred between the opposing picket lines, generally ending good-naturedly as it began, but sometimes the whistle of a bullet would warn some sharp-tongued Yankee that he had touched a sensitive point in his interlocutor's nature.

General Hooker's army was now much reduced in numbers. The total loss at Chancellorsville had been 17,197,—of which the Sixth Corps, leading all the others, had sustained 4,601. Some of these had been "missing" at the close of the battle and afterward returned, while others were but slightly wounded and soon reported for duty; but the permanent loss could not have been less than 15,000, while the term of service of the nine-months' and two-years' troops—the latter to the number of over 30,000 having been furnished by New York—was about expiring. From these two causes the Army of the Potomac had already lost or would within a few weeks lose considerably more than a third of its numbers. The army under Lee, on the contrary, was at this time strengthened by reinforcements and especially by the return of Longstreet. The latter had been dispatched soon after the battle of Fredericksburg to operate against General J. J. Peck at Suffolk, who with a small force was protecting the land approaches to Norfolk. Disappointed in his hope of surprising that vigilant officer, and unable to carry his defenses by assault, Longstreet spent the winter and early spring in a series of siege operations which proved so ineffective that they were finally abandoned on the 3d of May—the day of the fierce struggle between the rival armies on the Rappahannock.

The Confederate army, augmented in numbers and elated over the recent victory, was now organized into three corps under Lieutenant-Generals Longstreet, A. P. Hill and Ewell respectively. Each corps consisted of 13 or 14 brigades in three divisions, the major-generals commanding the divisions being: In Longstreet's corps, McLaws, Pickett and Hood; in Hill's corps, Anderson, Heth and Pender; in Ewell's corps, Early, Rodes and Johnson. The eight brigades of cavalry formed a corps under the command of General J. E. B. Stuart. This was the army with which Lee was to make the most important military move in the history of the rebellion,—ably officered, admirably organized, inspirited by a long series of victories, supremely confident as to the future. Clearly it was not the policy of the commander of such an army to act on the defensive. The foreign sentiment, from which so much was expected, would look for vigorous efforts on the part of the Confederacy to win a place among the nations of the earth. The apathy, the discouragement, the secession sympathy at the North might by a single brilliant stroke be so intensified as to paralyze the national government and force the abandonment of the war for the Union. It needed no prophet to show that before the harvest came the Confederacy would be in serious need of supplies, while the rich farming lands of Maryland and Pennsylvania, only a few days' march away, abounded in food for man and beast. Here were three good reasons for the invasion of the North, and there were possibilities behind them which the eye of faith could easily discern of dazzling brightness. An offensive campaign was decided upon.

As early as the 20th of May the authorities at Washington were warned of the intended invasion, and General Hooker suspected the purpose of his antagonist on the 28th, but it was not till the 3d of June that the mutual watchfulness changed to activity. On that day Ewell's corps of the Confederate army began to move toward Culpeper Court House, where Stuart's cavalry covered Lee's left, and General Hooker at once set about penetrating the design of his adversary.

In the camp of the Thirty-seventh that peculiar activity which had come to be recognized by the dullest intellect as the prelude to "marching orders," had been noticed for some time. On the 2d and 3d of the month the brigade had been drilled by Colonel Edwards, and at 2 o'clock of the morning of the 4th the regiment was called from slumber to pack up everything and be ready to leave camp at 5 o'clock with eight days' rations. The preparations were promptly made and the order to move awaited, but it did not come till early morning of the 6th, when camp was finally broken. "The model camp of the Army of the Potomac," it had often been called,—to which memory would often turn, but which was never again to be visited by the departing braves! The line of march was once more to the familiar "Franklin's Crossing," below Fredericksburg, where the command halted along the Riverside road.

Howe's division had already crossed the Rappahannock, the earthworks on the opposite bank being swept with such a cannonade that not a head could be raised above them to offer opposition till the bridges were completed and the Federal soldiers rushed across and captured the demoralized post with scarcely the firing of a shot. A rapid advance of the skirmish line, while it showed that the enemy was wholly unprepared for the visitation, also revealed him in what seemed full force, and this being the object of the reconnaissance, the two commands assumed a defiant attitude and waited. A heavy thunder-storm in the afternoon drenched everything effectually, and through the night and the following day only an occasional picket shot or a brief artillery duel broke the monotony.

A detail of a thousand men was made from the brigade on the evening of the 7th to cross the river and construct intrenchments, of which number the Thirty-seventh furnished 350, following this detail by that of 100 more to support a battery. The fatigue party worked faithfully, though very silently, through the night, and morning light showed to the surprised Confederates a line of earthworks extending from the Bernard ruins far above the bridge head. These works were continually strengthened during the day, notwithstanding the artillery protests from the hights, which did no material damage. Thus far, and for three days following, the regimental head-quarters were on the north bank of the river, though the men were almost incessantly on duty. On the evening of the 10th the brigade crossed the bridges, taking up a position in the rear of the entrenched line, relieving a portion of the troops who had been doing service there.

Constant details were now made for duty on the skirmish line, and the men, who were already thoroughly wearied, had little opportunity for rest day or night. Although a general quiet prevailed, with the exception of occasional artillery firing, the rival picket lines watched each other closely. On the left, in the vicinity of the Bernard house, there was no firing, and as the lines were but a few yards apart, exchanges of papers, tobacco and coffee were occasionally made, till strict orders to the contrary were issued by the Union officers. Toward Hazel Run, on the right, however, there had been sharp and incessant picket firing, in which the Confederates had the advantage. The buildings used as coverts by their riflemen were torn to pieces by the Federal artillery, without effect; but finally a detachment of the Second company of Massachusetts sharp-shooters, under Lieutenant L. E. Bicknell, were brought over to apply *lex talionis,* which they did so effectually that the annoyance ceased, a flag of truce from the Confederates humbly asking for mercy.

Thus in a state of expectant and wakeful inaction the days passed till the evening of the 13th, when in a heavy rain the division recrossed to the north bank, climbed the Stafford hills out of artillery range, where with everything about them soaked by the incessant pouring, the men enjoyed the first unbroken sleep for nearly two weeks. The skirmish line had not been notified of the contemplated withdrawal till their companions were safely across and the bridges taken up, when they were quietly retired and taken over in boats. Scarcely a man was left behind, but Lieutenant Loomis had a very narrow escape from that unpleasant fate. He was posted at the extreme right in a secluded position near Hazel Run, and with one or two men was overlooked when the general retirement was made. Being missed he was sought for by one of General Newton's staff and discovered, but in the intense darkness the party missed the waiting boat and wandered about for a long time before finding means of crossing the river. On reaching his regiment about daylight, the lieutenant was greeted as one recovered from the dead.

A movement of the Union cavalry toward Culpeper by the way of Beverly and Kelly's Fords had encountered the Confederates in such strength as to convince Hooker that his suspicions of the rebel intentions were correct. The indecisive cavalry action at Beverly Ford, or Fleetwood, was followed by the advance of the Third Corps up the Rappahannock in pursuance of the positive instructions from Washington, insisting that in no event must the national Capital be uncovered. In the mean time, the Confederate movement was being pushed with characteristic energy. Ewell's corps moved from Culpeper through the Blue Ridge at Chester Gap, thence by way of Port Royal toward Winchester, where on the 13th the advance confronted some 10,000 Federals under General Milroy. That officer, underestimating the strength of the force moving against him, hesitated at first to retire without offering battle, and when two days later he became convinced of the folly of resistance, a large part of his men were surrounded and captured in the effort to escape. On the same day that Milroy's force was demolished Jenkins's cavalry, feeling the way for the advance of the invaders, penetrated as far as Chambersburg, Pa., whence they fell back to Hagerstown and encamped. The Washington government was now awake to the gravity of the situation, and President Lincoln called for 100,000 militia from the nearest states to repel the invasion. The response was so tardy and inefficient as to show the wavering condition of public sentiment. Well might Lee's battle-hardened legions ignore the militia of the northern states as a factor in the great problem they were to undertake. On the 21st Ewell crossed the Potomac at Williamsport and Shepardstown, and on the 27th his divided column had on the one hand pushed forward its advance to within four miles of Harrisburg, the Pennsylvania Capital, while the division under Early had reached Wrightstown, opposite Columbia on the Susquehanna. A small force of militia was assembled at the latter place, and saved the city by burning the railroad bridge across the river, a fine structure over a mile in length. The village of Wrightstown was fired by the conflagration but the Confederates extinguished the flames and made no effort to cross the river. Hill, finding that he was relieved of the pressure of the Sixth Corps on his front, followed rapidly by the Shenandoah valley route, Longstreet placing his corps on the east side of the Blue Ridge to guard the passes and protect the flank of the marching column, —then following in turn and forming the Confederate rear. A sharp cavalry fight at Aldie on the 17th had developed the rebel position sufficiently to give Hooker a clear conception of the purpose of his antagonist and his own army was moved promptly and efficiently to check and defeat the wily schemes of the Southern commander.

We left the Thirty-seventh regiment sleeping in their wet blankets on the water-soaked earth, enjoying a profound slumber which continued till bugle and drum sounded the signal for the march toward Washington. And such a march! Considerable rain had fallen, and over the muddy Virginia roads the great army had been moving with its multitude of horses, wagons, artillery and ambulances. Let the reader who does not realize from actual participation picture one vast expanse of mud, in the midst of which runs a poorly defined highway, for in the search for better footing thousands of men and horses and wheels have made common way of the bordering lands. Far as the eye can reach a great blue throng surges hither and thither, but who can say whether it recedes or advances? No cavalry are there, for they are away on the outskirts, engaged in many a deed of daring, but infantry, artillery, ponton and wagon trains are mingled in one mass of confusion. The soft mud almost engulfs the heavily loaded wagons, and the ponderous wheels of the gun carriages sink deep in the mire. The drivers whip and scream and swear—principally the latter—and not infrequently the pressing infantry come in for a share of the maledictions. Nor are the latter backward in consigning to a place where no artillery could possibly be used the unwieldy vehicles which block the way. If the region is level and unobstructed the infantry take to the fields and make reasonable progress, but here is a defile through which all must pass, and the mud is especially deep. A great Parrot gun blocks the way, stuck fast in the slime. The horses and drivers and tugging artillerists who are striving to rescue their beloved piece occupy all the available room, and only now and then a common soldier can dodge past. Meanwhile the pouring infantry fill all the approaches, and when at length the cannon rolls on there is a rush from the impatient mass. Fortunate, indeed, if some luckless comrade does not lose his footing and roll over and over in the half-liquid sea. A few pass, and then another gun or cassion or wagon lurches into the same slough, and the struggle is repeated as the long day wears itself away. But at such a time day and night are alike, in so far that they must be subordinated to the orders of the general commanding. The corps must be at a designated point at a specified time, whether five hours or twenty be required to make the distance.

At 5 in the afternoon, on that 14th of June, the corps reached Stafford Court House, and halted for five hours, when the tramp was resumed. All through the night the column crept on at a snail's pace, the men keeping ever a sharp lookout for the bright camp-fires which would announce the approaching bivouac. But no camp-fires were lighted that night, and morning found the command at Aquia Creek, where a halt was made for breakfast. But not for rest! Not yet. Just a few moments in which to breathe after swallowing their coffee, and then "Forward!" once more on the interminable road.

The sun rose bright and clear and a sultry day ensued. Like magic the mud dried and crumbled under the multitude of feet, and a choking cloud of dust arose and settled in volume on every perspiring face and hand. It penetrated everywhere—eyes, nose, mouth and lungs, all were filled; thirst became intolerable, but water was not to be had. Even if by good fortune a little spring or stream was discovered, in a moment the banks were trampled and the water all too soon lost its purity and became mere liquid mud from the struggles of the rushing hundreds who swarmed about it, eager only to touch a finger's tip in the cool mass, if it was no longer possible to moisten the parching throat with the undrinkable mixture.

Dumfries was reached at noon, and on a south-sloping hillside, on the parched ground in the terrible glare of the sun, the men threw themselves to sleep, glad even of that opportunity. At midnight the march was resumed, and with a brief halt in the morning for coffee it was continued till noon, when Wolf Run Shoals on the Occaquan was reached. There a halt was made of some three hours, and very grateful was even that brief breathing spell to the exhausted men. There was opportunity for bathing their blistered feet in the clear waters of the creek, for cooling the throbbing temples and drinking satisfying draughts. Here was the outer line of the Washington defenses, garrisoned at this point by the Vermont nine-months' brigade of General Stannard, who had succeeded to the command of Colonel Stoughton, captured in his bed a few months before. The two commands mingled with hearty good fellowship, for the common home in New England made them feel an additional fraternity. Marching a few miles farther toward evening, bivouac was made near Fairfax Station, where the regiment remained all day of the 17th, the men generally making the most of their respite from the wearisome marches recently endured.

Quite an exciting incident occurred during the day, which at one time threatened serious results, but through the good offices of the Thirty-seventh bloodshed was averted. Trouble had arisen in the camp of the Thirty-sixth New York, quite a number of the members—dissatisfaction which had existed for some time being intensified by whisky which they had somehow obtained—refusing to do further duty, claiming that their time of enlistment had expired. The provost marshal was called upon and went among the men, striving to restore subordination, but he was promptly knocked down, when he called upon Colonel Edwards for assistance. The latter formed his regiment so quickly and silently that some of its exhausted members were left asleep on the ground but a few yards away, hastened to the scene and formed square about the revolters. They were then informed by Colonel Edwards that they would be required to serve till the expiration of the full two years of the last company of their regiment mustered into the United States service, and were given the alternative of stepping five paces to the front in signification of acceptance or of being put under arrest. Without much hesitation the entire command stepped forward, though earnestly asserting afterward that they would have fought any other regiment than the Thirty-seventh.

Next day, the 18th, the regiment marched to Fairfax Court House, and tents were pitched on the battle-field of Chantilly, not far from the spot where the brave Kearney fell. The march, though little more than five miles, was very trying, the day being sultry and intensely hot, so that many of the men fell from the ranks with sun-stroke or exhaustion. The location was far from an agreeable one, since both fuel and water were difficult to obtain, and the latter very poor when got, but six days were passed in this vicinity with slight changes of position, in perpetual suspense as to what the next hour might bring, and with no more exciting event than an assembly of the brigade on the 23d to witness the drumming out of camp of a worthless member of the Tenth regiment. During this time General Hooker had been anticipating an attempt on Washington from the west by the Confederates, but it was now evident that they were moving into Pennsylvania, and in that direction the Army of the Potomac began to seek them.

The Thirty-seventh marched to the vicinity of Centreville, some six miles, on the afternoon of the 24th, and the following day relieved a brigade, now ordered to join the Second Corps, which had for nearly a year, since entering the service, been very comfortably quartered there, enjoying all the luxuries of soldier life with few of its trials. While they had abandoned great quantities of camp conveniences, which the Thirty-seventh hastened to possess themselves of, it was remarkable to see the enormous knapsacks which the men started out with the intention of carrying on the sweltering marches before them. Their burdens were very much lightened before many miles had been passed. In the course of the day the regiment was comfortably settled with tents pitched near the old earthworks, fitted up in many instances with the equipage abandoned by the departing troops. Every foot of the ground in the vicinity was historic, and the men inspected with much interest the weather-worn intrenchments and the numerous soldiers' graves near by. Despite the rain which fell at night, a feeling of intense satisfaction prevailed. There was every indication that the regiment was to remain for a time in that place on permanent duty—which would be a very agreeable relief from active campaigning.

Alas for the soldiers' expectations! At 2 o'clock that night the familiar tones of Adjutant Colt were heard as he stumbled through the darkness to the different company head-quarters, calling out as each in turn was reached : "Captain, wake up your men, have them pack everything, make their coffee and be ready to march at 4 o'clock!" There was many an exclamation of disgust as the command turned out into the drizzling rain, folded such of their possessions as it seemed best to take upon the march, destroyed everything else that was destroyable, and then waited till near 8 o'clock before the signal for departure was given. Dranesville, 20 miles away, was reached that night, after an exhausting journey; the gentle rain, while saving from the tortures of excessive heat, making the roads exceedingly slippery and difficult.

Four o'clock next morning saw the command again under way, the day being cloudy and quite comfortable for marching. In the early part of the afternoon a halt for a couple of hours was made overlooking Edwards Ferry, where the troops in advance were crossing the Potomac once more into Maryland. Far as the eye could reach vast wagon trains wound over hill and through valley, or were parked beside the road waiting their turn to join the procession, and the vivid panorama gave to many a beholder a truer realization of the magnitude of that branch of the army service. Finally the tired infantry started forward once more, crossed the pontons on to loyal soil, made some three miles more, and at dusk turned into some vast clover fields, where the weary soldiers were not long in providing themselves with luxurious couches, on which they slept soundly till the sharp notes of the reveille broke through the darkness of the waning night. The day which was dawning when the tired column resumed its way at 4 o'clock in the morning of Sunday, June 28, brought little likeness to the quiet New England Sabbath of which many in the regiment could not help thinking by way of contrast as the tedious hours wore away. The line of march was through a fine agricultural region, where the thrift of the Maryland farmers contrasted sharply with the indifferent methods of Virginia, especially as the latter had been aggravated by two years of desolating warfare. Cherries were now ripening, and it was one of the relieving features of the march that the soldiers were occasionally able to spring into a tree loaded with the luscious fruit and gather a few handfuls, adding a delightful relish to the not especially appetizing army rations.

Very early in the morning the regiment went through Poolesville and later reached Barnesville, a pretty little village whose charm to the soldiers was enhanced by the fact that there for the first time since crossing into Virginia the previous November they were greeted by smiling faces and words of sympathy. Plainly they were now in the land of friends once more, and their hearts beat with fresh courage. Hyattstown was passed in the afternoon, and some distance beyond, five miles short of its destination, the exhausted corps halted for the night.

That evening the fact became generally known throughout the army that General Hooker was relieved of the command and succeeded by General George G. Meade, the commander of the Fifth Corps. The change produced scarcely a ripple of excitement among the rank and file or the minor officers. For many reasons which have been already suggested General Hooker had won the enthusiastic approval of his men; at the same time, it is but truth to say that his capacity to manage so vast a trust had come to be doubted, hampered as he was by the never coincident supervision of General Halleck. This divergence of views had culminated in outbreak when Hooker asked to have the garrison of Harper's Ferry, some ten or eleven thousand men under General French, added to his advancing columns. This demand Halleck refused, Hooker asked to be relieved and the request was granted. The troops in question were at once placed under the command of General Meade, who was given entire control of the movements of the army. That General Hooker continued to do valiant battle for his country sufficiently attested his patriotism—his bravery friend nor foe ever questioned.

The promotion of General Meade placed the Fifth Corps under command of General Sikes, at the head of its three divisions being Generals James Barnes, R. B. Ayres and S. W Crawford. Other changes in important commands had meantime occurred. When Lee's purpose was divined, and it was hoped to raise a strong militia force to oppose him, General Brooks, commanding the First Division of the Sixth Corps, had been placed in command of the Department of the Monongahela, with head-quarters at Pittsburg, and was succeeded in the corps by General Horatio G. Wright. General Couch was also taken from the Second Corps and placed in command of the Department of the Susquehanna, with head-quarters at Harrisburg, General Hancock taking charge of the corps, with its three divisions commanded by Generals J. C. Caldwell, J. Gibbon and Alexander Hays. The Third Corps was consolidated to two divisions under Generals Birney and A. A. Humphreys, the latter transferred from the Third Division, Fifth Corps. General Francis C. Barlow had succeeded General Devens in the command of the First Division, Eleventh

Corps, and the cavalry corps, which had been placed in charge of General Pleasonton on the return of Stoneman from his comparatively unsuccessful raid in early May, had its three divisions commanded by Generals Buford, Gregg and Kilpatrick. In the Sixth Corps, Colonel Burnham's Light Division had been abolished and the regiments composing it assigned to the First and Third Divisions.

The change in commanders caused not the slightest interruption to the movements of the army, nor were the plans under which Hooker had been operating essentially modified. Those plans may be in a few words thus outlined: The Union army, marching by way of Frederick, would thence be moved rapidly northward covering all the available roads to the eastward of the South Mountain range, till the line of its march should intersect that of the Confederates. Then, on Freedom's soil, with no advantages save those which Nature had provided and which the genius of the respective commanders might seize upon, the momentous battle would be fought.

It was not later than 3 o'clock in the morning of June 29 that the slumbering regiment was aroused, the few preparations necessary for another day's tramp hastily made, and then for long hours they waited expectant while brigade after brigade and division following division filed steadily past. Eustis's Brigade was to form the rear guard of the corps that day, and it was after 10 o'clock when the scene of bivouac was left. The long wait had worried the men not a little, as they knew that a late start meant a still later reaching of bivouac in the evening and greater personal weariness, since the rear of the column is ever the most trying position in a march. "Why couldn't we have spent some of these seven hours in rest?" many a poor fellow asked. "Because it wouldn't have been military!" some philosopher in the ranks was ready to reply. "You don't suppose old ―― cares whether his men live or die!" the officer animadverted on ranging from the colonel of the regiment to the new commander-in-chief, according to the speaker's dislike or distrust.

A few miles brought the regiment to the village of New Market, where a little incident lightened the spirits of the men wonderfully. Before reaching the place cheers were heard in advance, and on entering the town two or three young ladies were discovered standing in front of their home waving small Union flags. It was an electrifying sight, and the enthusiasm which had pervaded the troops in advance was emphasized from the strong throats of the Thirty-seventh. There was no question now that they were in the land of friends. A little further on the traditional town pump was encountered, but not as had often occurred in Virginia dismantled to prevent the thirsty soldiers from obtaining a drink of water. Its long handle was swung unceasingly up and down by a tall, tattered negro, his homely lineaments beautified by a smile of supreme happiness as he watched the surging throng before the pump, and caught their hurried words of heartfelt thanks. The sweat coursed down his massive features, for he had been thus engaged from early morning, declining all offers of assistance. "No, soldiers," he responded, "I don' wan' no help. Put yo' cup right under there and git some water—I'll gib yo' all you want if I hab to pump up de bottom ob dis yer well!" Bless his kind heart! No man in Maryland did nobler service for the cause of his country that day.

The afternoon was more or less rainy, and the progress of the column slow, so that the 28 miles which made the day's march were not completed till considerably past midnight for the regiments in the rear, after which, according to the custom General Hooker had instituted some time before, a day's rations were drawn from the supply wagons and distributed before the men slept. With morning light of the 30th the men were again aroused, poorly prepared by the few hours' rest for another tedious day's march, and at 8 o'clock, after the distribution of a mail and the preparation of such food as they possessed, their onward way was resumed. There was a heavy rain-fall during the forenoon, wetting everybody completely and making the roads quite difficult, though the afternoon was pleasant and comparatively comfortable for marching. Soon after noon the beautiful village of Westminster was passed through, where in the morning Gregg's cavalry had skirmished with a small force of Stuart's

Confederate horsemen, where the Thirty-sixth New York regiment also left the brigade and started for home. That night the Sixth Corps bivouacked near Manchester, about 20 miles from the starting point of the morning.

General Sedgwick had now reached the right of the position in the rear of Pipe Creek, a tributary of the Monocacy, where General Meade's plan contemplated the fighting of the decisive battle, and the following day was given to inspection and preparation for the expected strife. The other corps, covering the ground for thirty miles to the westward, were feeling for the enemy under instructions to fall back with a show of resistance when he should be struck, and take up position behind Pipe Creek. The opening blows of the great conflict were indeed struck while the men of the Sixth Corps were cleaning their weapons, sleeping or eating cherries about Manchester, but the outcome was so different from the anticipation that instead of remaining to fight in the position they had reached by such intense effort, they were called to still greater exertions in order to reach the field—to make, in fact, one of the most famous marches known to military history; and it must be borne in mind that they were not fresh for the effort, but already sadly exhausted by nearly a month of continual skirmishing and marching, having for five days made an average of 25 miles per day through alternate rain and intense heat, followed by 24 hours of comparative rest.

During the afternoon there had been a quite constant sound of cannon far to the northwest, but it only evoked the remark that the cavalry were having another brush. As dusk fell many of the men were asleep, for they were still weary, when the clatter of hoofs, the hurried dash of staff officers, the bustle of preparation at head-quarters, and the vigorous command to "Pack up and fall in!" drove away in a moment all hope of a refreshing night's sleep. Before the slower men are in their places, even, the column is in the road and sweeping back in the direction whence it came the previous evening. There is a hope which is more than half a belief that the destination may be Westminster, which is but ten miles away, and the men move out with cheerful step. Presently a kind-hearted farmer, who is giving each boy in blue a cup of milk, announces that a battle has begun at Gettysburg, nearly 40 miles away, and it is natural to suppose that to be the destination of the corps.

"*About* 40 miles—he said it was 40 miles—and what did he call the name of the town?" goes from lip to lip, and the step which has been light becomes heavy and mechanical, and the soldiers are transformed into mere machines, to plod on as steadily as possible all the interminable night. There is no moonlight, and only a pale glimmer of the stars, half obscured by clouds; but the long column presses forward and never halts, for if it stops the men will drop into heavy slumber and may be left behind in the darkness. As it is, some of the officers doze in their saddles, and the men as they walk are like those moving in a dream.

The night is well advanced, and the leading brigade has been toiling for miles along a narrow road, when a shouting aide presses through the struggling footmen. "Make way here, make way, for God's sake; you are all wrong!" Then reaching the head of a regiment : "Halt your men, colonel; you are on the wrong road!" Presently the head of the column comes slowly back, those who have dropped to sleep are roused, the regiment countermarches and plods back over the three or four miles that have taken so much of the soldiers' vital force all in vain. Two or three hours have been lost and six or eight miles of ground covered that the general historian will make no account of when he tells the story of the night.

Morning lights the east; dawn flushes the sky; day comes in its full glory; but the column does not halt. At last the advance brigade turns from the highway, and a hundred little fires for the preparation of coffee flash up in a moment. The water comes from a generous brook in the valley, and how grateful after the intense hunger is partly satisfied it will be to bathe the heated face and blistered feet in the cool stream! Vain hope! Even before the coffee is made the bugle rings out its unwelcome call and the weary procession is resumed. The half-made coffee is swallowed on the march or carefully poured into the canteen, for in many cases it is the only food or drink the soldier can hope to taste that day. With that care for the stomachs of his men which was characteristic of him, General Hooker had kept the army supplied with three days' rations, even on the march, the supply trains being brought up every night and food drawn for the third day in advance. In most cases the two or three days' rations which nominally were in the men's haversacks had quite disappeared, so that when under General Meade the order was issued that no more should be drawn until they were due by the commissary's records, it in effect obliged most of the enlisted men to subsist for three days on one day's allowance, supplemented by whatever individual skill or good fortune might add. Far out on either flank of the moving column the more ambitious went, searching out every dwelling that promised a mouthful of food, finding here a few cherries, there some half-ripened blackberries, and welcoming whatever would appease the cravings of hunger. These men had no money with which to buy, they could offer only a soldier's rude thanks and a promise to fight for the threatened homes when the enemy should be met; but whatever the loyal people could spare was freely bestowed, often to the last eatable morsel. Especially was this true of the village of Littlestown, ten miles southeast of Gettysburg, the only place of any size through which the Sixth Corps passed that day. The inhabitants there seemed actuated by a common impulse to empty their larders for the benefit of the soldiers, but not more than a brigade or two had passed when the last of the available supply was exhausted and they could only lift up empty hands in blessing of those on their way to defend their homes and property.

The Southern cavalry had scoured the country pretty effectually during the few days of their presence, and almost from the time the Federal column entered Maryland every officer who could be approached had listened to tales of especial hardship in the way of horses and other property ruthlessly appropriated with at the best no other compensation than the worthless Confederate scrip. As one such unhappy applicant turned away from the Thirty-seventh, at a temporary halt, he exclaimed, very vigorously, "Well, colonel, if you can't do anything toward getting back my colts, I hope when your men come across the rascals they'll give them hell!"

Only the participant in like experiences can realize the misery of the ceaseless march of the long, sultry hours. It was a hot, breathless July day. The sun poured down with merciless, unbroken heat, and the dust that rose in great lazy clouds from the highway enveloped man and horse, general and private alike, in its all-embracing mantle of torture. How the exhausted lungs panted for one full breath of pure, cool fresh air! Panted only to be mocked by the bitter, burning, dust-laden blast that seemed to come from the mouth of a furnace. What wonder that the sun-stroke was omnipresent along the line—that strong men gasped and staggered and fell, while the thick blood burst forth from mouth and nostrils and the tortured frame was placed tenderly in some shaded nook by comrades whose visions swam and who trembled on the verge of a like fate. But the winding column never paused, for not the life of one man but the life of the nation was at stake that day.

About midday the regiments filed into the fields beside the road and the men sank upon the ground. "Make no fires, for there will be no time to cook anything—only a few minutes for rest," was the instruction as the line halted, and every moment was devoted to the relief of the painful feet and weary limbs. All too soon came the summons to fall in again, and the men struggled to their feet. They had not realized before how tired they were, how sore and stiff their limbs.

From early morning the booming artillery had proclaimed the work of death to be still in progress, and each hour as the distance lessened the thunder grew louder. Already the corps was meeting the tide of wounded hastening with desperate energy to the rear—that most demoralizing experience to a body of troops approaching a battle-field. With scarcely an exception the tale they told was one of disaster to the Federal army. "You fellows will catch it; the whole army is smashed to pieces!" said more than one brawny fugitive with a bleeding arm or a bandaged head, glancing over his shoulder as though fearing the pursuit of a rebel column. Only a few miles remain, and occasionally through an opening between the hills what looks like a white bank of fog can be seen. It is the smoke that hangs over the scene of the great contest. There is a sharp hill in advance over which the pike winds, and when its crest is reached the field will be in view. The word runs back along the line, and what a transformation is wrought! Gone now the fatigue, the weariness forgotten; the blood bounds once more in the veins, the muscles harden, the eyes flash! Down into the valley—up the sharp ascent beyond, and with eager eyes the men of the Sixth Corps look upon the greatest battle of the rebellion. Yet it is not much that they see. A low range of hights, battery-crowned and partially wooded, with masses of soldiers that look like threads of blue drawn at hap-hazard across the green of the landscape; a cloud of smoke about the batteries at the left, with now and anon the white puff of a bursting shell—then they go down the slope, across Rock Creek, and turn into the fields beside the Baltimore pike on which they have been marching. "Rest!" is the brief and welcome command, and they drop on the unshaded ground, glowing with heat, though it is. Here and there one, less exhausted than his fellows, gathers as many canteens as he can carry and starts for a supply of water—a precaution that must not be neglected. A canteen of water is the wounded man's best friend, and who can tell what the remaining hours of the declining day may have in store? The column proper has halted, indeed, but there is no cessation of the procession coming up the pike. The thousands who have been unable to keep pace with the swiftly moving corps throng the highway in groups and masses, all actuated by a common motive—to find their respective commands and do their duty. The record of the Thirty-seventh in regard to straggling on this occasion is one to which it may well revert with pride. Out of its over 600 men only seven were absent when the roll was called on halting.

All too short has been the interval of rest, when a staff officer dashes down the turnpike. There is a momentary consultation, a hurrying here and there of orderlies, then the command, sharp and clear, "Fall in!" To their feet spring those who a few minutes before seemed helpless from exhaustion. Forgotten the pain, ignored the stiffness of limb, for help is needed, and never did the Sixth Corps fail at the call of duty. As by magic the line is formed, but the march is no longer by the broad highway; it is down across the fields and thence up into the forest toward Weed's Hill, where Sickles and his Third Corps are in a death grapple with the Confederates under Longstreet. There are hundreds of objects which attest the presence of the great battle-field—groups of men in gray guarded by those in blue, disabled cannon which have been dragged back from the front, and the other debris of war. The men can only glance at them as they go hurrying past. How heroically they hold their places —those sons of New England who after such mighty efforts to reach the scene are now going up toward the smoking crest to face death, mutilation,—all the horrible chances of the battle!

Presently a messenger comes galloping back from General Sedgwick, who is at the front. "Tell Colonel Eustis to bring up his brigade as soon as possible!" These words mean something, coming from that source. "Double-quick!" is the simple order, and the Thirty-seventh, which is leading the brigade, dashes forward in fine array with never a lagging step. "Fix bayonets!" and with a clash and clatter the steel is fitted to every musket, in readiness to force its way through whatever may oppose. In a few minutes Little Round Top is reached, the column is changed quickly to line of battle, the right resting close to General Sedgwick's head-quarters, thence extending back of the crest toward the southeast, ready for any duty which may be required. The fierce struggle of the afternoon was dying away with the daylight, only the occasional dropping of a bullet in the forest—one of which killed a sergeant of the Tenth regiment—showed to the waiting line how near it was to the scene of active service.

In that position the men laid on their arms that night, and most of them slept soundly, notwithstanding the surroundings and the ceaseless procession of stretcher-bearers passing through the line of the Thirty-seventh with their ghastly burdens.

CHAPTER IX.

THE TURN OF THE TIDE.

THE BATTLE OF GETTYSBURG.—THE THIRTY-SEVENTH TRIED BY FIRE.—THE PURSUIT OF LEE.—CLIMBING THE MOUNTAINS. —ONCE MORE IN VIRGINIA.

General Lee became convinced on the 28th of June that the rapid northward movement of the Army of the Potomac would cut off his communications with Virginia and seriously imperil his command should he cross the Susquehanna, as he had contemplated, and a concentration of his forces in the direction of Gettysburg was ordered to begin the following day. At that time Early's division of Ewell's corps was at York, to the northeast of Gettysburg, the other two divisions of the same corps at Carlisle, north of Gettysburg, and the two corps of Hill and Longstreet at Chambersburg on the west. Hill and Ewell moved leisurely toward the point of concentration and Longstreet prepared to follow. Meanwhile from the south and southeast the Union troops were approaching the same spot. General Meade, with the intention before referred to of fighting on the line of Pipe Creek, if possible, had established his head-quarters with the Second Corps at Taneytown, due south from Gettysburg. The Fifth and Twelfth corps were at Hanover, east of Gettysburg, the Sixth at Manchester, while the Third at Emmettsburg supported the advance of the First and Eleventh toward Gettysburg from that point.

General Buford occupied Gettysburg with his cavalry division on the 29th, pushing out pickets on the different roads running in the direction of the enemy, and awaited the arrival of General Reynolds. Shortly after 9 o'clock of July 1, the advance of Heth's division of Hill's corps began to press the Union cavalry on the Chambersburg turnpike, but a skillful use of Buford's artillery held them on the other side of Willoughby Run till General Reynolds arrived on the scene with the two brigades of Wadsworth's division of the First Corps. Cutler's brigade was formed across and on both sides of the pike, while the "Iron" Brigade commanded by General Meredith, went into position on its left and in the rear of the seminary which gave its name to the gentle swell of land between the scene of conflict and the village. The formation of the Union line had taken place under fire, and a desperate conflict at once opened, in which the Confederates met with serious loss. There General Archer and 800 of his brigade were captured by a flank move of the Iron Brigade, and two Mississippi regiments of Davis's brigade were obliged to surrender in the railroad cut parallel to the pike in which they had taken position; but all the Federal success was more than counterbalanced by the loss of the noble General Reynolds, killed by a sharpshooter's bullet at the very moment of greatest promise. The command of the field now devolved upon General Doubleday, who had come up with the other divisions of the First Corps, and soon his entire force was hotly engaged. The advance of Rodes's division of Ewell's corps was coming in on the Carlisle road, and connecting with Hill's left it extended the line of battle far around and beyond the Union right. General Paul's brigade very neatly captured three regiments of Iverson's North Carolinians, and the Union troops fought desperately and successfully against the immensely superior numbers that pressed them.

About 1 o'clock the Eleventh Corps came up, and General Howard, by virtue of his rank, assumed command of the field, turning his corps over temporarily to General Carl Schurz. The Eleventh was composed of three divisions of two brigades each. One division—Steinwehr's—was posted as a reserve on Cemetery Hill to the eastward of Gettysburg, while the other two were thrown into position to prolong the Union line around to the northward of the village. This line was now three miles in length, facing in two directions at nearly right angles, everywhere weak, and swept by the Confederate artillery posted on the commanding eminence of Oak Hill. The weakest point was at the junction of the two corps, or where the junction should have been, for they do not seem to have connected, and here Rodes forced in his division like a wedge and broke the right of the First and the left of the Eleventh Corps. Then the whole Confederate line pressed forward and crumbled the opposing force by the power of its blows, pushing on through the town, capturing several thousand prisoners and finally halting for the night at the base of Cemetery Ridge.

As soon as General Meade was apprised of the severity of the conflict and the death of General Reynolds, he sent forward General Hancock, who was with him at Taneytown, with instructions to assume command at the front. Hancock nobly displayed his powers as a commander in rallying the fugitives that came pouring over Cemetery Hill, forming them in connection with the small reserve already there in such firm array as to discourage the further advance of the Confederates. General Slocum arrived on the scene with the two divisions of the Twelfth Corps late in the afternoon, strengthening and extending the Union line, and turning over to him the command at the front, General Hancock rode back to Taneytown to consult with General Meade. On the way he met his own Second Corps, which Meade had ordered forward, and placed it in reserve as a protection to the flank and rear of the main position. The Third Corps under General Sickles also came up about the same time and went into position on the left. General Stannard's brigade of Vermonters likewise reached the scene and took position with Doubleday's division of the First Corps, to which they were assigned. Their ranks were full, and though they had never borne the test of battle, and their nine-months' term of service had almost expired, they were to prove themselves soldiers of the most heroic mold.

On reaching head-quarters General Hancock found that the Fifth and Sixth Corps had been ordered up, and Meade's disposition to fight at Gettysburg was strengthened by Hancock's report of the strong defensive position now occupied by the portion of the Federal army already on the field. At 1 o'clock that night Meade reached the scene, and early morning of the 2d of July saw the two armies facing each other and waiting for the terrible test which was now certain to come.

From the village of Gettysburg radiate no less than 11 important roads, and that the reader may correctly appreciate the relative positions of the armies and the more striking topographical features, he will suppose himself approaching the town by the Baltimore turnpike, by which the last part of the journey of the Sixth Corps to the spot was made. A mile southeast of the center of the town he will pause at the top of a considerable eminence, known as Cemetery Hill, its summit on the left of the beholder being occupied by Evergreen Cemetery, the village burying-place. Something more than two miles away as the bird flies, almost due south, rises the round wooded brow of Round Top, 164 feet higher than the crown of Cemetery Hill; a half-mile north of Round Top is a secondary elevation known as Little Round Top or Weed's Hill, 116 feet lower than the parent mountain, but still 48 feet higher than the cemetery, with which it is connected by an elevation or swell in some parts sinking so nearly to the common level as to require the practiced eye of an engineer to locate. To the rear, however, the slope was more pronounced, affording admirable shelter for the reserves, trains, hospitals and the like. Nearly parallel and about a mile to the westward of the range just described rose another, not so commanding in hight and less broken in outline, with its crest almost entirely wooded, extending in nearly a direct line north and south far as the eye could reach, known as Seminary Ridge. The valley between these two ranges broadens and stretches away toward the eastward at the village of Gettysburg, sweeping around to the northward of Culp's Hill, the latter a rocky, wooded, irregular eminence breaking back toward the rear a half-mile to the northeast of the cemetery. Along this valley ran the lines of Ewell's corps—the left of Lee's army—extending through the village and connecting at Seminary Ridge with the center under Hill. Here the Confederate line bent southward, following the course of the hights and connecting with the right under Longstreet, the latter's command reaching down opposite

THE BATTLE OF THE SECOND DAY. 181

to Round Top; Longstreet and Hill faced nearly east, Ewell almost south.

Cemetery Hill, commanding in hight every other eminence in the vicinity except the Round Tops and unlike them admirably adapted to occupation by bodies of soldiers and commanding every road entering Gettysburg, had been marked by the trained eye of General Reynolds when he rode rapidly to the front as the key point of the entire field, and by his direction Steinwehr's division was posted there when Howard's command came into action. On this reserve the broken battalions had been rallied as they streamed back through the town, and from this starting point had been built a battle front which the stoutest hearted chieftain might well hesitate to attack. The right of the Union line on Culp's Hill was formed by the Twelfth Corps, hastily intrenched in a position so naturally strengthened by rocks and by the swampy borders of Rock Creek at the right that it seemed almost impregnable. The First and Eleventh Corps, or what was left of them, prolonged the line to and covering Cemetery Hill, from whose commanding hight batteries looked grimly forth in command of the neighboring valleys, the town and all its approaches. The First Corps, commanded by General Doubleday during the first day, had now been placed under General Newton, who had left his own Third Division of the Sixth Corps in charge of General Wheaton, the latter's brigade in turn commanded by Colonel Nevin of the Sixty-second New York. South of the cemetery Hancock's Second Corps was placed, the Fifth, which arrived early in the morning of the 2d after a sharp night's march, being in reserve, while General Sickles's Third Corps formed the Union left.

Here was the critical point in the Union line. General Sickles, ordered to place his corps in the best position, found that at this point the center of the valley proper along which the Emmettsburg road ran was really higher ground than that in the rear which would have continued the Federal line directly toward Little Round Top, and there he placed his two divisions. This disposition of the corps has been much criticised, but it seems doubtful if with the force at his command Sickles could have made a wiser one. Had the impetuous blow of Longstreet that afternoon been received with the corps in the direct line to Little Round Top the line must have been weaker, it could scarcely have failed to yield before the assault, throwing both those commanding eminences into the hands of the enemy, which would instantly have rendered the whole Federal position untenable. Yet there was a fatal weakness in the formation of the corps, since after extending along the road to a peach orchard almost directly in front of Little Round Top and a mile distant it bent back at a sharp angle and ran toward that hill, ending "in the air," as the right of the Eleventh Corps had done at Chancellorsville. These points were noted by the Confederates, and Longstreet prepared to attack, opening his artillery fire shortly after 4 o'clock. General Meade was even then consulting with Sickles as to the possibility of correcting the faulty alignment, but as that was clearly impossible prompt measures for reinforcing the left were taken.

Hood's division led in the attack, striking a frightful blow on the angle at the peach orchard and crushing in the Union lines there while at the same time it enveloped the whole flank and crept around between Sickles's left and Little Round Top. The latter had thus far been used only as a signal station, and the occupants were folding up their flags to depart when General Warren, the chief engineer on General Meade's staff, apparently the first on the field to comprehend the importance of the hill, ordered the flags to wave while he hastened in search of assistance. The Fifth Corps was just coming upon the field to reinforce Sickles, and Warren took the responsibility of detaching Colonel Vincent's brigade and threw it forward to the imperiled hight. Hazlitt's battery was also secured and by tremendous exertion placed in position on the crest, the guns being lifted over the rocks by the men or dragged by ropes up the precipitous slopes. As Vincent's men climbed one side Hood's Texans scrambled up the other, and almost hand to hand the contest raged. The Confederates were driven back to the base of the hill, but there amid the rocks they clung with a dogged determination, working still around the exposed flank. Vincent and Hazlitt were both killed, with hundreds of their brave fellows, and the ammunition of the infantry was exhausted. Colonel J. L. Chamberlain's brave regiment—the Twentieth Maine—had extended its thin line till the men stood in single rank, then when their guns were empty bayonets were leveled and they rushed upon the foe. Maine met Texas, and New England won.

Meantime in the peach orchard a terrible conflict ensued. The enemy penetrated farther and farther the disrupted Union line, breaking off fragment after fragment and sending it bleeding and helpless to the rear. Reinforcements came in striving to regain the lost ground, fought desperately for a short time and gave way in turn. Cross, Zook and Willard commanding brigades were killed or mortally wounded; General Sickles suffered the loss of a leg, the command of the corps devolving upon General Birney. Steadily the terrible wave of fire rolled up toward the line of Cemetery Ridge till the Fifth Corps was fully enveloped From the Second, First and Twelfth Corps detachments came hurrying up to strengthen the line which was now assuming permanence and solidity, while the attack, so long continued and so desperate, was becoming spasmodic and weak. The Confederates, too, had lost heavily in men and officers. General Barksdale was fatally wounded, and Longstreet, riding to the front to examine the work still before his decimated legions, saw with dismay the firm ranks of undaunted blue.

It was at this time that the Sixth Corps—never more welcome—began to reach the scene. Nevin's brigade (lately Wheaton's), which had led the corps in that memorable march, swept over the hill, pushed the Confederates back and held the ground. Close in their wake Eustis's Brigade was in line of battle ready to test its mettle, but it was not needed. The Union line was now strong enough to defy any earthly foe, both the Round Tops were securely occupied, the flank and rear beyond them were held by the cavalry supported by the veteran Vermont Brigade and Torbert's New Jerseyans, and as dusk closed in on the long summer's day the sounds of strife gradually ceased and the demoralized assailants withdrew. Both sides regarded the result with satisfaction. The Confederates had fought desperately and had gained considerable ground, but they had secured no important advantage. Their assaults had finally been repulsed and their advance driven back. Said a wounded Federal officer as he was borne through the line of the Thirty-seventh that night to suffer the amputation of a terribly shattered leg: "I don't begrudge it a bit! We drove the graybacks a mile and a half, and it was worth a leg to see them go!" This spirit was manifest everywhere among the Union soldiers. They were on Freedom's soil, fighting her decisive battle, and no matter what the cost, victory must be won. " Boys, we have come here to *stay!*" said brave Colonel Stone to his brigade as they took position in front of the enemy in the first day's fight. That pregnant sentence was caught up and became the watchword of the loyal army.

The battle of the afternoon was not confined to the scene of the conflict just sketched. More or less fiercely it raged all along the line. Hill menaced the Union position in his front and Ewell attacked savagely with Early's and Johnson's divisions. The former advanced against Cemetery Hill, but was repulsed, though the batteries on East Cemetery Hill were penetrated by Hays's brigade, the artillerists fighting desperately with clubs, sticks and stones, over their beloved guns. Then reinforcements came to aid the imperiled gunners, the Louisianians were driven back into the fire of converging batteries where they suffered terrible loss, the "Tigers" as reported taking back only 150 of the 1,750 who joined in the charge.

Johnson's division directed its efforts against the northern face of Culp's Hill, and there the greatest Confederate success was won. The Twelfth Corps having been drawn upon to support Sickles before danger in that part of the field was anticipated, the determined attack pushed the defenders out of their earthworks, and though fighting continued far into the night, the Confederates maintained the lodgment thus made.

That night a council was held at the head-quarters of the Union commander and it was decided to continue the fight, though the loss on the Federal side had been at least 20,000 men already. The first work of the morning, therefore, was the recovery of the lost ground on Culp's Hill, and there, both sides reinforcing their troops already in position, a stubborn contest raged till nearly noon. Shaler's brigade of Wheaton's division was doing its best in conjunction with the Twelfth Corps, but Johnson held on doggedly, and a request was sent to General Meade for another brigade. "Send Eustis," was the order, and the brigade, which with scarcely a change of position had all the morning lain listening to the roar of cannon and the rattling fire of skirmishers in front, moved briskly away toward the right, the Thirty-seventh in advance. Again they were not needed. Johnson had retired while the orders were in transmission, so the brigade was halted for a time in a grove near Cemetery Hill, whence it presently started back toward the point from which it came. A terrible and wholly unexpected trial was in store for the Thirty-seventh. In going over, as in coming back, the Taneytown road had been followed part of the way. This road diverges from the Emmettsburg road at the outskirts of the village at the base of Cemetery Hill, winds around the hill and crosses the ridge a little distance south of the cemetery, running directly in the rear of the Round Tops. At the point where the Thirty-seventh entered the road the ridge to the westward sinks to a scarcely perceptible elevation, so that the movement of the column was fully exposed for a short distance to the Confederate artillery on Seminary Ridge, a mile away Suddenly, with no more warning than a preliminary shell or two that went so far overhead as to scarcely attract an upward glance of the eye, a murderous fire burst from the distant batteries, striking the regiment in the flank with wonderful precision and doing frightful execution. It was the opening of Lee's furious cannonade preceding his last desperate assault, and whether the missiles were aimed at Eustis's command or at the formidable array of Federal batteries just over the slope to the front is uncertain. Shells burst in the faces of the men, tore terrible, bleeding gaps through the ranks, crashed in resonant fury against the stone-wall and rocks bordering the road, rent the old board fence at the left into hurtling fragments,—there could have been no severer test of human courage, and there could have been no nobler response than was made by the Thirty-seventh regiment. Not a man faltered. "Steady, Thirty-seventh! Forward, double-quick!" rang forth from the lips of Colonel Edwards, and straight through that horrible tempest of death the regiment went with the steadiness of a battalion drill. It was only a few rods till shelter was reached—a rocky piece of woods sloping toward the east, and here the regiment halted. As it did so a staff officer rode to the side of the colonel and said in tones heard by all the members: "Colonel Edwards, I am directed by Colonel Eustis to express to you his compliments for the splendid conduct of your regiment under the most terrible artillery fire he ever witnessed." It was a prompt, unqualified and gratifying compliment, but it had been earned at a sad cost. Six men were killed or mortally hurt, while 25 others were wounded, an unusually large proportion of them having received disabling injuries. Never was the perfect organization of the medical corps better illustrated. Scarcely had the regiment come to a halt and the injured who had been able to keep their feet till a place of shelter was reached been conducted to the rear, where their wounds received such hasty treatment as was possible, when the stretcher-bearers began to arrive with their bleeding burdens. One after another was brought in and tenderly deposited upon the leafy ground. "We can find no more; are they all here?" is the report. A hasty consultation—then the name of a missing one is uttered. Back again over the shell-swept field the undaunted stretcher-men go, bending low to escape, if possible, the flying missiles, looking everywhere in the vain hope of finding the absent comrade. He is at the rendezvous before them. Struck in the head with a fragment of shell and stunned, he had recovered consciousness to find himself exposed to further wounds or death at any moment. Struggling to his feet and groping around till his gun is found, the unfortunate fellow staggers along the course taken by his uninjured comrades till he reaches the regiment, presenting a most ghastly spectacle, face, clothing and hands covered with blood, his appearance horrifying, though in fact his wound is not serious.

Suddenly a cry of horror breaks from the group of wounded and finds quick echo from their friends. A wounded horse at a mad gallop comes tearing straight toward them. His iron-clad hoofs strike the ground with a force which seems to shake the entire hill, and apart from the danger of being crushed beneath their terrible blows the sight presented by the poor wounded brute is a horrible one. A cannon-shot has torn through his lower jaw, leaving it hanging only by a few shreds. With head thrown high in air, uttering frenzied cries of pain, the severed jaw swinging and whirling at every stroke of the hoofs, his magnificent white breast covered with the spouting blood, he plunges straight toward the score or more of mangled human beings. "Shoot him! shoot him!" goes up from many a lip suddenly grown pale, but no shot can be fired without endangering life, nor is there time for deliberate aim till he has swerved somewhat from his course and goes harmlessly past through the forest.

While the ambulances are on their way to the spot to take the wounded back to the division field hospital, which has been established near Rock Creek, there is time to survey the group of sufferers. In Company A, Thomas B. Jenks, Josiah T. Hunt and George W Truell were wounded. In Company B the wounded were: Enos Besoncon (mortally), Almon Cadwell, George T. Carter, Calvin Goodbo and Charles A. Taggart. From Company C, Corporal John A. Hall, John Kelley, Frederick S. Shephard, James Ferry and John M. Taylor were wounded. The severest loss was borne by Company E, in which James H. Perkins was killed and Charles Gurney fatally wounded, with Sergeant Darwin R. Fields, James L. Bowen, James M. Fletcher, Daniel Lewis and Edwin E. Phelps wounded. Elihu Coville of Company F was mortally wounded. Lieutenant Andrew L. Bush of Company H received a severe wound in the thigh from a fragment of shell, and in his company Charles N. Clark, Horace C. Ramsdell and Alonzo F. Turner were wounded, as was Willard Armstrong of Company I. In Company K, Patrick Hussey was killed and James Crampton mortally wounded.*

---
*It is thought that a few others, whose names cannot be ascertained were wounded. No careful returns of casualties in the regiment seem to have been made till the campaigns of the following year were entered upon.

The escapes from death or severe wounds were especially numerous. Color-Sergeant C. S. Bardwell was knocked down by a fragment of shell which struck his pistol, bending the barrel and bruising the wearer, but doing no further harm. "Cap'n, I can't do much with sich a gun as that!" says a sturdy young Irishman, holding up his musket, through the breech of which a shell had made its way without knocking it from his hand. The coat collar of another was torn from the garment without damage to the wearer and without his knowledge.

While the wounded were lying in the ambulances ready to set forth for the hospital the Thirty-seventh was again summoned toward the right, but as before, the crisis passed without the necessity for its assistance, and again it moved back. The supreme effort of the Confederates had been made—and had failed. It was a mad attempt. General Lee seems to have been rendered desperate by the situation, especially after his lodgment on the right had been driven out in the morning. Against the judgment of his ablest officers he resolved upon a direct attack against the Federal left center. Prefacing the charge by a terrible cannonade of an hour and a half from 150 pieces of his artillery, to which 80 guns on the Union side made undaunted response, he finally at about 3 o'clock launched Pickett's division of Longstreet's corps across the wide plain against the Second Corps, located to the southward of the cemetery. The attacking division was composed principally of the flower of Virginia troops, had been the last to reach the field, and had not before been engaged. They were supported by Pettigrew's division and Wilcox's brigade of Hill's corps, while a co-operative demonstration was made by other troops from Longstreet's command farther toward the Union left. The latter was promptly frustrated by a very gallant attack on the charging lines by the cavalry command of General Kilpatrick, which made so valiant an assault as to completely check that part of the rebel programme, though at a loss of the brave General Farnsworth and the severe handling of his brigade.

The story of the war presents no grander example of devoted bravery than the charge of Pickett's command,—nor any more unjustifiable waste of human life by a commander. Moving unfalteringly across the wide expanse under a most terrible artillery fire, it swept on up the slope, struck and penetrated the thin line of Hancock's corps. For a moment its banners waved in a sort of triumph, then the lines of blue closed around and enfolded the wedge of gray till it was utterly crushed and destroyed. Pettigrew's supporting line had gone to pieces some time before, demoralized by the discovery that they were not operating against Pennsylvania militia, as they had been led to suppose, but their old enemy, the Army of the Potomac. Hays's division of the Second Corps gathered in from this mass of fugitives 2,000 prisoners and 15 battle flags. Wilcox's brigade having reached the shelter of the Emmettsburg road waited there for the storm to cease, and thus when Pickett's command reached Cemetery Ridge both its flanks were exposed. A part of Stannard's Vermont Brigade was moved promptly against the Confederate right flank where it poured in a terribly demoralizing fire. Entire regiments dropped to the ground and threw up their hands in token of surrender, while Pickett, unharmed though nearly every other officer in his division had been struck down, seeing the madness of further effort to pierce the Union lines, sadly gave the command to retreat. Of his three brigade commanders, Garnett was killed, Armistead mortally wounded after penetrating the Union lines, and Kemper severely so. Twelve colors and 2,500 prisoners from the division remained in the hands of the victors, while the remnant of those who had escaped death or wounds fled wildly back across the plain, again exposed to a terrible artillery fire. Wilcox now moved forward his brigade, with what object it would be hard to say, and it very speedily shared the fate of Pettigrew's command, being torn to pieces by the hot fire poured upon it and several hundred of its men made prisoners by two regiments of Stannard's brigade.

The last mighty shock of the battle of Gettysburg had been felt, and through that night and the following day the remnants of the Confederate army gazed sadly forth from their position on Seminary Ridge at the Union lines massed in firm array along the blood-stained hights from Culp's Hill to Round Top. Any further attack on Lee's part was utterly out of the question, and his preparations were at once made for a retreat to Virginia with whatever he could rescue from the disaster, though it was not till near daylight of the 5th that his picket lines were withdrawn. Blame has sometimes been attached to General Meade that he did not make the defeat of Lee more complete by a strong counter attack after the failure of Pickett's assault; but it should be borne in mind that he had only a few fresh brigades, that the Army of the Potomac had already lost 30 per cent of its numbers, including many of its most valuable officers—Hancock and Gibbon having been severely wounded in repulsing the final attack. Under such circumstances to abandon an impregnable defensive position to accept the chances of offensive warfare when it was not a matter of necessity would certainly not have been wise.

Even the reserve brigades were in no condition for severe duty. The Thirty-seventh, which had made so brave a record on the march to the field, was sadly exhausted before the close of that weary 3d of July. Back and forth in the rear of the line it had hastened from point to point wherever the danger was greatest, often at double-quick, through the terrible heat till many of its members were prostrated by sun-stroke, among the number being both the colonel and the lieutenant-colonel. The Second Brigade was soon after the repulse advanced to the front, taking position near the foot of the ridge and just to the northward of the scene of the terrific struggle of the day before. Late in the afternoon Crawford's division of the Fifth Corps, lying to the left of Eustis, charged forward over a portion of the ground wrested from Sickles, capturing a battery and driving the Confederates pell-mell back to their main line.

The night which succeeded was one of the saddest. Everywhere the field was covered with the dead and wounded, and after dark the soldiers of the two armies mingled freely on the ground between the skirmish lines; looking for fallen comrades or actuated by the promptings of a common humanity in seeking to allay the terrible suffering which no imagination could realize. A severe rain-storm during the night proved a blessing to many who were suffering from thirst, though under the circumstances it was a source of great discomfort to others.

The 4th passed with little of interest. About noon the Thirty-seventh were retired somewhat from their advanced position and ordered to intrench without delay, it being understood that artillery fire was shortly to be resumed. The men had only their bayonets and their hands for intrenching tools, but the former loosened the earth, while the latter, assisted in many cases by the owner's tin plate or cup, piled it up in a defensive form. Rails were gathered from the fences, and even dead horses utilized, till in a short time they had constructed a creditable line of breastworks behind which the regiment settled as comfortably as possible considering the nearly incessant rain. Lee during the day retired from in front of Culp's Hill and withdrew his forces from the village of Gettysburg, taking up a strong position along Seminary Ridge, where he seemed to be awaiting attack. The village was occupied by Howard's forces about noon, but no further demonstration was made upon either side.

Daylight of Sunday, the 5th, failed to bring the usual scattering fire from the picket lines, and the suspicion was at once awakened, which investigation confirmed, that the enemy had gone. The skirmishers were pushed forward till the fact was established and then the Sixth Corps was organized for the pursuit. Moving out by the Emmettsburg road through the center of the battle-field, a horrible spectacle was witnessed by the soldiers. Everywhere the sad debris of the conflict met the eye. The wounded had all been gathered into the vast field hospitals, but the dead were still unburied on every hand, though large details from the Second Corps were then at work on that sad duty, marking the resting place of each comrade with a piece of board which had recently formed part of a cracker box, bearing so far as it was possible to decide the facts the name, rank, company and regiment of the fallen hero. Great numbers of the Confederate dead still lay exposed to the elements, scores of horses were strewn around as they had fallen, weapons and equipments of every kind were scattered in every direction. As Gettysburg was left behind and the regiment pushed along the Fairfield road in the pursuit additional evidences of the terrible losses of the enemy constantly multiplied. Every building was filled with their wounded ; in sheltered spots in the corners of fences, wherever an approach to comfort could be found, the unfortunate men had been left to the tender mercies of the victors—mercies, be it recorded, which never failed to succor and care for the misguided men as tenderly as though they had fallen in defense of the Stars and Stripes. Yet Lee's long wagon trains had been packed to their utmost capacity with wounded, whom he was attempting to transport back to Virginia.

The day's march was short, not more than seven or eight miles being covered. The roads were muddy and very tedious, and early in the afternoon the advance came so close upon the rebel rear that it was necessary to proceed with caution. Evening showed the enemy's rear guard strongly disposed to dispute the passage of the pursuers through the South Mountains, which had now been reached, and a halt for the night was ordered. Many had been the demonstrations of delight along the route by the loyal people, some of whom came from miles away to look upon the valiant veterans who had freed them from the presence of the hateful foe. There was everywhere the realization of a crushing defeat sustained by the invaders, their own wounded and prisoners frankly admitting for the first time that they had been worsted by the Yankees in fair fight, but charging it all to the mistaken policy of leaving the defensive in Virginia and assuming the offensive on Northern soil.

The corps were early astir next morning, with many anticipations as to what the day might have in store for them, and presently moved forward toward the mountains. An inconsiderable advance was made, then a halt for an hour or two ; after which the regiment retraced its steps nearly to the starting point of the morning and deployed as skirmishers, in which position it remained till nearly evening. Then the march was resumed, but it was no longer in direct pursuit of the retreating foe. General Meade had changed his plan, if the purpose of a close, sharp pursuit had ever been entertained. Lee had taken the most direct route for the Potomac on leaving Gettysburg, the distance to

Williamsport by way of Fairfield being about 40 miles; but instead of following over the same route and pressing the retiring columns, the Union commander decided upon a circuitous route to the eastward, fully twice as long. Leaving a small force, principally cavalry, to watch the Confederate rear, the pursuing column proper was turned in the new direction, and the Thirty-seventh, having covered the withdrawal of the rest of the corps, followed it toward Emmettsburg. Passing through Fairfield, another halt was made till after dark, when the journey was taken up in earnest.

And such a night's march! None who had part in it can ever forget that terrible tramp. The men were hungry at the start, having received but a very limited supply of rations at Gettysburg. The road was narrow and rough, evidently but little traveled, and was literally a bed of mud resting on a foundation of small sharp stones. The soft mud soaked the men's shoes, all of which had seen much wear, and the flinty stones cut them to pieces till many a poor fellow was forced to plod along barefooted or with only his stockings to protect the blistered and bleeding flesh. Unhappy the naturally tender-footed! The long marches of the recent past had reduced all such to a condition of incessant suffering. Long after midnight the groaning column plodded on, passing through a dark piece of woods where the intense gloom seemed to add to the roughness and the muddiness, and where files and companies mingled in an inextricable mass. Officers sought in vain for their commands, or maintained bearings only by the familiar tones of some light-hearted private whose spirits no hardship could subdue. Finally they staggered rather than walked through Emmettsburg and half a mile beyond, halting in an open field at 3 o'clock and sinking down wherever it might chance to sleep during the few hours that remained before the bugles would again sound the advance.

Early morning of the 7th found the tired regiment once more astir. Those who had not been able to find their places during the night now did so, a limited supply of rations was drawn and many of the men ate their first food for 36 hours. A large mail —especially welcome at this time of great privation and exertion

—was distributed, and at 8 o'clock the march was resumed. Pitiful as was the condition of the men, and meager as had been the time allowed for rest, the day's programme contemplated a march of fully 25 miles, and as nearly as possible the distance was made. But it was not till midnight that the column halted, and then it were more correct to say that it merely dwindled away till there was nothing left to proceed further. The conditions during the day were rather favorable than otherwise save that the men were very weary; but near night the ascent of Catoctin Mountain began,—an experience which after the lapse of 20 years may well cause a shudder at the remembrance. A drizzling rain had been falling during the day, but as the men began to climb the mountain it increased till it seemed to descend in torrents. Nothing worse in the form of roads could be conceived of than that which infantry and artillery in a confused huddle were trying to follow. The darkness was intense—literally nothing could be seen. The mounted officers could not distinguish the men upon whom each moment their horses were in danger of stepping; neither private nor captain could tell who was struggling along at his side save as the voice made revelation. The plunging and crushing of the ponderous artillery forced the infantry to the woods and fields for the possibility of a passage, and there the apology for a column melted away and dwindled till there was no remedy but a general halt. The woods and fields everywhere were full of men, singly or in groups, who had given up all effort at further progress. Happy were they who by rare good fortune had succeeded in kindling a little fire, but they were few. In the darkness and pouring rain men who could stagger no further laid them down to die, unheeding whether their life might be trampled out by groping horsemen or their stumbling comrades on foot.

Very forlorn indeed was the column which at 7 o'clock next morning took up its way toward Middletown, some six or seven miles away. The rain still continued and the mud was steadily becoming more liquid and abundant. The way led down the mountain, and the road was terribly hard for the footsore soldiers, but they moved slowly, reaching Middletown about noon.

Soon after the halt it ceased raining, the sun shone brightly forth, and as no further march was made that day the opportunity for drying clothing and blankets was improved. A full supply of rations was now secured, the men prepared generous suppers for the first time in many days, after which they enjoyed a full night's rest which was highly appreciated. The 9th saw another advance of a few miles, the army pivoting on the right, composed of the Sixth and Eleventh Corps, while the left, extending to the Potomac, closed up toward the enemy. A halt was made at Boonsboro about noon, shelters were pitched and a comfortable afternoon and evening passed. As the Union cavalry had driven the enemy from that place the previous evening there could be no doubt of the proximity of the two armies, and the early opening of a great and decisive battle was confidently looked for.

Antietam Creek was crossed by the left the next day—Friday, July 10—while the right advanced to the vicinity of Funkstown, which was reached three hours after the enemy left. The pressure of the Confederate skirmishers against the Union advance now showed the near presence of Lee's entire force, and by noon the Sixth Corps was in line of battle, a portion of the Thirty-seventh being thrown forward to the outposts. The entire operations at this time took place in one of the richest and finest agricultural regions of Maryland, and the necessary destruction of grain and crops was immense. Untold acres of the finest wheat, nearly ripe for the harvest, were trampled by lines of battle, by marching columns or wagon and artillery parks, and well might the unfortunate citizens exclaim, "From friend and foe alike deliver us." Beyond a little skirmishing and artillery firing to develop the Confederate position the afternoon passed without event. The Southern army, forced to assume the defensive, was found to be well intrenched in front of Williamsport. Four days previous they had reached the river, almost before the roundabout Federal pursuit began, but found the stream too deep for fording and they had not pontons enough to construct a bridge. The incessant rains continually swelled the flood, so Lee had no alternative to facing about and assuming the boldest front possible. That the condition of his troops was critical their own warmest partisans admit. They had courage in plenty, but next to no ammunition. The 11th was passed in the same quiet way, with Companies A, I and G of the Thirty-seventh on the skirmish line, the left of the Army of the Potomac being moved a little nearer to Lee's right. Early the following morning the Thirty-seventh passed through Funkstown and after feeling its way for two or three miles took position in front of the enemy's intrenced line between Hagerstown and Williamsport.

The two armies were now in position, face to face, and it remained for somebody to give the order to strike. General Meade held a council of war and decided not to attack. All the following night was devoted to intrenching the Union lines and the 13th passed with only the exchange of a few shells by the opposing artillery. That night each commander reached a decision,—General Meade decided to attack next day, and General Lee—finding that it would be possible to ford the river and having also succeeded in constructing one ponton bridge at Falling Waters—decided to go back to Virginia—which he did. The Union army moved down to Williamsport through a disheartening rain, which added to the gloom felt at the escape of the foe whose complete destruction the rank and file had confidently hoped to see accomplished. With the evening a severe thunder storm came on, drenching out and washing away what little spirit still remained in the tired bodies.

Disappointing as was the escape of Lee across the river, it must be recognized that Meade had great reason for the caution with which he acted. While the Confederate army had suffered a decisive defeat at Gettysburg, his own had been sadly wounded, and he was even then unaware of the straitened condition of his antagonist. The close of the battle left the Army of the Potomac with but 47,000 muskets; and though General French with his division joined the Third Corps, of which he took command, on the 8th, Meade still believed the enemy fully equal to him in numbers, with the advantage of a selected and fortified defensive position of much natural strength. The Union soldiers were by no means in good fighting condition. The Sixth

Corps was counted as the main dependence of the army, since it was efficiently organized; had been but slightly engaged at Gettysburg, and its morale was ever admirable; yet it was perhaps more than the others worn out by almost incessant marches and hard duty. In the Thirty-seventh regiment 180 men at that time—nearly a third of the whole number—were entirely destitute of shoes, while their clothing was correspondingly demoralized. Other regiments were certainly in no better condition.

Ewell's corps forded the Potomac at Williamsport, while the Confederate right and center under Longstreet and Hill retreated by the ponton bridge at Falling Waters. The rear guard of the latter was vigorously attacked by Kilpatrick's cavalry, two guns, three colors and a large number of prisoners being captured and General Pettigrew mortally wounded, with slight loss to the assailants.

The direct pursuit of Lee's army was now ended, and was to be succeeded by a parallel scramble southward,—the counterpart of so many other movements, the Union army east of the Blue Ridge and the enemy in the Shenandoah valley. "Cover Washington and take up a threatening position!" were Halleck's directions to Meade, and early on the morning of the 15th the Thirty-seventh in its place in the corps moved back over the road it had come, through Funkstown and Boonsboro, halting near the latter place for the night and receiving rations for two days. Soon after setting out upon the march that morning an interesting meeting took place between the Thirty-seventh and the Forty-sixth Massachusetts, Colonel W S. Shurtleff, a nine-months' regiment from Springfield and vicinity containing many friends and acquaintances of the Thirty-seventh. During the closing days of its service the Forty-sixth had been moved from North Carolina to Baltimore, where it formed part of a brigade under General H. S. Briggs, moving to Frederick City and thence to the Army of the Potomac before Williamsport, where it was attached to the First Corps. A few days later Colonel Shurtleff's command left for Massachusetts, bearing many a warm message from the Thirty-seventh to friends at home. At 3 o'clock of the 16th the camps were astir, at half-past 4 the column was on the way, and at noon, having made a march of 16 miles, the Thirty-seventh halted within a mile of Berlin.

The associations of the place came vividly to the minds of all the members of the regiment. Less than nine months before they had stopped at the same place on the way into Virginia. During the interval what an epoch of history had transpired. Then as now the Union army was in pursuit of a demoralized, retreating foe. The adored McClellan was then in command. The disastrous experiments of Burnside and Hooker had succeeded, followed by the signal victory under the present conservative commander. Everywhere in the regiment, from field officers to privates, there was the feeling that the victory might and should have been made more decisive. There was a fear that the experiences of the previous year were practically to be repeated. The thought of another campaign in the desolate and unfriendly regions of Virginia, following the brief sojourn in a friendly country, was far from pleasant; yet underlying all preferences and wishes, there was ever manifest in the breasts of the soldiery a firm faith in the approaching triumph of the cause in which they were enlisted, and a disposition to accept patiently whatever of hardship and sacrifice might be necessary till the flag of the Union should float in triumph over the entire land.

It was Thursday noon when Berlin was reached, and no further movement was made till Sunday, the 19th. The two entire days of rest, free from care or anticipation of an immediate battle, were heartily appreciated by the men. Friday was rainy and disagreeable, but the men received a supply of rations and clothing, both very much needed, and Saturday proved sunny and pleasant. That evening found a marked improvement in the external appearance of the regiment. The river had given opportunity for bathing, the worn-out clothing was in many instances discarded for fresh suits, the barefooted ones had once more comfortable shoes and socks, generous mails had been received and dispatched, comfortable food had been prepared, and Sunday morning found the command, brightened and encouraged by these circumstances, cheerfully responding to the orders for an early march.

It was half-past 7 when the column moved on to the ponton bridge, across its swaying length, and was once more on the "sacred soil." Over the same route they had traveled the previous autumn the regiment pushed along some ten miles or more, passing through Lovettsville, the few visible inhabitants more scowling and ill-natured, if possible, than on the previous occasion. The halt for the night was made near the little hamlet of Wheatland, and though the march had not been long it had been very wearying, the sun seeming to shine with renewed fierceness after the weeks of almost constant cloud and rain. But if Sunday had been hot, Monday was hotter. That day's march took the regiment to Union, about ten miles further down the valley, past Snicker's Gap, through which, as so often before and after, the two armies played peep with each other. Fortunately General Meade was not in a hurry, the Thirty-seventh led the corps that day, marching leisurely with frequent halts, and the region was well watered by the various small streams tributary to Goose Creek. These factors combined to make the day's march quite comfortable considering the broiling heat.

The brigade halted for the night in a well-fenced lot of several acres, the sole occupants of which had been about a dozen lean, long-legged Virginia hogs. Never was the command to "Stack arms" more promptly obeyed, and what followed, the moment ranks were broken, can be pretty well imagined. The pigs were fleet of foot, and they ran for life, but the odds were fifty to one, and the boys in blue remembered that Lee's soldiers had recently been drawing rations at the expense of the loyal people north of the Potomac. The scramble was very exciting while it lasted, but within ten minutes the hundred camp-fires were sending up the aroma of roasting pork.

The 21st was given up to rest, the soldiers exploring the surrounding country in search of forage, though finding little except blackberries, which were abundant and delicious. Next day at noon the regiment again led the corps, marching to Upperville, near the base of the Blue Ridge, on the road from Fairfax via Paris to Winchester. Here a halt was made for the night, but at 3 o'clock the bugle rang out reveille and the line of march was soon taken up. The Thirty-seventh, however, now took its place as rear guard, following the wagon-train, and consequently, as a march of 20 miles or more was made, did not reach bivouac till 2 o'clock at night. The tired men dropped upon the ground and slept, almost wherever they chanced to be, during the two hours or so till daylight, when they were aroused to prepare a hasty breakfast and journey on again. The fires were lighted and the little cooking was about half done, when the sharp order to "Fall in!" came, and the half-cooked food was eaten as it best could be on the march. About 10 o'clock Manassas Gap was reached, where it was made known that a sharp skirmish had occurred the previous day, resulting in the driving back of the Confederate forces to Front Royal. The services of the Sixth Corps not being required, after waiting a few hours they marched back over the road they had come, and once more turned their faces in the direction of Warrenton, toward which the Army of the Potomac was concentrating. Halting for the night near Orleans, the march was resumed early next morning, Saturday, the 25th,—a day long to be remembered on account of the sultry, breathless heat. At Cliffe Mills a bridge was wanting, and a detail from the regiment, under direction of the engineers, soon had a substantial structure in place. Then forward again over the miserable roads, hungry, weary, the men continually falling by the way from sun-stroke, till at last a halt was made on a steep hill-side within a mile of Warrenton.

Here for four days the regiment remained and rested. The following day being Sunday, religious services were held by Chaplain Morse, for the first time in many weeks. The remaining days were devoted to explorations of the surrounding country, ostensibly in search of blackberries, though it was noticed that many a ration of fresh veal, pork and mutton found its way into camp without having passed through the commissary department. The men rapidly recovered from the exhaustion of their recent marches while the general health of the regiment, greatly improving, had now become remarkably good, considering the severe nature of the service.

Up to this time the following changes had occurred in the roster of officers: Second Lieutenant Harris was advanced to first lieutenant dating from June 3, and was assigned to duty with Company F. On the same day Captain J. P. Kelley of Company A resigned and First Lieutenant J. A. Loomis was made captain, continuing to serve with Company E. Second Lieutenant Bush, who was absent wounded, was commissioned first lieutenant, while Orderly Sergeant Albert C. Sparks of Company E was commissioned second lieutenant and assigned to duty with Company C. Sergeant Major Robert A. Gray was made second lieutenant and assigned to Company H. Sergeant Hubbard M. Abbott of Company G succeeded Gray as sergeant major. Second Lieutenant Morgan of Company B resigned June 19, and Color Sergeant Charles S. Bardwell was commissioned second lieutenant dating from June 20, and assigned to Company B.

CHAPTER X

THE REGIMENT IN NEW YORK.

THE UNION VICTORIES.—NORTHERN TREACHERY AND DIS-
LOYALTY.—THE RIOT IN NEW YORK.—THE THIRTY-SEVENTH
SENT TO THE CITY.—ITS CREDITABLE SERVICE THERE.

The night of July 2, 1863, closed upon the most momentous crisis in the history of the Southern Confederacy. At every principal point along the military frontier the opposing forces were locked in desperate and fateful struggle. At Gettysburg the most sanguine partisan of either army could only hope for victory; at Vicksburg, Pemberton's beleagured garrison were heroically struggling against despair while Johnston, with 30,000 men was seeking for an opportunity to strike the besiegers in the rear and make a way for the escape of the besieged; from the embrasures at Port Hudson the Confederate cannon still looked forth with grim defiance. With anxiety, there was still hope everywhere for the Southern cause. The night of July 3 found that hope shattered and the doom of the Confederacy clearly forecast.

At the very moment when Pickett's shattered legions were hurled back from Cemetery Ridge, Pemberton and Grant met between the lines at Vicksburg to discuss the surrender of that stronghold. For almost 50 days the siege had continued, pressed constantly with the indomitable energy of the Union commander, and repelled with characteristic determination by the Confederates. Twelve miles of trenches had been dug in the investment, and 89 batteries, mounted with 220 guns, constructed. The besieged and besiegers in many parts of the line looked each other in the face across the same parapet, and fought with hand grenades, bayonets and pistols. Twice had mines been exploded under the defenses with no greater result than the slaughter of a few men, but preparations were now made for a general and simultaneous assault along the entire line on the morning of the 6th of July.

Three days before the time appointed for the terrible attempt the flag of truce appeared. The condition of the garrison fully justified the step on the part of their commander. The men, closely confined to the trenches for seven weeks, much of the time on short rations, had lost health, courage and subordination. Consultation with his division commanders convinced Pemberton that they could not even be nerved up to attempt cutting their way through the circumvallating lines, while the danger of revolt could not but be recognized. General Bowen, with a flag of truce and a letter to Grant, appeared before the Federal lines on the morning of the 3d, and nearly 24 hours passed in conference and correspondence, Pemberton anxious to make the best terms possible for his command and Grant practically insisting upon unconditional surrender. These terms were finally accepted, and at 10 o'clock on the 4th the Confederates by divisions marched out in front of their works, stacked arms and colors and retired to the town. General Logan, receiving the surrender, marched his division into the town amid the wild enthusiasm of the Union army. The surrendered force comprised about 31,000 men, only 22,000 of whom were fit for duty in the trenches, and 172 cannon; making the total loss to the Confederates from the opening of the campaign not less than 46,000 men, 60,000 stand of arms and 260 pieces of artillery—a terrible blow to the Southern cause.

Johnston, meanwhile, had gathered as much of an army as possible about Canton, a day's march north of Jackson, where the first of June found him in command of some 36,000 efficient men. Instead of striking the best blow possible in aid of the beleagured garrison, he allowed them to starve and wear out in the trenches for four weeks while he maintained an argumentative correspondence with the Richmond government. On the 28th of June, with no increase of force, he moved toward Vicksburg, but found Sherman with 30,000 troops strongly intrenched

facing to the rear. Johnston's plan had been to make as strong
an attack as possible on the northern portion of the investing
line, in the hope of weakening the southern portion so that the
garrison could cut its way through and escape. The plan miscarried totally, for not only was Pemberton's force too much exhausted to throw itself upon the Federal bayonets, but Johnston
was unable to find any point where it would be less than madness to attack. He did not even begin to feel the Federal position till July 2, and while he was yet reconnoitering the ground
those whom he sought to succor surrendered. Sherman was apprised of the surrender immediately and directed to move vigorously against Johnston, which he did, but the latter did not
wait to receive the blow. Falling back rapidly to Jackson,
which he reached on the 7th, the disheartened commander proceeded to strengthen the fortifications while he appealed to Richmond for help. The victorious legions under Sherman closed
around the place on the 10th, and a strong reconnaissance showing it strongly intrenched, a regular investment was decided on.
But Johnston did not await siege. Despairing of any relief from
the Confederate government, he evacuated Jackson on the night
of the 16th and pushed rapidly to the eastward. He was followed
sharply for some miles, but as a scrub race was no part of Grant's
plan the pursuing column was recalled, the railroads about Jackson thoroughly destroyed, and Sherman took his elated forces
back to Vicksburg.

While these events had been transpiring in Mississippi another
substantial drop had been added to the nation's cup of rejoicing.
Port Hudson also had fallen, and the Mississippi "flowed unvexed to the sea." This place, whose works were of immense
strength, had been invested by the Army of the Gulf—the
Nineteenth Corps, under General Banks—on the 25th of May,
the garrison easily repelling determined attacks on the following
day and on the 13th of June, at a cost to the besiegers of fully
4,000 men. But day by day the lines drew nearer the doomed
stronghold, and the scanty supply of provisions rapidly disappeared till starvation stared the defenders in the face. Suddenly on the 7th of July, from the lines of the Union army broke

rapid discharges of artillery and ringing cheers which drove from the breasts of the defenders the last ray of hope. The news had been received of Vicksburg's fall, and when the authenticity of the tidings was assured General Gardner announced his willingness to give up the hopeless struggle, commissioners were appointed to arrange terms of surrender, and on the morning of the 9th the capitulation took place. It embraced some 6,500 men, 5,000 muskets and 51 cannon; but of vastly greater importance than the mere loss or gain of men and munitions was the breaking of the last barrier across the Father of Waters, giving to the Union fleet full command of that great waterway.

The Confederates had not relinquished these points without strenuous efforts to secure others, though all had been thwarted. While the siege of Port Hudson was being prosecuted the Confederate General Taylor gathered what force was available in Louisiana and moved down toward New Orleans, capturing a few small garrisons and threatening the Cresent City itself. General Emory, who was in command there, became alarmed and sent to Banks for help, but the latter held steadily on till Gardner surrendered when a competent force was dispatched down the river, which speedily dissipated all danger and sent the insurgents beyond pursuit into the interior.

A similar but more pronounced effort was made in Arkansas, where Confederate General Holmes with a strong force made an attempt to capture Helena, hoping thus to secure control of the river at that point. A resolute assault was made on the 4th of July, but was bloodily repulsed by General Prentiss, with a garrison of less than one-half the Confederate number, when Holmes also sought safety in the fastnesses of his department.

General Rosecrans, meanwhile, had been far from idle. His antagonist, Bragg, with his base of supplies at Chattanooga, had his field depot and a strongly intrenched camp at Tullahoma, with his advanced lines, also well fortified, a dozen miles in front. On the 23d of June Rosecrans ordered an advance of his army, pressing the front sharply with a single corps, while the bulk of his army moved around the Confederate right with the intention of flanking the entire position and at the same time threatening the enemy's communications. In the midst of a terrible rain-storm this movement was carried out with perfect success, and with trifling loss to the Unionists the Southern army was forced from its advanced line. The successful Rosecrans pushed forward in battle array against the main position, but on the 1st of July received the intelligence that Bragg was in full retreat toward Chattanooga. Having pressed his fleeing antagonist as closely as practicable, the Union general finally paused to rest his army and repair communications in his rear, presently advancing to the Tennessee river near Stevenson, Ala., freeing the state of Tennessee with the exception of the small corner about Chattanooga from the presence of the rival armies.

With success thus everywhere crowning the Union banners there came with midsummer a respite from the incessant thunder of actual conflict. Banks concentrated his forces at New Orleans; Grant remained at Vicksburg though his army was considerably scattered, the Thirteenth Corps going to Texas, while a considerable part of the remainder reinforced Rosecrans in his campaign against Bragg. How the armies in Virginia had settled down to watch each other across the upper Rappahannock we have already seen.

The political situation in the loyal states had meantime become critical. Added to the great number of actual sympathizers with disunion, there were very many well intentioned people who from one cause or another had become dissatisfied with the administration of governmental affairs, or the slow progress of the war with its immense cost of blood and treasure; while others were simply discouraged and despaired of the ability of the national government to reassert its authority over the seceded states, feeling that the sooner the war was terminated and peace restored on the best terms possible the better it would be for all parties. Everywhere through the loyal states the feelings of distrust and discouragement were nurtured and intensified by the disloyal element, whose boldness and bitterness increased as the gloomy days of the great crisis wore on.

President Lincoln had issued a proclamation on the 8th of May ordering a draft in July, and as the time approached the opposition to this vigorous measure was shown to be organized and formidable. The draft itself had been rendered necessary through the discouragement thrown over enlistments by the "Peace party," urged on by the activity of the "Copperheads," as the avowed Southern sympathizers were called. While this state of affairs was everywhere prevalent in varying degree, its centers seemed to be in Ohio and in New York city. In the former locality it was under the direct nurture of Clement L. Vallandigham, an ex-Congressman of Ohio, but who now loved to be called the "Apostle of Liberty." Vallandigham led all others in shameless disloyalty, his seditious utterances becoming finally so unbearable that it was decided to make an example of him. Ohio was at that time in the Military Department of the Ohio, under the command of General Burnside, with headquarters at Cincinnati. On the 13th of April Burnside had issued a proclamation for the suppression of seditious speech and action, and on the 4th of May Vallandigham was arrested, tried by court-martial at Cincinnati and sentenced to close confinement in a fortress during the continuance of the war. President Lincoln, ever merciful, commuted the sentence to banishment within the Confederate lines. This decree was carried out May 25, and the distinguished exile was dropped in neutral ground in front of Rosecrans's lines, Bragg declining to receive him under flag of truce. Not finding life in the Confederacy to his liking, Vallandigham soon escaped through the blockade to Canada, where he found plenty of congenial spirits among the renegades and plotters who swarmed in that convenient haven.

Everything tended steadily toward a crisis. With the draft at hand, with Lee's army in Pennsylvania and Morgan's cavalry raiding through Indiana and Ohio, with the ignorant and vicious classes in many of the larger cities ripe for open revolt, and urged on by unscrupulous foes of the government, open and secret, the closing days of June were portentous indeed to those who loved their country. But a great mistake was made by the Confederates in their armed invasion of the loyal states. Especially the raid of Morgan to plunder and destroy awoke many an indifferent citizen to active patriotism. The militia of the threatened states gathered in swarms about his path, cutting off his retreat when he sought to regain his own soil, driving him wildly from point to point till his force was utterly scattered and himself became a prisoner, with most of his men.

Through all this reign of foreboding and despair the sullen roar of the artillery at Gettysburg fell on the strained ears of the nation. How the people listened and hoped and prayed! How on that pregnant night of the 3d of July hearts true to the old Union dared to hope when the electric wire flashed the news that Lee's great attack was repulsed and the Loyal lines stood unshaken on Cemetery Ridge. Great was the joy on the following day—the Nation's Anniversary—when the intelligence was confirmed; while succeeding days heard the glad news from Vicksburg, with confirmation of the reported flight of Bragg from before the victorious Union forces in Tennessee. Surely that was joy enough for one week. A riotous uprising had been expected on the Fourth in New York city, but it did not come—the tidings were not congenial to disloyal demonstrations; it was delayed, not averted. Yet on that potent day, mixed with the rejoicings and the renewed consecrations to the service of the common country, were many covert or open denunciations of the government at Washington, many an insinuation cloaked in specious language, many a bold declaration that the war was a failure, was unjust, was wicked; many an exhortation to abandon the struggle for the life of the Union; and these came not from pot-house politicians or nameless demagogues seeking for notoriety, but from men enjoying high places in the confidence of the people, and wearing noble titles of honor. The seed thus sown bore fruit.

The draft was appointed to begin in New York city July 13, and on the morning of that day the officials having the matter in charge assembled and quietly proceeded to their unwelcome task in an office on the corner of Forty-sixth Street and Third Avenue. Almost simultaneously with the first revolution of the fateful wheel a pistol shot was heard in the street outside, a howling mob burst into the building, driving out the officers and their assistants, destroying everything on which they could lay hands and firing the building. The police were powerless to quell the disturbance, and the superintendent, Mr. Kennedy, who sought to restore order, was beaten almost to death. The firemen were not allowed to extinguish the flames which the insane rioters had kindled, and building after building was swept away. The telegraph lines leading from the city had already been cut, and in a moment the metropolis of America passed under the full control of a blood-thirsty, brutal mob, composed of emissaries, refugees, and the lowest and vilest of its own residents. The scenes which followed transcend description. The mob spread rapidly through the city, breaking into the manufacturing establishments and forcing the employes to swell its ranks, stopping railroad trains to search for soldiers, wounding and plundering the passengers, and finally destroying the Harlem bridge. The residence of Postmaster Wakeman was pillaged and burned, while that of the mayor was stripped of everything which could be carried away or destroyed. Plunder, violence, lust and murder rioted everywhere. Its most devilish fury, however, was wreaked upon the inoffensive colored people of the city, who were hunted down, maimed, mutilated and murdered with a fiendishness which even at this lapse of time makes the blood run cold. The poor creatures were hanged to lamp-posts, tortured, and in some cases fires were built into which they were thrown and kicked till they were burned to death. The Colored Orphan Asylum on Fifth Avenue, containing some 200 homeless negro children, was plundered and given to the flames, while the wretched inmates were hunted about the streets by the howling, drunken demons as though they had been so many dangerous wild beasts.

Thus Monday, Monday night and the forenoon of Tuesday wore away. At noon of the latter day, while the rioters, led by a Virginian emissary, were gathered in front of the *Tribune* office —the entrances to which were barricaded by bundles of printing paper, while the occupants were thoroughly armed for its defense, as was also the condition in the office of the *Times* and other loyal papers—contemplating its destruction, word was circulated that Governor Seymour was at the City Hall and would address them. At once the crowd surged that way, and the Governor stated that he had sent his Adjutant-General to Washington to have the draft suspended and stopped. In closing he said:—

I now ask you, as good citizens, to wait for his return, and I assure you that I will do all that I can to see that there is no inequality and no wrong done any one. I wish you to take good care of all property, as good citizens, and see that every person is safe. The safe keeping of property and persons rests with you, and I charge you to disturb neither. It is your duty to maintain the good order of the city, and I know you will do it. I wish you now to separate as good citizens, and you can assemble again whenever you wish to do so. I ask you to leave all to me now, and I will see to your rights. Wait till my Adjutant returns from Washington, and you shall be satisfied.

The mob applauded the Governor uproariously and promptly resumed their work of devastation and murder. During the day Governor Seymour issued a proclamation forbidding rioting, but the brutal wretches cared nothing for mere words.

By some unaccountable neglect no precaution whatever seemed to have been taken to guard against the riot, which had certainly given abundant notice of its probability. No military force was within reach, but when it became evident to the tardily awakened authorities that nothing else would suffice to restore peace such detachments as could be gathered were collected and directed to disperse the insurgents. Colonel F. H. O'Brien of the Eleventh New York Militia offered the services of his regiment, which were gladly accepted: but the gallant colonel, venturing far in advance of his command on his mission of peace, was brutally murdered, his body subjected to every indignity and finally hanged to a lamp-post by the human fiends. At first the troops, reluctant to resort to sterner measures, fired over the heads of the mob or used blank cartridges, but these discharges were greeted with howls of rage and desperate assaults upon the troops till in self-defense the volleys were sent home with a will. Gradually the bullet and the bayonet broke the ranks of the marauders, and by Thursday a measure of quiet was restored. Important points near the river fronts were protected by armed vessels whose guns commanded the streets, and the state militia which had been dispatched to Pennsylvania was by that time returning in such numbers as to insure efficiency.*

The number of lives lost during this wild carnival can never be known. Governor Seymour himself estimated it at 1000, but it it quite possible that these figures may be too high. Fifty buildings were wholly destroyed, in addition to many that were sacked and plundered, the city being obliged to pay $2,000,000 in damages.

The Governor demanded that the President should suspend the draft on account of its inequality of operation, and also that it should be postponed till the matter of its legality could be passed upon by the proper tribunals. On the former ground the President conceded an adjournment till the justice of its operation could be decided; but declined to commit the matter to the courts, since that course would utterly paralyze the efforts of the government to reinforce its armies to meet the exigencies of the occasion. The 19th of August was designated as the day for the resumption of the draft, and General John A. Dix succeeded General Wool in command of the Department. The well-known energy of the new commander left no doubt that whatever measures might be necessary to the public peace and the support of the authority of the general government would be vigorously adopted. Evidently the disturbing elements looked to New York as the center from which the cue for other cities was to be taken. In many of the cities there had been more or less disorder, notably at Boston, where a single volley at the critical moment saved the city from further turmoil; but nowhere else had open riot occurred to merit the name.

One of the first acts of the new commandant, General Dix,

---

*The writer, with a train full of wounded from the battle of Gettysburg, reached Jersey City on the morning of the 13th, destined for New York. As the steamer on which North River was crossed drew near the pier intelligence was received of the outbreak which rendered the landing of wounded soldiers in the streets impossible, since they would undoubtedly be murdered by the rioters. After a long delay the helpless cargo was taken to a nearly vacant convalescent camp on Bedloe's Island, where under the guns of Fort Wood they would at least be safe, though owing to the absence of provision for their coming many suffered severely for the want of proper care. From the island, by day and night, the smoke and glare of fires kindled by the mob could be seen and often the wild yells of the crowd came over the waters. Such of the wounded on the island as were capable of doing service were taken over to the city during the day, returning at night accompanied by others who had been hurt during the various conflicts. As the horrible scenes witnessed by the delegation were discussed in the wards during the evening, the vain wish broke from many lips for the presence of the speaker's "old regiment" from the Army of the Potomac to mete out proper punishment.

was to ask of the War Department a detail of four of the most efficient regiments in the Army of the Potomac for service in and about the city pending the draft, the preference to be given to New England and Western troops. The request having been granted and duly forwarded, selection was made of the Thirty-seventh Massachusetts and Fifth Wisconsin from the Sixth Corps, the Fifth New Hampshire from the Second Corps and the Twentieth Indiana from the Third Corps. The energy manifested in forwarding these troops to their destination was something quite out of the usual line, as we shall see by following the movements of the Thirty-seventh, with which alone this narrative will be concerned.

At midnight of July 30 the regiment with the exception of the few camp guards was soundly sleeping, when Lieutenant-Colonel Montague rode into camp. Following the battle of Gettysburg that officer had been detailed as inspector general on the staff of Brigadier General J. J. Bartlett, temporarily commanding the division, where he had just been notified of the detail and given permission to accompany the regiment. Colonel Edwards being thus informed of the selection, ordered the men aroused, and when an hour or two later the official notification came it found the command about ready for the march to Warrenton Junction, ten miles away, to take the cars for New York. At first the half-awakened men could scarcely realize that they were not being hoaxed, but the vigor of the preparations going on at regimental head-quarters and all through the camp dispelled the doubts. Coffee was made and a hasty breakfast, for which the unexpected good news left little appetite, was swallowed, after which the few possessions that the soldiers had been able to retain during their recent trying experiences were gathered in the most compact form possible, and the order for marching impatiently awaited. The line was formed at dawn, and with a glee such as they seldom before or afterward experienced the men obeyed the order to "March!" Already they had come to understand that the present favor was due to the high standing of the regiment in discipline, its reputation for excellence in drill, subordination and general morale, and many a kind word was spoken for the officers that morning by men who were not accustomed to the use of such expressions.

The Junction was reached about 11 o'clock, and cars were taken for Washington. The ride was a memorable one. Every foot of the ground traversed was historic, and about each insignificant station clustered the recollections of daring deeds performed by Blue or Gray. Back and forth over the region the tides of war had ebbed and flowed, leaving their traces everywhere in blackened ruins and desolated fields. There would have been no surprise if at any moment the train had come to an abrupt halt, and the fusillade of some marauding party had broken upon the ears of the passengers; but the ride was made without interruption, Alexandria was passed through near evening, and at 7 o'clock the Capital was reached. It was 3 o'clock before the train which was to continue the journey northward was ready, yet little sleep was had during the long hours of the wait; the men were too much elated, and had too keen a realization of the difference between their present journey by rail and the long, terrible marches recently endured, to give much heed to ordinary weariness or one or two nights of broken rest.

Baltimore was reached early next morning, August 1, and there another wait for transportation detained the regiment till about noon, but it was not an unpleasant halt. The name of the city had up to this time had a hateful sound in the ears of Massachusetts soldiers. It was not forgotten that more than two years before her streets had been consecrated by the blood of the first martyrs in the great contest; but the spirit which had demanded that sacrifice was no longer manifest. The streets were not filled with a riotous mob as in 1861, nor did the people wear the cold look of suppressed hatred which had been manifest in 1862 when the Thirty-seventh passed through on its way to the front; instead there was a cordial greeting and an earnest manifestation of loyalty quite surprising and very gratifying. . In fact, everywhere on the trip the regiment as representatives of the "grand old Army of the Potomac" were received with the utmost enthusiasm, and this greeting was doubly grateful to the recipients. It assured them not only of the fact that they were among friends, but that the loyal people of the great North were appreciative of the faithful but so often unfortunate work which the army that they represented was doing for the perpetuity of the government.

It was late in the evening when Philadelphia was reached, but the hospitality of that noble city was never wanting, at whatever hour of the day or night loyal soldiers could be ministered to, and the passage of the Thirty-seventh proved no exception to the general rule. A bounteous supper was provided, well seasoned with those kind words of cheer which the sons and daughters of Philadelphia so loved to bestow. At its conclusion the journey was resumed. As the Steamer Belknap bearing the regiment steamed up New York harbor toward noon of the following day, which was Sunday, August 2, the command was formed on deck and Colonel Edwards, as his keen glance ran proudly down the line, exclaimed in his most impressive tones: " We are going among friends—friends who may have to be treated as enemies! Battalion load at will—load!"

The grim smile with which the commander watched the execution of his order was reflected from the features of the men as the ramrods rattled merrily in the musket barrels, and when the steamer swung up to the pier every man was prepared for whatever might be demanded of him. But there was no call to duty of an unpleasant nature. The streets were filled, but as the regiment debarked near Castle Garden and stacked arms on the adjacent streets it experienced only a kindly greeting. What real sentiments lurked under the friendly exterior it might not in every case be easy to determine, and there were sullen faces in the background of which glimpses were sometimes caught, but these the sons of Massachusetts little heeded.

Colonel Edwards, on reporting the arrival of his command, was directed to proceed to Fort Hamilton, one of the defenses of the harbor, located on the Long Island shore at the Narrows. The regiment accordingly re-embarked during the afternoon, reaching its destination after a pleasant trip down the harbor which had all the zest of a holiday excursion. A satisfactory camping ground was selected a short distance from the grim walls of the fort, and immediate preparations were made for the comfort and creditable appearance of the regiment. An issue was promptly made of A tents for the entire command, and requisitions were filled for new dress suits,—the uniforms then worn giving unmistakable evidence of the severity of their recent experiences in march and storm and battle. During the evening most of the men seized the opportunity to bathe in the abundant waters of the harbor, and the beach presented an interesting picture as the scores of bathers plunged in and out of the water, the evening air echoing their fragments of laugh and jest and song.

The following day was devoted to settling the regiment comfortably in the new quarters and the pitching of the tents, which in comparison with what the Thirty-seventh had recently experienced seemed quite palatial. If any additional evidence of the changed order of things was needed it came that afternoon when rations were drawn, consisting of soft bread, fresh meat, vegetables in plenty, and many an unwonted article. While these provisions were being made for the immediate needs of the regiment the men had been making themselves acquainted with their surroundings. The entire force at the post was found to consist of a detachment of the Fifth United States and a battalion of the Twelfth Regulars under Captain Putnam. the "permanent guard," with two volunteer regiments, the Eleventh and Thirteenth New York Heavy Artillery. Colonel Edwards had on arrival at New York been assigned to the command of the post, succeeding Major Bruen, whose staff he retained, with First Lieutenant H. M. Stacey of the Twelfth Regulars as post adjutant. The Thirty-seventh were thus placed under the immediate command of Lieutenant-Colonel Montague, this being the first occasion when for any considerable time the regiment as such received its orders from any save its organizer and original commander. The relations of commander and command, then for the first time assumed, which were afterward to be cemented in bonds of enduring esteem on both sides by many a fierce trial by fire, seem to have been mutually pleasant, though rendered far different and more complicated by the changed surroundings than they would have been in the field.

The ensuing two weeks brought little of especial note to the organization, beyond the sharp change from the life the men had temporarily left to that upon which they had now entered. The carelessness inseparable from life at the front gave way to the most exact military discipline, the utmost neatness in quarters and dress, with faithful devotion to drill. Four hours daily were given to the latter whenever weather permitted,—company drills coming in the morning from 6.15 to 7.45 and from 9 to 10, with battalion drill for an hour and a half in the afternoon, followed by dress parade.

With this thorough practice following upon its previous efficiency, it is needless to say that the Thirty-seventh rapidly acquired fame for its excellence in drill, and many visitors from the city came down to the fort at the hour of dress parade to watch the Massachusetts regiment of whose skill they had heard wonderful accounts. No such were ever known to go away disappointed. while many a hearty compliment was left behind. all of which very speedily found their way to the ears of the men and officers, inciting to still further endeavor. Even the professional prejudice of the Regulars who formed part of the garrison at the fort gave way. and they were forced to admit that there was at least one volunteer regiment whose discipline, drill and general soldierly qualities were unexceptionable.

Inevitably the influence of the Thirty-seventh was exerted on the other regiments with which it was brigaded. Sergeants Chapin of Company C and Warner of Company H were detailed as "instructors in tactics" for the heavy artillery regiments, while Captain Loomis (whose own Company E was drilled in the management of the heavy guns in the fort as a recognition of its proficiency) was appointed instructor for the non-commissioned officers of those regiments.

As the regiment was so near the homes of most of its members, many friends took advantage of the opportunity to visit those in whom they were interested, and not a day passed that some familiar face from Massachusetts was not seen in camp.

The wives and families of some of the officers were with them during the stay of the Thirty-seventh in the city, while some of the men received short furloughs; in these ways many an opportunity for meeting was improved by friends who were never again on earth to join hands.

Thus, with no more exciting event than the drumming out of camp on the 14th of August of a worthless member of Company K, the days passed till the date fixed by the government for the resumption of the draft, August 19. On the previous day Colonel Edwards visited the police head-quarters and inquired as to the prospect for peaceful proceedings. He was informed that there was certainly danger of an outbreak; that the rioters claimed to have 20,000 men well armed and organized; that they had given the authorities to understand that they should probably offer no violence unless Massachusetts soldiers came into the city, in which event they declared that not one of them should leave it alive. No knight of antiquity ever accepted the gauntlet of defiance more unhesitatingly than Colonel Edwards resented this implied threat against his pet regiment. Hastening at once to the head-quarters of General Canby, who had command of the city, he reported what he had heard. "And now, General, I have a favor to ask," he added. Being asked to state his wishes, the impulsive colonel thus formulated them: "I wish to bring my regiment—the Thirty-seventh Massachusetts—to the city, to station them as special guard of the drafting proceedings, that no other troops be in sight, and that they display only the Massachusetts flag except in case of actual conflict, when they will also fly the United States colors." The request being promptly granted preparations were at once made for moving the regiment to the city. The men, finding that they were likely to see active service, requested that they might lay aside their dress suits and resume the well-worn raiment with which they had become so familiar, and such permission was given.

That evening, just after dress parade the orders were received to "Pack up and fall in!" and in a very few minutes, equipped for duty with 60 rounds of ammunition and three days' rations, the regiment marched down to the wharf, took the steamer which was in waiting and were transported to the city proper, where they bivouacked for the night on the ground at the Battery. Early in the morning of the following day the command was under arms and marched up Broadway to the Washington Parade Ground, where they halted and awaited the development of events. Companies G and C were detached for duty at the drafting rooms on Sixth Avenue, where according to orders they displayed only the Massachusetts standard. There was no hostile demonstration. Not a few eyed the lone Indian, the uplifted sword and the Latin motto on the strange banner and asked, "What flag is that?" or "What soldiers are these?" and the reply was civil but emphatic. "That is the flag of Massachusetts, and this is a part of her Thirty-seventh regiment —how do you like them?" Doubtless the presence of the soldiers, well prepared to meet any crisis, with the knowledge that several other regiments of veterans were within easy distance, influenced the rioters to submit quietly to the inevitable; let us also hope that time and conscience had shown them the terrible wickedness and the supreme folly of their previous conduct.

At the usual hour that evening several regiments of the New York militia marched on to the Washington Parade Ground for their dress parades. Their appearance was very fine in their untarnished and showy uniforms, accompanied by full brass-bands, exhibiting in a marked degree the fascinating phase of holiday soldiery. Their friends, many thousand in number, applauded loudly as they went through their various exercises in a highly creditable manner, the entire vicinity being packed by a deeply interested crowd. As the last regiment marched off the Thirty-seventh marched on. The contrast could not have been greater. From the holiday parade to an exhibition of the veteran fresh from the fields of deadly strife, the change was instantaneous and striking. The curious throng became silent in a moment, and every movement of the visiting regiment was watched with the most earnest and sympathetic curiosity. The men, women and children seemed to realize that they looked upon a leaf from the great book of war, startling in its vivid reality. Those sturdy, bronzed men were in the midst of their term of service.

Neither flushed with the ardor of departing volunteers, to whom hope and chance gave a rosy future, nor gladdened by the termination of an honorable service, with the blessed anticipation of a speedy return to the joys of home, the veterans who now came upon the stage could only look forward to continued sacrifice, to wounds and suffering and death. Their dilapidated garments, while made as presentable as possible, had protected their wearers in the trenches across the Rappahannock, in the terrible marches in pursuit of Lee, had been torn by the cannonade at Gettysburg, soaked and rent in the hand-built intrenchments of that fateful field and on the horrible by-ways of Catoctin Mountain. Marked, indeed, was the contrast between those rags and the holiday attire of New York's pet regiments.

Never did the sturdy arms of Drum Major Gaffney wake more animating response than when his drum corps performed its part that evening, and the entire command seemed nerved to its very best. From the first command given by the colonel every movement was executed as though by an automaton. From the assembled multitude burst an irresistible wave of applause, so earnest and long continued that the succeeding orders were delayed to allow it to abate. Finally the order was given to "Raise arms!"—the most difficult known to infantry tactics for a regiment to perform in perfect cadence. As though one intelligence animated the entire line, every back was bent as one and every form assumed its perpendicular. The enthusiasm of the surrounding multitude could no longer be restrained. Like a peal of thunder, applause and cheers burst forth, drowning every effort of Colonel Edwards to make his own vigorous voice heard, and the parade was summarily dismissed.

Through the following day and till afternoon of the 21st the Thirty-seventh remained on duty, with no serious menace of a riot, when they were relieved and returned to the quarters near Fort Hamilton. The days which succeeded were uneventful. The usual routine was strictly followed, the men going sometimes to the city on passes, but more frequently strolling away to gather blackberries, which grew abundantly at no great distance from the fort. On the 30th of August Colonel Edwards received a two-weeks' furlough, and Colonel Day was assigned to the command of the post. On the 11th of September Colonel Edwards returned, and the men having learned of his marriage during his absence thoroughly appreciated the following order, which was read that evening at dress parade :

> In view of the brilliant success attending the recent expedition to the West of our gallant and Union-loving commander, Colonel Edwards, and of his return to us with his fair bride, it is hereby ordered that all prisoners confined at this date in the regimental guard-house be unconditionally released and returned to duty.
>
> By order of Lieutenant-Colonel MONTAGUE, Commanding.

At the same time orders were issued for the regiment to hold itself in readiness to move at short notice, it being understood that it was to report for duty in New York city, but it was not till next day that transportation was furnished and farewell was bid to Fort Hamilton. The rumor as to destination proved correct, the command landing in the upper part of the city and marching to "Camp Canby," on Columbia College grounds, Forty-ninth Street between Fifth and Sixth Avenues. Neglecting to pitch their tents that night, the men sleeping upon the ground received the full force of a hard shower, but merely drew their rubber blankets a little closer with the remark that it seemed like Virginia to feel the rain once more driving in their faces.

Two days were devoted to getting the camp in order, and when it was done the Thirty-seventh found itself delightfully situated. The grounds were in the most pleasant portion of the city, being high and salubrious, the air pure and invigorating, the surroundings all that could be asked. It was at that time the general expectation among both officers and men that they would remain there through the winter. It was known that General Canby, after a critical inspection of each regiment in and about the city, had given the Thirty-seventh the award of the best order and discipline and had forwarded to the War Department a request to retain that regiment and the Fifth Wisconsin. On the 2d of September Captain Mulloy had been dispatched to Washington to bring on the company and regimental property which had been left behind when the regiment hurried through, and the command seemed now comfortably settled for a permanent stay. About this time Governor Andrew of Massachusetts visited the camp, his presence awakening no little interest among the members, while less noted citizens of the old Bay State continually sought out the regiment.

Three companies were detailed for special duty on the 15th,— D at the head-quarters of the Provost Marshal, F at the police head-quarters and G at the depot of government supplies. Smaller details of officers and men were made for other duties in various parts of the city between Central Park and White Street, and thus engaged the regiment passed a month of routine.

October 13 was a day of quiet bustle about the regimental head-quarters, the various detachments throughout the city were called in, and at dress parade that evening orders—the existence of which had already been suspected by the men—were read directing Colonel Edwards to report with his command to Major General Halleck at Washington. Hearty cheers were given for the Army of the Potomac, but it must be admitted that the tidings were far from welcome. It was simply human nature for the men to hope that they might pass a few months more, convenient to friends and the amenities of such a life as they had for a time been allowed to enjoy, rather than in the dangers and exposures of the trenches and the unending march through a hostile region. There was little sleep that night, from a multitude of causes, and early morning found the command in readiness to move.

Fortunately the regiment had been spared the necessity of shedding blood during its stay in the city, and it had performed faithfully every duty which came to it, winning high praise from all under whose notice it came; but it had none the less been exposed to serious dangers and had in a certain respect suffered. The scattering of the men about the city on duty and the laudable wish to allow them every privilege consistent with reasonable precaution for their well-being exposed them to the influence of the designing scoundrels and Southern sympathizers with whom the city was filled, and who spared no effort to corrupt and entice from duty. Citizens' clothes were furnished to all who could be induced to wear them and leave the service, while transportation to Canada—that land of refuge for deserters and traitors—was ready to take the refugee beyond danger of recapture and punishment. The total loss to the regiment from this cause was 47 during the 70 days of its absence from the Army of the Potomac. This was more than one-half of the loss of the Thirty-seventh by desertion during the entire service of the regiment, (as will be seen by reference to the Appendix,) and it must also in justice be stated that it was confined almost entirely to the foreign-born element. The victims—for in many cases they were more sinned against than sinning—fell among their countrymen, of whom the disloyal and riotous element in New York was so largely composed, were plied with vile liquors and viler persuasions, and in this way many who were naturally brave and true were led from their allegiance. But while this loss seemed so serious, coming within so brief a period,—a large percentage of the absentees disappearing after it was known that the regiment was ordered back to the front,—it assured the loyalty of those who remained. From that time forward desertion was almost unknown in the history of the Thirty-seventh regiment. All whose fidelity wavered, or could by any influence be made to waver, had now left the regiment; the loss had after all been far less than might have been expected, and the firm battalion which on that crisp October morning turned its face toward Washington was one of whose courage and steadiness any commander might well be proud.

CHAPTER XI.

AGAIN AT THE FRONT

THE RETURN TRIP.—THE FORTUNES OF THE ARMY.—THE VICTORY AT RAPPAHANNOCK STATION.—THE DISMAL EXPEDITION TO MINE RUN.—CHANGES AND PROMOTIONS.

Farewell was spoken to Camp Canby at 8 o'clock in the morning of October 14, and in their best attire the Thirty-seventh marched down Fifth Avenue and Broadway to the foot of Murray street. Here a steamer was in waiting near the Russian fleet which had for some time been lying in the harbor, and while the members of the regiment were awaiting the departure of their own boat much time was spent in watching the unfamiliar foreigners, whose sympathy with the United States government was thus agreeably manifested. It was not till 3 o'clock in the afternoon that all was ready for the departure, when the steamer left the wharf and moved steadily down the harbor to Port Monmouth, where the regiment disembarked, took the cars and rode through the night.

Philadelphia was reached at 7 o'clock next morning, and, in accordance with the unvarying custom of that City of Brotherly Love, a sumptuous repast was furnished at the Volunteer Refreshment Saloon. Not till noon was a train in readiness for the continuation of the journey, and it was after dark when Baltimore was reached. Supper was provided there,—not of the Philadelphia standard, but good and satisfactory,—and a few hours later the command was packed upon freight cars and crept toward Washington, which was reached soon after daylight of the 16th. With a halt of but a few minutes the regiment proceeded on its way, being directed by General Halleck to report to General Meade. Crossing Long Bridge and passing through Alexandria, it steamed slowly back over the route it had followed in coming north ten weeks before, but it is needless to say that the emotions of the men were quite different from those experienced on the upward trip. To add to the discomfort of the occasion, it commenced raining heavily just as the cars halted at Fairfax Station, shortly before noon. The officers suffered most. In their best dress, with no covering save their fine new overcoats, which had scarcely been worn, they were more exposed than the men, who generally possessed rubber blankets which gave them a partial protection. A laugh was raised and good feeling kept up by Captain J. L. Hayden, the best of campaigners and sanguine enough to find something cheerful in any outlook, who came up where the disconsolate group of officers were standing in the mud and jerked out with his habitual quick utterance, "Let us all cry!"

Stopping in the pelting storm for the men to draw rations,— a not very pleasant duty under the circumstances,—the march was taken up toward Fairfax Court House, which was reached about dark and a halt made for such a supper as was possible under the circumstances. The rain-fall, severe at first, had steadily increased in volume until it seemed an unbroken sheet, and already the clayey soil had become a spongy bed of mud several inches in depth, through which in the intense darkness it was next to impossible to travel. After stumbling on for a mile or two a halt was ordered, and the men with a refinement of irony advised one another to "make themselves comfortable for the night." Standing with heads bent toward the storm till the fury of it somewhat abated, a bivouac was made in the mud, the contrast from the carpeted tents in New York to which the mind would revert being disagreeable enough.

The storm ceased during the night, the following day proving as delightful as a Virginian October day could be, and although the mud remained in provoking quantity, it rapidly disappeared before the bright sunshine and the gentle breeze. The march was resumed at daybreak, in the direction of Chantilly, and about midday the Thirty-seventh sighted the Army of the Potomac, disposed in battle array on the ground swept over by the conflict of September 1, 1862. The arrival of the regiment being reported to General Meade, it was ordered to the Sixth Corps and by General Sedgwick assigned to its old place in Eustis's Brigade. Its return was gladly hailed by the other regiments, and with a feeling of being at home once more it took its place in the second line of battle.

While officers and enlisted men alike are busy during the uneventful afternoon in drying their clothing, writing letters to the friends from whom they have so recently separated, gossiping with acquaintances in the other regiments, or resting idly in the grateful warmth of the sunshine, let us see how it is that the Army of the Potomac is again almost at the gates of Washington in defensive position against an expected attack.

At the close of July, when the Thirty-seventh had set out upon its mission of peace, it had left the two armies concentrated respectively near Warrenton and Culpeper, with the Rappahannock as a dividing line between the outposts. On the 1st of August General Buford of the Union cavalry made a strong reconnaissance across the river, driving back the enemy's mounted outposts till his infantry lines were reached, and not long afterward General Lee retired to a stronger defensive position south of the Rapidan. Early in September Longstreet's corps was detached from the Army of Northern Virginia, Pickett's division being sent south of Richmond, while the other two went to the assistance of Bragg at Chattanooga. Although his own army was seriously weakened by the dispatch of so many of his best regiments to New York, while other detachments had been sent to South Carolina, Meade on learning of Longstreet's absence planned to move against his antagonist. Accordingly, on the 13th of September the cavalry, supported by the Second and Sixth Corps, crossed the Rappahannock, pushed the enemy's outposts before them and advanced to the Rapidan, where the infantry took position, while Buford's horsemen set out to feel the way for a movement of the army by the right flank via the upper Rapidan. Before this movement had taken form, however, it was checked by orders from Washington, while the Eleventh and Twelfth Corps were detached from the Army of the Potomac and dispatched under command of Hooker to operate against the Confederate army in Tennessee.

Meade's army having been somewhat strengthened by the return of a portion of his detached regiments, he was cautiously feeling the ground on his right when on the 9th of October he learned that some movement was being made by Lee, and the following day it became evident that the latter was moving past the Union right flank and threatening its rear and the communications with Washington. General Meade seems to have supposed that Lee intended to offer him battle near Warrenton, and moved his own army in accordance with that supposition ; but the mistake was discovered in season to make new dispositions before the enemy became aware of the error. Meade, finding that he could not fight on ground of his own choosing in the vicinity of Warrenton, resolved to take up a position at Centreville and Chantilly, north of the disastrous Bull Run fields, and accordingly moved his forces with all speed in that direction. It was a curious race which resulted. The opposing armies were moving over parallel routes, almost abreast, and so near each other that collisions of outposts and detached parties were constantly occurring, keeping both armies sharply on the lookout, yet neither aware of the purpose or the exact location of the other.

While this scramble for position was going on a remarkable incident occurred. On the 13th the Confederate cavalry leader Stuart, who was feeling the way in advance of Lee's infantry, came upon the head of General French's Third Corps and was obliged to retreat with his force of some 2,000 men. Halting for the night in a growth of scrub pines, the bold cavalryman was astounded to find that he had taken refuge between the two main columns of the Union advance, the Second Corps, now commanded by General Warren, interposing between his small force and the main body of Confederates, while Gregg's cavalry was on the other side. Sending scouts through the Union lines to make known his critical situation and solicit assistance, Stuart waited till near daylight when he opened fire upon Caldwell's division in his front, the men of which were just lighting their fires to prepare breakfast. Quite unprepared for any such hostile demonstration, the exposed troops were moved to shelter on the other side of the hill, where they were again fired upon by Ewell's advance, coming up in the other direction. In the confusion Stuart made good his escape with slight loss, and the imperiled division of the Second Corps found itself in turn almost surrounded by the enemy. Some very sharp fighting followed, before the entanglement was cleared up, but no general engagement ensued, since that was the farthest from the thoughts of either party at that time and place. Meade's several corps were striving to move up past Bristoe's Station before the Confederates should come down upon his flank with sufficient strength to cut his army in two, while Lee was straining the powers of his men to the utmost in the hope that he might reach that point in advance of the Federal columns. That object, indeed, failed, but Hill's corps, coming down from New Baltimore on the northwest, while Ewell advanced from the southwest, was in time to interpose between the Fifth Corps, which had just passed, and the Second Corps, the rear of the Union army, which had all day been skirmishing with and holding back Ewell's corps in their rear. Warren's command thus found itself attacked front and rear with the entire Southern army closing about it. A very gallant fight was made by the three brigades which Warren was able to bring into action, and the rebel attack was repulsed with the capture of 450 prisoners, five pieces of artillery and two Confederate battle flags. So prompt and effective was the resistance that all the remainder of the afternoon was spent by the Southern army in getting into position; but as soon as it was dark Warren with his wounded and prisoners followed swiftly in the tracks of the rest of the Union army, and morning of the 15th found all in position near Centreville, after four days and nights of almost incessant marching and fighting.

Here it was that two days later the Thirty-seventh had rejoined the army, the Sixth Corps holding the right of the line near Chantilly. A forward movement had been planned for the 16th, but the severe rain of that day prevented, and next day General Sedgwick reported the enemy still in his front. As

Meade wished to fight on the defensive, if possible, there was another wait in expectation of an attack. But none was made, the Southern commander also feeling a strong preference for the defensive unless he could find an opportunity to strike a sharp blow with the promise of almost certain victory. Companies F and G of the Thirty-seventh were detailed for picket on the 18th, the line being established about a mile in advance of the main position. Everything was quiet in front, and during the day all indications of the presence of the enemy ceased, quite unexpectedly, since during the previous night the picket line had become frightened at some real or supposed demonstration by the foe and was ordered to fall back upon the camp, calling the corps to arms before daybreak, the line being re-established after the excitement, with no further demonstration. In fact, Lee having failed in the principal object of his expedition, now contented himself with destroying as much as possible of the Orange and Alexandria railroad and falling back nearer his own base of supplies. His purpose being penetrated by the Union commander, orders were issued Sunday evening, the 18th, for an advance in pursuit next morning, the men, owing to the uncertain nature of the communications being provided with eight days' rations. In respect to this matter of rations, it was not in human nature to refrain from fault-finding, since in addition to the enormous load which the men were required to carry, the quality was of the poorest—the crackers being wormy and the meat consisting of salt ham of very indifferent quality.

The pickets were called in at daybreak Monday morning, and the men made an early breakfast preparatory to the march. While they were thus engaged a sudden and furious shower burst, tearing down tents and drenching everything in a flood of rain: but such experiences had become too common to elicit more than passing remark. The exposed soldiers merely protected themselves and their possessions as well as they could till the first fury of the storm abated, when the order to march was issued.

Passing to the westward of Centreville and taking the Warrenton turnpike, the column pushed steadily forward all day with no event of importance to thrill the jaded frames, though there was much in the region passed through to interest the members of the Thirty-seventh, covering as it did the scene of the two battles of Bull Run and so many minor encounters and strategic movements extending over almost the entire period of the war. In every direction were to be seen strong fortifications standing as they had been left by one or the other of the contending parties, wasting away by the slow erosion of time and storm; graves, marked or unmarked, were scattered everywhere; while skeletons of animals and even of men once partially buried dotted the neglected and desolate fields. Gainesville was reached near night and the men, well exhausted by the heavy march of 14 miles, had pitched their shelters, eaten their suppers, and were about lying down to sleep, when heavy artillery firing was heard at the left, and almost simultaneously the command to "Pack up and fall in!" rang sharply forth. It was obeyed, the column made a rapid march of half a mile, stood in line for an hour, then returned to the former bivouac. It was merely "the cavalry again!" Kilpatrick had during the afternoon been pressing the enemy's rear guard sharply, inflicting considerable damage, but toward night was drawn into a trap and attacked from two or three directions by a superior force, driven back to and through the lines of the First Corps, the pursuers following so closely as to "gobble up" quite a number of the disordered infantry and take them away in triumph. Satisfied with what they had accomplished, the triumphant Confederate horsemen wheeled about and the retreat of Lee was without further resistance continued beyond the Rappahannock.

Eight o'clock next morning, the 20th, saw the Thirty-seventh again on the road, and after a leisurely march till about 2 in the afternoon a halt was made near New Baltimore, not far from the spot where they passed several days the previous fall at the time of Burnside's taking command of the army. About dusk, after the bivouac was well disposed for the night, the unwelcome order to "Pack up!" was once more heard, and the column dragged along through the darkness toward Warrenton, which was reached at 10 o'clock, the regiment halting for the night about half a mile east of the town. There the following day and night were passed, but on the 22d camp was changed to the hills a mile or so to the northwest of the town, very near the point of the regiment's location at the time it was summoned to New York. Here the camp was more carefully located and a week of quiet ensued, with very little duty for the men, while the railroad was being repaired and other preparations made for the continuation of the campaign. At this time General Meade wished to change his base to Fredericksburg by a rapid movement, but permission for the transfer was not granted by General Halleck.

Ten days passed with no other change than the visible waning of the year. While the days were generally pleasant and bright, the nights were frequently so cold as to make the duties of the pickets and guards anything but pleasant; and it was evident that whatever campaigning was to be done before winter must be undertaken soon. Nor were other evidences of an intended movement absent. A brigade review and inspection was held on Sunday, the 1st of November, and the following day there was a division review by General Sedgwick. Tuesday the camp was changed about a mile, being located nearer Warrenton on the Salem turnpike, and then came another respite till Friday, the 6th, when definite orders were issued for a movement at an early hour next morning.

As before stated, the Confederate army had retired behind the Rappahannock, and was at that time engaged in building huts for the winter quarters of the men, Lee evidently anticipating no further trouble from the Army of the Potomac. General Sedgwick with the Fifth Corps in addition to his own, forming the right of the army, was directed to move against Rappahannock Station, while General French with the First, Second and Third Corps was to attempt a crossing at Kelly's Ford, a few miles to the south. The latter column moving from Warrenton Junction while Sedgwick advanced from Warrenton, the routes were almost parallel and of practically equal length, and the march being unopposed by the enemy, there was every probability that the two crossings would be reached at about the same time, and the importance of vigor in all subsequent proceedings was impressed upon all concerned. The initial operations were remarkably successful.

Reveille broke the dark air at 4 o'clock on the morning of the 7th and the Thirty-seventh was soon in readiness for the orders to move, which were not received till 7 o'clock. The morning was bright and pleasant, but not even the rich sunlight could remove the gloom of desolation which hung over the town of Warrenton, which had so long lain in the path of receding and advancing armies. The business which had formerly made its streets lively had entirely disappeared, and a large proportion of the inhabitants seemed to have gone with it. Many of the houses were uninhabited and more or less wrecked, while the few inhabitants who were visible seemed to have abundant cause for the sourness and sadness written upon their faces. Poor Virginia! She had taken the sword, and terribly was she perishing by the sword : her homes shrouded in one universal pall of mourning, her fields desolate and her streets deserted. Brave indeed were her sons, and no less heroic her daughters in the cause of their mistaken espousal; the world will ever accord them that just praise, and none more cheerfully and fully than those who bore arms against them; yet none can look back upon those desolate scenes, even after the lapse of a generation, without a vivid realization of the wickedness and pity of human warfare.

The sharp chill of the night and early morning disappeared as the day advanced, and the column pressed steadily on till about noon, when the thunder of artillery but a few miles in advance showed that the head of Sedgwick's column had struck the Confederate outposts. The pace was at once quickened, a strong wind and dusty roads making the movement anything but agreeable. A part of the way the march was beside the railroad, or rather the road bed, for every rail and tie had been removed by the enemy, as a precaution against their use by the Yankee army. At 2 o'clock the scene of action was approached and soon the shells from the enemy's batteries began to explode in the vicinity of the Thirty-seventh. Close column by divisions was formed and the regiment advanced under the shelter of a slight hill, lying in the rear of a battery which was doing fine execution. The fight was already in earnest progress, and as the Thirty-seventh was moved to its place in the supporting line the enemy's skirmishers were driven back, but it was not till dusk that the Confederate works were assaulted.

The position occupied by the detachment of Lee's army which Sedgwick now confronted was an unusual and as the result proved an unfortunate one. On the north bank of the Rappahannock at this point some earthworks previously constructed by the Union army had been taken possession of by the Confederates and altered and strengthened so as to form a formidable barrier in case the Federals should approach the river at that place. They could only be reached by a front attack over low ground swept for half a mile by the Confederate artillery. On confronting them, General Sedgwick deployed the Sixth Corps to the right of the railroad and the Fifth to the left, and obtaining possession of commanding ground near the bank of the river on each flank posted his heavy guns and endeavored by a severe artillery fire to drive out the defenders. This attempt, however, proved fruitless, as the Confederate guns sent back shot for shot with unabated vigor. The garrison in the works when Sedgwick's forces deployed in their front consisted of Hays's Louisiana brigade of Early's division of Ewell's corps, and Hoke's brigade of North Carolinians of the same division was sent over to reinforce them—making a force of about 2,000 men, and as the Confederate commanders believed enough to hold the position in the face of all the Yankees who could be brought against it.

General Sedgwick having command of the entire operations at this point, the Sixth Corps was in the immediate command for the first time in action of General Horatio G. Wright, of the First Division, General David A. Russell of the Third Brigade taking charge of the division. Russell, after a thorough inspection of the ground in his front, decided that an assault was practicable, and on receiving permission to make it selected his own brigade and the Second of the same division, commanded respectively by Colonels Ellmaker and Upton. With a heavy artillery fire from both flanks covering the movement, the assaulting column advanced through the gathering dusk, crossed the ditch, scaled the parapet and poured into the works almost before their intent was comprehended. General Russell went over the works with the men of his command, and in the fierce hand-to-hand fight that briefly followed one of his colonels, thinking his general in too dangerous quarters, called out to his soldiers to "Rally on the General!" To which the brave leader replied, "Rally on the rebs, men, rally on the rebs!" The Sixth Maine and Fifth Wisconsin led in the principal attack, supported by the other regiments of their brigade, while the One Hundred and Twenty-first New York and Fifth Maine of Upton's brigade carried the rifle pits to the right and completed the occupation. The skirmish line of the Fifth Corps, also, catching the enthusiasm of the moment, broke through on the left of the railroad, and almost in a moment more than three-fourths of the garrison were killed, wounded or captives, the remainder having succeeded in escaping across the ponton bridge to the south side of the river, including General Hays, who escaped by his horse taking fright after the general had been made a prisoner. The total Union loss was 371 in killed, wounded and missing, while General Early reported his loss at 1,672 men, four cannon and eight battle flags. Considering that the defenders fully equaled in numbers the assaulting column, and that the attack was everywhere successful at the first attempt, the capture of Rappahannock Station must be regarded as one of the most brilliant actions of the war.

The mission of General French had been equally successful. Arriving in the vicinity of Kelly's Ford about noon, he found the crossing guarded by a detachment from Rodes's division of Ewell's corps posted behind rifle-pits on the south bank of the river. The Third Corps, commanded by General Birney, while French had the general command, was in advance, and acted with commendable vigor. Posting his artillery to sweep the southern bank, where a wide plain was commanded by the higher ground on the northern side, Birney forded his First Division across the river, the water up to their waists, and immediately charged the rifle-pits with six regiments, capturing 500 prisoners with next to no loss on his own part. The initial operations had thus been eminently successful at both points; the Confederates had sustained a loss of over 2,000 men, and the crossing of the river had been accomplished under circumstances to inspirit the Federal soldiers in the highest degree. But the early promise was not to bear its fruit.

The Thirty-seventh remained during the night in about the position it had taken on reaching the field. Late in the evening, after the fighting was over and the fruits of the victory secured, permission was given to build fires sufficient for the making of coffee, and the little warmth which they were thus enabled to obtain was very grateful to the chilled, weary and hungry soldiers. With rapid wings the news of the good work in front traveled to the supporting lines, which could only judge of the progress being made by the sound of the firing and cheering, and presently squads of prisoners came trooping back to the rear, showing that the favorable reports were in no wise exaggerated. "Where is your army going now?" asks a good-natured Yankee as the long string of captives files past. "Going to see Father Abraham and get some soft bread." replies one; "To see the drafted men from New York!" retorts another with a little bitterness in his tone.

Daylight of the 8th found the Thirty-seventh again on the march, making its way down the river toward Kelly's Ford, from which the additional good news of French's success had been received during the night. Before noon a halt was made in the woods not far from the Ford, the men improved the opportunity of fuel and freedom to cook as good a dinner as their stores of provision would allow, and then waited all the afternoon for further orders. These came near sunset when the regiment was moved a short distance and assigned the duty of picketing the road leading to the Ford. in which position it remained during the night, and, contrary to all expectation, for two days and nights ensuing. Lee had again escaped, fearing to await the attack of Meade's elated army, and retired beyond the Rapidan, making Gordonsville his base of supplies.

Early Wednesday morning, November 11, the regiment retraced its steps to Rappahannock Station, crossed the river on a bridge which had been constructed by General Meade's ponton corps on the site of the one burned by Early after his disaster, advanced some six miles to the vicinity of Brandy Station, where camp was pitched and the men directed to make themselves as comfortable as possible, as they would remain there for at least two weeks and perhaps more. This intelligence was not greeted with cheers, since the location was scarcely an ideal one for a camp, the situation being exposed and wood having to be brought a long distance. But the days wore away with their dull routine, the chills of early winter sharpened the air more and more, cold, heavy rains made day and night alike uncomfortable, and November approached its close, while uncertainty and expectation hung over the camps. Yet there was no indication of an intention on the part of General Meade to put his army into winter quarters till he had again crossed swords with his wily antagonist. A regimental inspection on the 16th was had by Captain Young of the Second Rhode Island, the brigade inspector, and on the 20th a review of the Sixth Corps was held by General Sedgwick. Meantime the paymaster had visited camp, but brought little money to the members of the Thirty-seventh, as their extra expenses for clothing and other supplies while in New York had drawn heavily upon their allowances.

During this interval of inaction General Meade had not been idle. While waiting for the completion of the railroad to Rappahannock Station, which was made his base of supplies, he had gained pretty accurate knowledge of the position of Lee's army, which he found to be spread out for some 20 miles over the country beyond the Rapidan, with the fords of that river imperfectly guarded. Meade's plan of operations contemplated a rapid movement of his own army by different routes, penetrating between the separated corps of his antagonist and fighting and defeating them in detail. Orders were issued on the 23d for a movement the following morning; the men were provided with several days' rations, as the plan contemplated the moving of the army without wagon trains or any incumbrance which could by any possibility be avoided. The morning of the 24th brought a cold, disagreeable storm, which lasted most of the day, and though camps were struck before daylight and the men in shivering squads awaited orders to fall in, none came during that day or the next. The storm had caused a delay till the roads had opportunity to settle somewhat, but the orders were renewed for the 26th, and that morning knapsacks and haversacks were slung and the "Mine Run movement" began.

It was Thanksgiving day in Massachusetts, as the sons of that State well remembered—was that a fortunate omen for their expedition? Before setting forth the men were cheered by news of the success of General Grant in the West, and there was need enough of whatever encouragement they could receive at the outset, for they found little enough afterward. The roads were still muddy, and as the Sixth Corps followed the Third they found the way more trying than it would otherwise have been. Making slow progress, though at great expenditure of physical energy, the column toiled along all day and far into the night. The latter portion of the journey was the more unpleasant as it was through a dark wood where the uncertain road was rough and extremely muddy. The movement had now become very spasmodic, the column halting and starting at uncertain intervals but with no indication of approaching bivouac. The woods were filled with stragglers who had issued their own orders for a halt, kindled fires and were cooking their suppers and making themselves generally comfortable. Finally at about 10 o'clock the Rapidan was crossed at Jacob's Mill Ford and a mile beyond the thoroughly exhausted regiment came to a halt, those who were not too much exhausted making fires over which their "Thanksgiving Dinner" of coffee and "hard tack" was prepared. The most sumptuous repast could not have been more welcome. An early start next morning was expected, and the camp was astir betimes, but the entire day wore away, as well as the early part of the night, with no change of the regiment's position. Heavy firing could be heard in front at intervals, giving evidence that the advance was being contested, but only surmises came back to the listeners. The situation was terribly uncomfortable. The weather was cold, chilling and almost freezing the men, especially at night, while the momentary expectation of orders to continue the march precluded the possibility of making themselves more comfortable.

Silence at last reigned over the forest, the men were sleeping and the fires had generally burned out, when at 1 o'clock the bugle rang its unwelcome call, the men scrambled to their feet, packed their frozen blankets as best they could, and presently moved forward. Under the circumstances the march was necessarily slow, but it continued till daylight when a halt was made for breakfast, followed by a rest of an hour, after which the slow toil was resumed and continued till near noon. The route followed—if route it could be called—was an extremely difficult one, leading through the forest, often filled with undergrowth which the column could with difficulty penetrate, generally along some obscure by-way and often through regions where apparently the foot of man had never before wandered. A considerable conflict was evidently going on in front, and the regiment had reached a point in the immediate rear of the Union lines from which the men expected each moment to be ordered into action, though the all-enveloping thicket prevented any view of what might be transpiring in the immediate vicinity, when a heavy, cold rain began to fall and the firing very soon ceased, with the exception of an occasional cannon shot and the inevitable fusillade of the skirmishers. The Thirty-seventh fell back into the forest for a short distance, built fires and remained through the afternoon and part of the night. Let us see what had been transpiring in the mean time.

General Meade's intention, as we have said, was to pass the right flank of Lee's army, penetrate between the corps of Hill and Ewell before they could unite, and defeat them in detail. Lee's front at that time extended from Barnet's Ford, northeast of Orange Court House, down the Rapidan to Mine Run, a small stream entering the river at a point almost due south from Kelly's Ford on the Rappahannock. Leaving the Rapidan there, the Confederate line bent sharply to the south along Mine Run, occupying a strong position which had been well fortified for some miles back from the main stream. Evidently considering this a sufficient defense of his right flank, Lee had left the fords of the Rapidan from that point to its junction with the Rappahannock undefended, save by small cavalry outposts. South of the Rapidan and nearly parallel to it, at a distance of six or eight miles, run the old turnpike and the plank road leading from Fredericksburg to Orange Court House and passing to the rear of the rebel intrenched line. Meade's programme was for the Army of the Potomac to cross the Rapidan at the different fords, push quickly by the cross roads to these highways, and joining forces press rapidly westward, scattering the different sections of the Confederate army as they were encountered. In pursuance of this plan the Third Corps, followed by the Sixth, was to cross at Jacob's Mill Ford, a mile or two below Mine Run, and proceed to Robertson's Tavern on the turnpike. There the Third Corps, whose movements were to time those of the others, was to be joined by the Second under General Warren, which was to cross at Germanna Ford, some two miles below Jacob's Mill Ford. The Fifth Corps, followed by the First, was to cross at Culpeper Mine Ford, still further down the river, push on to Parker's Store on the plank road, at that point some two miles south of the turnpike. Such was the well-laid plan; like many another it was to meet unexpected obstacles in the execution.

In a scheme so complicated it was essential that there should be a perfect execution of the plans. The Third Corps, upon which so much depended, failed at the start, being behind time in reaching the Rapidan. Then it was found that the engineers had miscalculated the length of bridge necessary for the crossing and time was wasted in piecing out the structure with poles. At best the approaches to the bridge were so difficult that the artillery of the two corps was obliged to go down the river, cross at Germanna Ford and make its way back on the south side of the stream to rejoin the column. It was morning of the 27th, therefore, when the army found itself across the Rapidan. The Fifth Corps pushed forward with the cavalry along the plank road, reaching Parker's Store in the middle of the forenoon, encountering there the enemy's outposts, which were steadily driven back for several hours till New Hope Church was reached, where the cross road from Robertson's Tavern on the turnpike intersects the plank road. Here Sykes was directed to halt his command and await co-operation. The Second Corps had reached the Tavern shortly after noon, encountering the Confederates in considerable force, and the opposing forces were quickly thrown into line of battle, but hours passed with no tidings from French and the two corps under his command. In fact, he had proceeded but a few miles from the crossing when he became confused in regard to the road which he was expected to follow, took the wrong one, came upon the enemy, who made vigorous demonstrations against his flank, creating apprehensions of an attack in force, so that the entire day was wasted without sufficient advance on his part to allow the Sixth Corps to take the road at all, as we have seen. Finding it impracticable by the roundabout communication which alone was possible to bring the Third Corps forward promptly, General Meade sent a dispatch to General Sedgwick to move his command immediately to Robertson's Tavern, and French was directed to follow the Sixth Corps. Sedgwick needed no second bidding; hence the midnight reveille and the consequent march which had brought the Thirty-seventh so near to the front.

The Union army was at last in position, the demonstrations in French's vicinity having ceased, allowing his corps to come forward; but it was a position which should have been occupied at least 24 hours before, and those hours had not been wasted by the Confederate chieftain. Early apprised of the movement of the Army of the Potomac, and divining its intent, Lee had rapidly strengthened his line in the rear of Mine Run, extending it so as to fully cover the turnpike and the plank road. Having by the preliminary skirmishing gained time for this purpose, he now withdrew to his main position and with smiling confidence awaited the onset of his antagonist.

The position of the Confederate army was along a range of hights half a mile or more in the rear of Mine Run. The stream itself was difficult of passage, its banks being marshy and fringed with bushes and vines. Beyond it a gentle slope led up to the enemy's position, swept every foot of the way by their fire and filled with abatis and other obstructions. Having advanced as far as practicable without a conflict, General Meade disposed his army in front of the Run in this order: General Newton's First Corps formed the center, lying just south of the old turnpike, with the Fifth Corps on its right and the Third on its left. General Sedgwick with his First and Second Divisions was thrown well to the right, while his Third Division, which had for some time been under the command of General Terry, was detached to co-operate with the Second Corps in feeling for a more vulnerable point to the left.

Accordingly the men of the Thirty-seventh found themselves aroused at 1 o'clock in the morning of Sunday, the 29th, drew a small additional supply of rations, and before daylight were on their way, passing Robertson's Tavern, through to the plank road and beyond it, around the head of Mine Run, the advance skirmishing continually with the enemy's outposts and driving them back till near night, when General Warren, believing that he had found a comparatively weak point, so reported to Meade and disposed his forces for the attack whenever it should be ordered. General Sedgwick from the right also reported that he deemed an assault in his front practicable. General Warren was strengthened with two divisions from the Third Corps and directed to attack at 8 o'clock next morning in connection with a heavy artillery fire from the center, while Sedgwick was to "go in" an hour later.

The Thirty-seventh were in reserve during the night of the 29th, lying on their arms and sleeping as much as possible in the intense cold, which had now become so intolerable that men were frozen to death on the picket line. Early in the morning the regiment was moved forward to the front line, taking position on the extreme left. It was terribly uncomfortable lying upon the frozen ground hour after hour waiting for the signal to spring to their feet and dash forward into the face of death, and the men would almost have welcomed the command, since it would have stirred the blood and warmed the benumbed limbs;

but it did not come. The morning's inspection of the works in his front revealed to Warren that his intention to attack had been anticipated, that the enemy had used the entire night in extending and strengthening the fortifications, that the latter were filled to the utmost capacity with exultant defenders and bristling with cannon which had not been there the previous evening. Warren reported the discouraging outlook to his commander and awaited orders. Meade sent a hasty order to Sedgwick, who was waiting the passage of the few intervening moments to hurl his human avalanche against the foe, directing him to suspend the attack, and hurried to a personal consultation with Warren.

The judgment of the lieutenant was confirmed on inspection by the general commanding. The plan of attack which on the previous afternoon had seemed feasible was now seen to be hazardous to the degree of rashness. The two points of assault were fully five miles apart, rendering perfect co-operation very difficult; there were no reserves to follow up and secure any advantage which the attacking columns might gain; but above all there was the extreme doubt of any lodgment being made in the hostile works. The common soldiers saw the desperate outlook as clearly as their generals. They had never shrunk from the call of duty—they never would; but with firm fingers each man had written his name and pinned it upon his blouse that his dead body might be identified when the burial parties should do their sad work!

To make other dispositions of the army—to search for an undefended flank or a practicable point of attack on a concentrated foe whom Meade believed his equal in numbers—would require time, while the rations with which his men set out were nearly exhausted, and his supply trains were under cavalry guard beyond the Rapidan. The steadily increasing cold weather seemed to indicate the setting in of a severe winter, and reluctantly the orders were issued which should record upon the movement the verdict of "failure."

All day the Thirty-seventh remained in their uncomfortable position, the skirmishers and sharp-shooters in front keeping up an incessant fusillade, though by rare good fortune the loss was only one or two men wounded. There were plenty of narrow escapes, as always at such times, among them being that of Chaplain Morse, who on one of his several visits from the hospitals in the rear to the regiment at the front was fired at and narrowly missed by a sharp-shooter on two occasions. At night the regiment was relieved and with the rest of the division marched back to the turnpike, some three miles, where the Sixth Corps was reunited, the other two divisions having been recalled from their advanced position at the right. Large fires were made and the men went to sleep about them, but as soon as the flames died away the torturing cold reasserted its cruel power, and long before daylight the camp was voluntarily astir, building fires and preparing breakfast, in the expectation of being presently called to sterner duty.

But all that day, December 1, wore away with no summons till evening, after many of the men had disposed themselves to sleep, when the familiar invitation to "Pack up and fall in lively!" rang through the oak forest, and at 9 o'clock the column sped swiftly back toward the Rapidan, but not by the route which it had traversed in coming through the wood and which had proved such an entanglement to the Third Corps. Following the turnpike back to its junction with the Brock road, a mile or so east of the Old Wilderness Tavern, and then turning nearly due north, the regiment crossed the Rapidan at Ely's Ford about daylight, and after making a mile or two on the north side of the river halted for breakfast and rested till noon. Most of the men and the officers as well slept during the wait, for the night's march had been swift and continuous and they were severely exhausted. The mounted officers had shared their horses with line officers, enlisted men and servants, who were unable otherwise to accompany the column, and thus nearly every member of the command was in his place when the regiment halted, and the few who were behind soon came up.

The march was resumed at midday, and the tottering column, sore, stiff and weary, plodded along till after dark, crossing Mountain Run where they had crossed it a week before in going out, and soon afterward the Thirty-seventh halted in a piece of woods for the night. The ground was low and marshy, with frequent pools of water into which the men stumbled, but they gave little heed to the discomforts. Wrapping themselves in their blankets, officers and men alike threw themselves upon the ground and slept the sleep of exhaustion till morning. As it was now certain that the regiment was near the old camp, and hence probable that they were to return there, the men devoured for breakfast what little food remained in their haversacks, in many cases ardently wishing it were more, and shortly afterward resumed the march, which led directly back to the old camp,— quitted seven days before for one of the most tedious, exhausting, depressing and apparently fruitless expeditions in the history of the army. History will justify,—it has already justified, —the wisdom of General Meade; but the thinking men who made up the army could not then comprehend as they now do the unfortunate combination of circumstances which conspired to defeat the skillful plans of the general commanding, and it was not remarkable that there was bitterness of feeling and of speech among those who had endured the severe sufferings of the bootless campaign.

Tents were hastily pitched during the afternoon and three days' rations drawn, but the camp was not at once to settle into dull routine. When in possession of the new supply of rations, the men prepared bountiful suppers and crept into their tents under the warning to be ready to move at a moment's notice. A little later they were called up to draw more rations and took the occasion to eat some more supper, after which they returned to their blankets and were not again disturbed that night. Next day details were made for guard and picket, the camp lines were established and a settled conviction began to be felt, despite all manner of camp rumors as to possible expeditions in the near future, that winter quarters would now be established. Within a few days that conviction deepened into certainty, the site for a new camp was selected and the men set to work upon it, patterning closely after "Camp Edwards," the famous habitation of the previous winter.

Up to this time several additional changes had taken place among the officers of the regiment. Second Lieutenant Harrigan of Company K resigned October 30, and as that company, like most others in the regiment, was reduced below the number for which the government allowed the muster of a new second lieutenant, the latter vacancy remained unfilled, as did other vacancies in the same rank, except when promotion is noted. First Lieutenant Charles Phelps of Company I resigned November 17, Second Lieutenant F Edward Gray of the same company being advanced to fill the vacancy. Major Eugene A. Allen resigned November 25, and was succeeded by Captain Marcus T. Moody of Company G, whose commission bore date December 5 though he was not mustered to the new rank until January. First Lieutenant Bliss of Company G was at the same time commissioned captain, but before the receipt of the commission he resigned as first lieutenant, December 23, being influenced by family considerations, among them the death of his only brother, Captain George S. Bliss of the Fifty-second Massachusetts regiment. Second Lieutenant James C. Chalmers of Company A was promoted from December 5 to first lieutenant and assigned to Company G. The resignation of Lieutenant Bliss making another vacancy in the roster of captains, First Lieutenant John C. Robinson of Company C was promoted to date from December 24, taking command of Company G. Second Lieutenant Jones of Company F was made first lieutenant of Company C.

CHAPTER XII

WINTER ON THE RAPIDAN

THE CLOSING YEAR.—PROGRESS OF THE WAR.—THE WINTER
CAMP AND THE LIFE IN IT.—A FUTILE EXPEDITION.

Mention has been made of cheering news which came from Grant in the West as the troops of the Army of the Potomac were about to set forth on the Mine Run expedition. To see what it was we must return to Bragg and Rosecrans, whom we left, the former at Chattanooga, Ga., with the principal Confederate army west of Virginia, the latter near Stevenson, Ala., preparing to cross the Tennessee river in pursuit of his antagonist. In co-operation with Rosecrans, General Burnside took the field actively in Eastern Tennessee, capturing Frazer's brigade and Cumberland Pass September 9, thus interposing his own army between Bragg and Virginia, besides dispelling the fragmentary forces of armed Secessionists who had been maintaining a reign of terror in the region about Knoxville, and the faithful Unionists who had been obliged to flee for their lives now ventured to return to their homes again.

Bragg's position at Chattanooga was one difficult of approach by a hostile force from any direction, since it was shut in by commanding mountain ranges, with numerous creeks and rivers; but Rosecrans decided to push straight across the Tennessee, over the mountains beyond, and threatening the enemy's communications either drive him toward the interior of the Confederacy or force him to a decisive battle. With numerous feints completely deceiving Bragg as to his real intentions, the Union commander crossed the Tennessee at four different points, and the first days of September saw his army pushing its way over the ranges to the eastward. Bragg immediately evacuated

Chattanooga, moving due south some 15 or 20 miles and establishing his army along the east bank of West Chickamauga Creek, facing the advancing Union army. By this movement General Rosecrans was sadly deceived, thinking that the Confederates were in full retreat. Fearing that Bragg might attempt to escape to the westward, and again carry the theater of war into Tennessee, Rosecrans sent to Sherman for co-operation to prevent such a result, and scattered his own forces for 40 miles through the mountains to operate against the supposed fugitives.

But nothing was further from Bragg's mind than flight. He had been heavily reinforced by the merciless conscription which was being carried on through the South, by most of Johnston's available force, and finally by the two divisions from Lee's army commanded by Longstreet in person, who had made their way through the Carolinas and were now coming up via Atlanta. Most of these troops were veterans, they vastly outnumbered the Union army, even if the latter had been consolidated, while in its present scattered condition there was every hope that it might be broken up in detail with little cost to the Confederates. Rosecrans did not know of these reinforcements, but he became aware of the presence on the Chickamauga of the enemy in strong force, and easily divined Bragg's intention. By skillful dispositions and great exertions he succeeded in rescuing the scattered detachments of his army, and by the time the Confederates were ready for the attack their antagonists were tolerably ready for the defense. In fact the initial blow was struck by the Union army, though with no conception of the results which were to follow. The morning of September 19, 1863, opened the struggle. General Thomas, commanding the Union left, had thrown out a detachment in search of an isolated brigade of the enemy which had been reported on that side of the creek, but after a brief engagement found that a strong force was developing in his front. In fact Bragg had intended to throw his right under General Polk with crushing weight upon the Union left, but the engagement which ensued showed that he had somewhat mistaken the position of his antagonist, whose flank extended farther to the northward than he had anticipated. The Southern army was across the creek, however, in much stronger force than Thomas had in readiness for immediate operation against it, and the boys in blue were driven back. They were speedily reinforced and drove their antagonists in turn, and so through the day, with the advantage favoring first the Stars and Stripes and then the Stars and Bars, the battle raged with terrible desperation but without decisive result. The Union right was also repeatedly assailed, but on that part of the field every attack was repulsed and the lines stood firm.

That night Longstreet came up with a division and two brigades of fresh troops and took command of the Confederate left, in place of Hood, who had the immediate command of that wing during the first day. The fight of the 20th opened by a determined effort on the part of Polk to turn Thomas's left flank and interpose between the Union army and the Rossville Pass through Missionary Ridge to Chattanooga, but every attempt was stubbornly contested and defeated with the assistance of troops drawn from other parts of the line. On the right, meantime, owing to misunderstood orders in connection with the reinforcements sent to the left, a considerable gap was left in the line, and Longstreet's quick eye grasped the opportunity. Hood's command in overwhelming force was pushed into the opening, cutting off five brigades and inflicting upon them terrible loss. Then the whole right crumbled before the riving of this monstrous wedge of exultant victors. Brigade after brigade was struck in the flank and swept back in confused masses; Rosecrans and his corps commanders, McCook and Crittenden, were carried back with the flood which they had no power to stem ; while General Garfield, the chief of staff, was dispatched to Thomas to bear the news of disaster, urge that general to maintain his ground as long as possible, and then to hold Rossville Pass at all hazards while Rosecrans disposed his scattered forces for the defense of Chattanooga, on which they were in full retreat.

It was during the closing hours of this disastrous day that General Thomas won the sobriquet of "The Rock of Chickamauga." With a force not exceeding 25,000 men, in a position strengthened by such slight intrenchments as circumstances would permit, he received attack after attack without flinching or yielding, holding his ground determinedly against the pressure of at least twice his numbers; finally retiring one division at a time to Rossville Pass in accordance with orders,—the last to leave the field being Wood's division, whose faulty movement had opened the way for the breaking of the right. The Pass was firmly held during the following day, when all retired to the fortified lines about Chattanooga.

The battle of Chickamauga was one of the bloodiest known to modern warfare. Out of some 55,000 men engaged, the Union loss was 16,336; from the best data attainable it is estimated that Bragg lost from his 70,000 effectives present over 20,000, though in this as in so many other important battles no official report of the aggregate Confederate loss is made.

The victors did not press the vanquished, but contented themselves by taking position on the mountain ranges within a few miles of Chattanooga, whence they could look down upon the Union camps, while their position upon Lookout mountain completely closed the Tennessee river, so that Rosecrans was obliged to throw a ponton bridge across in the rear of the town and haul his supplies over the mountains 50 or 60 miles by the most wretched roads, which as soon as the autumn storms began to prevail would become utterly impassable. As it was, the army almost at once was distressed for rations, and many thousand horses and mules were lost from want of forage and by excessive work upon the roads. Clearly this situation could not long be borne without the utter overthrow of Rosecrans's command, and the Washington authorities acted with commendable promptness. The Eleventh and Twelfth Corps were withdrawn from the Army of the Potomac, as we have seen, put under the command of Hooker, and placed in position to protect Rosecrans's long lines of communication,—having marched to Washington and been transported thence by the roundabout route necessary in eight days from the time of leaving the Rappahannock. They were sadly needed, since the immense Union wagon trains, in addition to all other drawbacks, were constantly exposed to the raids of the vigilant Confederate cavalry, from which serious losses were suffered. General Burnside was also directed to move to the assistance of the Army of the Cumberland, as was Sherman from his position in Mississippi. There was change in all directions. On the 28th of September the Twentieth and Twenty-first Corps were consolidated into the Fourth and placed under command of General Gordon Granger, while McCook and Crittenden, the relieved corps commanders, were ordered north to await the result of a court of inquiry.

The crowning change was made, however, on the 16th of October, when the Departments of the Ohio, the Cumberland and the Tennessee were consolidated as "the Military Division of the Mississippi," and placed under the command of General Grant. At the same time General Rosecrans was relieved of the command of the Army of the Cumberland, to which General Thomas was assigned, the former issuing a farewell address to the command on the 19th and at once departing for his home at Cincinnati. General Grant's first order to Thomas on taking command was to hold Chattanooga at all hazards, to which Thomas, whose army had already been on half rations for a month, made answer, "We will hold the town till we starve." The important events which followed were so entirely governed by the remarkable conformation of the region about Chattanooga that a general idea of the geographical features becomes necessary.

The town is situated at the head of the valley of the same name, through which flows Chattanooga Creek, emptying into the Tennessee a few miles below the town. This valley extends in a direction somewhat south of west, and its eastern boundary is formed by Missionary Ridge, a well-defined range extending far past the town at a distance of three or four miles to the eastward. Half a dozen miles south of Chattanooga was Rossville Pass, opening through the Ridge into Chickamauga Valley, in which the battle of that name had taken place. Bending southward around the town the Tennessee flows three or four miles till it reaches the base of Lookout Mountain forming the western boundary of Chattanooga Valley, when it turns almost due north in the shape of the letter U, the inclosed tongue of land being known as Moccasin Point. Lookout Mountain, which rises very abruptly, has at the top a table land of varying width, extending back for several miles, upon which, near the northern extremity, was situated the village of Summertown. Near the western base of the mountain ran Lookout Creek, giving name to the valley through which it flowed. Beyond this valley rose the less elevated Raccoon Mountains, on the other side of which the Tennessee again resumed its general southwestern course. The Confederate main force was disposed across the valley in front of Chattanooga, their pickets close up to those of the Union army, their right extending to the northward along Missionary Ridge, while their left ran over and along the northern and western faces of Lookout. It was this left wing, composed of part of Longstreet's troops, which commanded from their elevated positions so much of the river and of the roads beyond as to necessitate the interminable mountain transportation from which the Union army was suffering.

The first movement of the campaign was planned before General Grant took command, and, as he approved it, was immediately carried out. Its object was to open a line of communication from the rear of Chattanooga across Moccasin Point and Brown's Ferry, thence through Lookout Valley, crossing the Tennessee again at Bridgeport, Ala., thus avoiding the mountains and reducing the distance one-half. To gain possession of the left bank of the river at Brown's Ferry a very brilliant night expedition was planned and successfully executed. At 3 o'clock in the morning of the 27th of October 50 squads of 24 men each were quietly embarked in as many ponton boats under the command of General W B. Hazen and without the use of oars floated down the current as near the right bank as possible till the ferry was reached. For seven miles the flotilla drifted past the Confederate picket lines without receiving a shot or being noticed, but as the oars were used to bring the boats to the landing the picket post at that point delivered a volley. The little force promptly landed, took a position to cover the ferry and began to intrench, while the boats hastened to bring over the brigade of General Turchin which had marched overland to the opposite bank. A sharp attack was made on Hazen's command, but the gallant fellows held their own and the bridge was soon completed.

At the same time General Hooker set out from Bridgeport to cross the Tennessee and open the route through Lookout Valley. General Geary's division of the Twelfth Corps was in advance and during the 28th penetrated to Wauhatchie without encountering serious opposition. After midnight, however, it was savagely assaulted by McLaws's division of Longstreet's corps, which crept upon it in the darkness hoping to take the sleeping camp by surprise. Geary and his men were wide awake, well realizing the danger of their position, and though enveloped on three sides fought unfalteringly till one brigade of Schurz's division of the Eleventh Corps, encamped some miles in the rear, came up on the double-quick and relieved the pressure upon Geary's left. The other brigade had been detached en route to operate against a second body of Confederates who were advancing against the camp of the Eleventh Corps. As Steinwehr's division was moving to join in the fight nearest it fire was opened by a strong force of the enemy posted on an almost inaccessible hill 200 feet in hight. Two regiments under Colonel Orlando Smith,—the Thirty-third Massachusetts, Colonel A. B. Underwood, and Smith's own, the Seventy-third Ohio,—were ordered to clear the hill with the bayonet, which was magnificently done. Colonel Underwood was severely wounded, and at the request of General Hooker received a promotion to a brigadier generalship for his gallantry. Probably no more picturesque night battle than that of Wauhatchie was ever fought. All along the valley and up the slopes of the hills the bursts and flashes of fire ran, while from the frowning hights of Lookout, as though from batteries built amidst the clouds, the Confederate artillery joined in the strife. But the attack was everywhere repelled, and within a day or two the route though the valley was opened and firmly held. The partial freeing of the river also allowed the employment of a small steamer which some of the Michigan troops in the army had built and named the "Chattanooga," by which supplies were brought to the ferry.

A considerable force had meantime been sent from Bragg's army under command of Longstreet to operate against Burnside, to prevent him from reaching Chattanooga and if possible to destroy or capture his command. The latter, making the best defense possible en route, fell back to his intrenchments at Knoxville. Longstreet made a sharp attack November 18, getting possession of some outposts and killing General W P. Sanders, who with a small command had bravely defended the place till Burnside's arrival. Finding that the works were too strong to be carried by assault, Longstreet immediately began siege operations, hoping to bag the garrison before assistance should reach them, as he knew Burnside's stock of provisions to be small. While the siege was yet in progress the country was electrified by the tidings from Chattanooga.

Late in September General Sherman with the Fifteenth Corps had moved from Vicksburg by water to Memphis and thence by rail toward the Tennessee, in support of Rosecrans, but when Grant's plans for a campaign against Bragg were perfected he was ordered forward to Chattanooga and on his arrival operations at once commenced, the first offensive movements being made November 23. On that day Sherman crossed the Tennessee and the Chickamauga, after various demonstrations to mislead the enemy, and moved forward along the line of the latter stream against the Confederate right at the upper end of Missionary Ridge, making his way slowly but holding tenaciously whatever ground was gained. On the afternoon of the same day General Thomas formed a strong line of his own command which was advanced against the Confederate center in front of Chattanooga, carrying everything before it as far as Orchard Knob, a minor elevation some distance in front of the Ridge but beyond the first line of rebel rifle pits. Here a battery was placed and intrenchments thrown up to hold the ground thus gained.

The first decisive blow was struck by Hooker on the 24th. From his position in Lookout Valley he was directed if possible to drive the Confederates from their occupancy of Lookout Mountain. The force at his command consisted only of Geary's division of the Twelfth Corps, Osterhaus's of the Fifteenth and two brigades from the Fourth,—troops that had never fought together and whose numbers seemed wholly inadequate to the terrible undertaking; but at 4 o'clock in the morning he reported readiness and shortly afterward the movement began. Almost from the brink of Lookout Creek the mountain side sloped upward so sharply that it seemed almost impracticable for the unimpeded foot of man, breaking finally into a perpendicular palisade from 50 to 100 feet in sheer ascent to the table land forming the summit of the mountain. At every available point below the palisade this slope was filled with abatis, rifle-pits, breastworks and epaulments defended by McLaws's veterans. The stoutest heart might well have shrunk from the struggle which must ensue, but Geary's division never faltered. Crossing the creek and extending its lines up the mountain side till the palisade protected the right flank it faced northward and assisted by the fire of the batteries from the valley began to press forward. A heavy mist hung over the face of the mountain almost concealing the struggling heroes from the sight of their anxious friends, but now and then through a rift their advancing banners could be seen, the line of fire moved steadily forward with never a retrograde, and at noon the utterly demoralized defenders were driven around the sharp northern end of the mountain and the pursuers looked over upon the lines of their fellow-Unionists in the Chattanooga Valley. Here Geary was directed to stop and reform his lines, but there were indications that another stand would be made as the eastern face was turned, and his victorious command, necessarily broke into an exultant rabble, rushed forward with never a pause and sent their antagonists in a mad scramble over the rocks and through the gullies into the valley beyond. Then the line was established, the right still resting against the palisade and the left reaching to near the mouth of Chattanooga Creek in the valley, facing and enfilading the Confederate position on the right of Thomas. During the night an attack was made on Hooker's right but it was easily repulsed, and at daylight next morning the Stars and Stripes waved from the summit of the mountain, which had been hastily abandoned, Bragg concentrating his entire force on Missionary Ridge, with his pickets still clinging to the eastern shore of Chattanooga creek.

Hooker's command was now ordered forward across the valley to the Rossville Gap, which it reached and occupied about the middle of the afternoon, having been delayed on the way by sharp skirmishing and missing bridges. Then facing northward it advanced steadily till sunset, driving the enemy from one position to another with resistless force. All day Sherman had been battling sturdily at the north end of the Ridge, with his face to the south, though making but little advance owing to the difficulty of the ground and the tenacity of the resistance. As the afternoon wore away without sufficient progress to satisfy General Grant he ordered Thomas to assault the enemy's center in front of Orchard Knob. The position here was very strong. At the foot of the ridge, half a mile from the Knob, was a strong line of works; half way up the ascent was a second, consisting chiefly of rifle-pits ; while the summit was very strongly fortified, with 50 pieces of cannon in position. The four divisions of Baird, Wood, Sheridan and Johnson were formed from left to right in the order given and at half-past 3, under orders to carry the first line of works if possible, advanced at the booming of six signal guns.

Through a terrible fire of shot and shell, grape, canister and musketry, the lines moved firmly across the plain to the base of the mountain, captured the works which were their objective point and sent such of the defenders as could escape rushing frantically up the hill. Then the victors endeavored to halt and lie down at the foot of the Ridge in obedience to their orders, but there was no shelter from the plunging fire rained on them from above, and presently detached groups following the lead of some dauntless standard-bearer began to climb the hill-side. The movement spread like wildfire. Officers cheered on their men, color-bearers waved their flags and shouted back for their fellows, till presently a hundred detached groups with a common object went scrambling up the ravines and gullies, dodging from one partially sheltered covert to another, screaming, cheering, shouting like so many madmen. General Grant looking on from Orchard Knob, was astonished. "By whose command is that movement?" he asked the equally surprised Thomas. "It looks like a spontaneous advance," was all the reply that the latter could make. "All right if it comes out well ; if not somebody will suffer for it !" the chieftan growled as he watched the progress of the disorderly scurry up the hill.

Sheridan's men were the first to reach the summit, and for a time they found themselves with plenty of occupation, but soon a lodgment was made, some of the batteries captured and the guns turned upon the breaking lines of the Confederates. In one hour from the firing of the signal from the Knob the entire crest in their front was in possession of the Boys in Blue. Wood's division, to the left of Sheridan, met a more determined opposition, and the struggle there continued till after dark, when the Confederates broke before the repeated assaults, the panic extending even to the troops in front of Sherman to the north, so that when night settled over the mountains it found Bragg's army in full retreat toward Dalton, while that officer himself barely escaped capture with the other generals at his head-quarters. This was the news which next morning was read to the Army of the Potomac as it set forth on its dismal pilgrimage toward Mine Run.

That night a force of 20,000 men under General Granger set out for the relief of Burnside at Knoxville, while Hooker, Sherman and Sheridan pressed the retreating Confederates. Several sharp actions occurred between the pursuers and the rear guard, especially at the mountain passes near Ringgold where Hooker dislodged Cleburne after a very stubborn engagement, following which the pursuit was abandoned and the Union army concentrated near Chattanooga, in the vicinity of which they enjoyed a a winter of well-earned rest. General Sherman joined Granger's column on the march toward Knoxville, taking command. On the 3d of December the advance entered the Union lines at Knoxville and the siege came to an end. Longstreet on hearing of the disaster to Bragg realized that time was becoming precious and resolved upon carrying the works in his front by assault, which was made and bloodily repulsed on the 29th of November. From Knoxville he retreated in the direction of Virginia, where we shall find him presently.

As the news of Grant's magnificent victory, following so closely upon his successes in Mississippi, was made known to the country, he became everywhere the hero of the year. Thanks and a gold medal were voted him by Congress, while the public and private expressions of appreciation were of the most flattering nature. The finger of destiny seemed unmistakably pointing to him as the chieftain ordained to lead the Union armies to triumph, and his subsequent promotion to Lieutenant-General, with command of all military movements, was everywhere regarded as one eminently fitting.

The other military operations of the closing year were scarcely noteworthy. In North Carolina, General Foster as Burnside's successor was engaged in a more or less desultory strife with small bands of Confederates, with no important advantage accruing to either. In South Carolina all efforts were concentrated against Charleston harbor, and these under General Gillmore and Admiral Dahlgren, were of the most earnest nature and some progress was made. Morris Island was wrested from the Confederate grasp after the blood of Colonel Shaw and his colored troops of the Fifty-fourth Massachusetts, with others, had been poured out in vain in the ditches of cruel Fort Wagner; Fort Sumter had been pounded to a shapeless mass of ruins, and shells from the "Swamp Angel" had gone screaming into Charleston, "The Cradle of Secession." General Banks having restored a satisfactory degree of quiet in Louisiana had turned his attention to other points in his department, and had made some progress toward re-establishing the old flag in Texas, operations in this quarter continuing while winter had locked up the armies in other sections.

On the whole the outlook had brightened wonderfully during the last six months of the year, and the improved military situation was reflected in the autumn elections by a stronger expression of confidence in the National government. Vallandigham, the opposition candidate for governor of Ohio, who from Canada was posing as a martyr to military despotism, was buried under a loyal majority of a hundred thousand; New York gave a substantial Union majority, as did Maryland, where the question of emancipation caused sharp strife.

In the Confederacy, on the other hand, the outlook was continually darkening. Following the defeat of Lee and the losses in the Mississippi valley, President Davis had ordered the conscription of all able-bodied men in the Confederacy between the ages of 18 and 45, and before the close of the year the latter limit was extended to 55. During the winter General Bragg was made general-in-chief of the Confederate armies by Davis, but the appointment was not one to inspire hope or produce satisfaction. The pressure of the continually strengthening blockade was more and more crippling the southern resources, the hope of foreign assistance was daily waning, the finances were becoming seriously crippled, and the abundant Confederate "paper money" had a varying specie value of from four to six cents per dollar.

To return to the winter quarters on the Rapidan; directly after the Mine Run fiasco, the Thirty-seventh, as we have seen, selected the most favorable spot available and began the build- of their winter quarters—"Camp Sedgwick." The result was a model production, noteworthy among the multitude of camps which dotted the face of the country for miles around, though confessedly not so complete and perfect as its prototype of the previous winter, since the facilities for construction were by no means equal. Desirable material was scarce, having to be brought a considerable distance even at the beginning, and the entire work was done under the omnipresent feeling that the location of the army, or still more probably that of the regiment, might be changed at almost any hour. So while the camp was made complete and comfortable, more individuality was displayed in the construction of the different cabins and in their fitting up. The huts when completed and occupied on the 10th of December numbered 140, exclusive of officers' and other general quarters, 18 less than were vacated in May, showing the net decrease in the number of men to be provided for to have been over 70 since the building of "Camp Edwards;" and this despite the liberal number of new recruits received during the autumn, who had taken their initial campaigning experience in the very trying days of Mine Run.

One very cold Sunday soon after the occupation of the camp the men were supplied with reading matter from the Christian Commission in lieu of religious services, and the colporteur thus interestingly writes of the tents visited :

> It is a curious task to go through the regiment and call at every tent. The tents are made of logs with shelter tents for a roof. I commence at a company street, for instance, on the right. At the first tent I find a door rudely constructed from rough boards, through which I can pass quite readily by stooping low. At the next I find a handsome paneled door cut off at both ends and hewed at both sides, and having a beautiful glass knob attached ; taken probably from some secessionist's dwelling. These doors are at the end of the hut. At the next I find the entrance at the side, and made from the boards of a cracker box. At the next I find the door at the back end, and I get in by pushing aside a rubber blanket which is hung up to stop the opening. At the next tent I look for the door at one end, then at the other, then at each side, and I fail of finding any anywhere. Finally I call out to those inside, "Where do you get in?" And behold I get in as the sick man got in where Christ was, to be healed, that is through the roof. At another tent I find a door made of small round poles framed together and covered with an old grain sack. The tents inside present some attractive features. Among other things I saw to-day in the various tents a surveyor's rule, a cane-seat chair, a mahogany table, a drawer from a bureau, a rosewood box of small articles from a young lady's toilet, a pair of tongs, a spear for catching eels, and a great variety of articles which I cannot remember. They are brought in by foraging parties from various places beyond our picket lines. * * * * The moral aspect of the regiment is now very good. I have to-day spent about half the day in the regiment among the men, and I did not hear a single oath.

The winter on the Rapidan was marked by an unusual religious interest throughout the Army of the Potomac. Apart from the earnest efforts put forth by the various chaplains for the spiritual and moral welfare of the men with whom they were associated, the Christian Commission had many agents actively at work in co-operation. One of their creditable efforts was the furnishing to each brigade in the army of a "fly" for covering a chapel tent. In Eustis's Brigade, as in some others, it was thought better to assign the gift to one of the regiments, the choice being made by the chaplains drawing lots. The Thirty-seventh was fortunate in securing the tent, and during the early part of January a chapel was erected and furnished, capable of seating about 150 persons. The structure was unique in construction, though answering admirably its purpose. The sides were built of split logs fixed upright in the ground, forming a stockade some six feet in hight to the eaves of the canvas. The crevices being closed by a liberal application of mud, the interior, 20 by 24 feet, could be comfortably warmed by the small stove with which it was provided. Seats were obtained by splitting logs, hewing the upper side to passable smoothness and mounting them upon legs; while the desk was quite tastefully fitted up, bearing on its front the Greek cross of the corps in evergreens; above it the state and national colors were draped, while in front were two crossed muskets, each bearing a small copy of the Stars and Stripes.

As soon as the building was habitable it came into use each Sabbath and nearly every evening in the week, prayer-meetings being held either there or in the chaplain's tent several times during the week; while a spelling-school and a lyceum attracted many who did not care especially for the religious gatherings. The latter, however, grew in interest, and during the winter a regimental church was organized, adopting a creed and a covenant suitable to the circumstances. This church, beginning with a few earnest members, grew continually, especially toward the close of winter, reaching a membership of 55. Baptism was performed on several occasions, and some notable conversions were made. The chapel was dedicated by quite impressive services on Sunday, February 7, 1864, though it had been in use for some time previous. The chaplains of other regiments were in attendance, the regimental choir under the lead of Lieutenant Edwards sang appropriate hymns, and the dedicatory sermon was preached by Chaplain Beugless of the Second Rhode Island. Much reading matter was furnished by the friends of the regiment in Massachusetts, in addition to that provided by the Christian Commission, a box of books being sent to the Thirty-seventh by the Sunday-school of the Congregational church in

Lee, and a large bundle by Mrs. E. L. Edwards of Springfield, among other contributions. In connection with the debating association, which was presided over by Corporal Shepardson of Company A with Sergeant Warner of Company E for secretary, a weekly paper called "The Reveille" and contributed by different members of the regiment was read, thus reproducing some of the dearest features of New England village life and furnishing the men healthful mental discipline and moral training.

In connection with this mental exercise the members of the Thirty-seventh provided liberal physical recreation. Nearly every pleasant day in the intervals between drills a game of baseball or "wicket" formed a center of attraction for the unemployed members of the brigade; these games becoming largely inter-regimental, a variety of "teams" were organized throughout the brigade, some of which became very proficient. If a fall of snow prevented the regular pastime, it only furnished the opportunity for another, and many a battle of snow-balls was conducted with an energy and skill worth of the more deadly conflict to which the combatants might at any time be called.

Yet with all these and many other alleviations of the hours which otherwise might have proved monotonous and demoralizing, the lot of the soldier was by no means an enviable one. The season seemed unusually inclement. Storms were many and severe, and the cold often intense. At such times, especially if a strong wind prevailed, even the most comfortable quarters did not suffice to prevent suffering on the part of the occupants. The supply of fuel was inadequate at the beginning of winter, and it became deplorably short as the months wore away. The region had been previously occupied by soldiers of both armies, who had cut off the best of the wood, but the stumps had been cut so high and so much waste had been made in other ways that for a time a comfortable supply could be obtained by taking off another section from the stumps and otherwise gleaning the field. But this soon exhausted the immediate vicinity, and then the men were obliged to bring all supplies from the distance of two or three miles. Very naturally no advance supply was ever gathered, and when a long storm came on it invariably found the occupants of a large proportion of the tents casting lots or taking turns in going forth through the inclemency with some wonderfully dull apologies for axes to obtain a supply of firewood. During February the trials in this respect were especially severe, the weather being piercing and the wood having to be drawn three miles, the companies being put upon an allowance of one small load each per day. Inadequate as was the supply in quantity, it was even more so in quality, being for the most part green pine, which only burned through perpetual coaxing. The discomfort of some of those cold nights is graphically described in a letter written to a fellow-clergyman by Chaplain Morse, which also shows that the misery was not all endured by the enlisted men, as they sometimes felt. Says the chaplain:

Imagine your humble servant sleeping on two horizontal poles with barrel staves laid across, with two thicknesses of blanket between him and the staves, with the wind blowing powerfully and the thermometer several degrees below zero. Add to this the constant fear that the tent would blow away. * * I laid on one side, then on the other side, then on the upper side and then on the lower side; then I would bend myself up double and rub my feet with my hands, then stretch out again; then I would double up and undouble in rapid succession and throw myself into all sorts of spasmodic convulsions to get up a circulation. Well, I circulated myself pretty generally, and circulated the bed-clothes about the tent promiscuously. How patriotic I felt just then! I would have given three rousing cheers for the Union only I was afraid of waking up the quartermaster in the tent adjoining, who was snoring like an earthquake. * * Finally I concluded to arise and so I proceeded to unbag myself, and presently "Chaplain 37th Mass. Vols." was emptied out on the floor. Dressing was a slow process, so I untied my tent and out I went under flying colors to get some kindling wood. I came back again and hacked a full hour with an old dull hatchet, shivering in the mean time and suffering the most excrutiating agony. Finally I got a fire, and wasn't it a luxury? Then I bagged myself again and located myself longitudinally on the barrel staves. I rolled, tumbled, whined, sneezed, grunted, doubled up and undoubled and then did it again, and the third time, and kept doing it. I don't know how I got through the night, but I found myself here this morning in the body. I got breakfast, went to Brandy Station to chaplains' meeting, and as scarcely any one else came I concluded the rest fared worse than I did, and I came back singing, "The soldier's life is always gay."

With such uncomfortable experiences in camp, it scarcely needs to be said that the trials and sufferings of guards and pickets were much greater. But between the storms there were many bright and sunny days, which were fully occupied in drill; in addition to the usual routine, many of the non-commissioned officers laboring with the new recruits to bring them up to the high standard of the veterans of the regiment. Frequent and rigid inspections kept the standard of soldierly excellence high, while there was comparatively little sickness and few deaths from disease during the winter.

The inclement season was not to pass without more or less rumors and attempted "movements" against the enemy. Early in the morning of February 6 the Thirty-seventh was roused with orders to be ready to march at 8 o'clock, but the entire day passed with nothing in addition except suspense and the sound of distant cannonading. It proved to be another "mud march," not quite so disastrous as that of the year previous, and in which fortunately the Sixth Corps was not called to take a part.

A few days before General Sedgwick, commanding the Army of the Potomac in the absence of General Meade, received a request indorsed by the Washington authorities to make a demonstration against Lee on the 6th to aid a scheme of General Butler for making a dash on Richmond with the intention of freeing the Union prisoners confined there. The movement was a complete failure, the column which undertook the enterprise finding their advance confronted by a strong force and an important bridge gone. Sedgwick, however, knew nothing of this, and carried out his part of the programme as thoroughly as the storm which came on almost at the moment of moving would allow. General Kilpatrick was to demonstrate with his cavalry at Culpeper Mine Ford, General Merritt at Barnett's Ford, General Warren with the Second Corps at Morton's Ford, and General Newton with the First Corps at Raccoon Ford. The mud prevented getting forward the pontons and some of the half-dozen batteries of artillery which the two corps attempted to take with them, but the soldiers themselves reached the assigned positions: at Morton's Ford the enemy were surprised and Caldwell's division of the Second Corps crossed the river, gaining some advantages. Hays's division was sent over in support, but both withdrew during the night and after another day of skirmishing and demonstrating across the stream the expedition returned to camp.

Nothing had been accomplished beyond the loss of a few hundred men by the Army of the Potomac, but the reports received convinced General Meade and the military directors at Washington that a properly managed movement of similar nature might succeed, and late in the month General Kilpatrick with a picked cavalry force of 4,000 men and some horse artillery was sent forth upon the undertaking. His purpose was to move by the most direct route possible past the right flank of Lee's army and by way of Spottsylvania Court House straight to Richmond, release the Union prisoners there and conduct them to Williamsburg, distributing on his way the recently issued amnesty proclamation of President Lincoln. At the same time a strong demonstration was to be made around the left of the Confederate army by the Sixth Corps, which was to move as far as Madison Court House, where Custer's cavalry would pass it and push forward as far as the Rivanna river near Charlottesville. Birney's division of the Third Corps was to move to James City in support of the Sixth, and the entire army was to be held in readiness to march at a moment's notice if wanted. This part of the movement was under the direction of General Sedgwick, and it scarcely needs be said that it was promptly and efficiently carried out.

The Thirty-seventh received its preparatory orders in the afternoon of the 26th, and about 9 o'clock next morning the line was formed and the column moved away toward Culpeper, which was passed during the day and bivouac made for the night at James City,—a characteristic Virginia town, consisting of one dwelling, a deserted building which had once been a store, and a few dilapidated out-buildings whose excuse for existing at all no one seemed able to determine. The men were quite weary with the march of 17 miles and slept soundly, though the camp was early astir in the morning. The forenoon was well advanced before the march was resumed, however, nor was it pursued vigorously during the day. Shortly after noon Robertson's river was reached, on the banks of which the regiment cooked coffee, rested for an hour or two and then pushed forward within a mile of Madison Court House, where the corps was disposed in order of battle and bivouacked for the night.

Forty-eight hours were passed in this position, the last 24 of which were supremely uncomfortable, as it stormed incessantly, a snowy, sleety rain which froze as it fell, and from which the men had very inadequate protection, having left their shelter tents behind. About dark the regiment was ordered under arms and moved back across Robertson's river, going into bivouac after marching a mile further. It was a very cheerless resting place for human beings, as it was in an open field where the mud seemed to reach a uniform depth of about a foot, the mingling snow and rain was still falling, and it was so dark that the nearest objects were barely distinguishable. Sleep or rest was out of the question, and the men passed the dragging hours as best they could. Next morning, March 2, the faces of the wearied corps were turned toward "home"—for it thus they felt and spoke of Camp Sedgwick—and at 6 o'clock that night, after an intensely wearying march of 20 miles over muddy, slippery roads which seemed simply interminable they entered the familiar streets. Many had fallen behind in the last few miles, unable to retain the speed with which their more vigorous comrades were pressing toward the old camp and its comparatively comfortable quarters. One of their number, Private Henry A. Mell of Company F, fell exhausted and died on the way, but apart from his sad fate the regiment met with no direct loss during the expedition.

The storm had made of what would otherwise have been an agreeable break in the monotony of camp life an exceedingly trying experience. The men could see no fruits of their labor. There had been nothing approaching the nature of an engagement, only a wearying trip through a desolate region. No wonder that an irreverent sufferer when asked by an invalid in camp where he had been replied with a snarl and an oath, "Fourteen miles beyond God's knowledge!" But presently the tidings came that Kilpatrick, though failing to enter Richmond, had actually been within its defenses and had inflicted serious injury on the railroads in the rear of Lee's army, and it was then understood that the purpose of Sedwick's movement had been fully accomplished.

For some weeks many of the officers in the army had enjoyed the presence in camp of their wives and other friends, among the number being the wives of Chaplain Morse and Captain Edwards, who had been left in camp during the absence of the regiment, but soon afterward all visiting friends took their departure and the signs of the camp pointed unmistakably in the direction of a resumption of active campaigning. In fact though the actual time for movement was still some distance in the future, events of the greatest importance to the army were constantly transpiring.

With the close of February Congress had revived the rank of Lieutenant-General in the Army of the United States, President Lincoln at once nominated General Grant to the office, he was promptly confirmed by the Senate and a few days later—having been summoned to Washington—was by the President assigned to the command of all the armies in the field. On the 11th of March he visited the Army of the Potomac, and the rumor that he intended to make his head-quarters with that army was heard with gladness. As the rumor became a certainty, and the soldiers marched past him in review, hope swelled in every breast. With the prestige of almost unvarying success in the scenes of his former endeavor, it was but natural to hope that decisive victory would crown his efforts in the larger field, that the object of the war would speedily be accomplished and the citizen soldiers return once more to the homes and friends they had left at the call of duty.

A few changes in the regimental roster of officers had occurred during the winter and early spring prior to the opening of the campaign. First Lieutenant Andrew L. Bush of Company H, disabled after once returning to duty by the outbreak of the wound received at Gettysburg, was discharged February 5; dating from the 9th of the same month Second Lieutenant John S.

Bradley of Company G was made first lieutenant and mustered into Company H. Sergeant Joseph Follansbee of Company G was commissioned second lieutenant vice Bradley, and First Sergeant George E. Cooke of Company F was made second lieutenant of that company, both being mustered April 28, though their commissions dated from the occurrence of the vacancies they filled. Assistant Surgeon Thomas C. Lawton resigned February 23, and March 27 Dr. Elisha M. White of Boston was appointed to the vacancy. Captain John B. Mulloy of Company K was honorably discharged by Special Order of the War Department April 4, and on his refusal of a reinstatement which was offered, First Lieutenant Charles L. Edwards received promotion and was mustered as Captain of Company D. Second Lieutenant Walter B. Smith, who had previously been transferred from Company E to Company C, was promoted to first lieutenant of Company D. Among the officers on detached service at this time were Captain A. S. Flagg on recruiting duty in Massachusetts and Lieutenant C. S. Bardwell in command of the brigade pioneer corps. Captain Flagg did not return to duty in the regiment, being honorably discharged for disability May 14.*

---

* Captain Flagg was immediately recommissioned as captain by Governor Andrew and assigned to staff duty, serving with Generals Thomas, Sherman, Meagher, Schofield and Howard, the latter for a period of more than a year, till his final muster out in June, 1866.

CHAPTER XIII.

NINE DAYS OF CARNAGE.

THE REORGANIZATION OF THE ARMY.—THE GRAPPLE IN THE
WILDERNESS.—BY THE LEFT FLANK TO SPOTTSYLVANIA.—
DEATH OF SEDGWICK.—"THE ANGLE."

During the latter part of March, 1864, the Army of the Potomac was largely reorganized, the five corps being consolidated to three,—the Second, commanded by General Winfield S. Hancock; the Fifth, under General Gouverneur K. Warren; and the Sixth, General John Sedgwick—the latter the senior corps commander. The old Second Corps had been consolidated into two divisions of four and three brigades respectively, the First commanded by General Francis C. Barlow and the Second by General John Gibbon. The 35 regiments of the Third Corps were consolidated into four brigades, two each of which formed the Third Division of the new Second Corps, commanded by General David B. Birney, and the Fourth Division, General Gershom Mott. The old Fifth Corps was likewise reduced to two divisions of the new,— the First of three brigades under General Charles Griffin and the Third (Pennsylvania Reserves) of two brigades under General Samuel W Crawford. The Second and Fourth Divisions of three brigades each were made up of the old First Corps and commanded respectively by Generals John C. Robinson and James S. Wadsworth. The old Sixth Corps was likewise consolidated to two divisions, the Third being broken up. Wheaton's brigade was made the First of the Second Division and Eustis's became the Fourth, while Shaler's was known as the Fourth Brigade of the First Division. The corps organization was thus modified as follows: First Division, General Horatio G. Wright, composed of the brigades of Colonel Henry W Brown

(New Jersey Brigade), Colonel Emory Upton, General David A. Russell and General Alexander Shaler; the Second Division, General George W Getty, had the brigades of General Frank Wheaton, Colonel Lewis A. Grant (Vermont Brigade), General Thomas H. Neill and General Henry L. Eustis. The new Third Division was made up of the troops which had been attached to the First Corps as a provisional division directly after the battle of Gettysburg, being at that time commanded by General H. S. Briggs, now placed under General James B. Ricketts, the two brigades being commanded by General William H. Morris and Colonel Benjamin F. Smith—the latter being relieved May 5, by General Truman Seymour. The artillery of the corps consisted of nine batteries under Colonel Charles H. Tompkins. General Kilpatrick having been relieved from the command of the cavalry of the Army of the Potomac, that important arm of the service was placed under the command of General Philip H. Sheridan, who had commanded an infantry division in the Army of the Cumberland with signal ability. The three divisions of the corps were made up as follows: First, General A. T. A. Torbert, composed of the brigades of General George A. Custer, Colonel Thomas C. Devin, and General Wesley Merritt; the Second Division, General David M. Gregg, had the brigades of General Henry E. Davies, Jr., and Colonel J. Irving Gregg; the Third Division, General James B. Wilson, had also two brigades under Colonel T. M. Bryan, Jr., and Colonel George H. Chapman.

The transfer of Eustis's Brigade to the Second Division was made March 24, and the men exchanged for the white the blue crosses which they had worn since the adoption of the corps badge system. The brigade was now one of the smallest in the army, the consolidation making many brigades consist of from eight to ten regiments. In fact the tendency everywhere was to consolidation and concentration, to such a degree that from this time onward the general reader must lose sight of all the minor organizations. Troops were moved in the campaigns which followed by corps and divisions, brigades were rarely spoken of, regiments passed out of consideration in the magnitude of the struggles between what were henceforth to be the principal contesting armies of the government and its would-be destroyers. Through this maze we must follow the Thirty-seventh as it goes forth to win its greatest renown and prove its quality as "a fighting regiment." Up to this time it had scarcely felt the supreme shock of battle. Placed often where its discipline and firmness were well tested, and never with other than the highest credit to itself, it had still in a remarkable degree escaped the horrible decimation which was henceforth so often to tear its serried ranks into mere bleeding fragments. It was not to be expected that the future should bring to the regiment as an organization the good fortune which had thus far attended it, and this feeling was voiced by many a thoughtful man, whether wearing a sword or bearing the musket. There was the general feeling that Grant would strike no uncertain blow, and past experience in conflict with the Army of Northern Virginia gave the best possible assurance that the foe would give back blow for blow to the last desperate extremity.

The closing days of March and the early part of April were marked by severe and successive storms, rain and snow alternating and making the roads very bad. While the armies were thus weather-bound the general commanding was perfecting his plans for the campaign which was to open as soon as the roads were practicable. His scheme contemplated the active and simultaneous employment of all the Union armies in concert, thus requiring of the enemy a similar use of his forces and preventing the drawing of troops from one army to reinforce another, as had so often been done in the past when the action of the Union armies had been without concert. Accordingly the command of all the troops between the Alleghanies and the Mississippi river had been bestowed upon General Sherman, and he was directed to move upon the Confederate army, intrenched near Dalton, Ga., and commanded by General Johnston since the promotion of General Bragg to general-in-chief. The objective point of Sherman's advance was to be Atlanta, the railroad, manufacturing and military center of the state. Grant's own head-quarters were to be with the Army of the Potomac, whose objective was to be the Confederate army commanded by

General Lee, the Army of the Potomac to remain under the immediate command of General Meade. Burnside with the Ninth Corps, which had been strengthened by a division of colored troops, was to join the Army of the Potomac, but for a time remained under the direct command of Grant. At the same time General Butler with the Tenth and Eighteenth Corps, some 30,000 in number, was to move against Richmond from the south by way of the James River and City Point, while General Sigel was to operate in the Shenandoah Valley, detaching a portion of his command for service under General Crook in the Kanawha region. The part taken by these co-operating columns will be referred to at the proper time: for the present the narrative must follow the Army of the Potomac and especially the fortunes of the Thirty-seventh regiment as a factor of that army.

At the close of April General Lee's army occupied practically the position of the previous autumn,—the right resting on the intrenched line of Mine Run, the left extending some 18 or 20 miles up the Rapidan. While this front line was held by a strong picket, the bulk of the army was encamped several miles in the rear, nearer the base of supplies, and Longstreet with his two divisions returned from East Tennessee was posted near Gordonsville, ready to move in either direction as the Union army should attempt the right or left flank movement.

The Confederate position was simply impregnable to a front attack, and it only remained to decide whether to move the Union army around its right or its left, and General Grant decided upon the former. The orders were accordingly issued for the beginning of the advance directly after midnight on the morning of the 4th of May. The Second Corps, preceded by Gregg's cavalry division, forming the left column, was to cross the Rapidan at Ely's Ford and advance to Chancellorsville ; the right column, composed of Wilson's cavalry division, the Fifth Corps and the Sixth, was to cross at Germanna Ford and advance to Wilderness Tavern. It was intended by moving at midnight to bring the columns to the river soon after daylight, to effect a crossing without serious opposition; and it was further hoped that by a vigorous forward movement the two columns might pass through the thickly wooded region known as "the Wilderness" and reach more favorable ground for military operations before the enemy should be able to concentrate in sufficient force to necessitate any heavy fighting. The first part of the programme was perfectly carried out ; the second part failed, owing to the vigilance and promptness of movement of the enemy.

As the Sixth Corps followed the Fifth the men were allowed a little longer rest on their last night in camp, but at half-past 2 the bugles called from slumber, the tents were taken down, knapsacks packed, breakfast prepared and eaten, and as the light of coming day began to brighten the East the column moved forward. It was some 15 miles from the camp of the Thirty-seventh to the crossing of the Rapidan at Germanna Ford, and as the day proved quite sultry and the march was made rapidly the men suffered much. The bridges were reached and crossed early in the afternoon. Two had been laid at each ford,—one of canvas and one of wooden boats, while one of the latter had been laid at Culpeper Mine Ford, between the crossings of the two columns, for the use of the trains. After the passage of the troops the canvas boats were taken up and accompanied the army, the wooden ones being left for the use of the trains, the Ninth Corps and Torbert's division of cavalry forming the rear guard. Strong works commanding the fords had been constructed on the southern bank, but were not fully manned and only a few scattering picket shots opposed the Union advance.

The head of Hancock's corps reached its destination at Chancellorsville about 10 o'clock in the forenoon, and as the column came up the troops were concentrated and halted for the night. Warren was an hour or two later in reaching Widerness Tavern, and the Sixth Corps went into bivouac along the plank road leading from Germanna Ford, the rear near the ford, the Thirty-seventh having advanced some three miles.

Just after sunset religious services were held by the chaplain, in which a considerable portion of the regiment joined, not a few of whom were never again to enjoy such an occasion. Warm as had been the day, the night was uncomfortably cool, as the mountains to the westward had but a day or two before been covered with snow. At an early hour the encampment was still, the men seeking rest to fortify them for the unknown trials of the coming day. Here and there a group might be seen after the majority had gone to rest holding earnest conference as men might well do over whom the shadow of death rested; while others, without thought save of the present moment, were engaged in games or enjoying the luxury which some fortunate foraging enterprise had provided.

At 6 o'clock of the morning of the 5th the regiment marched, in its place in the column, moving slowly till about noon when it reached its destination at Wilderness Tavern. It was intended that Hancock and Warren should push forward to points on the Catharpin road to the southwest of the positions they then occupied, orders to that effect had been issued and the troops began to move accordingly in the morning; but it was soon found that Confederates in considerable numbers were within a short distance on the turnpike in Warren's front, and both columns were halted till they should be dispersed. It proved to be Ewell's corps coming down in force to strike the Union army in the flank, and when Sedgwick reached the Tavern he found the battle developing in a serious manner.

The point of contact was about midway between the battlefield of Chancellorsville and the scene of operations at Mine Run, all three movements covering more or less of the same ground. We have already noticed that through this section of the country the old Orange turnpike and the Orange or Gordonsville plank road run nearly parallel and from two to three miles apart, the course being a little to the south of west. The Germanna plank road, coming in from the northwest, crosses the turnpike a little to the west of Wilderness Tavern and continues through to the Orange plank road, which it joins near Hickman's house. Something less than a mile west of this junction the Brock road comes up from the southeast, crosses the Orange plank road, and running thence in a general northerly direction across the Germanna Ford plank road continues through to the turnpike, which it enters some three-fourths of a mile to the east of Wilderness Tavern. With the exception of the roads described the region was traversed only by various by-ways and wood roads, little better than trails, in one of the best of which General French's command had become hopelessly entangled the previous November. These were all well known to the Confederate commander or to soldiers in his army, while they were wholly unknown to the Federal officers and soldiers. Add to this that the entire region was covered with a forest so dense that no use could be made of artillery, choked with underbrush in many parts so thick that a line of battle could scarcely be discerned at 10 paces, and it will be seen against what obstacles the Union soldiers contended in the battle of the Wilderness.

General Lee seemed to have divined very nearly the time and direction of the contemplated movement of the Army of the Potomac. At any rate he was fully prepared for it, and when on the morning of the 4th his signal corps reported Grant's army in motion he promptly dispatched Ewell by the turnpike and Hill by the plank road to fall upon the moving columns before they should reach open ground, while Longstreet was summoned up from Gordonsville in haste.

Half a mile southwest of the Tavern was Lacy farm, a cultivated tract in the midst of general desolation, which covering an extensive knoll commanded a view of the wide-spreading tangled forest. Here Grant and Meade took up their positions, while Warren moved Griffin's and Wadsworth's divisions of his corps westward along the pike in search of Ewell's advance. At the same time the report of Hill's column on the plank road left no doubt that a general engagement was at hand. Hancock had started out early in the morning, marching nearly due south, and his advance was beyond Todd's Tavern, moving directly away from the scene of conflict, when he received the order to halt, followed presently by one to march by the Brock road to its junction with the Orange plank road and place his corps in the path of Hill's advance. Meantime Sedgwick, coming up the Germanna road, was ordered to connect with and prolong the right of the Fifth Corps, or rather of Griffin's division of it, to the north of the turnpike. This was promptly done with Wright's division, Neill's brigade of the Second and Seymour's brigade of the Third Division. Morris's brigade remained at the Ford covering the bridges till the arrival of the Ninth Corps, while General Getty with his remaining three brigades was sent down the Brock road to the Orange plank road with instructions to advance along the latter and if possible drive the Confederates whom he might encounter back beyond Parker's store, some three miles to the westward.

About noon the fighting began in earnest. Griffin's division, making its way as best it could through the tangled undergrowth, came suddenly upon a Confederate line of battle, charged impetuously and drove it back. This was Jones's brigade of Johnson's division, and Jones was killed at the time that his force was scattered, but strong reinforcements were encountered immediately and the Federal advance was in turn driven back. The only two pieces of artillery which Griffin had been able to get into action, advancing them along the turnpike, were abandoned, the horses being killed, and finally fell into the hands of the enemy. General Wadsworth's division was ordered forward through the thicket south of the turnpike to connect with Griffin's line and prolong it to the south. The result strikingly illustrates the terrible difficulties encountered in moving troops through such a jungle. The division was formed in front of the Lacy House and was instructed to move due west, which would bring it into the proper position. Unfortunately its direction was faulty at the start, inclining toward the northwest, and as it progressed the error was aggravated, so that it came into position with its flank almost directly toward the Confederate line of battle and in that situation received its fire. There was nothing for the men to do but to scramble out of the awkward predicament the best way they could. The lines finally being somehow re-established, both Ewell's and Warren's troops intrenched at about the point where the struggle began, the works being some 300 yards apart.

Later in the day Sedgwick's lines, creeping through the brush, came in contact with the foe and a serious engagement resulted. Colonel Upton's brigade, forming the left of the Sixth Corps line, reached a part of the field which had already been fought over, where the dead and wounded of both armies were still lying on the ground and the woods in his front were on fire, so that his further advance was checked. The rest of Wright's division, however, struck the enemy a well-directed blow, routing two brigades, killing General Stafford, the commander of one, and capturing many prisoners. With this achievement the day closed on the Union right.

General Getty with his three brigades had moved promptly to the junction of the plank and Brock roads, and with a strong skirmish line in front advanced along the former for some distance until he confronted the enemy in so strong force that he felt the hopelessness of attempting to do more than hold the ground till Hancock should come up. Wheaton's brigade was formed on the right of the road, Grant's Vermonters on the left, with Eustis's Brigade in support, the Thirty-seventh on the right and the Tenth on the left of its front line, with the Seventh and the Second in their rear. Hancock's troops soon began to arrive and went into position to the left of Getty, and as soon as the line was reasonably well formed the order to advance was given. Obedience was not so easy Both sides had intrenched as much as circumstances would permit during the pause, and when Wheaton's and Grant's veterans attempted to advance they were met by a terrible musketry fire which they returned with interest. For a long time the two lines at close quarters poured a deadly fire into each other without wavering on either side. Hancock's strong lines were pushed forward but without avail. A stream of wounded men poured to the rear, and the Thirty-seventh, though not engaged, began to lose men from the dropping musket shots. The first man killed was Corporal Theodore A. Church of Company G, who had volunteered to join an observation detail from the regiment sent out near the skirmish line to watch the progress of events in front, and while thus engaged he was shot through the head. Captain J. L. Hayden of Company H received a musket ball in the thigh inflicting a severe wound, from the results of which he was a few months afterward obliged to resign the service, and 11 enlisted men were wounded.

Thus far the battle had taken the character of two independent engagements, General Warren with the assistance of Sedgwick doing the best he could in the vicinity of the turnpike, and Hancock with Getty's three brigades doing likewise on the plank road. Late in the afternoon it was attempted to insure connection and some degree of co-operation between the scattered Union forces by directing General Wadsworth to move his division of the Fifth Corps through the forest toward the plank road and strike Hill's command on the flank in concert with Hancock's attack. The movement was accomplished with great difficulty, and it was dark before the designated position was reached. Finding himself in the vicinity of the enemy, General Wadsworth halted his command for the night, the two lines being so close together that representatives of each looking for water in the darkness wandered into the other and were made prisoners.

There was little movement during the night. Troops simply could not be handled in that abominable jungle in the darkness; but General Burnside with the Ninth Corps was ordered up to fill the gap between Hancock and Warren, and the order to each corps commander was simply to attack along the entire line at 5 o'clock next morning. Yet the decisive energy embodied in that simple direction was fully matched in that of the Confederate commander. Just before the appointed hour, as General Sedgwick was making his final dispositions for the advance, Ewell's divisions came streaming through the forest and dashed against the firm lines of the Sixth Corps. It was as though a wavelet had struck a rock. The recoil threw the charging columns back in disorder, and the Union right, guided and controlled by the calm power of General Sedgwick, drove back the demoralized foe and established its lines several hundred yards in advance. Then the intrenched position of the enemy was reached, and human valor could carry men no farther. So it proved in the case of Warren. Along his front the Confederate position had been made so strong that a direct attack—the only one possible—resulted in no advantage to the Union arms, although valiantly delivered and repeated with fearful persistency all the morning.

Burnside, either because his troops were not in position or for some other reason, did not attack at the appointed time, nor in fact till afternoon. Not so with Hancock. At the appointed moment his troops were launched against the foe, though his line at the left was hampered and held back by the expectation that Longstreet or a portion of his command might come up the Brock road to strike the Federal left flank. Pivoting upon the left, therefore, the Second Corps with the other commands which had been attached to it swung forward its right, covering the important plank road. Here General Birney of the Third Division, Second Corps, was in command, his own division, supported by Getty's three brigades (now commanded by General Neill, Getty having been wounded the previous afternoon), moving along both sides of the plank road. In the advance of the morning Eustis's brigade formed the third or fourth line, the Thirty-seventh supported by the Seventh on the right of the road with the Tenth and Second on the left. After stubborn resistance the Confederate lines gave way everywhere in Birney's front and a considerable advance was made and held, though his left was pressed back from its farthest point. At the same time General Wadsworth's division, coming in upon the Confederate flank forced its way across to the plank road, faced in the line of the general advance and drove the enemy still further back. It was the critical moment of the battle. If the Federal movement could have continued it must have torn Hill's entire corps to pieces, but owing to the nature of the ground it became necessary to make a complete readjustment of the lines. The men were scattered and mingled in almost inextricable confusion; officers were without command, detached knots and groups struggled here and there, the whole expanse swarmed with fugitives pressing not from but toward the enemy. It was no trifling task to gather commands, form lines, establish connections and put the forces in condition for effective work, and while this was being done Longstreet's two fresh divisions came up on the Confederate side. Their presence was unknown till Hancock, strengthened by Stevenson's division of the Ninth Corps, which with Wadsworth's was now placed formally under his command, attempted a further advance. By this time Longstreet was in position, and though Birney, Mott and Wadsworth fought their divisions gallantly they were held in check by the firm lines which they encountered. While the battle was still raging fiercely and when the Federal troops had nearly expended their ammunition they were taken in the flank by five brigades which Longstreet had moved around to the unfinished railroad and thence nearly due north, striking Mott's thin lines, which crumbled at the shock. Before Wadsworth's brigades were prepared for this new trial the wave swept over upon them and they too, unable to hold their ground, rushed back in confusion toward the Brock road, throwing other troops into disorder.

Eustis's Brigade was coming up in column of regiments at this moment, when General Wadsworth, seeking for some force to stay the disaster, rode to the Thirty-seventh, which was in front, and directed a charge against the exultant Confederates. Colonel Edwards received the order and moved his regiment by the right flank till it stood full in the path of the victorious legions; then facing the terrible work before it the frail line heard undismayed the order to charge ten times its own number, and with a cheer and a dash as one man the gallant battalion threw itself against the advancing line. The remainder of the brigade halted.

It was like a charge through the wildest regions of Dante's "Inferno"! The forests which once covered the entire region with a magnificent growth had been cut over repeatedly to furnish fuel for the mines which had been worked in the vicinity since the early days of Virginia, and instead of the natural growth there had sprung up everywhere a dense thicket of scrub pine, oak and walnut saplings, hazel and other bushes and briers so dense that it was next to impossible to force one's way through them without tearing flesh and clothing. Interspersed with rocky tracts on which only a gymnast could maintain his footing were marshes even more impassable. But over the swamps, between the saplings, through the bushes and briers the men forced themselves, firing as they went, clearing the human opposition away with the bayonet, catching a gleam now and then of the loved colors—Massachusetts and the nation side by side—as they steadily pressed through the wilderness, driving back the enemy, line after line in disorder, inflicting serious loss, but marking the path of the advance with brave men fallen along the way.

Still onward sweeps the line! Only the Thirty-seventh Massachusetts regiment is fighting Hill's and Longstreet's corps. It was a charge of Six Hundred; not as on the famous field of Balaklava a swift cavalry dash, but a forlorn hope of infantry, throwing itself unsupported into the face of twice ten thousand foeman. Hotter and hotter comes the fire! Ah! the colors—the Stars and Stripes—sway and seem to fall; but before they touch the earth they are held erect again, though in other hands. Color Sergeant John W Field of Hatfield, wearing his white Greek cross as bravely as knight of old ever bore the Christian cross against the Infidel, falls dead, shot through the head, but his flag is caught and borne still forward in triumph.

"You have made a splendid charge!" said the noble, white haired General Wadsworth to Colonel Edwards. "Your regiment alone has done all that I wished and more than I hoped. I will go now to reform my lines and you must fight your way back as best you can." They were the hero's last known words. Riding to the left of the regiment in search of his scattered division, he came under fire of the enemy, was mortally wounded in the head, fell into their hands and died within their lines.

The regiment had advanced some 900 yards, the left resting on the road and the right "in the air," when there was a momentary halt. A little break in the tangle in front showed some kind of earthworks. "We must go at those with a rush!" suggested Lieutenant-Colonel Montague to Colonel Edwards; but just at that moment Captain Lincoln came in from the right with news that the rebels seemed to be getting around that flank. "Refuse your right and hold your position," was the command; but as it became evident that the regiment was being enveloped the order to fall back was given. The charge had been a magnificent one—the men had responded to the sacrifice demanded with unsurpassed devotion and courage. The return exhibited still higher qualities of heroism.

With wonderful coolness one-half of the regiment marched some 25 paces to the rear, loading as they did so, when they faced to the front delivering a steady fire till the others fell back. Thus in alternate movement, with an unbroken front to the foe, with a persistent courage that refused to be hurried into a double-quick, those who were left, in sadly shortened line, rejoined the brigade and at once set to work in the construction of a line of rifle-pits on either side of the plank road. Before the task of intrenching had proceeded far, however, new dispositions were made and the brigade advanced to the crest of a hill some distance to the right and rear of the scene of the recent attack. Here under a severe fire which was returned with energy the position was held while Hancock's lines were established in the vicinity of the Brock road, to which it had been decided to fall back. The Second Corps being finally in position the brigade withdrew to the main line, forming Hancock's right, and while awaiting the expected renewal of the Confederate attack there was time to note the extent of the loss already suffered. This was serious enough, as the terrible shortening of the regimental line had proclaimed. In addition to the loss of the previous afternoon, 34 enlisted men had been killed and over a hundred officers and men wounded.

Among the killed were many of the bravest and best beloved of the regiment, the full list being as follows: Company A—Sergeant Sylvanus Muller, Oliver C. Hooker. B—Edward W Coope, Gordon Dunn, George King, Eugene Murphy, George F. Phinney, James B. Rudd. C—John W Newton, Egbert Pexley, John Walcott. D—George C. Clark, John S. Hyde, John D. Smith, George M. Wolcott. E—Sergeant John M. Partridge, Urbane H. Crittenden, Richard Fulton, Joseph Rivet, Francis Sherman. F—Color Sergeant John W Field, Corporal John M. Dunbar, Orange Bardwell, Joseph J. Rogers. G—Sergeant William M. Knapp, Joseph Bushman, Maurice Moore, Henry D. Temple, William Whitney. H—Arthur T. Merritt, Sumner Warner, Sidney P. Wood. I—John Wilcox. K—Timothy McNamara.

The wounded officers comprised Major Moody, slightly in the

head; Captain Lincoln in the side, and First Lieutenant Chalmers in the hand, producing disability from which he was subsequently discharged. It was at the beginning of the retrograde movement that Major Moody was wounded, and at first the hurt seemed to be a severe one. But the plucky major not only did not leave the field, but rendered invaluable service in preserving a firm front against the enemy. With hat off and the blood streaming over his face and breast, he skillfully maneuvered the left wing, worthily exemplifying in his own bearing the unflinching persistency and courage of the regiment of which he was a modest and worthy officer. Lieutenant Chalmers had during the winter preceding been one of the foremost in the athletic sports of the regiment, as was recalled by the unwavering tones of the brave Scotchman when, extending the mangled member toward the lieutenant-colonel near by he sang out, "No more base-ball for me, Colonel!" (The full list of wounded, accurate as it can be made by diligent research, will be found in the Appendix.)

The expected onset by Longstreet's corps was delayed on account of the severe wounding of that chieftain by his own men almost in precisely the manner in which a year before Stonewall Jackson had received his mortal hurt, though Longstreet was shot down in broad daylight while riding in front of his command arranging for the attack on Hancock. General Lee at once took personal direction of the preparations, but it was several hours before he was ready to order the advance. In the mean time Leasure's brigade of Burnside's corps charged across in front of Hancock's position, encountering little opposition; and as it seemed possible that the enemy might have given up the idea of a further struggle Hancock and Burnside were ordered to attack in force at 6 o'clock.

At 4 o'clock, however, the Confederate onset came, their lines advancing within a short distance of the Union breastworks and giving and receiving a heavy fire for a long time, the assailants in their exposed position suffering most severely. A singular circumstance, as it chanced, gave the latter a temporary advantage near the close of the engagement. In front of the Union lines, where the ground had been fought over several times, a fire had been burning since early in the day, and had communicated to the logs forming the breastworks. Fanned by the breeze it spread rapidly for hundreds of yards, the smoke and flame carried back into the faces of the defenders checking their fire and finally driving them out of position. The assailants discovering this fact pushed forward a brigade or two and made a temporary lodgement in the works, sending a part of the Federal soldiers to the rear in disorder; but a determined attack by a portion of Colonel Carrol's brigade regained the lost ground and the entire Confederate line withdrew from the hopeless contest. Hancock's men having nearly exhausted their ammunition were in no condition to deliver a counter attack, and the fighting on that part of the line ceased, not to be renewed.

But Lee, with his usual determination, had not given up the idea of inflicting further damage on his antagonist, and soon after the conflict ceased on the Union left it broke out at the extreme right. By skillful effort Ewell succeeded in massing Gordon's Georgia brigade and Johnston's North Carolinians in strong force on Sedgwick's flank. The lines of the Sixth Corps had been weakened to strengthen those further to the left, and Shaler's brigade were assiduously building breastworks near sunset when they were surprised by a vigorous onset and gave way in some confusion owing to the suddenness of the attack. Shaler himself was made prisoner, as was General Seymour, whose brigade was likewise broken, and for a time a critical state of affairs existed. The entire Sixth Corps' front was attacked vigorously, and as the troops present consisted of but four brigades in addition to the broken ones on the right there was danger that the impetus of the blow might force a further giving way. Fortunately for the Union arms, the jungle prevented the effective moving of troops by the enemy, and in the opening of the engagement the Confederate forces became scarcely less broken than the brigades receiving the shock, so that there was every danger of the temporary success turning into a disaster if fresh Federal troops should come upon the scene. The officers on each side, therefore, set themselves at once to reorganize their commands. General Wright held his remaining brigades firmly to their work, while General Sedgwick never displayed his qualities as a popular officer better than in bringing order out of the threatening chaos. Riding in the path of the fugitives and interposing the power of his presence like an insurmountable wall, he called upon the demoralized ones to "Remember the honor of the Sixth Corps." The appeal, uttered in those warm-hearted, manly tones which no battle tempest ever disconcerted, was the most potent that could be made. The men, ashamed of their temporary demoralization, halted, faced about and under the personal superintendence of their beloved commander, in hastily formed lines, went steadily back to regain the ground they had lost. This done, in the early darkness a new and stronger line, somewhat to the rear and better adapted to the occupation of the diminished force that was to hold it, was selected, fortified and occupied later in the night.

The danger of thus weakening the Union right being forcibly shown to General Meade, the five brigades which had been detached were ordered to rejoin their corps, and with the rest Eustis's Brigade, which had been relieved from the front to obtain a little rest, was roused and marched for a time in the direction of the right wing, halting at length till daylight the better to find its way through the maze.

Early next morning—the 7th—the brigade in two lines took position on the left of the corps, and through the forenoon waited in constant expectation of a fresh outpouring of blood; but the morning passed in comparative quiet. The Union skirmishers were pushed forward to feel the foe, but everywhere the report was practically the same,—Lee had withdrawn his forces to their strongly intrenched lines some three-quarters of a mile from those of the Union army, and having secured the advantages of some openings where artillery could be placed was awaiting the Federal attack. This it was decided not to make. For two days the contestants had grappled with stubborn fury, each gaining at some time certain advantages, to be quickly offset by equal disadvantages. No great contest could with more propriety be called a drawn battle. While Grant had taken the initiative, his movement had not contemplated or intended a battle where it had taken place. Lee had forced the encounter, had inflicted upon the Union army severe loss, but had himself received the first of the crushing blows which were to be continued with the merciless persistence of remorseless warfare till the military power of the Confederacy should crumble in ruins. Having engaged for two days in a deadly struggle in a region where common humanity—if considerations of humanity ever entered the councils of military commanders—should have forbidden the joining of battle, each side was now quite ready to select and to accept some other location for the continuation of the strife. The men of both commands were utterly exhausted by the arduous experiences of the past few days, yet as neither knew the purposes of the other it was necessary that every man who could be spared for the purpose should be engaged with pick and spade in fortifying so that no sudden attack should bring disaster at an unprotected point.

Thenceforth, indeed, so far as Lee's army was concerned, spades were to take the place of bayonets. While there were occasional sorties and dashes, the steadfast principle governing the tactics of the Confederate chieftain was to plant his army in the path of the enemy, intrench heavily and maintain the best possible positions of defense. This course made the prosecution of the war on the part of the Army of the Potomac bloody and at times disheartening, but it was at the same time so practical a confession of weakness on the Southern side as to proclaim to the whole unprejudiced world that the beginning of the end had come.

About noon Eustis's Brigade was relieved from its position at the left of the corps, but instead of falling to the rear as the men fondly hoped for rest and relief from the constant apprehension of the front, it moved over to the extreme right, where it formed in a single line and remained till near dark, when it was set to work constructing a line of earthworks, built of logs, and whatever could afford protection from hostile bullets. This work was naturally very difficult in such a country. The soil was filled with roots and stones interlaced in an impenetrable net work; and to all other considerations must be added the exhausted condition of the men. Yet the works were built and manned, and the defenders sank behind them in the hope of a night's unbroken rest.

Never was hope more vain, General Grant had decided, as soon as it became evident that Lee had settled into the defensive, to push on to the southward and interpose between the Confederate army and Richmond. Already were his trains in motion and the orders issued directing the movements of the various corps. According to these instructions, as soon as darkness made the movement practicable the Fifth Corps was to move by the Brock road and Todd's Tavern to Spottsylvania Court House, a march of some 15 miles, followed by General Hancock's command to Todd's Tavern, about half way from the recent battle-field. The Sixth Corps was to move by way of the pike and plank road to Chancellorsville, whence taking the cross roads by Aldrich's and Piney Branch Church it was to come in upon the Spottsylvania road between the Fifth and Second Corps, forming the center of the army. The trains of the Fifth and Sixth Corps were to follow the latter during the march, being previously parked at Chancellorsville. All movements, as well as the withdrawal of the army from its position in front of the enemy, were to be protected by cavalry outposts and skirmishers.

Such was the plan in pursuance of which the Thirty-seventh were placed under marching orders about dusk and soon afterward drew quietly to the rear, taking up the march which with more or less interruption continued all night. Daylight found the regiment near Chancellorsville, and for some distance the march was continued in the direction of Fredericksburg along the plank road. Then the main road was quitted and the column turned sharply southward. The march, which was steadily kept up till afternoon, proved one of intolerable severity. In addition to the worn condition of the men, consequent upon the incessant tax on nerve and body during the previous few days, the weather was most trying. The heat had now become intense and enervating, the roads were dry as tinder, and the dust rose in stifling clouds which hung with torturing persistency close to the earth, choking the lungs, the throat, the eyes, and settling in disgusting quantity upon the sweaty flesh wherever it could penetrate.

Added to these physical tortures, there was the constant expectation of a renewal of the battle. The army was simply feeling its way through the wilds of a sparsely populated region, and the growling cannon along the flanks gave oral demonstration that the movement was not being made free from observation. In fact the two armies were moving in almost parallel columns toward the same point, the Confederates being in advance. As was anticipated, the removal of Grant's trains the previous afternoon gave the enemy notice that the Army of the Potomac was to follow suit, and Lee gave Anderson, who had succeeded to the command of Longstreet's corps after that leader was wounded, directions to march in the morning to Spottsylvania Court House, to be in readiness to meet the new movement if it should prove to be of a hostile nature. As the woods in the Wilderness were on fire in various directions and a favorable bivouac could not be found, Anderson marched that evening and early next day planted his corps across the road leading to the Court House, in a position some two miles to the northwest of the village.

In the mean time Warren had been making the best of his way with the Fifth Corps toward Spottsylvania by the Brock road. His task proved by no means an easy one. The cavalry of the two armies had been in conflict there, fighting sharply at Todd's Tavern the previous day ; so that when in obedience to the new programme General Merritt attempted to clear the way for the advance of Warren's infantry he found the road barricaded and Fitz Hugh Lee's horsemen still in force in his path. So persistent was the opposition of the rebel cavalry and so difficult the nature of the ground for the operations of mounted men that the task of opening the route was finally turned over to the infantry, and all through the morning Warren's advance struggled along. Soon after passing the junction of the Piney Branch Church road, by which Sedgwick was to come with the Sixth Corps, the ground became more open and favorable, and Robinson's division, which had the advance, attempting to push forward promptly through the clearing at "Alsop's" found its progress checked by a furious fire from a strong intrenched line of the enemy. General Robinson himself being severely wounded, his command, utterly unfitted by the exhausted condition of the men for going into an engagement, fell back in some confusion, and Griffin's division, taking up the attack to the right, shared a like fate. At this time General Crawford's division of Pennsylvania Reserves, well tried on many a bloody field and understanding the nature of the work before them, came up and established the Union lines in spite of the vigorous protests of the enemy. General Warren, not feeling strong enough to attempt to do more, waited for the coming of General Sedgwick, and that officer on reaching the scene took command of the field. Hancock was still detained at Todd's Furnace where the Catharpin road connects the Brock road with the Shady Grove Church road by which the principal Confederate columns moved toward Spottsylvania. At this point it was feared that an attack might be made on the Federal rear, and in fact there was more or less desultory fighting during the early portion of the day; but Lee's entire army was hurrying as rapidly as possible toward Spottsylvania, where it was practically all assembled and put in battle array before night.

In Lee's front General Sedgwick was disposing his forces for the opening of battle, but the afternoon was well spent before his arrangements were completed. Then an advance was made by Colonel Brown's New Jersey Brigade of the First Division, Sixth Corps, but it encountered a strong force and was obliged to fall back without having accomplished anything. Near sunset a more successful movement was made by General Crawford's division, supported by Eustis's Brigade, which crossed the open ground, pushed into the woods in front, and coming upon a force of troops from Ewell's corps marching by the flank drove them a considerable distance, capturing quite a number of prisoners. Falling back to the opening the troops were placed in position for the night, the Thirty-seventh in the front line, and profound was the sleep into which the weary men sank the moment they were permitted to do so, continuing till the crashing of cannon at morning light called them to a tardy realization of their position.

The day which had dawned, Monday, May 9, 1864, was one never to be forgotten in the history of the Sixth Corps. Early in the morning the skirmish line, composed of a detail from the Thirty-seventh regiment, was ordered to advance, which it did in the most determined manner, driving back the opposing skirmishers for half a mile till the fortified main line of the enemy was encountered. A terrible fire broke forth from the earthworks, the bullets sweeping over the frail array of skirmishers as though to destroy every living thing within range, but the men in blue hugged the ground, gave back a fire of defiance as rapidly as they could load their pieces, and waited anxiously for the supporting charge which their own orders had seemed to promise. None came, however, and at length a retreat was reluctantly ordered. Then a partial quiet settled over the opposing forces, broken now and then by the experimental firing of some battery taking up a new position, or the faint report and sharp hiss of some sharp-shooter's deadly efforts.

It was from the latter that the catastrophe of the day was to come in the death of the beloved Sedgwick. That officer was standing in the rear of the rifle pits occupied by his command, with a few members of his staff, directing the strengthening of his lines, when the group were fired upon by some sharp-shooters far in front, whose bullets whistled so near as to cause an involuntary shrinking on the part of the staff officers. "Don't be afraid, boys, they couldn't hit an elephant at that distance!" said Sedgwick, with a glance at the location of the marksmen. Almost as the words left his lips he was struck beneath the eye by a bullet which passed entirely through his head, and without a word, with only a sad smile lighting his noble features, the brave soul which had never known fear or dishonor quitted its earthly tenement. Of the sad scene which ensued when the terrible loss was reported at head-quarters Sedgwick's adjutant general, Martin T. McMahon, says:

Each one in that tent, old gray-bearded warriors, burst into tears and for some minutes sobbed like children mourning a father. They built a bower of evergreen among the pine woods and laid him out upon a rough bier made for him by soldier hands, and all day long there were strong men weeping by this funeral couch. They came from all parts of the army, the old and the young, the well and the wounded, officers and men, to take their last look at the beloved chieftain. Many thousands of brave men who composed that army were familiar with death in all its forms. Not once nor twice had they seen strong men stricken into sudden death. Not once nor twice had they beheld men of high rank, in high command, fall amid contending hosts. They had, perhaps, grown hardened and indifferent to what was necessarily of frequent occurrence and the common expectation of all. But when the news went that day, like an electric shock, along the lines of the Army of the Potomac that John Sedgwick was dead, a great loneliness fell upon the hearts of all, and men that scarcely ever heard his voice, many that scarcely knew him by sight, wept bitter tears as if they had lost an only friend, and all recalled how on many occasions, hearing on right or left or rear the thunder of hostile guns, all anxiety passed away from the minds of men at the simple remark, "It must be all right, Uncle John is there."

No commander in the army, it is safe to say, had a closer hold upon the affections of his subordinates, from the musket bearers in the ranks to those officers who commanded his divisions, than the general now dead. The perfect incarnation of human bravery, he was at the same time modest to the point of diffidence, while his great heart overflowed with tenderness to the men of his command. Their fortunes and their fare were his own. On the march, if not in front he was in their midst, sharing their trials. His last night of life was passed among his faithful soldiers, like them sleeping upon the earth without tent or blanket. Whatever the duty to which his command might be called, they knew that his hand was firmly upon the helm, that his brain was clear and his purpose developed. As was the officer, such were the troops with whose organization he had been so long identified. Where he led they would follow, and their only fear had been that under the pressure to take a higher position he might at length yield, and leave the immediate command of the corps. They had never thought of the terrible blow which had now fallen.*

---
*General Sedgwick was a native of Connecticut, graduated at West Point in 1837 and served with much distinction in the Mexican war, reaching the rank of major, serving afterward in Texas till the outbreak of the rebellion. In March, 1861, he was made lieutenant-colonel of the Second

In accordance with the known wish of General Sedgwick, General Horatio G. Wright, the able commander of the First Division, was given command of the Sixth Corps, General David A. Russell taking the First Division. From casualties and other causes constant changes were transpiring among commanders of every grade, and at this juncture one in which the Thirty-seventh was peculiarly interested occurred in the transfer of General Eustis† and the permanent assignment of Colonel Edwards to the command of the brigade. In this promotion to a broader field of usefulness Colonel Edwards received a merited recognition. His qualities were eminently those of a general officer. Quick to discern, prompt in execution, brave to a fault, knowing intimately the troops with which he had to do, it was morally impossible that Colonel Edwards should fail to win a high measure of success. As a regimental commander he had written the impress of his character firmly on the Thirty-seventh. If in the desire to attain absolute perfection for his loved command he had sometimes been hasty and consequently unjust to his subordinates, he had bitterly regretted that injustice. The interests of his regiment had invariably been safe in his hands, since no commander could have been more jealous of the welfare of those intrusted to him.

In Lieutenant-Colonel Montague the regiment found an able and acceptable successor to its promoted colonel. The methods of the officers differed essentially. If Edwards was born to command, Montague was intended by nature for a leader. His personal power and influence were unbounded, his military qualities admirable, and his perfect knowledge of the regiment in detail assured a worthy record for the future.

These changes had taken place during the 9th, and meanwhile the Army of the Potomac had developed and completed its lines

United States cavalry and in August was given command of a brigade in the Army of the Potomac and was afterward assigned to command the Third Division, Second Corps, doing noble service on the peninsula and with Pope in his disastrous campaign. At Antietam his division fought with desperation, and he was twice wounded, but refused to yield the command till he fainted from loss of blood. In January, 1863, he was given command of the Ninth Corps, but the 5th of February following was assigned to the Sixth.

†General Henry L. Eustis was a graduate of West Point in the class with General Pope, standing first in his class, and at the outbreak of the war was a professor in the Lawrence Scientific School at Cambridge, Mass. He was at this time temporarily assigned to the command of the Fourth Brigade, First Division, Sixth Corps, but resigned the service June 27 following.

facing the Confederate position. The Union right was held by the Second Corps, which had been brought down from Todd's Furnace when it became apparent that there was no real danger in that quarter. The Fifth and Sixth Corps formed the center, with the Ninth on the extreme left. While the front was strongly held a line of earthworks was thrown up just in the rear, to which the troops presently retired to obtain shelter from the incessant fire which the enemy's sharp-shooters kept up. During the afternoon General Hancock was directed to move his corps across the Po, which at that point ran between the two lines, the immediate objective being an extensive Confederate wagon train which was seen to be moving toward Spottsylvania. A sharp engagement had begun to result next day when he was called back in order that his troops might be disposed to assist in an attack upon the enemy's center which had been decided on. It was not easy to withdraw troops from the immediate face of the foe with a conflict in progress, but this was done till only two brigades were left to sustain the contest. To complicate their situation, the woods in their rear caught fire, but the gallant fellows hurled back the force that was pressing upon them and then extricated themselves, though obliged to abandon their wounded comrades to perish by the flames. On both sides the impression left was that of a Federal defeat.

The attack which followed was unmistakably a disaster, the troops of the Fifth Corps throwing themselves against the enemy's intrenchments repeatedly, and at some points gaining a footing upon them only to be driven back with terrible loss, while comparatively little injury was inflicted upon the assailed. A little later in the day—that is, about 6 o'clock—a charge was made by Upton's brigade of the Sixth Corps which was more successful. That officer struck and penetrated the intrenchments of what afterward became so horribly famous as the Angle, captured a large number of prisoners, several flags and guns, making a lodgment with his unaided brigade in the second line of works; but the expected support did not come and after dark his line was retired, having inflicted as well as sustained serious loss. Further to the left General Burnside made a strong reconnaissance without result, but with the loss of General T. G. Stevenson commanding his First Division killed.

During these disastrous attempts the Thirty-seventh took no active part as an organization, though its men were on the skirmish lines in liberal detail, doing good service and suffering some loss, as did the men behind the intrenchments, from the constant firing of the Confederate sharp-shooters. Artillery had now come into use on both sides, and the guns of the Sixth Corps in many cases occupied the same works with the infantry. Yet so exhausted were the men from their incessant trials that many of them slept beneath the muzzles of the guns being fired directly above them.

The results thus far had not been very encouraging, but the indomitable energy of General Grant knew no such word as discouragement, and the following morning he sent to Washington a brief summary of his operations, closing with the famous sentence, "I propose to fight it out on this line, if it takes all summer!" Through the 11th there was little fighting, the day being devoted to preparations for the terrible struggle of the 12th. Toward night the Thirty-seventh, with the rest of the Second Division, were relieved from the rifle-pits by the Third Division, moved to the rear and massed in an open field where, despite a steady fall of rain, the exhausted troops slept soundly.

Very early in the morning they were awake, and with the coming of light the terrible crash of battle which seemed to fill the air bespoke a renewal of the struggle. In fact the Second Corps under the determined lead of Hancock had undertaken to do what Colonel Upton with his brigade had shown to be practicable—penetrate the Confederate line at the Angle. This Angle consisted of a peculiar formation of the enemy's defenses, located almost directly north of Spottsylvania Court House. Beginning at their left, the general direction of the Confederate front till this point was reached was about due north. Here it turned and faced the east, running irregularly till the right rested on the river Po to the southwest of the Court House. At the Angle, however, the formation of the land was such that the line of defense instead of turning sharply in the new direction bent out forming the two sides of a blunt-nosed triangle. Along what would have been the base ran the second line which, like each of the sides may be described as about a mile in length. The ground sloped up to these works from the front, and for some distance before they were reached it was cleared of standing timber, though the approach was more or less obstructed.

As soon as the morning light became sufficient to allow his guides to take the point of direction, Hancock, whose corps was massed near the Landrum house in front of the Angle, ordered the charge. Through the rain and fog of the early morning the Second Corps in two irresistible lines swept up to and over the works. Johnson's division of Ewell's corps held the lines— three brigades of Virginia and one of Louisiana troops, the very flower of the Confederate army. Men could not have fought better than these men did, hand to hand in the trenches; but the enveloping force closed about them forcing the surrender of over 3,000 soldiers, with 20 cannon and 30 battle flags. Johnson himself and Steuart, one of his brigade commanders, were among the captives—both being former army friends of Hancock. So far all was well, and Hancock reported back to Grant, "I have used up Johnson and am now going for Early." But it was not easy to achieve further success. The Second Corps was disorganized by its experiences thus far, and when it reached the second line, at the base of the Angle, it was unable to make any further advance. Here the enemy was met in force, prepared to recover the ground that had been lost. Despite the gallantry of his men Hancock's advance was checked and thrown back, and it soon became evident that the supporting lines must be relied upon to hold what had been won. This work was to be done by the Sixth Corps.

As already described, Russell's and Neill's divisions of that corps had been moved to the rear and massed the previous evening, ready either to support Hancock or to attack in their own front, as developments might seem to justify. At half-past 4 the bugles rang out the assembly and an aide from General Wright announced that the brigade first under arms would take the lead.

Edwards's Brigade (as it must henceforth be known) was first in motion, and moving toward the left near the Landrum house, advanced to the edge of the clearing in front of the contested intrenchments where it was formed in a single line, the Tenth, Second and Thirty-seventh from right to left—the Seventh having been left on the skirmish line in front of the Third Division. Moving up the slope to the recently captured works under a deadly fire which swept over the entire region, the brigade connected with the Excelsior Brigade of Mott's division of the Second Corps, taking position against the outer face of the Confederate intrenchments. These works were built of logs, strengthened with an embankment of dirt, and having a "head-log" at the top to protect the heads of the defenders while delivering their fire through the crevice beneath it. They were thus about equally available for defense in either direction.

Scarcely had the Thirty-seventh taken position when the first of the desperate efforts of the enemy to regain possession of their lost works was made. A division in three lines swept forward magnificently, their approach covered by a ravine till they were within a very short distance. A ripple of fire ran along the line of blue and the battle front of gray melted away into broken fragments which scrambled back into the ravine, leaving the ground strewn with their dead and disabled. But the determination of madness seemed to possess the Southern generals. Again and again were their solid columns pushed into the fatal Angle, only at each renewed effort to be sent back in disorder, leaving more and more of their bravest dead upon the scene till the slain actually lay piled upon each other. All authorities competent to speak from intelligent observation agree that nowhere else in the entire war was such slaughter as within this comparatively limited arena.

Finding that the plan of assaulting in heavy columns was a useless waste of life, the Confederates resorted to every device to accomplish their purpose. In some parts of the field lines of skirmishers were rushed across, those that lived to make the passage hugging one side of the works while the Union soldiers occupied the other and fighting obstinately across in that way, each thrusting his gun over the crest and firing down into those on the other side; but in front of the Thirty-seventh the fire was too hot and well directed to allow of approach to such narrow quarters.

It was during this struggle that the Thirty-seventh captured its first battle flag. Following a temporary lull in the conflict a line of battle appeared in its front and swept forward with a slightly diagonal inclination directly toward the crouching regiment. "Hold your fire, men! Not one shot till I give the order!" said the indomitable Montague. Three hundred dark muzzles looked grimly out from beneath the head-log, each covering its chosen victim. Not till the nearest Confederates were within a few yards was heard the anxiously awaited order to "Fire!" There was a flash, one simultaneous crash, and a cloud of white smoke spread like a curtain before the breastworks. When it dissipated that beautiful line of battle had entirely disappeared, the color-sergeant lay dead in the midst of his guard, and his flag, falling upon his dead body, became the well-earned prize of the Thirty-seventh.

The incessant firing in connection with the prevailing rain-storm soon choked and fouled the heated muskets till they were almost unserviceable, and as the line could not be relieved weapons were exchanged with a regiment which marched up in the rear, and so without a break the merciless fire was kept up. Finally at 4 o'clock, after ten hours of incessant engagement, the regiment was relieved and fell back a few rods behind a sheltering ridge to allow the men to take their first food since the few hasty mouthfuls of the morning and obtain a fresh supply of ammunition. Soon after dark one of the relieving regiments unaccountably broke and huddled to the rear, wildly ejaculating, "The rebels are in the works!" The Thirty-seventh, many of the men asleep and entirely out of ammunition, were lying in the mud a few rods away, close by brigade head-quarters. Colonel Edwards and Lieutenant-Colonel Montague sprang to their feet, startled by the rush. Quick as a flash came the orders of the soldierly Edwards, "Advance the Thirty-seventh and hold the line with the bayonet!" At once rang out the clear tones of the lieutenant-colonel, "Forward, Thirty-seventh to the breast-works! Fix bayonets!" Guided by his voice, the officers and men of the valiant regiment scrambled to their feet, and, undaunted by the losses of the doubtful day, undismayed by the incipient panic, equal in courage to confront in the darkness an unknown and unseen foe—more trying because unknown and unseen,—they hurriedly but with magnificent spirit pushed through the broken abatis to the unguarded section and crowned the crest with a strong wall of steel. Then a fresh supply of ammunition arrived and through the long night hours till almost morning the ripple and splutter and crack of the musketry fire never abated. About 3 o'clock on the morning of the 13th the fire from the enemy slackened and finally ceased, and a patrol sent out by Colonel Edwards discovered that the enemy had retreated from the immediate front. They had in fact fallen back to the new line at the base of the angle. A skirmish line was promptly advanced which brought in a considerable number of prisoners, and in the morning the brigade was relieved by one from the First Division, retiring to the vicinity of the Landrum house where it stacked arms and bivouacked for the day, the men dropping upon the muddy ground in the drenching rain and falling asleep at once from exhaustion.

There was opportunity now to review the work of the regiment during the trying period just passed, and the Thirty-seventh had cause for pride in the part it had taken. Both General Meade and General Neill in their reports spoke in the highest praise of the services of the brigade, and Colonel Edwards, while complimenting his entire command, after speaking of Captain Lincoln, who though suffering from the wound received in the Wilderness six days before fought with his company and received a severe wound in the side, says, " Great credit is due Lieutenant-Colonel Montague for the manner in which he fought his regiment." The latter in fact, received the brevet of colonel for "distinguished gallantry at the battle of Spottsylvania Court House," the first brevet bestowed in the regiment.

The fire of the Thirty-seventh had probably been the most remarkable delivered by any regiment during the same length of time, over 400 rounds per man having been expended, and this in the midst of a continuous rain-storm. Where this fire swept over the enemy's line the bullets cut off the trunk of an oak tree 21 inches in diameter, so that the tree fell within the Confederate works, injuring several men of the First South Carolina regiment of McGowan's brigade. The trunk of this tree is still preserved in the War Department at Washington as a memorial of the terrible struggle at the Angle.

Intense as had been the strain on the men for so long, their morale had shown no sign of weakening. Especially was their heroic endurance tested when at one time a call was made for 50 volunteers to undertake an enterprise from which none could hope to escape alive. The full number including Captain Tyler, promptly stepped from the ranks, but the plans were changed and the sacrifice was not demanded.

The loss of the regiment had been severe, especially in officers. Lieutenant-Colonel Montague, after being knocked down by a bullet which struck him upon the arm, inflicting a severe bruise, was wounded in the foot while leading the regiment up to hold the works with the bayonet as previously described, and after seeing the men in position was obliged to leave the field. Major Moody had previously received a severe and disabling wound in the thigh, leaving the regiment in command of Captain Donnelly. Captain Pease, the kind-hearted Christian and commander of Company B from its formation, had received a wound from which he died two days later. Second Lieutenants George S. Cooke and Joseph Follansbee, but recently promoted—brave and true men who had worthily won their shoulder-straps—were mortally wounded; the former already dead, and the latter clinging to life till the 23d. Besides these Captain Lincoln was seriously wounded; First Lieutenants Champney and Wellman were struck, the former in the leg and the latter in the hand with a disabling injury; while Second Lieutenant Albert C. Sparks had suffered a terrible wound in the chest, but fighting bravely for life he finally triumphed, contrary to all expectations.

The killed thus far since the change to Spottsylvania comprised the following: Company A, Edward Bergley; B, George

N. Barnes, John McNerny; C, Sergeant George D. Chapin, Corporal Michael Moren, Thomas McCabe, 2d; D, Corporal William M. Kingsley; E, Colonel D. Halsey; F, Martin S. Hubbard; H, Lyman C. Bartlett, Edmund H. Sears; I, Corporal Josiah B. Hawks, Albert R. Clark, Edwin O. Wentworth; K, Michael Freeman.

The wounded, of whom several were fatally hurt, (see Roll of Honor for the classified list,) reached nearly 50, so that the regiment was reduced to little more than 300 members present—a trifle over half the number with which it had set forth from Brandy Station ten days before.

CHAPTER XIV

A GLANCE TO THE REAR.

THE WOUNDED AND DYING.—HOSPITAL SCENES AND INCIDENTS.—THE CHRISTIAN AND SANITARY COMMISSIONS.

Any picture of soldier life, such as it is the purpose of this volume to present, would be incomplete if it did not at some time turn from the battle line, from the march and the bivouac, to glance at that vast assemblage in the rear of every battle-field where the horror and the brutality of war can best be learned—where also may be gathered some of the noblest lessons of human charity, some of the most touching examples of patriotic devotion, some of the truest exhibitions of heroism. There had been abundant aggregations of human sacrifice before. The bloody horrors of Bull Run had come to the sensibilities of the startled country with an unveiling of what war really meant of bloodshed and suffering; but this proved only a drop in the bucket of what followed in ever increasing volume through the peninsular campaign, Manassas, Antietam, Fredericksburg, Chancellorsville, Gettysburg,—in conjunction with the great fields of the West where in almost equal numbers the bravest of the nation were giving their lives and their life-blood in unstinted measure on the altar of a united country.

Yet all these, it seemed, had but paved the way for the terrible outpouring of this spring campaign of 1864. The strong regiments which went into the Wilderness on that sunny May morning in magnificent array, trusted because proved on many a trying field, shrank to mere fragments in the ordeal to which they were subjected; yet the incessant rattle and turmoil of battle did not cease. When one body of troops became too much decimated to continue the struggle longer another relieved it, fresh men were hurried forward from every available point to fill the places of the fallen, while the thunder of cannon and the rattle of musketry by day and by night, now receding, now advancing, kept up the chorus of death which was never to cease till the military power of the enemies of the Union should crumble away and dissolve.

The struggle in the Wilderness had many peculiarities. The fighting was mostly done at close range and by infantry; hence the wounds were almost entirely inflicted by bullets, which while perhaps equally fatal did not present the horrible mangling of artillery fire. Each army had its main intrenched line and between the two most of the fighting was done, charge and counter charge sweeping over the same ground in some cases a half-dozen times. This entire region was therefore filled with the dead and wounded, those of the two armies mingling. Such as could crawl to one side or the other did so, since even if captivity resulted it presented in the prospect less terrors than continued suffering from undressed wounds, while the victim lay exposed to the hot sun and the fire of both friend and foe: or more dreadful still, to be burned alive by the forest fires which even the flash of a musket might kindle, and by which means it was estimated that not less than 200 Union wounded perished. Unavoidably the fate of many a poor fellow remains to this day wrapped in mystery. Whether in struggling through the tangled undergrowth, separated momentarily from his comrades, some hissing missile struck him dead, whether through untold agony his life passed slowly away with none to soothe or know the sad fate: or borne away to the wretched prison pen to yield up his life in its awful precincts,—one thing is sure, that in the great army of martyrs each name shall be sacredly enrolled and faithfully treasured.

Yet while this terrible sprinkling of stricken humanity carpeted the ground between the two lines of battle, the great bulk of the injured managed in some way to reach the rear, where every provision possible under the circumstances was made for their relief. In some convenient spot to the rear of each division or corps engaged, will be found the hastily improvised hospital. The command has perhaps marched miles on the double-quick and is "ordered in" to hold some important position. Before the column seems to have halted the bleeding victims begin to hurry back or are borne on stretchers, seeking the prompt attention which may stanch the flow of blood and save' life. The surgeons, with such assistants as are available, have selected a location for the hospital, sheltered from fire and convenient to water if possible. Perhaps they have been able to pitch a few fly tents to protect from the storm or the scorching heat of the sun; more likely there may be nothing beyond the shelter of a tree, and at the best the only couch will be the bare ground, muddy or dry and parched. If a few leaves and boughs can be obtained for the worst cases there is so much in the way of luxury. Before even these simple preparations can be completed the freightage of misery begins to arrive. Let a surgeon speak for himself and for his class in regard to the work which follows:

At the field hospitals the work of destruction is seen in all its horror. There wounded men by thousands are brought together, filling the tents and stretched upon every available spot of ground for many rods around. Surgeons, with never tiring energy, are ministering to their wants, giving them food, dressing their wounds or standing at the operating table removing the shattered fragments of limbs. Men wounded in every conceivable way, men with mutilated bodies, with shattered limbs and broken heads, men enduring their injuries with heroic patience, and men giving way to violent grief, men stoically indifferent, and men rejoicing that it is *only a leg*. To all these the surgeons are to give such relief as lies in their power, a task the very thought of which would overcome physicians at home, but upon which the army surgeon enters with as much coolness and confidence as though he could do it all at once. He has learned to do what he can, contenting himself with working day and night without respite, and often without food, until by unremitting but quiet toil the wants of all are relieved.

While it is unquestionably true that among medical officers, as elsewhere in the army, there were those who were unworthy and a disgrace to the service, it is equally true that the devoted surgeon often did a work quite as trying as the facing of hostile rifle-pits, and in a way to win the undying affections of those for whom he labored. A prominent officer of the Sanitary Commission, who with the best of opportunities for observation spoke no hasty word, says in regard to the services performed by the medical staff at the time of which we write:

The devotion, the solicitude, the unceasing efforts to remedy the defects of the situation, the untiring attentions to the wounded upon their part were so marked as to be apparent to all who visited the hospitals. It must be remembered that these same officers had endured the privations and fatigues of the long forced marches with the rest of the army; they had shared its dangers, for one medical officer from each regiment follows it into battle and is liable to the accidents of war, as has been repeatedly and fatally the case ; that its field hospitals are often, from the changes of the line of battle, brought under fire of the enemy, and that while in these situations the surgeons are called upon to exercise the calmest judgment, to perform the most serious and critical operations, and this quickly and constantly. The battle ceasing, their labors continue. While other officers are sleeping, renewing their strength for further efforts, the medical are still toiling. They have to improvise hospitals from the rudest materials, to surmount seeming impossibilities. The work is unending, both by day and night, the anxiety is constant, and the strain upon both the mental and physical faculties unceasing.

Chaplain Morse of the Thirty-seventh, whose time was divided between his regiment at the front and the hospitals in the rear, writes interestingly of the scenes at the Wilderness, from which a few extracts will be read with interest. Referring to the engagement of the 5th, he pays a deserved tribute to the bravery with which the men bore their sufferings and notices the little complaining heard. One of the wounded men was in great pain when brought in, but after his wounds were dressed and a comfortable couch provided he began singing in sweet and touching tones, "Who will care for mother now ?" All about the hospital worked till late into the night and by dividing their number into reliefs the labor was carried on all through the night. After a season of duty with the regiment, Mr. Morse returned with the hospital steward to the division hospital on Saturday morning, learning that numbers of his own regiment were there in need of care. He adds :

> Our aid was very timely. There were some flies pitched but they did not afford space enough to protect a tenth part of the number from the scorching heat of the sun, which was almost insufferable. I provided myself with a canteen of water, a cup, a pair of scissors, bandages and lint, and went to work. I first sought out the men of my own regiment and rendered them all possible relief. All the men I found disengaged who were well I employed in putting up screens of shelter tents to afford the wounded men a shade. Such a field of labor I never saw before.

Wherever I went or in what direction I turned the men would beg in piteous tones for water, or to have their positions changed, or their wounds moistened, or for some other favor. I found several who had been wounded two days or more and their wounds had not been touched at all. I will give a single instance of the kind of relief I was enabled to furnish. I found a man in terrible agony. He had received a charge of buck shot in the calf of the leg. Fearing it might bleed too much he put a suspender around his leg just below the knee and buckled it tightly. Below that his leg was badly swollen and turning black and blue. His pants, drawers and stocking were thoroughly saturated with blood and had dried and adhered closely to the skin. I cut the suspender, and then cut off all the bloody clothing, washed his leg thoroughly, put compresses soaked in water upon the wounds, secured them with bandages, had a shelter tent put up to make a shade, and in a few minutes the man fell asleep. You can imagine how grateful he felt and how much satisfaction I experienced. So it was in numerous instances. There were wounds of all possible kinds and in all parts of the body. I worked so hard and so long that finally I became so faint and dizzy that I was obliged to go one side and lie down, fearing I might fall headlong upon wounded men. In the afternoon we loaded the ambulances as fast as they came. I remained till I succeeded in getting every man of the Thirty-seventh loaded. It was then after dark and there was to be no more transportation. About 60 poor fellows were left there on the ground. They begged piteously to be taken away, and actually cried. Surgeons and nurses remained with them, expecting to be immediately taken prisoners. Nothing has seemed so hard to me since I have been in the service as to go away and leave those suffering comrades to fall into the hands of the enemy.

This abandonment was rendered necessary when the flank movement to Spottsylvania was decided upon, all for whom any description of transportation could be provided being sent to Fredericksburg. Those who could walk had meantime started on in advance and were first to reach the city. Their treatment on entering the place can only be recalled after the lapse of 20 years with a thrill of indignation. Some 300 of them were surrounded by the inhabitants, led by Mayor Slaughter, and turned over to a Confederate cavalry force, who immediately marched the poor fellows to Richmond as prisoners of war. In fact the citizens of Fredericksburg displayed throughout extreme bitterness and hostility to the Union wounded and those who ministered to them, though motives of prudence prevented any further outrages.

Very rapidly the little city filled to its utmost capacity with the wounded. A never ceasing train of wagons wound down over the famous hights, each with its ghastly, bleeding burden. Before the tide from the Wilderness had ceased to flow that from Spottsylvania began. It was a terrible jaunt for the poor fellows. Fifteen miles of jolting ride by day and night, over abominable roads, constantly growing worse under the incessant use to which they were subjected, was no light trial for men wounded almost to death, as were thousands of those who thus came. Many died on the way. An unbroken train of army wagons went rumbling and rattling to the front loaded with supplies for the active army, and came rumbling and rattling back loaded with the wounded for whom there were no other means of transportation. To attend the 30,000 sufferers 40 surgeons had been sent from the front. The number was utterly inadequate, yet it was all that could be spared, for the armies still confronted each other and the work of death was constantly going on. The handful of medical officers worked faithfully, but they were already worn out with incessant labor and many broke down entirely and had to be sent to Washington for care and rest. The assistants and nurses were obliged to devote much of their time to burying the dead, of whom the number was great. To quote the words of another devoted surgeon at this trying time:

We are almost worked to death; my feet are terribly swollen; yet we cannot rest for there are so many poor fellows who are suffering. All day yesterday I worked at the operating table. That was the fourth day I had worked at those terrible operations since the battle commenced, and I have also worked at the tables two whole nights and part of another. Oh! it is awful. It does not seem as though I could take a knife in my hand to-day, yet there are hundreds of cases of amputation waiting for me. Poor fellows come and beg almost on their knees for the privilege of having the first chance. It is a scene of horror such as I never saw. God forbid that I should ever see another. * * * I see so many grand men dropping one by one. They are my acquaintances and friends. They look to me for help and I have to turn away heart-sick at my inability to relieve their sufferings.

In this vast assembly the Thirty-seventh regiment was represented by nearly a fourth of its members, scattered throughout the town wherever it might chance; order there was none.

Anxious friends came to the city seeking loved ones who were supposed to be there, but they had no guide and could only wander about scanning each face and inquiring everywhere. Food and supplies of every kind were scarce for a time, but the government promptly forwarded an abundance, and the two noble Commissions of practical charity,—the Christian and the Sanitary,—were early on hand with supplies of delicacies and a strong corps of physicians and surgeons from civil life. Each of these organizations was a model in its way, and no sketch of the great civil war can be written without appreciative mention of their inestimably valuable work. The Sanitary Commission, especially, had at this time developed its hold upon the hearts of the people and the soldiers to a wonderful degree. For the first year and a half of the war its operations though faithful had been on a comparatively small scale from want of funds, but at that time $200,000 was received from California, stimulating contributions from other states, so that thenceforth it never needed money. In the spring and summer of 1864 numerous extensive fairs were held in the cities of the North, netting large sums and enabling the Commission to render invaluable relief to the suffering and destitute. The entire amount received and used by the Commissson was not far from $5,000,000, and apart from the relief and care afforded, its work in the institution of soldiers' homes, the preparation of vital and sanitary statistics, the furnishing of information as to missing soldiers, and the collection of their pay, deserves and will ever have the gratitude of the American nation. The Christian Commission, no less devoted, in addition to its labors for the spiritual welfare of the men, lost no opportunity to minister to their physical needs.

In the lull in the great struggle at Spottsylvania one of the best-known press correspondents with the army spent a day at Fredericksburg, and a few extracts from his impressions will be of especial interest to many readers of this book :

The city is a vast hospital; churches, public buildings, private dwellings, stores, chambers, attics, basements, all full. There are thousands upon the sidewalk. All day long the ambulances have been arriving from the field. There are but few wounded left at the front, those only whom to remove would be certain death.

A red flag has been flung out at the Sanitary Commission rooms,—a white one at the rooms of the Christian Commission. There are 300 volunteer nurses in attendance. The Sanitary Commission have 14 wagons bringing supplies from Belle Plain. The Christian Commission has less transportation facilities, but in devotion, in hard work, in patient effort, it is the compeer of its more bountifully supplied neighbor. The nurses are divided into details, some for day service, some for night work. Each State has its Relief Committee.

How patient the brave fellows are! Not a word of complaint, but thanks for the slightest favor. There was a lack of crutches. I saw an old soldier of the California regiment, who fought with the lamented Baker at Ball's Bluff, and who had been in more than 20 battles, hobbling about with the arms of a settee nailed to strips of board. His regiment was on its way home, its three years of service having expired. It was reduced to a score or two of weather-beaten, battle-scarred veterans. The disabled comrade could hardly keep back the tears as he saw them pass down the street. "Few of us left. The bones of the boys are on every battle-field where the Army of the Potomac has fought," said he.

There was the sound of the pick and spade in the church-yard, a heaving-up of new earth,—a digging of trenches, not for defense against the enemy, but for the last resting-place of departed heroes. There they lie, each wrapped in his blanket, the last bivouac! For them there is no more war,—no charges into the thick, leaden rain-drops,—no more hurrahs, no more cheering for the dear old flag! They have fallen, but the victory is theirs,—theirs the roll of eternal honor. Side by side,— men from Massachusetts, from Pennsylvania, and from Wisconsin,—from all the states, resting in one common grave. Peace to them! blessings on the dear ones,—wives, mothers, children whom they have left behind.

Go into the hospitals;—armless, legless men, wounds of every description. Men on the floor, on the hard seats of church pews, lying in one position all day, unable to move till the nurse, going the rounds, gives them aid. They must wait until their food comes. Some must be fed with a spoon, for they are as helpless as little children.

"O that we could get some straw for the brave fellows," said the Rev. Mr. Kimball, of the Christian Commission. He had wandered about town, searching for the article.

"There is none to be had. We shall have to send to Washington for it," said the surgeon in charge.

Straw! I remember two stacks, four miles out on the Spottsylvania road. I saw them last night as I galloped in from the front.

Armed with a requisition from the provost marshal to seize two stacks of straw, with wagons driven by freedmen, accompanied by four Christian Commission delegates, away we went across the battle field of December, fording Hazel Run, gaining the hights, and reaching the straw stacks owned by Rev. Mr. Owen, a bitter rebel.

"By whose authority do you take my property?" "The provost marshal, sir." "Are you going to pay me for it?" "You must see the provost marshal, sir. If you are a loyal man, and will take the oath of allegiance, doubtless you will get your pay when we have put down the rebellion." "It is pretty hard. My children are just ready to starve. I have nothing for them to eat, and you come to take my property without paying for it." "Yes sir, war is hard. You must remember, sir, that there are thousands of wounded men,—your rebel wounded as well as ours. If your children are on the point of starving, those men are on the point of dying. We must have the straw for them. What we don't take to-night we will get in the morning. Meanwhile, sir, if anybody attempts to take it, please say to them that it is for the hospital, and they can't have it."

It is evening. Thousands of soldiers just arrived from Washington have passed through the town to take their places in the front. The hills around are white with innumerable tents. A band is playing lively airs to cheer the wounded in the hospitals. I have been looking in at the sufferers. Two or three have gone to their long home. They will need no more attention. A surgeon is at work upon a ghastly wound, taking up the arteries. An attendant is pouring cold water upon a swollen limb. In the Episcopal church a nurse is bolstering up a wounded officer in the area behind the altar. Men are lying in the pews, on the seats, on boards on top of the pews.

Two candles in the spacious building throw their feeble rays into the dark recesses, faintly disclosing the recumbent forms. There is heavy, stifled breathing, as of constant effort to suppress cries extorted by acutest pain.

Passing into the street you see a group of women, talking about *our* wounded,—rebel wounded, who are receiving their especial devotion. The provost marshal's patrol is going its rounds to preserve order.

Starting down the street, you reach the rooms of the Christian Commission. Some of the men are writing letters for the soldiers, some eating their night-rations, some dispensing supplies. Passing through the rooms, you gain the grounds in the rear,—a beautiful garden once,— not unattractive now. The air is redolent with honeysuckle and locust blossoms. The prunifolia is unfolding its delicate milk-white petals; roses are opening their tinted leaves.

Fifty men are gathered round a summer-house,—warm-hearted men, who have been all day in the hospitals. Their hearts have been wrung by the scenes of suffering, in the exercise of Christian charity, imitating the example of the Redeemer of men. They have dispensed food for the body and nourishment for the soul. They have given cups of cold water in the name of Jesus, and prayed with those departing to the Silent Land. The moonlight shimmers through the leaves of the locusts, as they meet at that evening hour to worship God.

After singing, a chaplain says, "Brethren, I had service this afternoon in the First Division hospital of the Second Corps. The surgeon in charge, before prayer, asked all who desired to be prayed for to raise their hands, and nearly every man who had a hand raised it. Let us remember them in our prayers to-night."

A man in the summer house, so far off that I cannot distinguish him, says, "Every man in the Second Division of the Sixth Corps hospital raised his hand for prayers to-night."

One who was on the spot thus speaks of the work done at Fredricksburg by Mrs. Barlow, the accomplished wife of General Barlow, who died at Washington, July 27, 1864, of fever contracted in this work:

She had in some way gained possession of a wretched-looking pony, and a small cart or farmer's wagon, with which she was continually on the move, driving about town or country in search of such provisions or other articles as were needed for the sick and wounded. The surgeon in charge had on one occasion assigned her the task of preparing a building which had been taken for a hospital, for a large number of wounded who were expected almost immediately. The building was empty, containing not the slightest furniture or preparation for the sufferers, save a large number of bed-sacks, without straw or other material to fill them. On requisition a quantity of straw was obtained, but not nearly enough for the expected need, and we were standing in a kind of mute despair, considering if it were indeed possible to secure any comfort for the poor fellows expected, when Mrs. Barlow came in. "I'll find some more straw," was her cheerful reply, and in another moment she was urging her tired beast toward another part of the town where she remembered to have seen a bale of the desired article earlier in the day. Half an hour afterward the straw had been confiscated, loaded upon the little wagon by willing hands and brought to the hospital. She then helped to fill and arrange the sacks, and afterward drove about the town in search of articles which, by the time the ambulances brought in their freight of misery and pain, had served to furnish the place with some means of alleviation.

Of the visit of a ministering angel of another type, Dr. Reed, a surgeon, says:

One afternoon, just before the evacuation, when the atmosphere of our rooms was close and foul, and all were longing for a breath of our pure northern air, while the men were moaning in pain or were restless with fever, and our hearts were sick with pity for the sufferers, I heard a light step upon the stairs, and looking up I saw a young lady enter, who brought with her such an atmosphere of calm and cheerful courage, so much freshness, such an expression of gentle, womanly sympathy, that her mere presence seemed to revive the drooping spirits of the men, and to give a new power of endurance through the long and painful hours of suffering. First with one, then at the side of another, a friendly word here, a gentle nod and smile there, a tender sympathy with each prostrate sufferer, a sympathy which could read in his eyes his longing for home love and the presence of some absent one—in those few minutes hers was indeed an angel ministry. Before she left the room she sang to them, first some stirring national melody, then some sweet or plaintive hymn to strengthen the fainting heart, and I remember how the notes penetrated to every part of the building. Soldiers with less severe wounds, from the rooms above, began to crawl out into the entries, and men from below crept up on their hands and knees to catch each note, and to receive of the benediction of her presence—for such it was to them.

Let it not be supposed that these brave men and women confined their ministrations to the great hospitals in and about the cities or far from the fields of strife. Wherever there was suffering from wounds or sickness they went, to the field hospitals and even along the lines of battle. The Sanitary Commission alone was represented on at least 500 of the 600 battle and skirmish fields of the war, and an authority already quoted ("Carleton") thus speaks of the work in the field hospitals a little later in the campaign:

I recall in this connection, a hot, dry, sultry day. The sun shone from a brazen sky. The grass and shrubs were scorched, withered, and powdered with dust, which rose in clouds behind every passing wagon. Even the aspens were motionless, and there was not air enough to stir the long, lithe needles of the pines. The birds of the forest sought the deepest shade, and hushed even their twitter. It was difficult for men in robust health to breathe, and they picked out the coolest places and gave themselves up to the languor of the hour. It required an earnest effort to do anything. Yet through this blazing day men crouched in the trenches from morning till night, or lay in their shallow rifle-pits, watching the enemy,—parched, broiled, burned, not daring to raise their heads or lift their hands. To do so was to suffer death or wounds.

The hospital tents, though pitched in the woods, were like ovens, absorbing and holding the heat of the sun, whose rays the branches of the trees but partially excluded. Upon the ground lay the sick and wounded, fevered and sore, with energies exhausted, perspiration oozing from their faces, nerves quivering and trembling, pulses faint and feeble, and life ebbing away. Their beds were pine boughs. They lay as they came from the battle-field, wearing their soiled, torn, and bloody garments, and tantalized by myriads of flies.

The surgeons in charge were kind-hearted and attentive. They used all means in their power to make their patients comfortable. Was this the place where the sick were to regain their health, far from home and friends! With nothing to cheer them, hope was dying out, and despondency setting in; and memory, ever busy, was picturing the dear old home scenes, so painfully in contrast with their dismal present.

There were no clouds to shut out the sun, but the brazen dome of the sky glowed with steady heat. The Christian Commission tent had been besieged all day by soldiers, who wanted onions, pickles, lemons, oranges,—anything sour, anything to tempt the taste. A box of oranges had been brought from City Point the night before. It was suggested that they be distributed at once to the sick and wounded. "Certainly, by all means," was the unanimous voice of the Commission. I volunteered to be the distributor.

Go with me through the tents of the sufferers. Some are lying down, with eyes closed, faces pale, and cheeks sunken. The paleness underlies the bronze which the sun has burned upon them. Some are half reclining on their elbows, bolstered by knapsacks, and looking in vacancy, —thinking, perhaps, of home and kin, and wondering if they will ever see them again. Others are reading papers which delegates of the Commission have distributed. Some of the poor fellows have but one leg; others but the stump of a thigh or an arm, with the lightest possible dressing to keep down the fever. Yesterday these men, in the full tide of life, stood in the trenches confronting the enemy. Now they are shattered wrecks, having, perhaps, wife and children or parents dependent on them; with no certainty of support for themselves even but the small bounty of government, which they have earned at such fearful sacrifice. But their future will be brightened with the proud consciousness of duty done and country saved,—the surviving soldier's chief recompense for all toil and suffering and privations of the camp and field.

As we enter the tent they catch sight of the golden fruit. There is a commotion. Those half asleep rub their eyes, those partially reclining sit up, those lying with their backs toward us turn over to see what is going on, those so feeble that they cannot move ask what is the matter. They gaze wistfully at our luscious burden. Their eyes gleam, but not one of them asks for an orange. They wait. Through the stern discipline of war they have learned to be patient, to endure, to remain in suspense, to stand still and to be torn in pieces. They are true heroes!

"Would you like an orange, sir?" "Thank you." It is all he can say. He is lying upon his back. A Minie bullet has passed through his body, and he cannot be moved. He has a noble brow, a manly countenance. Tears moisten his eyes and roll down his sunken cheeks as he takes it from my hand.

In one of the wards I came upon a soldier who had lost his leg the day before. He was lying upon his side; he was robust, healthy, strong and

brave. The hours dragged heavily. I stood before him and yet he did not see me. He was stabbing his knife into a chip, with nervous energy, trying to forget the pain, to bridge over the lonely hours, and shut the gloom out of the future. I touched his elbow; he looked up.
"Would you like an orange?" "By jingo! that is worth a hundred dollars!" He grasped it as a drowning man clutches a chip. "Where did this come from?" "The Christian Commission had a box arrive last night." "The Christian Commission! My wife belongs to that. She wrote to me about it last week,—that they met to make shirts for the Commission." "Then you have a wife?" "Yes, sir, and three children." His voice faltered. Ah! the soldier never forgets home. He dashed away a tear, took a long breath, and was strong again.
"Where do you hail from, soldier?"
"From old Massachusetts. I had a snug little home on the banks of the Connecticut; but I told my wife that I didn't feel just right to stay there, when I was needed out here, and so I came and here I am. I shall write home and tell Mary about the Christian Commission. I have been wishing all day that I had an orange; I knew it was no use to wish. I didn't suppose there was one in camp; besides here I am, not able to move a peg. I thank you, sir, for bringing it. I shall tell my wife all about it."

These expressions of gratitude were not indifferent utterances of courtesy, but came from full hearts. Those sun-burned sufferers recognized the religion of Jesus in the gift. The Christian religion, thus exemplified, was not a cold abstraction, but a reality, providing for the health of the body as well as the soul. It is easy to converse with those men concerning their eternal well being. They could not oppose a Christianity that manifested such regard for their bodily comfort. Such a religion commended itself to their hearts and understandings. Thus the Commission became a great missionary enterprise. Farina, oranges, lemons, onions, pickles, comfort bags, shirts, towels, given and distributed in the name of Jesus, though designed for the body, gave strength to the soul. To the quickened senses of a wounded soldier parched with fever, far from home and friends, an onion was a stronger argument for the religion that bestowed it than the subtle reasoning of Renan, and a pickle sharper than the keenest logic of Colenso!

An extensive branch of the Fredericksburg hospital was established at Belle Plain, and there also the work of organization was largely in the hands of the Sanitary Commission. The materials at hand out of which to construct anything approaching comfortable quarters for the sufferers were terribly inadequate. Given a large building, generally quite bare, and a quantity of empty bed-sacks, the tireless workers were expected to do the rest. The cooking had often to be done in the open air with a collection of the most inadequate utensils, and the finding of a cast-away stove that in other scenes could only have provoked derision was a piece of rare good fortune.

But these establishments were only temporary. As rapidly as possible the wounded were sent forward by transports to Washington, whence they were distributed to the comfortable hospitals in the northern cities, a portion being furloughed to their homes, while many of the slightly wounded were enabled to return to their regiments. The last transport load left Fredericksburg May 26, and the surgeons returned to their duties in the field.

CHAPTER XV

SPADES AND BULLETS.

THE CLOSING STRUGGLES AT SPOTTSYLVANIA.—"BY THE LEFT FLANK."—CROSSING SWORDS AT NORTH ANNA.—THE DEATH HARVEST AT COLD HARBOR.

We have said that on the morning of May 13 the Thirty-seventh regiment fell back from the Angle to a point near the Landrum house, where it remained that day and into the following night with but trifling changes of position, most of the men finally putting up their shelter tents for protection against the incessant rain and sleeping whenever there was opportunity. In fact there was a lull all along the line. The Confederates had settled themselves behind their earthworks, strengthened by abatis and slashings in a manner to make them quite formidable. The defenders, too, had the advantage of formation, and with numerous good and convenient roads could concentrate their troops at any threatened point very speedily, their entire position forming a vast angle, inside which it was very convenient to maneuver.

In connection with the main struggle at the Angle on the 12th, in which Hancock's and Wright's corps had borne the brunt, Burnside on the Union left and Warren on the right had been ordered to attack in force and had done so sufficiently to show that there was no hope of making any promising lodgment. It was decided during the 13th, therefore, to swing the Fifth and Sixth Corps around to the left, connecting the former with Burnside's left, in the hope that some undefended point might be found on the enemy's right flank where a telling blow could be struck. The Fifth Corps, leaving a thin line to make a show of strength in the works, started on its pilgrimage at 10 o'clock that evening. The orders contemplated a circuitous march far enough to the rear of the Union lines to be secure from observation, using forest by-roads, fording the Ny river, making the way across fields to the Fredericksburg road, up which they were to advance, again crossing the Ny, and going into position from which to attack, or in case of no serious opposition being encountered to advance against Lee's flank and rear, early in the morning. The Sixth Corps was to follow and prolong the line to the left.

The elements seemed to oppose the plan. The rain still fell heavily and the mud became terrible. The entire region seemed to be soaked into one vast quagmire; the night proved utterly and intensely dark, and the exhausted men floundered about sadly in the effort to make their way through the unfamiliar forest. Guides had been provided and fires lighted to show the way, but the former were dazed by the difficulties of the march, and the latter were extinguished by the driving rain and the impossibility of obtaining proper fuel. As a result, at the time appointed for the attack but a few hundred men, and those almost without organization, were feeling their way against the enemy's skirmish lines.

It was after midnight that the Thirty-seventh were roused, tents struck, and the men, benumbed and almost senseless from their exhaustion and broken sleep, waited for the signal to march, which came about 2 o'clock. Through the few remaining hours till daylight the column plodded slowly along, the regiment halting in the early morning, near the hospitals of the Ninth Corps to prepare breakfast. In fact no further movement was made till late in the afternoon. It took a long time to gather the fragments of the Fifth Corps, so seriously scattered by the floundering through the darkness and the mud the night before, and by the time a force was collected adequate to strike a blow worthy the name, the enemy, in force and well intrenched, was ready to receive it in the old way. In consequence the fighting was nowhere very serious. The most important event of the day was the occupation of the Jett farm, a considerable eminence to the left of and commanding the position of the Fifth Corps.

This was seized upon early in the day by a small force of Regulars, who drove away some of the Confederate cavalry and began to intrench, when they were relieved by Upton's brigade, which under the personal direction of General Meade proceeded to make a permanent occupation of the locality. While the brigade was thus engaged it was assailed by a strong force of rebel infantry, Upton's men being precipitately scattered and General Meade himself narrowly escaping capture.

At about 3 o'clock in the afternoon the Thirty-seventh were ordered under arms, Neill's division being directed to support Ayres's brigade of the Fifth Corps in retaking the Jett hill. Moving near to the Ny, the men were ordered to unbuckle their cartridge boxes and hold them with their muskets above their heads in case they should be called upon to ford the river and charge the enemy beyond. But the latter seemed to have abandoned the place, making no attempt to hold it longer, and after some maneuvering and a brisk shelling of the woods in front, Edwards's Brigade went into position and threw up a line of rifle-pits.

Here the Thirty-seventh remained for three days without further engagement, merely confronting the enemy, each army on the alert, seeking for an opportunity to strike an effective blow, but finding none. Sunday, May 15, was a bright, calm day, in every way in marked contrast with those which had immediately preceded it. The location of the regiment was on a fine plantation which had hitherto escaped the desolations of warfare. Its fields were cultivated and charming to an unusual degree, and everything about it seemed instinct with the better life of Virginia's happy days. It occasioned more than a sigh of regret to see the beautiful inclosures trodden by the marching columns, torn by the spades of the fortifying squads, desolated by the axes of the pioneers.

That afternoon a religious service was held by Chaplain Morse, which was largely attended by the members of the regiment, as was a prayer-meeting in the evening held just in the rear of the rifle-pits. These were the first religious services since the day of leaving the camp at Brandy Station—not a long period on the calendar, but how eventful in the history of the Thirty-seventh! During the afternoon there was a very severe thunder shower, renewing the full volume of mud which had begun to abate in some degree. Possibly some demonstration had been contemplated but for this deluge, as the men were ordered to pack up, and the skirmish line was advanced some distance without encountering opposition. If there had been any intention of a movement it was abandoned. The command waited till night-fall for further orders, then pitched their shelter tents once more or laid down upon the wet ground to sleep.

The regiment now found itself for a time under the command of Lieutenant-Colonel Franklin P Harlow of the Seventh, an officer whose sterling qualities had been well proved during his term of service, especially in the desperate storming of Marye's Hights a year before. Detailed at this time to command the Thirty-seventh, whose own officers had been so generally wounded, he discharged the duties of that delicate position in a manner to win the admiration of the regiment and the respect of all with whom he came in contact.

The soldiers were early astir next morning, and after drawing rations waited in expectation of important orders of some nature, but none were received. The day passed in quiet, and after a prayer-meeting in the early evening the men slept without disturbance till morning. Nor was the programme varied for the following day, so far as the Thirty-seventh was concerned, till evening. Two days before the Second Corps, with the exception of Birney's division, had been swung back to the Fredericksburg road, leaving the Ninth Corps and Birney to form the Federal right. It was now decided to quietly return the Second Corps to its position at the Angle and attack early next morning on the scene of the terrible struggle of the 12th, with the Sixth Corps co-operating. After dark of the 17th, therefore, the Thirty-seventh, in common with its fellow-regiments of the corps, received orders to prepare to move, and all night was spent in a slow, intermittent, wearisome creeping through the woods and fields, by trails and by-ways, morning finding the brigade with Wheaton's near the Landrum house, deploying for the attack.

These two brigades covered the right flank of the Second Corps, and when the preparations had been completed, at about 5 o'clock, under cover of a tremendous artillery fire from the Federal batteries planted in the front line of the Union works and firing over their heads, the devoted lines moved forward to the assault.

It was a memorable scene. From right to left, for miles, the artillery crashed and roared, the woods and fields all about were filled with howling shot and bursting shell, to which the assailed made little reply, but not because they were dismayed or absent. Crouching behind their works, they waited till the assailants should enter the abatis and become disorganized in the struggle through the slashings and impediments of every sort which filled the entire ground to be charged over. Then, as the Confederate skirmishers were swept back before the strong lines of blue, the restrained tempest broke forth and with shriek and scream and hissing poured its death blast in the faces of the Union soldiers. As the hostile works were approached Wheaton's brigade moved to the right, uncovering Edwards's, which went straight forward, up to and over the first line of the Confederate intrenchments. The brave veterans would have gone directly into the jaws of death at the command, and they were not far from that allegoric spot at this particular moment. Hugging the ground and clinging tenaciously to what they had gained, the dauntless fellows waited in terrible suspense for the co-operating lines to make a corresponding advance and relieve them from the furious cross fire to which they were now exposed. They waited in vain. The task undertaken was too trying, the slaughter would be too terribly certain, the prospect of success was too remote. The troops to the right and left were breaking into fragments and scrambling to the rear as best they could; the order to fall back came to the Thirty-seventh. It was about as trying as one to advance, but commander and men knew each other better from that moment. "Steady, Thirty-seventh!" cautions Colonel Harlow, as though guiding an alignment on the drill-field, and with the firmness of review the regiment faces to the rear and moves back through the tempest of fire to the sheltering earthworks from which it had come.

"We went in, lost some men and came out again—that is all there was to it," said a gallant officer speaking of the part taken in this assault by the Thirty-seventh, and that was true of the entire operation. It had cost some six or seven hundred men and had amounted to nothing. The regiment had been very fortunate in having but two men killed—Sergeant Ira Larkins and Charles T. Wing of Company H—and 19 wounded, including Sergeant Major Hubbard M. Abbott in the hand. So with its rapidly shrinking line shortened by ten files for which it could only point to the fact of having penetrated further into the deadly jungle than any other portion of the assaulting lines, the Thirty-seventh turned its face once more toward the left, and used up the rest of the day in marching back to the vicinity of the Anderson house, crossing the Ny once more and getting into line of battle on the extreme Federal left.

By this time the tired men, who had been without sleep for 40 hours and incessantly marching and fighting for 24, were quite ready to lie down anywhere and sleep, but at 2 o'clock they were again called up and soon as it was light moved some two miles to the left and front, near the river Po. Formidable rifle pits in the rear of the advance line were constructed by details from the several regiments of the brigade, and for two days the Thirty-seventh, with the exception of continual duty upon the skirmish line, occupied these works in peace. Each evening a prayer-meeting was held in the grove of pines close to the rifle pits, and, as so often thenceforth to the close of the struggle, the bronzed and bearded warriors turning from scenes and thoughts of bloodshed to hold reverent communion with their Maker formed a touching and impressive picture.

On the 19th Ewell's corps of Lee's army sallied out from behind its breastworks and by a rapid movement swung around upon the Fredericksburg road, now used as the direct line of communication by the Army of the Potomac with its base at Aquia Creek, and pounced upon a wagon train. A sharp fight at once ensued in which the principal part was taken on the Union side by a division of heavy artillery fighting as infantry, which under the command of General R. O. Tyler had recently been attached to the Second Corps. This being the first battle in which these men had taken part, they went into it with an enthusiasm which was simply irresistible, and, though at heavy loss on their own part, drove the assailants back to their works, several hundred prisoners being taken.

The struggle which had continued for 15 days was now ended and preparations were made for a further movement by the left flank toward Richmond. Thus far during the campaign the losses of the Union army had amounted to over 40,000 men, and even these enormous figures do not adequately express the magnitude of this continual carnival of horrors. During all this time the men had been fighting by day and marching and maneuvering by night, constantly under fire, until many had utterly broken down from want of sleep and the continual strain upon the nervous systems. According to the best estimates the Confederate loss had been not far from 20,000; and this, though numerically so much less than the Union loss, was unquestionably a more serious blow to the government behind the army.

The Sixth Corps had been selected to cover the withdrawal of the army from in front of Lee, and till noon of the 21st remained in its intrenchments. The Second Corps started on its march early in the night of the 20th, the Fifth Corps followed next morning, and that afternoon Burnside also went, leaving Wright alone on the old battle-field. But a like movement had been made on the part of the Confederates, Anderson's corps moving out during the night of the 20th and Ewell's in the morning, so that as the day closed Hill alone confronted Wright. The march of Lee's column was straight toward his Capital by the Telegraph road, parallel to the movement of the Army of the Potomac, but as the latter had to take a less direct route, more to the eastward, General Lee intended to interpose across the line of the Federal advance in time to prevent immediate danger to Richmond, and this he was able to do, as we shall soon see.

About noon General Wright concentrated his forces in the strong works on the elevated ground about the Gayle house, and later General Hill, thinking to feel the retiring corps, made a vigorous attack, driving in the skirmishers and at one point making a lodgment in the line. But his forces were speedily driven out and the magnificent firing of the Sixth Corps artillery sent his four lines of battle back to their works in confusion. The loss of the Thirty-seventh in this little engagement was James Moran of Company C killed and six men wounded.

About 10 o'clock that evening the corps withdrew from its intrenchments and followed in the track of those that had preceded it, the skirmish line under command of Captain Loomis being extricated in the darkness with much effort but without loss. The march continued all through the night, but had the advantage over some of the night marches which had preceded it that steady progress was made without the vexation of frequent halts and delays; yet even at the best the men were sadly jaded and worn and welcomed the halt of early morning at Guiness Station for coffee, followed by a rest till 2 o'clock in the afternoon. The men generally devoted these hours to sleep, the day proving oppressively warm, though not all could resist the temptation to make limited excursions in the neighborhood in the interests of the individual commissary department.

The present movement of the army was through one of the richest and finest sections of Virginia, and one which had thus far experienced no more serious visitation than the occasional dash of a cavalry column; the country was gently undulating, with frequent fine estates and extensive plantations, the wide fields being generally in a state of cultivation quite charming to the eye.

During the respite cannonading had been heard in the direction of Bowling Green, but the roar of artillery had smitten the ears of the men so long and incessantly that this fresh outbreak scarcely provoked speculation. As the column moved in the afternoon in that direction, some reminiscences of the campaign of the previous May—which now seemed removed by such a distance of time and event—were recalled by passing the house in which "Stonewall" Jackson had died a year before of the wounds received at Chancellorsville. Bowling Green was passed and the column turned due south, pressing on till Calker's Store was reached, where a halt was made for the night, much to the relief of the men, who were quite exhausted from the heat of the day, their previous condition and the scarcity of food, which among officers and men was generally quite consumed. •At the close of the day's march the First Division, which had been in the advance, fell to the rear and the Second Division, going to the front, formed in line of battle and built temporary breastworks of rails behind which they slept soundly till morning.

Next morning the march was resumed soon after 8 o'clock, the Army of the Potomac moving toward Hanover Junction in three columns,—the Fifth Corps, followed by the Sixth, on the right, the Ninth in the center and the Second on the left. Late as was the hour of starting, the men of the Thirty-seventh went without their breakfasts, simply because they had nothing to eat except in the rare cases where they had been able to obtain something by purchase or forage ; but at noon a halt was made and five days' rations were drawn—a serious addition to the burdens carried by the men, though a very welcome one. An hour later the march was resumed, and as the afternoon wore away the unmistakable crash of battle was heard in front.

At Hanover Junction the Fredericksburg and Richmond railroad, which ran nearly due south, was crossed by the Virginia Central coming in from the northwest, whence the two, a few miles apart, ran nearly parallel to Richmond. A mile or two before reaching the Junction the North Anna river was encountered, which like most of those in that part of Virginia runs in a general southeasterly direction. A few miles below the North and South Annas unite, forming the Pamunky, which before reaching the sea joins the Matapony, and the two lose their identity in the York river. Parallel to the North Anna and some two miles from it flows Little river, a tributary of the South Anna, and between the two first named, in a position strong by nature and which he hastened to improve by fortifications, General Lee had again planted his army across the path of the Union advance.

Hancock's column struck the North Anna at the Fredericksburg railroad and the turnpike bridge a mile above, the latter being the only passage practicable for his troops, and the approach to this was commanded by some earthworks which had been built at the time of the Chancellorsville campaign and were now manned by the Confederates who had just reached the scene. A charge was made by Birney's division which resulted in the capture of the works with some of the defenders, and gave the Union soldiers command of one end of the bridge while the enemy held the other. This position was held during the night, frequent efforts of the rebels to burn the bridge being frustrated. On the right General Warren had reached the river at Jericho Mills, four miles above, where a very difficult ford was found, guarded only by a skirmish line. Scrambling down the steep rocky banks and wading the stream waist deep, General Bartlett's brigade of Griffin's division secured footing on the other side, a ponton bridge was hastily laid, and the whole corps, part wading and part using the bridge, crossed and established a line half a mile from the river. While the intrenching was being done a characteristic Southern assault was made by Wilcox's and Heth's divisions of Hill's corps, which at one point gained some advantage; but a well-directed artillery fire drove them back in confusion, and the Sixth Corps, which had by this time reached the north bank of the river, was not needed and did not cross the river till the next morning. General Warren had established his position, had captured nearly a thousand prisoners, and the prospect was regarded as quite cheering. At 3 o'clock in the morning of the 24th the Thirty-seventh crossed the river in connection with the rest of the corps and quietly waited through the day for developments. At that part of the field there was no considerable engagement, and many of the soldiers seized the opportunity to bathe in the North Anna—a privilege, it does not need to be said, of which they had long felt the need. At 5 o'clock the regiment advanced to relieve a portion of the Fifth Corps in the front line, and remained in their intrenchments through the night, exposed to a very severe thunder shower, the vivid lightning and loud thunder flashing and crashing through the forest in a remarkable manner while the rain poured down in torrents.

The promise of the initial movements had not been borne out

by the events of the day, and it was found that the Confederate army was really in a position of exceptional strength. Lee's center still rested upon the North Anna between the two crossings made by the Union wings; his left had been thrown back to Little river upon which it rested securely, the line facing about due north and extending from river to river, a distance of about a mile and a half, like a wall of iron. His right was protected by the Hanover marshes, south of the Junction, the general facing of his right wing being to the eastward. Lee's position was thus compact, admirably adapted for the concentration of force to any threatened point, and assailable only by direct front attack. The two wings of the Union army were separated by miles of distance and two crossings of the river, effective co-operation between them was out of the question, and the generals commanding were reluctantly forced to the conclusion that some more promising field must be sought. The retiring of Lee's left to Little river had obliged him to uncover the Central railroad, and this Meade proceeded to destroy for several miles, while Warren still strove to push his left through to connect with Hancock. But the enemy had been reinforced, both from the Shenandoah valley and by Pickett's division from south of Richmond, and his lines were everywhere firmly maintained.

At 8 o'clock in the morning of the 25th the Thirty-seventh marched toward the front, crossing the Central railroad at Noel's Station and advancing to the Anderson plantation, where the brigade in two lines formed on the right of Sweitzer's brigade of the Fifth Corps. In the afternoon the whole line moved a short distance to the left, when the men were set to work building fortifications, laboring all through the night and tearing down three negro cabins to obtain logs for the purpose. A heavy shower occurred during the night, and much rain fell the following day, when most of the men not at work on the pits were detailed for duty on the skirmish line, where a brisk firing was kept up, though fortunately none of the Thirty-seventh were hurt.

The movement of the Army of the Potomac " by the left flank toward Richmond " was resumed that evening, and the march which resulted proved one of the hardest of the many hard marches of the campaign. The regiment proper, or rather the handful of men accompanying the colors, moved soon after dark and marched steadily and as rapidly as possible all night. A large part of the men, however, were on the skirmish line and did not get across the river till daylight, when they pushed on at the top of their speed to overtake their fellows. The rain of the previous day had softened the ground, making all the roads difficult and exhausting, especially to the men of the Thirty-seventh, who were now passing their second consecutive night entirely without sleep. As usual, the Union army was obliged to make a long detour to reach roads which would secure the movement from observation, and in consequence they went across lots, through woods and by cross roads, over ditches and fences, through fields of corn and grain, crossing the Fredericksburg and Richmond railroad at Chesterfield Station. But the difficulty of the route was not the only tax upon the endurance of the soldiers. Again they were without food. For two days they had nothing to eat except two rations of fresh beef, and during this time they were being taxed to the utmost both day and night. It scarcely needs to be said that of the 311 members of the Thirty-seventh at this time present for duty, not one could have been properly termed a well man; yet the exigencies of the service were recognized by all, and each was making heroic exertions to meet the terrible and incessant calls.

The march continued all through the 27th, General Russell's division leading the corps, preceded by a strong cavalry force which during the forenoon reached and occupied Hanover Town, the immediate objective point of the army. The day being very warm, the mud was soon tolerably dried, the roads being in fair condition otherwise and leading through a charming section of the country, but the suffering soldiery had little eye now for nature's beauty; oh, that they might lie down in the cool shade in those green fields to sleep and rest!

A halt was made for the night a few miles from the Pamunky, and the men slept heavily till early morning when they were aroused and at 5 o'clock the march was resumed, the Thirty-seventh leading the corps. The river was crossed at half-past 8, and some two miles beyond the line of battle was formed, the Thirty-seventh being deployed as skirmishers and the remainder of the brigade proceeding to intrench, the lines running through a vast corn-field. There the entire corps remained till the rest of the army crossed the river and went into position, while the cavalry pushed to the front to ascertain as definitely as possible where the Confederate army was next to be encountered; for there was no doubt that Lee, having the shorter route and perfect knowledge of the country, had interposed between the Army of the Potomac and Richmond, which was now less than a day's march distant.

The crossing of the Pamunkey had placed the army on the famous "Peninsula," and the Federal advance had already reached the ground occupied by McClellan's outposts two years before. The cavalry found the enemy in considerable force at Hawes's Shop on the Hanover road, a severe engagement resulting in which Sheridan held the ground, and next day the different corps were pushed forward on reconnaissances to develop the intentions of the foe.

Late in the afternoon of Sunday, the 29th, the Thirty-seventh received the orders they had all day been cautioned to expect, knapsacks were slung and the column moved away toward Hanover Court House. A halt was made at midnight; the men threw themselves down beside the road or wherever opportunity presented and rested till early morning. The march thus far had been in support of General Russell's division, but on the morning of the 30th the Thirty-seventh took the lead, moving down the railroad as far as Peake's Station, cutting the telegraph wires, destroying the track and burning the buildings at the station.

A few hours later the corps commenced retiring, Edwards's brigade, strengthened by four additional regiments and a battery, being constituted the rear guard. These moved back slowly to Crump's Mills, skirmishing with the Confederate horseman all the way, and on reaching that point went into position on the extreme right of the corps, the Thirty-seventh supporting a battery. Here the night and the following day were passed with no further incident, though the sounds of continual artillery firing came up from the left. In fact the other corps, which had advanced on the direct roads leading to Richmond, encountered such opposition as to show the Confederate army in force along the Totopotomy, and after some sharp fighting it was decided to move still further to the left, since if Lee was forced from his present position it would only be to take a stronger one behind the Chickahominy and the impregnable Richmond defenses. A movement was therefore planned by way of Cold Harbor,* a hamlet where many important roads converged. The place was seized by Sheridan's cavalry on the afternoon of the 31st, preliminary to its occupation by the Sixth Corps leading the Army of the Potomac and by a column from General Butler's command south of Richmond.

A brief sketch must now be given of the operations of the Army of the James and of the Union cavalry up to this time.

It will be remembered that early in February an attempt had been made at the suggestion of General Butler to force a small, swiftly moving column from his army through the Richmond defenses for the purpose of liberating the Union prisoners confined in that city and on Belle Island and in the James River near it. This attempt had failed, as had a cavalry movement from the Army of the Potomac direct a few weeks later under General Kilpatrick and Colonel Dahlgren, the latter being killed. The enemy were found on the alert and the works proved too strong to be forced. But with the deadly grapple between the main armies in full progress and Butler's forces also operating from the other side of the Confederate Capital, it seemed that a bold, strong dash might prove successful, and after clearing the way for the advance of the infantry to Spottsylvania, General Sheridan with a powerful cavalry column made his way directly toward Richmond. Destroying railroads, public property and stores, he pushed on with slight opposition till Yellow Tavern was reached, not more than ten miles due north of Richmond. Here, on the 11th, Sheridan found himself confronted by General J. E. B. Stuart at the head of a strong force of Southern

---

* This name is variously given by different authorities as Cold Harbor, Coal Harbor, Cool Arbor, etc. I have used the first spelling as probably the more correct.

cavalry. A severe battle ensued in which the Confederate leader and General James B. Gordon, commanding one of his brigades, were mortally wounded. The loss of Stuart was a very heavy blow to the Southern army, his abilities as a cavalry leader being recognized through both armies. Lieutenant-General Wade Hampton was his successor in the command of Lee's cavalry. Having driven the enemy from his path, Sheridan pushed straight toward Richmond, and Custer's brigade succeeded in carrying the first line of works and capturing a hundred prisoners; but, as in other cases, the inner lines proved too strong to be forced. The column swept away to the southward, defeating every force which attempted to oppose it, made a junction with the Union troops on the James, procured supplies and returned leisurely to the Army of the Potomac, which it rejoined on the 25th in the vicinity of the North Anna. One of the best results of the raid was the recapture of 400 Union prisoners on their way to Richmond from the Wilderness.

Simultaneously with the advance of the Army of the Potomac against Lee, General Butler began his prescribed operations on the south side of Richmond. His force, comprising some 35,000 men of all arms, consisted of General W F. Smith's Eighteenth Corps, containing the divisions of Generals Brooks, Weitzel and Hinks—the latter colored troops,—and General Q. A. Gillmore's Tenth Corps, summoned for the occasion from South Carolina and comprising the divisions of Generals Terry, Ames and Turner, General Kautz commanded the cavalry division attached to the Army of the James. Making a demonstration as though he intended to operate on the peninsula by McClellan's old route, Butler suddenly transferred his troops by transport to the James, up which he advanced to City Point, within 15 miles of Richmond, where he landed and proceeded to intrench strongly at Bermuda Hundred, a small peninsula in the vicinity, where his flanks rested on the river and were protected by the gun-boats of the fleet. From this stronghold raiding parties were pushed out to strike the Richmond and Petersburg railroad, only a few miles in front, but found themselves confronted by Beauregard's command, which had been hurried up from South Carolina with all the reinforcements that could be gathered on the way. Several engagements of minor importance occurred, the road was effectually destroyed and Kautz's cavalry set forth on a raid to the westward, while Butler with his main force faced toward Richmond and advanced, pressing back the enemy's outposts, till his further immediate progress was checked by a strong line of works. While the two armies thus confronted each other Beauregard struck his antagonist a severe blow at Drewry's Bluff on the morning of May 16. Everything favored the Confederates. A heavy fog prevailed, covering perfectly their movement; their forces were advantageously disposed to strike the Union army in front, flank and rear; while the Federal line was so extended as to be everywhere weak and about as badly disposed as possible for defensive purposes. The Southern commander's plans were well laid for the complete overthrow of his antagonist, but some of them miscarried, while the stubborn resistance of the Union soldiers prevented a rout in any part of the line, though General Smith was obliged to fall back to protect his communications. As a result General Butler retired again behind his defenses at Bermuda Hundred, where his position was quite impregnable. Beauregard, constructing a parallel line of works, sat down to watch his foe, dispatching one division of his army to Lee's assistance.

General Grant, on hearing of the result of General Butler's movement, directed the latter to send him all the troops of his command save such as might be necessary to hold the position at City Point, and accordingly General Smith was dispatched with four divisions under Generals Brooks, Devens, Martindale and Ames—the two former well known and honored in the Army of the Potomac. These went by transports to White House, Grant's new base of supplies on the Pamunkey, whence they marched to Cold Harbor. Beauregard at the same time sent another division to reinforce Lee.

Sheridan having gained possession of favorable ground at Cold Harbor on the afternoon of the 31st of May was directed to hold it at any cost, while Wright was instructed to hurry with his corps from the right at Hawes's Shop to his support. The Sixth Corps was ordered to be at Cold Harbor by daybreak if this were possible,—which it manifestly was not. The orders were not received till well into the night, the distance to be marched was more than 15 miles over a region intersected in every direction by narrow, half-defined and unmarked roads, puzzling even in broad day and quite untreadable in the darkness of a moonless night.

The Thirty-seventh were called from slumber at midnight, the officers' horses were saddled and the men packed their blankets ready for an immediate start, but as the orders were not received to move one after another settled down to sleep again, and so the night passed till morning came. Then the march was taken up and steadily pursued, and seldom had the brave men struggled through a more severe ordeal. The day proved intensely hot, the sun burning down with a lurid, brassy glare that seemed to broil the human flesh on which it fell; the way led through sandy plains, heated to the intensity of a vast furnace, from which the most terrible clouds of dust arose, not only high into the air, disclosing every movement to the watchful enemy, but as well choking the breath and blinding the vision of the gasping men who were marching through them. Everywhere the sun-stroke did its deadly work—men fell blinded and gasping from the ranks, strong, brave men who on a dozen deadly fields had looked death in the face without quailing, conquered now by the long, unceasing strain to which they had been subjected and the mighty power of the elements.

As the Sixth Corps approached its destination it met the advance of Smith's column, which had been hurried forward without waiting for its wagons or ammunition, but by a mistake in its orders had marched several miles out of the way, and was now coming in through the sultry heat in a fearful state of exhaustion owing to its inexperience in heavy marching. Yet its spirit was as brave and true as any in the service, as it had just proved in one of the most ferocious contests of the war; and now it was only anxious to fight by the side of the veterans of the Army of the Potomac and win their approval.

A furious effort had been made that morning by Kershaw's division to drive Sheridan from his position, but the plucky cavalry leader dismounted his men and fought them as infantry with such address that the assailants with broken ranks were glad to retire. Meanwhile the Confederates had become aware of Grant's intention and when Wright's corps marched for Cold Harbor Anderson's did the same, while Lee's three divisions already at or near that point closed down to present a strong front. As the Sixth Corps moved up the road leading from Old Cold Harbor to Cold Harbor proper it went into position on the left of the road, Ricketts's division next the road, Russell's on its left and Neill's covering the flank and in reserve. The Vermont Brigade formed the extreme left and was supported by Edwards's Brigade in one line. On the right of the road was Smith's column, Devens's division connecting with the Sixth Corps and Brooks's on its right, while Martindale's was refused to cover the Bethesda Church road, General Ames's being detached for other duty.

As soon as the lines were formed and the men had rested somewhat after their severe exertions in getting there the order to advance was given and nobly responded to. The enemy was posted in a heavy forest behind the shelter of rifle-pits, to reach which it was necessary to cross a wide open field; but the firm battalions of Devens and the right of the Sixth Corps went across with a cheer, drove the rebels from their works and held them, capturing some 600 prisoners. The heaviest fighting was in the vicinity of the Cold Harbor road, naturally enough, but the shock was felt along the whole line. As the advance was made it was found that the Vermont Brigade was flanked by the enemy's extended line, especially endangering the Fifth regiment. The Fourth Brigade was at once hurried at double-quick to the threatened flank, throwing out a heavy line of skirmishers and holding the enemy in check till night, when a line of rifle-pits was quickly thrown up. During this movement the Thirty-seventh lost Corporal Thomas J. Crandall of Company H killed and five or six wounded.

Finding it impossible to carry the second line of Confederate works with the force at hand, Generals Wright and Smith took prompt measures to secure what had already been gained, intrenching strongly in the edge of the woods. The pickets fired incessantly and the artillery furiously from both sides, and even nightfall did not close the contest. Repeated efforts were made by the Southern soldiers, lasting far into the night, to regain what they had lost, but they found their purpose anticipated as often as repeated and finally they gave up the useless sacrifice of life.

The Union army was now concentrated for the inevitable trial of battle. The Second Corps was brought from its position far to the right to prolong the Union line to the left, and their arrival the following day relieved Neill's division, which passed to the right of the Sixth Corps and took the place of Devens's division. Throughout the Fourth Brigade there was the greatest anxiety to catch even a glimpse of General Devens, the former brigade commander, and after the commands separated there was renewed interest in the fact that Edwards's Brigade was brought close to Stannard's brigade of Martindale's division, in which were the Twenty-third, Twenty-fifth and Twenty-seventh Massachusetts regiments. The latter was composed of friends and school-mates of the members of the Tenth and Thirty-seventh, having been raised in the western counties of the state, and during the following days there was many a hearty greeting as acquaintances and relatives grasped each other by the hand. This regiment had proved itself worthy of its origin, having done faithful duty whenever called on, suffering especially at Drewry's Bluff and severely in the action of the first day at Cold Harbor; but a still greater trial was in store for it on the following day, when it was to lose its gallant commander, Major Walker, and near half its remaining members in the vain attempt, thrice repeated, to penetrate the enemy's lines.

General Devens's division was placed on the right of Smith's line, the Second Corps was moved down to connect with it, and the Ninth placed in Warren's rear. The Union army was thus made compact and strong and orders were issued to each corps commander to assault with his entire force next morning at half-past 4. The night of June 2 was marked by a severe rain storm, which was rather welcome as affording a grateful relief from the terrible heat and dust which had lately prevailed, and the men had long since ceased to regard a drenching as of any consequence. All night long the sputter and crack of the picket firing could be heard through the storm, and sometimes a line of battle would for real or fancied cause send its volleys hurtling through the darkness. It was a wild, restless night, fitting prelude for the day which was to come.

It may be doubted if the history of modern warfare contains a parallel of the battle of Cold Harbor on the morning of June 3, 1864, in the briefness of the struggle, the extent of the movement, the bloodiness of the repulse and the want of definite purpose in the attack. General Lee's position was some six miles in front of the main line of the Richmond defenses. His right rested on the marshy bank of the Chickahominy, whence his lines ran in nearly a straight course over favorable ground a little to the west of north, his left covered and protected by the swampy regions about the head-waters of the Totopotomy. Attack was therefore only possible in front and the entire space between the two lines was swept by a cross fire of the Confederate artillery and infantry. The corps of Warren and Burnside were practically out of the conflict, for the line of the former was so long and weak and the ground in his front so difficult that he was doubly estopped from offensive operations, while the Ninth Corps had been thrown to the rear of the Fifth as a protection to the weak Federal right flank. The ground to be fought over was almost exactly that of the battle of Gaines's Mills during the Peninsular campaign, with the difference that Lee now occupied the ground which McClellan then held, though the line of battle of the latter had faced nearly north with his left resting on the Chickahominy.

Upon Hancock, Wright and Smith, therefore, devolved the task of attempting to break the enemy's lines and drive him back into the strong works about Richmond, and at the appointed hour, almost at the moment designated, the three corps swept over the works in their front, into the valley of death. The Federal artillery behind them was worked with desperate energy, but it could not at once silence the Confederate batteries, which sent their mangling storms through the advancing ranks, while the flashing ripples of the still more deadly musketry fire lighted up the crests of the breastworks for miles away to right and left. How the crash and roar of innumerable cannon resounded and echoed ! How the missiles of every description tore through air and forest and earth ! How the great clouds of white smoke rose like a friendly veil to shut out the sights too horrible for mortal vision !

In a few minutes—minutes which seemed ages—the struggle was over. Everywhere the result had been the same. The main intrenched line had been found too strong for human valor to penetrate ; great numbers of the bravest and best of the Sons of Freedom had laid down their lives in the unequal contest, and then the shortened and decimated lines had fallen back. But only for a few yards—only to the nearest point where the brave fellows, lying prone upon the ground, could burrow themselves into the sheltering earth and hold fast to what with such sacrifice they had been able to gain. How quickly with the most inadequate tools this work was done ! How perfect the heroism which, halting within a stone's throw of an enemy's impregnable position, from which they had just been bloodily repulsed, enabled men to perform such work ! All through the remainder of the day these advanced positions were held, in some cases not more than 15 yards from the enemy's lines, though the Confederates made strenuous efforts to dislodge the persistent occupants. The day passed without further attempt to advance, and after dusk some of the more exposed detachments were withdrawn to more favorable positions, and a furious counter attack by the Confederates met with a firm repulse by the troops of Hancock's and Wright's corps.

During the engagement of the 3d the Thirty-seventh was in the supporting line, Edwards's Brigade being formed in the rear of Wheaton's in two lines, and when the latter pushed forward impetuously Edwards's advanced and occupied the line which Devens's division had charged on the first day of the fight. Here the regiment remained through the day, exposed to a severe fire which was almost incessant, losing Erastus B. Pease of Company

I killed, with 13 wounded, several fatally. The night was devoted principally to strengthening the lines, and the following day passed without other excitement than guarding against the bullets of sharp-shooters, who had now become so active and numerous that momentary exposure on any part of the Federal lines was an invitation to wounds or death. Even the hospitals were placed behind rifle-pits, and the whole camp became one vast system of burrows. At night of the 4th the Thirty-seventh were relieved by the Second Rhode Island, went a short distance to the rear and enjoyed one night's sleep freed from the burden of equipments and undisturbed by flashing muskets and hissing bullets.

The following day saw the brigade line further shortened by the departure for home of the Second Rhode Island, their term of service having expired, leaving behind the re-enlisted men and recruits which were temporarily attached to the Thirty-seventh and formed into an independent battalion of three companies under Captain Rhodes, a veteran and an excellent officer.

Large details from the regiment were now kept continually on the picket line, where the duty was especially dangerous and considerable losses were sustained. On the 5th Robert Elder of Company H and Clarkson H. Decker of Company I were killed and several wounded, including Captain Donnelly of Company I and Lieutenant George N. Jones, at that time serving on the staff of Colonel Edwards,—the former in the head and the latter in the arm. More perhaps to be dreaded than the bullets was the stench of the unburied corpses lying between the lines in the hot sun, but it was not till a change in the wind bore the effluvium to the Confederate nostrils in full force that they would consent to a truce for the purposes of burial. Assent was finally given on the afternoon of the 6th, picket firing ceased for a few hours, and the entire region between the lines was filled with a throng of wearers of the Blue and the Gray, shaking hands cordially and conversing as they proceeded with the horrible work which had brought them together. They would return to their works in a short time and immediately resume their best efforts to kill each other, but there were thanks for even this rift in the horrible cloud of war. Finally the men were separated by threats of opening upon them with the artillery from both sides, and the work of slaughter was resumed.

During the night of the 6th the regiment was relieved from duty at the front and went back again for rest, which continued through the 7th, the men being well supplied with rations and clothing during the day. The army was at this time well provided for in every way from the new base on the Pamunkey, and but for the terrible dead-lock at the front, the incessant screaming of shot and shell and the sharp-shooting, together with the stench inseparable from the vicinity of the great battle-field and the malaria from the marshes, which seriously affected the health of the men, the position would have been quite satisfactory. At 2 o'clock on the morning of the 8th the regiment was again called up and relieved the troops at the front, sending three companies on the fortified skirmish line while the remainder were posted as a reserve in the next line of works; the following night the relieved troops came back and exchanged places giving the Thirty-seventh another opportunity for rest, and thus the days wore away.

In the mean time more or less attempts were made by the Confederates to drive away the hated Yankees, but they invariably ended in disaster. The Federal intrenchments had been carried forward by regular siege approaches till they were close upon those of the enemy, but there was no probability of the army being able to accomplish anything at Cold Harbor and preparations for a move still further southward began to be made and noised about the camp. "The attack at Cold Harbor," said General Grant in his report, "was the only one in the entire movement from the Rapidan to the James which did not inflict damage to compensate for its cost." In fact the General-in-chief freely referred to the battle of Cold Harbor as one of the three great mistakes of the war.

On the night of the 10th, just after the Thirty-seventh had been relieved from a tour of duty at the front and the men had settled themselves to sleep, the brigade was called up and moved to the left a short distance, where it occupied the works vacated by the troops of the Vermont Brigade, next to the First Division. The fire of the sharp-shooters was found to be very annoying and dangerous at this point, and during the following day the regiment lost John Maloney of Company K killed, James Davis of Company E fatally wounded, and two men from Company I who received disabling wounds. Davis was struck by a sharp-shooter's bullet while drawing rations nearly a mile from the enemy's line in a position of supposed safety, and other casualties occurred in like manner. Thus steadily and sadly was the regimental line wasting away, the loss at Cold Harbor having now reached 35 officers and men, though the regiment had not been engaged in the thick of the fight.

During the 11th Lieutenant-Colonel Montague returned to the regiment and resumed command, having recovered sufficiently from the wounds received at the Angle a month before to again take the field, and he received a warm greeting from his command. At the same time there was keen regret at parting with Lieutenant-Colonel Harlow, who during the four weeks in which he had been in command of the regiment had won the high regard of its officers and men. The esteem had been mutual. "I look back to the brief period during which I had the honor to command the Thirty-seventh," said Colonel Harlow many years after, "with the most perfect satisfaction of any portion of my military career. No matter in what position they were placed, they could be depended upon to do all that mortal man could do." Such words of praise from such a source, spoken in the confidence of friendly conversation, will not be lightly regarded.

The loss of the regiment in officers had been quite as marked as in enlisted men. Besides the casualties of battle and sickness, several were at this time on detail, including Captain Hopkins before mentioned, Captain Tyler upon General Neill's staff, and Lieutenant Jones on Colonel Edwards's. Few of the companies, consequently, had more than a single commissioned officer present with them for duty, and frequently they were found in the charge of sergeants for considerable periods. Many of the latter were in these trying days winning promotion which was well deserved, and which was to come in due time.

CHAPTER XVI.

GOING TO MEET EARLY

IN FRONT OF PETERSBURG.—AT REAMS STATION.—EARLY IN
MARYLAND.—FORT STEVENS.—THE "SPENCER RIFLE."

No sooner was it evident to General Grant that the Confederate position at Cold Harbor was impregnable than he resolved upon a continuation of the movement "by the left flank" which had now become a by-word in the army as well as elsewhere. In accordance with this plan his right was gradually refused and shortened, the Ninth Corps relieving the Fifth and the latter taking position beyond Hancock on the left, extending that flank till it rested on the York River railroad at Dispatch Station, within ten miles of Long Bridge, at which it was his purpose to cross the Chickahominy. Once across that famous stream two courses were open to the Union commander—to advance against Richmond up the peninsula in the tracks of McClellan's movement of 1862, or by crossing the peninsula and the James River to operate against Petersburg, the strategic key to the Southern seat of government. The latter was the one selected.

The movement began soon after dark of the 12th of June, and was conducted with celerity and skill. General Warren's corps was thrown across the Chickahominy and deployed in line of battle covering all the roads leading to Richmond, while behind the strong front thus displayed the other corps marched directly across the peninsula. General Lee discovered the withdrawal next morning, but made no effort to follow. He evidently looked for an attempt to pass his flank and strike another blow for the possession of Richmond, and this suspicion was strengthened when a reconnaissance down the New Market road by a body of his infantry came upon Warren's line of battle checking further investigation in that direction.

The Thirty-seventh regiment had been resting through the day and the indications of an intended movement had been so unmistakable that no surprise was felt at the final orders to pack up everything and fall in. The Second Corps having followed the Fifth on the most direct route, the Sixth and Ninth took a course more circuitous and farther to the rear, while General Smith's command, marching back to White House, took transportation for Bermuda Hundred, and was again placed under command of General Butler. All night long the columns plodded on, the moon, which was at the quarter, lighting them indifferently till midnight. The weather was cool, and in that respect the men were comfortable, but the dust was terrible. A drought had set in, not a drop of rain having fallen for some ten days, and the condition of the region through which the march extended may be easily imagined when it is borne in mind that the country was generally a sandy plain through which the roads at such times greatly resembled beds of ashes.

At daybreak a halt of some ten minutes was made, fires were lighted and coffee hurriedly prepared, after which the journey was resumed. All day with brief intervals of rest the monotonous tramp was kept up through a region presenting little of interest. The York River railroad was crossed at Summit Station, above Tuntsall's, and Hopkins Mills were passed, then followed a monotonous toiling along all day till near night when the Chickahominy was reached and crossed at Jones Bridge and about a mile beyond bivouac was made for the night. The march was resumed early in the morning of the 14th and before noon a halt was made in the vicinity of Charles City Court House, where the regiment remained during the rest of the day and the succeeding night. On the 15th a move was made of some two miles only, bringing the regiment within a mile of the point selected for the crossing of the James River, where the brigade remained till late in the afternoon of the following day, it having been selected to form the rear guard for the artillery and trains of the corps.

While resting here during the 15th the Seventh Massachusetts withdrew from the brigade line and marched toward home, their term of enlistment having expired. The recruits and re-enlisted men of the regiment whose time had not expired remained behind as a detachment temporarily attached to the Thirty-seventh, the whole numbering nominally 76 men, of whom but a small part were present for duty.

Shortly before dark the order to march was received, the column filed down the river bank to and across the ponton bridge, then away into the darkness and dust on that most disagreeable of all duty, a night's march with the trains. Morning brought no relief save that of light, and with it came the terrible heat of the sun and increased discomfort from the dust. The command accompanied the trains till they reached their destination at noon, when the Fourth Brigade marched away toward Petersburg, halting during the afternoon within some three miles of the city. Supposing that they had reached bivouac for the night, the weary men were not long in wrapping themselves in their blankets to sleep.

In fact the exhausted brigade had merely halted in front of what was to be the most famous and deadly of all the Confederate intrenched lines, over and about which for 42 long weeks struggle and battle and siege were to rage. Petersburg, at which the Federal blow was aimed, was situated on the south bank of the Appomattox River, ten miles from its junction with the James and 20 miles south of Richmond. Apart from its relations to the latter place, the city was an important center on account of the railroads and turnpikes which radiated from it. The principal of these may be thus briefly described: The Appomattox River runs in a general easterly direction at this point, bending to the northeast after passing the city, and practically parallel to it lies the City Point railroad, running to the station of that name on the James River which was henceforth to be Grant's base of supplies. Leaving the line of the City Point road just east of the city limits, the Norfolk railroad ran to the southeast. Over the roads between these two lines of railway Grant's army had approached the city. South from Petersburg extended the

Weldon railroad, passing directly through North Carolina to Wilmington, with numerous important connections en route. The Jerusalem plank road ran nearly parallel three or four miles to the eastward, the Halifax road followed the railroad closely, the Vaughn road branching from it some four miles south of Petersburg and running to the southwest. The Squirrel Level road ran for several miles nearly parallel with the Vaughn a mile to the westward, finally connecting with the latter at a westward bend in its course. Three or four miles still further to the west ran the Boydton plank road, its course being in the same general direction. Some nine miles southwest of the city White Oak road branched from the Boydton and ran nearly due west, while crossing the latter near this point of junction and extending in a southeasterly course across the Vaughn road also was Hatcher's Run, a small stream which farther on its course connected with Gravelly Run forming Rowanty Creek. Westward from Petersburg, parallel to the river, ran the Southside railroad and the Cox road, leading into the heart of the Confederacy. To the north extended the Richmond railroad and the turnpike, threatened by Butler's force at Bermuda Hundred and strongly defended by Beauregard.

Before the arrival of the Sixth Corps important movements had taken place about Petersburg. On the 9th of June General Butler sent a force of infantry under General Gillmore, accompanied by a small cavalry force under General Kautz, to the south side of the Appomattox to attempt to seize Petersburg and destroy the railroad bridge across the river; but these forces moving by the City Point and Jerusalem roads respectively, encountered fortifications manned by Wise's brigade and such other defenders as he could get together at short notice, presenting so formidable an appearance that no attack was made. On the return of General Smith's command from Cold Harbor on the 14th it was at once set in motion on a like expedition, crossing the river seven miles below the city on a pontoon bridge. Early on the morning of the 15th the column pushed forward and at a distance of two miles from the river encountered a line of rifle-pits which was soon carried by General Hinks's colored division. Then a few miles more brought the troops in front of the fortifications which had checked Gillmore, strengthened and better manned in apprehension of the movement which had now begun, but not yet occupied by the veterans of Lee's army. The approach to the works was found to be across a wide valley, difficult to pass on account of ditches and ravines, while the enemy's perfect artillery fire drove away all Union batteries that attempted to take position in front. It was therefore decided to send across heavy skirmish lines, and in this manner the colored division actually captured some redans with the connecting rifle-pits in the first line of works. This done and the ground gained occupied in force, the attack ceased for the night.

By this time General Hancock's corps had arrived on the scene and proceeded to relieve Smith, while not long after the advance of Lee's army came pouring through Petersburg for its defense. During the following day Hancock gained some ground and more on the 17th in conjunction with the other troops which had come up; but the possession of the outer line, obtained at serious cost, simply revealed a stronger inner line, which Lee's army was busy in extending and strengthening. The Sixth Corps on reaching the vicinity had relieved most of the troops of Smith's command, which returned to Bermuda Hundred.

The tired members of the Thirty-seventh were sleeping soundly at 9 o'clock on the evening of the 17th, after their arrival within sight of the spires of Petersburg, when the bugle sounded the unwelcome call to "Fall in!" and as soon as the column could be formed it trudged away to the vicinity of the Jordan house, near the City Point railroad, to support the Vermont Brigade, and in the orchard and grounds surrounding the fine mansion the rest of the night was passed. Next morning the command moved to the right across the railroad and toward the Appomattox to develop the position of the enemy, but as it proved the latter had abandoned his front line and retreated to the inner and stronger one, so that the order for a general attack all along the line was postponed till afternoon. About 11 o'clock the brigade recrossed the railroad, occupied the vacated works near the railroad bridge and threw out a skirmish line, after which Colonel Edwards was directed to connect with the right of General Wheaton's brigade, move forward and attack at 12 o'clock. The connection was made and the advance took place, but the troops on the left obliqued so much to the right that Wheaton's brigade was forced in front of Edwards's, and the latter on reaching the crest of the hill formed under cover of it in two lines. Meantime the skirmish line of the Thirty-seventh found itself in especially hot quarters. Not only was it exposed to the fire of the enemy in front, but Wheaton's men through some misunderstanding were directing their fire upon the brave fellows from the rear. At this juncture occurred one of those instances of quiet heroism which live long in story. "Will any one volunteer to go back and stop that fire?" asked Lieutenant Gray. The only way to reach the source of danger was by a direct climb up the slope across a plowed field, exposed all the way to the bullets of both armies. "Yes, I'll go," said Sergeant Edwin Leonard of Company I; "I'd just as lief go as not!" and throwing his musket to a right shoulder shift he sprang away on his noble mission. Half way up he was noticed to fall to the earth, and more than one exclamation of pity for his supposed fate was uttered. But he had only thrown himself upon the ground for a moment to escape the myriad of flying bullets; when the fire slackened a little he was up and on again, reaching his destination and averting the fire of the brigade.

At 3 o'clock another advance was ordered and Neill's division of the Sixth Corps pushed forward along the railroad some 400 yards. (General Wright with his First and Third Divisions was at this time co-operating with Butler north of Petersburg.) The Second Corps on the left did not advance, and the men of the Greek cross were thus exposed to a severe enfilading fire: but they would not retreat. Rifle-pits were hastily thrown up and the ground was held. Nowhere else was any progress made except by Martindale's division across the railroad, which seized and held the enemy's skirmish line. The Second, Fifth and Ninth Corps attacked later in the day with heavy columns, losing severely, but everywhere the story was the same.

The loss of the Thirty-seventh in killed consisted of Florence

Burke of Company A, Paschal Janes of Company G, Corporal William C. Stockwell of Company I and Christopher Harding of the Seventh attachment. The list was increased the following day by the killing of Michael Keyes of Company B.

After holding their intrenchments through the day of the 19th Edwards's command was relieved by the Vermont Brigade at dark and retired to a position near the railroad bridge where the night was passed. The time of service of the Tenth Massachusetts having now expired after three years of faithful and creditable service, they bade adieu to their comrades in arms and marched to City Point on their homeward way. The re-enlisted men and recruits, nominally numbering 160, were, like the veterans of the Seventh, attached to the Thirty-seventh as an independent detachment awaiting further orders. Early in the morning the brigade was shelled out of its camp, one or two men being killed in the Tenth just as they were in the act of setting out for home. Shelter was taken in a ravine where rations were drawn, letters received and written, and a day of rest enjoyed.

At night-fall the brigade—now reduced to the Thirty-seventh regiment with its attachments and the Second Rhode Island battalion—again went to the front and with the Ninety-third Pennsylvania of Wheaton's brigade occupied a part of the line held by Gibbon's division of the Second Corps, running from the railroad to the left along a sunken road. At this point the two lines of works were separated by scarcely more than a hundred yards in some parts, the opposing lines grimly watching each other through the following day with an occasional outbreak of sharp-shooting,—the Thirty-seventh losing Frederick B. Crocker of Company F killed.

Evening brought marching orders, the line being relieved by troops from Martindale's division, and a monotonous night march ensued, the column feeling its way slowly to the left. That being the second night that the regiment had been without sleep, it was difficult to prevent the men from lapsing into utter insensibility at each of the frequent temporary halts. The object of this expedition was to reach and cut off effectually the Weldon railroad. With this purpose in view General Birney, commanding the Second Corps in the absence of General Hancock, (again disabled by the wound which he had received at Gettysburg,) was directed to throw his corps to the left of the Union line, connecting with General Warren's left and going into position as near the enemy's main works as circumstances would permit. General Wright was then to take up the prolongation, and it was expected that the Sixth Corps would reach and hold the railroad. The scheme signally failed. The two corps were ordered to proceed without reference to each other, Birney swinging forward toward the Confederate intrenchments while Wright pushed straight on toward the Weldon railroad. A gap was thus formed between the left of the Second and the right of the Sixth Corps through which two divisions of Hill's corps moved quickly and skillfully and fell in overwhelming force upon the flank and rear of Gibbon's division of the Second Corps. A considerable portion of this division was captured, while the Sixth Corps suffered less severely. Apparently satisfied with the advantage gained, the Confederates finally withdrew, taking their prisoners and the captured artillery. The Union lines were then adjusted and fortified, the Second Corps extending to the Jerusalem plank road and the Sixth running to the rear along the highway.

At daylight of the 22d the Thirty-seventh halted a short time for breakfast, after which they marched again and at 7 o'clock went into position on the extreme left of the corps. Companies F and G were sent to guard a bridge across a swamp a little distance in advance, while the remainder of the regiment divided its attention between supporting a battery and building works across the road. The sound of battle from Hill's assault at the right gave evidence that a severe conflict was raging not far away, but such sounds had become too familiar to elicit more than passing remark. The day and the night passed without event, and other days and nights of quiet followed. The army was simply too exhausted, broken and disorganized to do more than face the enemy, hold its intrenched position and seek to regain its energies. In the latter direction remarkable efforts were put forth. Everything in the way of rations and supplies that could minister to the comfort and health of the men was furnished, the Sanitary and Christian Commissions co-operating heartily with the Commissary Department of the army. There was need of all these kind provisions. The drought still continued, the heat was frightfully oppressive and the dust which rose at the slightest provocation was unbearable, though not to be escaped.

On the afternoon of June 29 intelligence came to General Meade that General Wilson with his cavalry division, which had been engaged in an extensive raid against the enemy's railroad communications to the westward, had been cut off and hemmed in at Reams Station on the Weldon road by a superior force of the enemy. The Sixth Corps was immediately ordered to march to his relief. The companies at the bridge were hastily recalled and at 3 o'clock the regiment set forth upon its dusty march of some ten miles. With the waning light the destination was reached, but Wilson was not there to need their aid. With considerable loss he had succeeded in freeing his command, and the Confederate forces, consisting of cavalry and infantry, did not await the onset of the Sixth Corps. The Thirty-seventh crossed the railroad near the Station, formed a line of battle and intrenched parallel to the road, passing the night with no further disturbance than occasional picket firing. Before the soldiers settled down to sleep, however, a considerable portion of the railroad had been destroyed, though some of the buildings were reserved for occupation by the officers.

Next morning what had been spared over night was given to the flames and details moved out several miles destroying the road and whatever could give comfort to the enemy, but meeting no opposition. Toward evening the commands gathered at the rendezvous and at 6 o'clock started on the return march. After several hours plodding through the darkness, there being no moon, bivouac was made in a plowed field where the dust seemed of fathomless depth; but the men, having had little rest since the start, were too weary to be critical. Moving a short distance in the morning to more favorable ground the regiment remained through the day and night, setting out in the morning of July 2 for the position on the Jerusalem plank road which had been quitted when starting upon the expedition. It was fortunate that the distance was but a few miles, for the day proved dreadfully hot and oppressive. The destination being gained, company streets were laid out and the encampment made as neat as circumstances would permit. Then followed a few days more of quiet.

The brigade was now reduced to but a trifle over 500 officers and men, a report of this period showing the following returned for duty: Thirty-seventh proper, 14 officers and 285 enlisted men; Seventh attachment, 1 officer and 21 men; Tenth attachment, 50 men; Second Rhode Island, 2 officers and 139 men; total, 512. On the 6th of July the Fourth Brigade, Second Division was discontinued and the troops under command of Lieutenant Colonel Montague were transferred to the Third Brigade, First Division, of which Colonel Edwards took command. The other regiments of the brigade were the Forty-ninth, Eighty-second and One Hundred and Nineteenth Pennsylvania, the Fifth Wisconsin Battalion and a detachment of Twenty-third Pennsylvania veterans. The waste of the campaign thus far will be realized when it is stated that with the exception of three New York regiments transferred to other brigades, Colonel Edwards now commanded all that were left to the service of three brigades composed of 13 regiments that had started out from the camp at Brandy Station two months and two days before, the Fourth Brigade, First Division, having also been included in the consolidation. As in the case of the old brigade, the time of several regiments had expired and their organizations had disappeared, while in other cases a handful only remained to guard the torn and shreded colors.

Meantime events were transpiring of great importance to the Sixth Corps, as they were to call it to a new field of duty. In fact the Third Division had already taken transportation to Baltimore to guard against a threatened raid into Maryland by a strong Confederate force under General Early, and in the evening of the 9th orders were received for the remainder of the corps to march at once to City Point, en route for Washington. It was scarcely a welcome order. The new dispositions had just been made—the red crosses had taken the places of the white on the soldiers' caps, satisfactory camps had been secured, the officers were comfortably settled in their new quarters, there was no appearance of an immediate serious movement. These thoughts flitted through the minds of many and were then dismissed, the few essential preparations were made, and in a remarkably short time the well-tried corps had turned its face toward the James River, 15 miles away. And by such roads! For six weeks no rain had fallen; for one-half that time the roads had been incessantly traversed by columns of cavalry and infantry, by artillery and wagons and vehicles of every description. Marching as rapidly as they well could, it seemed that the men must suffocate in the terrible clouds of dust which filled all space. But they had learned to endure all things, and morning found them at the wharf; but the transportation was not ready, nor was it provided till near night, and all day through the terrible heat of the sun the men remained packed on the bare sand with no relief save to watch the lazy flow of the broad river.

Leaving the Thirty-seventh and detachments under Lieutenant-Colonel Montague to embark at length, to creep down the river during the night, next day passing Fortress Monroe and its famous surroundings, encountering something of a storm in Chesapeake Bay, anchoring during the following night, then steaming up the Potomac past Mount Vernon—sacred to every American,—reaching Washington about noon of the 12th, let us see what had been transpiring in the region of the Upper Potomac.

At the opening of the campaign General Sigel, commanding a force in the Shenandoah valley and a co-operating column under General Crook in the Kanawha region, was directed to begin active operations in common with all the other Union armies. The movement of General Crook was measurably successful. He defeated an opposing force under General W E. Jones at Cloyd Mountain, pushed on to Newbern, where he destroyed an important bridge on the Richmond and Tennessee railroad and retreated safely, though an expedition of his cavalry under General Averell was not able to destroy the salt works at Saltville against which it was sent. Sigel himself was less fortunate.

Advancing as far as New Market, he was attacked on the 15th of May and signally defeated, by General Breckinridge, retreating some 30 miles down the Valley. He was at once removed from command by General Grant, and General David Hunter was appointed his successor. Hunter at once began to move toward Lynchburg, subsisting his army on the country through which he passed. At Piedmont he encountered a force under General W E. Jones which he thoroughly defeated, the Confederate commander being killed and a large part of his troops captured.

Hunter was now joined by the forces of Crook and Averell, with which he moved toward Lynchburg, meeting with some success on the way but also encountering delays which prevented his arrival at the point of destination in time to occupy it. Mention has been made of Lee's having received reinforcements from the Shenandoah Valley at the North Anna. These consisted of two brigades which he had called down from Breckinridge's command after the latter had defeated Sigel, supposing that a period of quiet would follow in that region. The disaster at Piedmont showed how much of an error had been committed, and not only were those brigades returned but the veteran corps of Stonewall Jackson, now commanded by General Jubal A. Early during the disability of General Ewell, was dispatched to the scene to operate against Hunter. As the latter approached Lynchburg on the evening of June 17 from the north Early came up from the south and hurried his troops through the town to the redoubts in front of Hunter. Sharp fighting ensued the following day which, though giving no decided advantage to either army, convinced Hunter that he was thwarted, and he at once retreated to the westward through Buford's Gap. A sharp pursuit was made for a time, inflicting no serious damage, after which the retreating column was left to make the best of its way to the Kanawha valley. Hunter was now in a very deplorable condition, having but a partial supply of ammunition, no food except some beef driven on the hoof, and being at least six days' march from any available supplies. As a factor in the pending struggle, therefore, he had ceased to be of the least account.

Early's original instructions had contemplated the defeat of the Union army and an advance into Maryland; Hunter by getting into his unfortunate predicament had rendered the former unnecessary and threw open wide the doors of the latter. Early had now four infantry divisions commanded by Rodes, Gordon, Ramseur and Echols, Ranson's division of cavalry, comprising four brigades, and an artillery force of over 50 guns. General Sigel was at Martinsburg with a small force protecting a quantity of government supplies, and an attempt was made to surround and capture the post; but Sigel, ably assisted by Colonel Mulligan at Leetown, who drove back the Confederate advance and gained valuable time, removed much of his property, destroyed the rest and with his garrison retired to the strong works on Maryland Hights where, though unable to take the offensive, he could defy attack from the enemy while his artillery and sharp-shooters prevented Early from occupying Harper's Ferry and making it his starting point for Maryland. Meantime the Southern horsemen had been raiding, plundering, levying contributions and destroying railroad, canal, bridges and other structures wherever they could penetrate, and on the 5th of July Early with two of his divisions crossed the Potomac at Shepherdstown.

As the invaders moved steadily toward and through Frederick, threatening equally Baltimore and Washington, the alarm became general. President Lincoln called upon some of the loyal governors for troops to serve for 100 days; General Lew Wallace, in command at Baltimore, gathered all the disciplined troops which were available or which could be relieved by Home Guards or the 100-days' men and formed a brigade under command of General E. B. Tyler, with which he took post at the crossing of the Monocacy, a few miles east of Frederick, where the roads to Washington and Baltimore diverge and where also he covered the railroad. On the 6th of July General Grant dispatched Ricketts's division of the Sixth Corps with some dismounted cavalry by way of Baltimore, which they reached the evening of the 7th and were at once hurried forward to Wallace's assistance. These went into position on the left, covering the railroad and the road to Washington, while Tyler's command was posted to hold the Baltimore turnpike, two or three miles to the northward. The Union position was in no sense a strong one, since the river was everywhere fordable, the flanks could not be protected, and Wallace had but eight pieces of artillery and less than 6,000 men all told.

Yet the battle of the Monocacy, July 9, was a stubbornly contested little engagement. Early advanced from Frederick in the morning, the divisions of Rodes and Ramseur against Tyler and Ricketts respectively, while Gordon crossed the Monocacy a mile below the Union left and struck the defending line in the flank. Yet the two brave brigades from the trenches in front of Petersburg held on tenaciously against the double attack till over one-half their numbers were killed, wounded or missing. The force of the blow had fallen upon Ricketts, since Early was principally concerned to clear the road to Washington, and about the middle of the afternoon, when it was evident that no further successful resistance could be made, Wallace concentrated his defeated forces on the Baltimore turnpike, along which he retreated. Pursuit was made for a little distance, but was abandoned before night-fall, and next morning the victors pressed on toward Washington. Their cavalry was very busy; scouting parties rode far and wide, seizing everything which could be made useful to the Confederacy. Hagerstown had been made to pay $20,000 in cash and Frederick ten times that amount, while cattle, horses, forage and provisions were seized and dispatched by the various fords into Virginia, all the crossings of the river being held by strong detachments. The telegraph lines from Washington in all directions were cut and many railroad trains stopped, on one of which General Franklin was found and made prisoner, but he managed to escape soon after through the negligence of his guards.

On the morning of the 11th Early's advance marched from Rockville toward Washington, coming down the Seventh Street road on the north side of the city. The day was fearfully hot and oppressive and the Confederates, worn out by their recent severe marching, fell out and straggled to such an extent that it was well toward night before the lines in front of the defenses began to show much solidity. Earlier in the campaign Washington had been surrounded by a circle of detached forts, usually connected by strong lines of rifle-pits and so arranged that even should one be captured it would be commanded by its neighbors on either flank and so be practically of no value to the captors. Early's advance brought him in front of Fort Stevens, to the east of which was Fort Slocum; on the west was Fort De Russy, beyond which was Fort Reno, its guns commanding the Georgetown road. Between Stevens and De Russy ran Rock Creek, through a ravine which seemed to promise something of a shelter for storming parties in case an attack should be decided on.

General Augur, commanding the defenses of Washington, had gathered in the fortifications such troops as were available for the service, but they were few in numbers and chiefly raw, being poorly adapted to withstand such veterans as Early would hurl against them. At half-past 1 in the afternoon of the 11th the fight opened by an artillery fire from the fort upon the Confederate skirmishers, driving them back, and half an hour later the glad news ran quickly through the city that the advance of the Sixth Corps was debarking at the wharves. At the same time came a steamer load of the troops of the Nineteenth Corps, a division of which had been ordered to Washington from the Department of the Gulf. These troops were met at the wharf by President Lincoln, and through a cheering throng they made their way at once toward the booming guns north of the city. Early and his officers through their glasses saw the reinforcements filing into position behind the works and realized that the tide of their success was to go no further.

It was near noon of the following day, the 12th, when the Thirty-seventh and its attachments debarked from the propeller Perit and took their way through Pennsylvania avenue and Seventh Street to the front. They were met at the wharf by Captain Colt of Colonel Edwards's staff, who informed them of the presence of the enemy near Fort Stevens. The men had been glad to begin the voyage as a relief from the heat and dust of the Petersburg trenches; they were now glad to stand upon the firm earth once more as a relief from the close quarters of the vessel. The populace gave frequent manifestations of their joy at the appearance of the veterans of the Sixth Corps, and the soldiers were by no means indifferent to the friendly faces and warm words which formed so marked a contrast to the sullen silence of Virginia. The sight of Fort Stevens recalled many a reminiscence to some of those in the regiment. Near it was Brightwood, the camp of the Tenth regiment up to the opening of the peninsular campaign, and the fort was built by that regiment. It was then named Fort Massachusetts, but had been renamed in honor of the gallant General Stevens who fell at Chantilly.

The fort at this time presented an interesting spectacle. In its safe inclosure were gathered cabinet officers and citizens of both sexes who had come out from the city to see the Sixth Corps whip Early, while in an embrasure beside General Wright and a surgeon stood the tall form of President Lincoln. General Russell, commanding the First Division of the Sixth Corps, with two of his brigade commanders, General Upton and Colonel Edwards, had just entered the fort and mounted the parapet to select positions for their commands, which were to join with a portion of the Second Division in an attack on the enemy. The turning of their field-glasses toward the enemy's line was a signal for his sharp-shooters to open and one of their bullets almost immediately entered the embrasure, struck a wheel of the siege gun and wounded the surgeon standing almost directly behind and close to the President. The latter was then induced by General Wright to sit down out of range, and a chair was placed for him against the parapet. Somewhat later as he sat there one of his cabinet said: "Mr. President, if you will look over in that direction," pointing with his finger, " you can see just where the rebels are." His reply was characteristic: " My impression is that if I am where I can see the rebels, they are where they can see me." But in spite of this theory as the lines advanced that unmistakable form was discerned watching their progress from over the parapet.

The attack being arranged, the Union lines pushed forward steadily for a mile, driving back the Confederate skirmishers and their reserves, though the latter made a stout resistance and inflicted a serious loss, especially upon the Third Brigade, Second Division, every regimental commander of which was killed or disabled. The Thirty-seventh was on the right of the line and was not severely engaged, only two members of the regiment proper being wounded—Michael Ploss of Company A and John Sandling of Company H. In the Tenth attachment Patrick Lovett was killed, while Lieutenant William H. Cousens and Patrick Mullen were wounded.

About midnight the regiment was relieved and fell back a short distance for bivouac, but the expected renewal of the struggle did not come in the morning. The enemy had disappeared. General Wright had been appointed to command the forces in the field, and soon after noon orders were issued for an advance of the Sixth Corps and Emory's Division of the Nineteenth in pursuit. The line of march led past Forts De Russy and Reno, as well as other fortifications in the line of defenses, thence through Tennallytown to Orcutt's Cross Roads, where the day's march ended. Everywhere sad and abundant traces of the great raid were visible. The previous night had been passed in the beautiful grounds of J. W Morrison, in the midst of which lay the blackened ruins of his mansion. Near by a like fate had befallen Montgomery Blair's fine residence; other buildings had been destroyed, some by shells thrown into them to drive out the enemy's sharp-shooters.

The afternoon march of some 17 miles was a very trying one, as the weather was intensely hot; but an abundance of good water was to be had, and the roads were much better than the ordinary Virginia article of the same name. As the horses of the command had been sent by a different vessel which had not yet come up, the "field and staff" as well as the rest of the regiment were obliged to make the march on foot that day, and there were blistered feet in plenty when the column halted. That evening the animals arrived, however, in charge of the servants who had been left with them, and as they brought also the officers' blankets and other camping conveniences they were very welcome.

The regiment was detailed as rear guard for the trains next day, the 14th, and as it consequently did not march till afternoon the early part of the day witnessed an important change in its equipment. The Springfield rifle muskets with which the men had been armed from the first were now turned in to Lieutenant Smith, ordnance officer for the regiment, and in their places an issue was made of the Spencer repeating rifle, or "seven-shooters," as they were familiarly termed. This was a new weapon of the magazine breech-loading order, with which but few regiments in the Army of the Potomac and none in the Sixth Corps had thus far been armed. While the regiment was marching through Washington toward Fort Stevens, the chief ordnance officer came to greet Colonel Edwards, and in the course of the conversation asked if he could do anything for him. "Yes" was the reply, "you can arm Colonel Montague's regiment with the Spencer rifle." "Make out your requisition for them and I will see that you get them," was the response. Within 24 hours the quartermaster had carried the papers to head-quarters, and with wonderful promptness the demand had been honored.

This new rifle was undoubtedly at that time the most formidable weapon that could be placed in the hands of infantry. Though somewhat shorter than the Springfield, it had wonderful range, shooting with accuracy and immense force. It used metallic cartridges and the method of loading was comparatively simple, as was necessary for successful use in the field. A tin tube containing a strong spiral spring held the cartridges, and this being thrust into place in the breech of the gun, the operation of the breech mechanism caused the upper cartridge to be pushed into the barrel ready for firing. The piece was cocked and fired in the usual manner. The guard being pulled down opened the breech of the gun and threw out the exploded shell, being returned to its place the gun was closed and the spring in the tube threw another cartridge into the barrel, when the piece was ready to be cocked and fired again, and so on till the last cartridge in the tube was used. Then the reloading occupied no more time than the placing of a single charge in a muzzle-loading weapon. With this construction it will be readily seen that the Spencer rifle in actual service was a great improvement upon the muzzle-loader, especially in "tight places," and the men of the Thirty-seventh were not a little flattered that they were the first in the Sixth Corps to be thus armed. They were not long in learning, however, that the repeater required a vastly increased supply of ammunition. The former complement had been 40 rounds, in place of which they were now expected to carry 100, and on some of the tedious marches that followed words of complaint more expressive than elegant were apt to be heard, and it is to be feared that sometimes the bundles of cartridges were surreptitiously lightened.

The weapon with which the Thirty-seventh now found itself equipped, and which was one of the most important pioneers in the revolution of modern small arms, was the invention of Mr. C. M. Spencer, at that time a young mechanic in the employ of the Cheney Brothers, the noted silk manufacturers of South Manchester, Ct. Mr. Spencer had been experimenting and developing his idea from 1857, and in 1860 produced the first working gun. The time was opportune, if not even providential; the first mutterings of the rebellion were giving notice of the storm to come. The importance of the invention was manifest to any intelligent observer of the national situation, and through the influence of a member of the Cheney firm a company was organized at Boston for the manufacture of the rifle. A part of the Chickering piano manufactory was leased for work-shops and half a million dollars was expended in furnishing stock and machinery.

Mr. Spencer meantime was making diligent efforts to bring his invention to the attention of the proper national authorities, and finally a test was arranged at the Washington navy-yard where 1,000 rounds were fired to show the capacity of the new claimant for official favor. During this test 21 shots were fired in 62 seconds, and the Secretary of the Navy was so favorably impressed that he gave an order for 1,000 of the rifles for trial in actual service on shipboard. During 1861 the number ordered amounted to 10,000, but their use was still confined to the navy.

Gradually, as it was seen that they were valuable in this limited field, they came into use among cavalry and mounted infantry, the western armies being the first to use any considerable number. During the Tennessee campaign of Rosecrans against Bragg in 1863 the Spencer rifle received commendation, but it was not till the following spring that it became known among the infantry of the Army of the Potomac, one of the first regiments to adopt it being the Pennsylvania Bucktails, who took it at the opening of the Wilderness campaign instead of the Sharpe rifles which they had previously used.

A rifle made for the purpose was presented to President Lincoln in August, 1863, by Mr. Spencer, who relates interestingly the almost boyish eagerness with which the President on a subsequent day in his presence examined and tested "the machine" in the White House grounds. The target made by Mr. Lincoln on that occasion—a piece of pine board six by eight inches with a black spot in the center—is preserved in the military museum at Springfield, Ill. Every bullet went through the "bull's eye," and a memorandum in pencil on the board says the target was made by seven consecutive shots at a distance of 40 yards.

Altogether 200,000 Spencer rifles were made, and it is worthy of remark that every one was an exact duplicate of all the others. Practical test in actual service did not suggest a single change from the original model in the way of improvement.*

---

*Those who carried the Spencer rifle during the war will be interested to know that Mr. Spencer has recently established at Windsor, Ct., a factory where the rifle in an improved and still more efficient form is made. It has recently been introduced to leading military powers throughout the world and very favorably received, and it is safe to predict that it is destined to win still higher place among the destructive enginery of modern warfare. The same principle has also been applied to shotguns with marked success.

CHAPTER XVII.

THE CAMPAIGN UNDER SHERIDAN

THE WAGON TRAINS—FOLLOWING EARLY BY MARCH AND COUN-
TERMARCH—SHERIDAN AT THE HELM—THE SKIRMISH AT
CHARLESTOWN—THE BATTLE OF THE OPEQUAN.

Not before 3 o'clock in the afternoon of July 14 did the Thirty-seventh regiment start upon the march as wagon guard, after having to a certain extent mastered the peculiarities of the Spencer rifle. There was plenty of time to study the new weapon en route, as the train barely crawled along and often seemed to have come to a dead halt. The trouble was that everything was new, raw and green. When the Sixth Corps was ordered to Washington its old train, which from long service had become experienced and valuable, was "turned in" at City Point, to await the return months later, and when the pursuit of Early was taken up the corps was provided with a fresh outfit, and "fresh" enough mules, drivers and wagon masters proved. The drivers and masters were "citizens" hired for the service, self-important, lazy, worthless fellows almost without exception; when put in connection with half-broken mules the scenes which transpired form admirable material for camp-fire yarns.

The trouble began at the outset. The raw mules would go where and when they pleased, or not at all; the drivers were indifferent or helpless and the bosses worse if possible. Teams were stalled or upset on level ground, and the night wore away in making a very few miles. During one of the stoppages of the train Colonel Edwards rode along and seeing a wagon upset, the driver sitting on the ground near by smoking and a wagon master on horseback paying no attention to the matter, inquired the reason. Getting an impudent answer from the fellows, who felt at liberty to be insolent on account of not being enlisted men, the colonel ordered the wagon master to set his men at work to right the vehicle. "You go to hell!" was the surly answer, repeated in more offensive form in response to the sharp "What?" which broke from the lips of the quick-tempered brigade commander. There was the quick whirl of a saber through the air, a tumbling bully rolling in the dust with a sore and bleeding head, followed by the colonel's voice in its most convincing tones: "There, now, you men get to work and take this train out of here!" For once, if the only time in their lives, the men *did* work, but it is doubtful if any permanent reformation was wrought.

Thieving from the wagons was a common offense, and a little later in the campaign Lieutenant-Colonel Montague found that his private satchel had been robbed and reported the loss to Quartermaster Sergeant Sears, who had charge of the two wagons containing the stores of the Thirty-seventh and its attachments including the Second Rhode Island—Quartermaster Bridgman having been left in charge of the brigade train at City Point. Suspicion at once fell on a spare wagon boss who had been very fond of lounging about and riding in the Thirty-seventh wagons, and a trusty soldier was detailed from Company A with orders to allow no stranger about the regimental wagons. Presently the intruder appeared and made his way toward the favorite resting place. "It's against orders to ride in these wagons, sur!" was the courteous protest of the guard. The familiar army expletive was grunted out as the intruder settled himself in the most comfortable position possible. "Me go to hill!" roared the soldier, his Celtic passion all aflame. "By me sowl, now ye'll come out o' that!" and a Spencer rifle at full cock turned its persuasive muzzle full between the fellow's eyes. The speed with which the rascal tumbled from the wagon and sought more hospitable quarters convulsed the few spectators with laughter; neither he nor any of his ilk troubled the wagons more, and there was no more stealing.

Now that the matter of wagon trains has been broached at

some detail from the necessities of the case, it may be well to call the attention of the general reader to the importance of this branch of military economy. With an army so often on the move and for great distances as was the case during the rebellion, the efficiency of the train service became a matter of supreme moment. Wherever the men went, the trains must follow them with such supplies as would be needed. If a battle was imminent, an hour's brisk firing would empty the soldiers' cartridge boxes, and the ammunition wagons must be near to furnish a fresh supply, even under the enemy's fire if necessary. The ambulances must be at hand to bear the wounded to hospitals for treatment. At such moments of supreme trial the ordinary wagons must be kept back out of the way, ready to lead the retreat at a moment's notice if the exigencies of the battle-field should so require; or to supply the needs of the men during the pauses in the conflict, wherever the fortunes of war might have taken the command to which the wagons were attached. On the ordinary march, wherever the corps or division or brigade was ordered to report,—if the expedition was anything more than a temporary one with rations in haversacks,—no matter what the condition or the nature of the roads, the trains were to follow and keep within such distance as would enable them to provision and otherwise supply the camps whenever they were formed. If the supplies had to be hauled any considerable distance the work of the trains was correspondingly increased, and often in stormy weather, when the roads became bad from the excessive use to which they were subjected, terrible hardships were endured by animals, train men, and those they sought to succor. When to this is added the danger of sudden raids by scouting parties of the enemy, the ease with which portions of trains could be cut off at favorable points and either driven away or plundered and destroyed before assistance could be summoned from guards who might be miles away and possibly worthless if on the scene, it will be understood that the life of an army teamster, especially if he sought to be to any extent conscientious in his work, was by no means an enviable one.

The number of wagons and the extent of the trains required

to supply an army would seem surprising to the general reader. The wagon train of the Army of the Potomac when it started on the Wilderness campaign would have occupied at least 60 miles of road, as closely as it was possible to drive the wagons over the imperfect roads. From this general basis it is easy to estimate the equipage properly belonging to each corps, division or brigade. But the trains never had the good fortune to proceed "decently and in order." A thousand accidents were liable, any one of which must annoy and delay those in the rear. Yet it was possible for an accident to be a blessing in disguise, as the quartermaster of the Thirty-seventh found on at least one occasion.

As was unavoidable after a long series of campaigns, the invoices of that officer's department called for many an article which the most diligent search would have failed to reveal. They were in fact "short," but were borne "on hand," pending final settlement. As the trains of the Sixth Corps were crossing the Chickahominy on the way to Petersburg, a pontonier who was washing his red shirt at the side of the bridge gave the garment a snap as one of the Thirty-seventh teams approached. The check mule shied violently, pushing the off leader over the side of the bridge into the water, and was of course drawn over with him. Their plunge drew over the next pair—the "swings" —and the weight of the four sank the end of the canvas boat so that the "wheelers" and the wagon were tumbled into the river, 20 feet in depth. One or two of the mules were cut loose and fished out after a series of laughable performances; the wagon and its contents were a total loss, but that loss simplified the quartermaster's accounts wonderfully.

The march of the Thirty-seventh on the afternoon of July 14, though lasting from 3 o'clock in the afternoon till after dark, covered not more than four or five miles, and finally a halt was ordered in a pleasant pine grove, where the command remained till the following noon. As an extensive blackberry tract was discovered in the immediate vicinity, the men made the most of the delay in securing a palatable feast. In the march of the succeeding afternoon more satisfactory progress was made;

Seneca Mills were passed and the halt for the night was made at Poolesville. Here evidence of a military execution was witnessed in the body of a deserter hanging from a gallows in the center of the village. In the little affair at Reams Station he had deserted from the First Long Island, and when his regiment made a dash soon after he was captured on the enemy's skirmish line, firing upon his late comrades.

Morning of the 16th found the Thirty-seventh in its place in the column with Edwards's brigade in the advance, and a hard day's marching ensued. The route led toward the Potomac by the Conrad's Ferry road, but some three miles short of the river a cross road was taken leading to White's Ford, being the route followed by Early in his retreat. On reaching the Potomac, which was here a half-mile in width and from one to three feet in depth, the enemy's cavalry vedettes were observed on the opposite bank, though too few in numbers to offer serious resistance. A battery was put in position and a few shots sent across which precipitated their withdrawal, after which the corps crossed without further molestation.

The column now turned nearly southward, passing the battlefield of Ball's Bluff where nearly three years before one of the lamentable tragedies of the war had occurred, thence to the beautiful village of Leesburg, which like very few Virginia villages was strongly reminiscent of New England thrift. Here no halt was made but the course was changed to the westward and the slopes of the Catoctin range were climbed, the exhaustion being well offset by the beauty of the panorama which was unfolded as the hights were gained. The entire day's march had been through a charming region. The fertile soil, stimulated by thrift and enterprise, had spread before the dusty soldiers a succession of delightful farms, the water-courses were abundant, the springs frequent, cold and refreshing. The weather, too, was comfortably cool, but the ground was still very dry and dusty, as there had been no rain for more than six weeks, and when the regiment halted for the night in a beautiful oak grove some three miles west of Leesburg and on the opposite slope of the mountains the men were quite ready to welcome the order.

General Wright had now been joined by two divisions of the Nineteenth Corps, and Hunter's command under General Crook, which had entered the Shenandoah Valley a few days previous by way of Harper's Ferry, was ordered to join him and co-operate in the pursuit of Early. The latter had that morning quitted Leesburg when Wright started his column toward the place from Poolesville, and barely succeeded in slipping through between the converging Union columns, Crook's cavalry capturing a considerable section of his wagon train at Purcellsville as it was making its way to Snicker's Gap, en route to Winchester.

The following day, Sunday, July 17, was one of rest for the Sixth Corps. Religious services were generally held, the Thirty-seventh uniting with the Fifteenth New Jersey, the chaplain of the latter officiating in the illness of Chaplain Morse and a brass-band giving its aid in the services. While the infantry were enjoying this respite the cavalry of Crook's column were searching for the enemy and that evening General Duffie reported Early on the west bank of the Shenandoah disputing the passage in force. As the instructions to General Wright were to pursue Early till he felt certain that the latter was really retreating southward and then hasten his own and the Nineteenth Corps back to Petersburg in time to strike a powerful blow there before Early's arrival, he ordered a forward movement the following morning to ascertain the exact state of affairs. Crook being at Purcellsville moved on in advance, while the Sixth and Nineteenth Corps followed.

The Thirty-seventh marched early in the morning, passing through Hamilton, Purcellsville and Snickersville, near which a halt was made about noon. In the mean time Crook's troops had passed the Gap, and from the western slope of the Blue Ridge could see the Confederates in considerable numbers beyond the Shenandoah. Colonel Thoburn's division was ordered across the river at Island Ford, a mile or so below Snicker's Ferry, while the Sixth Corps was directed to push forward and cross at the Ferry. The first part of the latter order was duly executed, the column moving through the Gap and down to the river, but before the crossing could be made a severe attack upon the right of Thoburn's line forced a body of dismounted cavalry and his own brigade back into the river. General Ricketts, in immediate command of the Sixth Corps (General Wright commanding all the troops in the field), did not think it advisable to attempt a crossing under these circumstances, and Thoburn's remaining brigades were ordered to retire, which they did as creditably as could be expected, since they were subjected to a heavy fire from the Confederate lines on the bank, while the latter were punished by the Union batteries on the opposite hills.

It was now near night and the two armies settled down on their respective sides of the river, each lining the bank with a cloud of sharp-shooters. Companies E and G of the Thirty-seventh were detailed for picket, Lieutenant-Colonel Montague being officer of the day and in charge of the picket line, and in the gloom of that July evening the first test of the Spencer rifles was made by a few members of the regiment scattered along the border of the dark river. There was a lively interchange of shots by the picket lines during the 19th, but the Confederates found themselves at such a disadvantage when opposed to the Spencer that they called out asking what kind of a "shooting-iron" it was. During the day there was some fraternizing between members of the Thirty-seventh and the Thirty-fourth, the latter being in the First Brigade of Thoburn's division. There were many friends in the two regiments and the experiences of each formed interesting topics for rapid question and answer.

With morning of the 20th the Thirty-seventh was ordered to force a crossing, and Lieutenant-Colonel Montague selected a point observed the day before while on the picket line, where in the middle of the river was considerable of an island with the side toward the enemy heavily fringed with bushes. A portion of the regiment was posted here under cover to open fire if necessary when the skirmishers started to cross. The latter were deployed and at the signal jumped into the river and waded across as rapidly as possible, with the water up to their waists. As there were distinguished lookers-on there was much rivalry, and each strove to do his best. Captain Loomis was the first to set foot on the coveted shore, with Lieutenant-Colonel Montague on horseback by his side and closely followed by the whole skirmish band. Up the little bluff they rushed, expecting each moment the flash of hostile rifles in their faces, but no enemy was visible. It was a bloodless victory, as the last of the rebels had left less than an hour before; but none the less it was to those engaged a thrilling episode. While Early's attention had been directed to the force in his front, Hunter at Harper's Ferry had pushed Averell's cavalry and some other forces up the Valley so that they were almost upon Early's rear before they were discovered. The wily Confederate at once retreated toward Strasburg, at the head of the main valley, and when the fact was established the Sixth Corps was ordered to advance to Berryville or beyond on the direct road to Winchester. Owing to a heavy thunder storm which occurred during the afternoon, the Thirty-seventh had not made more than about three miles after crossing the river when it was ordered to halt.

At this stage of proceedings General Wright reached the conclusion that as Early had retreated southward his instructions required him to return to Washington and thence to Petersburg without delay. The soldiers, who were either already asleep or preparing to sleep, were accordingly startled by the order to pack up and fall in at once. Toward midnight the column turned its face back toward the Shenandoah and marched to and across it, but it did not halt. Up the slopes of the Blue Ridge it went, to and through the famous Gap, down the eastern declension and back toward Leesburg over the road by which it had come. After marching 17 miles a short halt was made for breakfast near Hamilton, and when the meal was over the column resumed its tedious way. "I shall bivouac to-night on the south bank of Goose Creek," General Wright telegraphed to Halleck at Washington, and the promise was kept. At Leesburg the turnpike to the south was taken, a march of some four miles from the village placed the command in the designated location, and late in the afternoon a halt was ordered and ranks were broken. It had been a long and tedious tramp, but, as a few hours of daylight still remained, the banks of the creek were presently lined by busy men who took the first opportunity presented for four weeks to wash their clothes and bathe in the clear waters of the stream.

A grateful night's rest followed and at 8 o'clock next morning the marched was resumed. The experiences of this day were not so trying as those of the day before. At noon a halt of some two hours was made near Dranesville, after which the corps marched leisurely till after dark, crossing Difficult Run and halting for the night within 15 miles of Washington. The regiments were early astir next morning, and at 4 o'clock the Thirty-seventh began to march. At 9 o'clock the brown earthworks of the Washington defenses rose to view; Fort Marcy, standing guard over Chain Bridge, was passed, the bridge itself was crossed, and about noon the regiment went into camp near Fort Gaines, half a mile from Tennallytown, two or three times that distance from the battle-ground of Fort Stevens and five miles from Washington.

During the afternoon the men drew five days' rations and made requisition for fresh supplies of clothing, which it scarcely need be said were much needed by most of the command. The next day was Sunday, the 24th, and after an inspection by Captain Tyler officers and men devoted much of the time to perusing the large mail which had been brought in and to writing letters. In the afternoon religious services were held, the brigade band assisting, the men were cautioned to be ready to move at short notice, and after they had retired for the night were called up to receive the clothing subscribed for the day before. A generous rain fell during the night and the early part of Monday, but ceased before noon, and the day passed without further event than an order to be ready to march in the morning.

It was noon of the 26th, however, before the regiment quitted its camp, when it went through Tennallytown and turning its face to the northward took the road to Rockville. That town was passed at 6 o'clock and at 9 the regiment went into camp five miles beyond, the men seriously exhausted by their march of 15 miles, notwithstanding their three days' nominal rest. Let us look for the cause of this apparently aimless marching and countermarching through the deadly heats of July.

The want of competent direction had been sadly felt in the matter of meeting Early's raid. General Grant was supposed to direct in general terms with regard to the movements of all troops; but he was at City Point, while Halleck, serving as his chief of staff, was in Washington. Neither could judge intelligently of the situation of affairs in the Valley, since one series of reports was likely to be contradicted by another within a few hours. Grant had decided that it would be better to have General Wright and his corps returned to the Army of the Potomac while the Nineteenth Corps was retained at Washington for a time. Almost simultaneously with this decision the aspect of affairs in the Valley became so changed that Wright and his troops were again hurried up the Potomac. On the day that Wright had turned back toward Washington, Early sent Ramseur's division to drive away Averell's force a short distance north of Winchester. Averell had but 2,700 men, about half infantry, but with these he attacked and utterly routed the Confederate division, driving it in disorder from the field. Reinforcements were sent on to cover the retreat; during the night Early withdrew to Strasburg, while Averell advanced to Kernstown, south of Winchester, where he was joined by Crook. Early learned on the 23d that the Sixth Corps had withdrawn and the next day he fell upon Crook with the impetuosity characteristic of Southern attack, defeated and pursued him to the Potomac, Crook halting his forces at advantageous positions at the South Mountain passes in Maryland.

The Confederate cavalry under McCausland was now launched across the border and early in the morning of the 30th entered the city of Chambersburg, Pa., which, as it could not pay the $500,000 in currency or $100,000 in gold demanded as the price of exemption, was burned, leaving the greater part of the people homeless and helpless. Averell was but a few miles away with his troopers, riding in hot pursuit of the marauders now that their whereabouts were known, and McCausland, leaving the town in flames, moved rapidly away toward the southwest. The way of retreat was not an easy one, the Union cavalry pressing McCausland so closely that he had little opportunity to demand exemption money or apply the torch. On the 7th of August he was attacked near Moorfield at the junction of the north and south branches of the Potomac by Averell and utterly defeated, a large part of his command, with all his artillery and most of his wagons being captured, while the fraction which escaped was scattered in broken fragments in every direction. From this blow Early's cavalry never recovered.

While these events were transpiring, it was but natural that the loyal people, especially those exposed to the incursions of the desperate raiders, should be filled with alarm, and the news of Crook's disaster was the signal for the "about face" on the part of the Sixth Corps. We left the Thirty-seventh in camp beyond Rockville at the close of the first day's march. The onward way was resumed early in the morning of the 27th, the column passing through some pretty villages, including Nealsville and Clarksburg, and halting near Hyattstown early in the afternoon. The day's march had been only some 13 miles, but the weather was excessively hot and the men were foot-sore and dispirited at the prospect before them. Fortunately they were again in a country where blackberries abounded and many of them flavored their army rations with a delicious if informal dessert.

Starting at 7 o'clock in the morning of the 28th, the column passed through Hyattstown and to and beyond Urbana, halting about noon near Monocacy Creek on the scene of the recent battle between Wallace and Early. Resting through the severest heat of the day the regiment marched again at 5 in the afternoon, fording the creek, and leaving Frederick to the right and rear halted a little short of Jefferson at midnight. Only a few hours could be devoted to rest and sleep, sadly as these were needed by the exhausted soldiers; then up and on again, through Jefferson, Centersville, Petersville, to Knoxville on the bank of the Potomac; thence up the river to and across the ponton bridge leading into Harper's Ferry, and four miles beyond to Halltown where the command halted in line of battle. The day's march had been but 15 miles, yet it was estimated that 30 men in the corps had died of sun-stroke during the day.

The forces of Wright and Crook were now reunited with their

faces in the supposed direction of the enemy, when news was received of McCausland's raid and the burning of Chambersburg. Hunter was at once ordered by Halleck to send the troops back to Frederick to prevent the enemy from moving southward by that route. General Wright protested that his men were unfit to march, but the order was insisted upon and at 3 o'clock the movement began. At Harper's Ferry a long halt was made, and the whole army being packed into the narrow valley exposed to the direct rays of the burning sun—the day being one of the hottest ever experienced—suffered terribly. Many men had already fallen from the ranks of the Thirty-seventh with sun-stroke, and while waiting here Edward Dunn of Company I died from the heat and exhaustion.

The entire army was obliged to cross the river on a single ponton bridge, and the process was a tedious one ; but once across the column wound its way along through the greater part of the night, passing Sandy Hook and Knoxville, finally halting near Petersville, where the command rested till afternoon. Then the bugles sounded, the individuals fell into their places almost automatically and the great mass of suffering, despairing humanity moved out into the withering heat and the stifling dust. It passed through Jefferson, climbed the tedious slopes of Catoctin Mountain, looked out from the summit over the vast expanse of country which seemed but an invitation to perpetual journeying; then it wound down into the valley till within little more than a mile of Frederick, when the welcome orders to stack arms and break ranks were received. Ten miles had been accomplished, and short as was the distance one-half the members of the Sixth Corps—that organization whose powers of endurance had won the admiration of the world—had fallen out by the way. Many were still toiling along as best they could, but others in fearful number were quite broken down or had been prostrated by the deadly sun-stroke.

Thus closed the month of July, 1864,—one of the most trying experienced by the regiment. The first two days of August were devoted to rest, though on the 2d marching orders were again promulgated ; the Thirty-seventh packed up and had proceeded about 20 rods when the time of moving was postponed to next morning, rations were drawn and the camp settled down for the night. During the day Chaplain Morse rode to Frederick, and while there lost his much-prized horse by theft.

At sunrise of August 3 the Thirty-seventh took the lead of the corps in the day's march, which proved much less serious than was contemplated. Passing through Lime Kiln Station and Buckeystown, five miles south of Frederick, the Monocacy was forded half a mile beyond and on the southern bank the camp was established. Here, in a pleasant camp followed two days more of quiet. The 4th being the day appointed by President Lincoln for a national Fast day was observed by services in front of brigade head-quarters.

The day following General Grant visited General Hunter at his head-quarters at Frederick, and an important change was the result. Two divisions of cavalry from the Army of the Potomac had been ordered to join the forces already available against Early, such of the Nineteenth Corps as was at Washington had been sent up and the rest of it was under orders for the same destination, while General Sheridan had been relieved from duty with the Army of the Potomac and was then at Washington awaiting such command as it should be decided to give him. After consultation between Grant and Hunter the latter was relieved of his command and Sheridan was at once telegraphed to take command of all the forces in the field. At the same time the Middle Military Division was constituted, composed of the four departments of West Virginia, the Susquehanna, Washington and the Middle Department, Sheridan being assigned to the command of the new Division. Organizing his cavalry into a corps under the command of General Torbert, the new commander was prepared with a stronger force than had ever before operated in the Valley to take up the work assigned him.

Simultaneously with the arrival of General Grant at Hunter's head-quarters marching orders were promulgated. The Thirty-seventh received theirs during the evening of the 5th, tents were at once struck and everything packed, when it was found that the regiment was to serve as wagon guard and consequently it would be some hours before it would move. Rain fell during the night but ceased in the morning, and finally about 8 o'clock the long-expected summons came and the command trudged away in the rear of the trains. After making a few miles the now familiar Harper's Ferry road over the Catoctin Mountain and by way of Jefferson was struck. The march continued all day with no halt for dinner, nor did it cease till the evening was far advanced, when the regiment sank down to sleep on the tow-path between the canal and the river, eight feet in width, along which the last part of the march had been made.

With daylight of the 7th the regiment was again on the way. In an hour or two it toiled through Harper's Ferry once more, and passing Bolivar Hights took its place with the corps, which had gone into position the day before. A considerable detail went out on picket two or three miles in advance, and with no further incident than the advent of the paymaster with four months' wages two days passed while Sheridan was preparing for his forward movement. Torbert's cavalry arrived on the 9th, and next morning the advance began.

The Thirty-seventh broke camp soon after daylight, and during the forenoon passed through Charlestown, the county seat, made famous by the conviction and execution of John Brown in December, 1859. As the different drum corps and brass-bands entered the streets of the forlorn village each took up, with an energy regardless of the terrible heat, the air of "John Brown." At 4 o'clock the regiment halted near Clifton, where the left of the infantry line was established, facing toward Winchester, and bivouacked for the night in a forest.

The second stage of Sheridan's movement contemplated the advance of his army to the Opequan, all the fords of which were to be seized, and this part of the project was carried out early in the morning of the 11th. It was then intended to throw the Union army rapidly around in the rear and to the south of Early, who had been left the previous morning near Bunker Hill, forcing him to fight in that unenviable position; but the shrewd commander had already divined the intention and marched his command to the south of Winchester, as Sheridan learned early in the day. The latter halted at Opequan Creek till further investigation could be made, the Thirty-seventh being sent forward some miles on a reconnaissance. Finding nothing, they returned to the corps and a slow march to the southward ensued, lasting till about sunset, when the regiment encamped in an open field not far from White Post. Here Nathan J. Hedger of Company C died from illness and the hardship of the campaign.

Edwards's Brigade was detailed on the morning of the 12th to return to Winchester and escort the trains, which it was not safe to move without a strong guard. The city was reached about noon; Lieutenant-Colonel Montague was at once made provost marshal and Companies C and G were detailed as provost guard. Considerable numbers of wounded cavalrymen from both armies were found in the place, and though the general sentiment was intensely Southern, it should be stated for the credit of the citizens that the best of care was given regardless of the sufferers' allegiance. The wagons started toward the front about noon of the next day, the Thirty-seventh as rear guard once more, taking the Strasburg pike toward the south. Kernstown, Newtown and Middletown were passed in due order, and at 10 o'clock the brigade rejoined the corps near Cedar Creek, where the two armies were again confronting each other.

With no greater excitement than the skirmish lines afforded, the time passed till evening of the 16th. Sheridan had now become satisfied that Early, whose principal position and a strong one was at Fisher's Hill, had received heavy reinforcements from Petersburg, and directed a retreat down the Valley to the position on the Opequan to which he had first moved out from Halltown. It was 10 in the evening when the Thirty-seventh marched to the turnpike, along which it plodded all the rest of the night, reaching Winchester about sunrise of the 17th. Halting there for a while the march was continued till the Opequan Creek was crossed, when a halt was directed on the eastern bank. A night's rest did not follow, however, for about midnight the regiment was called up, sent back across the creek and deployed as skirmishers.

Morning saw the march continued toward Charlestown, by way

of Berryville, and when the way was clear the Thirty-seventh rallied and followed. It rained most of the day, some of the time severely, and the jaunt was a hard one, more especially as the men had been practically without rations for two days. Near night a halt was reached in the vicinity of Charlestown and a four-days' supply of food obtained, after which two days of inaction ensued, the second being rainy.

The Sunday morning quiet of August 21 was rudely broken by the long roll giving notice of the enemy's presence. Early had in fact been reinforced by Kershaw's division of infantry, one of cavalry and some artillery, and when Sheridan fell back had followed sharply, taking up his former position at Bunker Hill, leaving Anderson with the fresh troops at Winchester. A combined attack was planned for the morning of the 21st, Anderson to advance by the direct route from Winchester while Early came in from the west. The former found the cavalry in his front too strong and gave up his part of the programme; but Early came on impetuously, brushed away the cavalry outposts and struck a swift and heavy blow upon the Sixth Corps skirmish line.

The Thirty-seventh were quickly under arms and were ordered to strengthen the picket line. Lieutenant-Colonel Montague led his command at a double-quick to a sunken road commanding a wide field in front, where they were judiciously posted, and almost immediately the spiteful crack of the Spencer rifle began to be heard. The new weapon was having its first general test, and grandly did it meet the expectations which had been raised. It was at first supposed that the enemy was beyond the reach of musket fire, but on trial being made it proved that the Spencer bullets could be sent there with remarkable precision considering the distance, and the firing became general. A severe artillery fire was directed upon the Union skirmishers, and the southern sharp-shooters did their best to dislodge the obnoxious Yankees, but the line never wavered. The skirmishing continued all through the day, the Confederates making numerous efforts to advance their lines and post artillery in front of the seven-shooters, but wherever they appeared they were greeted with so hot and well-directed a shower of bullets that they were forced to retire. To the left some progress was made, and at one time there was danger that the men of the Thirty-seventh would be flanked out of their position, but a detachment faced that way and sent in so lively and accurate a fire that the danger was soon averted. The new rifle was somewhat shorter and heavier than the old, but the range was found to be superior; indeed, there seemed no limit to the distance to which the bullets might be sent with reasonable accuracy. The regiment fired during the day some 200 shots per man, and when darkness fell had the satisfaction of knowing that not an inch of ground been yielded.

But this brave resistance had not been made without loss. Five men had been killed : Corporal Levi Davis and Ithamer Woodin of Company A, Silas Miller of Company B, Corporal John E. Banks of Company G, and Robert Reinhart of the Tenth detachment. Fifteen others were wounded (see Appendix), including Captain William M. Hale of the Seventh detachment. The four sergeants of Company F were all wounded, First Sergeant Joseph K. Taylor fatally. Sergeant Taylor was a young man of fine promise, who left the sophomore class of Amherst College, a home of affluence and charming social relations, to offer his life on his country's altar.

Finding his position at Charlestown not so good for defense as that at Halltown, Sheridan moved his army back to the latter during the night. The Thirty-seventh vacated at daylight the skirmish line which they had so well maintained, and followed the movements of the main body, finding the army posted in an impregnable position with the right, the Sixth Corps, resting on the Potomac, the left, Crook's Eighth Corps, on the Shenandoah, the Nineteenth occupying the center.

For several days there was more or less skirmishing, in which the Thirty-seventh had no active part. Early seemed to be feeling the front of the other corps in the hope of finding some weak spot, and that failing he made demonstrations to right and left as though intending another invasion of Maryland; but the Union cavalry in strong force was watching his every movement, and he presently retired again to his favorite location at Bunker Hill. Sheridan, then, on the 28th, moved back to his Charlestown position, and on September 3 advanced up the Valley to the former position near Berryville, where he proceeded to intrench.

The same day General Anderson with Kershaw's division started from Early's camps to return to Richmond by way of Berryville. As Crook's men were going into camp Anderson came marching in among them. Both parties were wholly taken by surprise, but managed to get up a brisk skirmish, which lasted through the following day, Early coming up to the assistance of Anderson, when the latter returned to camp and waited for a week, when he again set out for Richmond, taking a safer route, by way of Front Royal.

The two weeks which followed the establishment of Sheridan's lines near Berryville were marked by no incidents of especial importance to the infantry of the Sixth Corps. Frequent clashes of arms occurred between the cavalry and the enemy, and sometimes scouting and foraging parties were sent out on foot, meeting with more or less adventure ; but the usual routine of camp life generally prevailed, drills were resumed to some extent, and the men, invigorated by the cooler weather, recovered from the exhaustion and illness induced by their recent terrible marches. On the 16th the veterans of the Tenth and Seventh regiments were consolidated into the companies of the Thirty-seventh proper, increasing its effective force by 73 men, and entitling the regiment to additional officers, commissions for whom were promptly fowarded.

On the 17th General Grant was in consultation with Sheridan. Kershaw had now left the Valley, it seemed possible for Sheridan to strike such a blow as would free the region effectually of the force which remained, and Grant's instructions to his lieutenant were comprised in the two words—"Go in !" Sheridan needed no second invitation. His orders were at once issued, the troops were supplied with rations on Sunday, the 18th, and next morning at 3 o'clock the Sixth Corps was on the road. Sheridan supposed Early's force to be divided, as a column had been reported moving northward the day before, and instead of planting his army across the line of the Confederate communications, as had been the original purpose, the Federal commander aimed his blow directly at the enemy's main body. The supposed division had not taken place, however, as Gordon's command had merely gone up to Martinsburg to drive away Averell's cavalry and returned in time to take part in the battle.

The column which moved out in the darkness of the waning night consisted of Wilson's division of cavalry, the Sixth Corps with Getty's division in front and Russell's in the rear, the Nineteenth Corps to follow directly and the Eighth being held in the rear to await developments. The line of march was along the Berryville and Winchester pike, which crossed the Opequan Creek at a difficult ford near the mouth of Abraham's Creek. The latter stream flows in from south of Winchester, while Red Bud Run, which empties near the same point, rises to the north of the city. On the section of land between these two streams the battle was principally fought. After crossing the Opequan the pike runs for some two miles through a narrow wooded ravine, at the western entrance to which, where the ground becomes more open and possible for military operations, the enemy's outposts were encountered.

Through this gorge Wilson's cavalry swept like the wind in the early morning's gray, captured the outposts and secured ground for the deployment of the infantry and thus successfully accomplished the first stage of the battle. Then through the long hours they held on till the head of the Sixth Corps came in sight. Getty's division went into position on the left of the turnpike and Ricketts's on the right, Russell's in rear of the latter in reserve. Then came another long wait for the Nineteenth Corps, which had followed the trains of the Sixth. During all this time the enemy kept up a heavy artillery fire, as they had throughout the deployment, but the troops were sheltered by the ground so that the loss was trifling. Finally the Nineteenth came up and went into line on the right of the Sixth, when the order to advance was given. Russell's division remained in reserve. At once the crash of battle broke with terrible fury. And a deadly battle it proved from opening to close. Neither side had field works or other protection than the natural contour of the ground afforded, and the loss of life was heavy.

At first the forward movement of the Union forces promised well, and the enemy was forced back by the strong blow delivered. But the two divisions of the Sixth Corps, guiding on the pike which ran between them, were deflected to the left, and the connection of the two corps became weakened. No sooner was this defect discovered than the Confederates took advantage of it. Rodes's and Gordon's divisions, led by Battle's brigade of the former, were driven like a wedge against the weak point and the two imperiled divisions of the Federal army—Grover's of the Nineteenth and Ricketts's of the Sixth—were broken and fell back with considerable loss. As a consequence the entire Union line drew back from the point of its farthest advance.

The Thirty-seventh was on the right of the brigade, and the quick eye of Colonel Edwards comprehending at once where the work of checking the Confederates must be done, he ordered the regiment to move to the right. The movement was made by the flank under cover of the ravine which extended at nearly right angles to the pike, bending a little to the rear. A position was taken somewhat in advance of ·Stevens's Fifth Maine Battery, which was doing excellent service, the line of direction being changed so that when halted the command faced to the northwest instead of west. Looking out of the ravine, which was barely deep enough to conceal the movements of his regiment, Lieutenant-Colonel Montague saw about 60 yards in front a body of Confederates, which proved to be the old "Stonewall" Jackson Brigade, advancing and evidently making for the battery in rear of the Thirty-seventh.

The enemy's line was somewhat ragged, both from the opposition it had already received and because in an advance of any troops for a considerable distance the more adventurous or excitable get ahead while those less anxious for close quarters lag behind, and the command becomes broken so that it cannot act, either on the offensive or defensive, with its full strength. This was the condition of the brigade which the Thirty-seventh with their Spencer rifles were now to face alone. There was no doubt in the mind of their commander of the course to pursue, or what the result would be. Instantly the message was passed down the line to each company commander that not a shot must be fired till the order was given, and that at the word every man must charge the rebels at a run.

"Forward!" at length rings out, and from the little ravine the regiment emerges, steady and firm, with its 296 rifles and seven times that number of deadly shots within them. The Confederates were astonished to see a regiment emerging as it were from the ground, but they were more astonished at the severity of the fire which opened upon them. One crashing volley followed the order to fire, supplemented by such a rapid succession of shots that by the time half the distance had been passed the magazines were emptied of their seven cartridges.

The demoralization of the Confederate line was speedy and complete. While the greater part, fighting more or less, struggled back to the position from which their advance had been made, a large number threw themselves upon the ground wherever a ditch or gully gave promise of protection from the terrible fire poured upon them by the repeating rifles, and were taken prisoners by the Thirty-seventh. For fully half a mile the pursuit was kept up, and it is believed that the number of prisoners taken by the regiment was fully equal to the number of muskets it carried into the field that day. Among the trophies captured was the battle-flag of the Second Virginia regiment, inscribed with the names of 17 battles, including the First Bull Run, in which the regiment had taken part.

A halt was finally called upon the brow of a hill at the extreme end of a little triangular piece of woods, beyond which the strong line of the enemy was clearly observed. A short distance to the left and in front was a thick wood and at once the left company under Captain J. A. Champney was sent to observe the enemy, so that they should not come unheralded upon the new position of the Thirty-seventh. In a few minutes Captain Champney returned, quite out of breath, having been obliged to make a considerable detour at the top of his speed to avoid the hostile fire, and reported that he was on the flank of a Confederate battery which, with more assistance, he could silence. As Captain Champney came in on the run to report to his regimental commander what he had discovered, he met General Upton, who was just coming up, and who, mistaking the motive of the captain's haste, sternly ordered him back to his regiment. Too full of the importance of his discovery to weigh his words, or to regard the possible consequence to himself, but filled with anger at the imputation upon his courage (of which no member of the regiment had greater measure), the brave and excited subaltern screamed out at the top of his voice and without checking his speed "Go to hell!"

Captain Hopkins (who had recently returned to service in the regiment, taking command of Company C) was sent with his company and a few of the best shots of the regiment to the scene, and under his direction a stream of bullets made the place too hot for even Early's veteran artillerists. The men were driven away and the horses killed, but later some Confederates crawled up through the grass, attached ropes to the guns and dragged them away.

Already the Thirty-seventh had lost many of its brave men and officers killed or wounded. As it went into position Color Sergeant Patrick Dunnivan of Company H received a wound through the shoulder, but the colors were caught by Corporal Edward D. Hooker of Company D, who bore the Massachusetts flag. Corporal Hooker was promptly promoted to sergeant and carried the national colors to the close of the regiment's service. Very soon after Captain J. A. Loomis of Company E received a bullet through the thigh, inflicting a severe wound which cost the regiment the services of a brave and efficient officer.

The Confederate success was now thoroughly checked, but it had been done at the cost of one of the noblest officers in the Union army,—General David A. Russell, who while hurrying his troops to the occupation of the crest just referred to and riding in the rear of the right wing of the Thirty-seventh regiment, after having received a severe bullet wound in the left breast of which he made no mention, was struck from his horse by a piece of shell. The missile passed directly through his chest, inflicting a wound from which he died after a few minutes' terrible suffering. General Upton succeeded to the command of the division.

It was about half-past 12 when Lieutenant-Colonel Montague halted his regiment in the position referred to, and for some 30 minutes afterward the Thirty-seventh held the vantage ground alone, till some troops of Upton's brigade came up. As the other regiments of Edwards's Brigade had advanced beside the pike while the Thirty-seventh changed its direction, the latter regiment found itself considerably to the right of its fellows.

About half-past 3 Lieutenant-Colonel Montague discovered from the position of Captain Hopkins's command on the flank that the rebels, broken on the right by the pressure which General Crook was bringing to bear upon them, were hurrying past in squads at a point some 80 rods in front of his command. Determined to cut off this avenue of escape, and having no time to obtain orders from superior officers, Montague moved the companies from the woods, reunited the regiment and with slight loss planted it across the path of the fugitives, picking up a few prisoners on the way.

Along the entire line the tide was now setting strongly in favor of the Union arms; officers and men alike thrilled with the excitement of the coming victory. The impetuous young General Upton chafed at even the temporary stands being made by the enemy. "What regiment is this?" he asked, galloping in front of the Thirty-seventh. Being answered he grasped the colors and shouted: "You are the boys I want; come on, and I will put you where you can whip them in ten minutes!"

Away went the gallant officer, straight toward the enemy's line, with the colors of the Thirty-seventh fluttering about his head. "Come on, boys!" shouted Lieutenant-Colonel Montague springing in front of his command, and the whole line swept forward, officers and men cheering, shouting, swearing, each striving to be first to reach the destination. Line officers and file-closers forgot their accustomed positions and pressed through the rushing line if possible, but there was no work for them in the rear, for during the whole terrible day not one man in the regiment was missing from his place unless killed or wounded.

It was a mad race till the enemy halted and rallied once more at the top of a considerable hill. A sharp-shooter's bullet struck the staff of the flag, General Upton was seriously wounded and the colors dropped to the ground. Captain Donnelly and Color-Bearer Hooker simultaneously seized the banner and it was up again in a moment, while the regiment rapidly rallied about it. The Thirty-seventh were now in a perilous position, for they were far in advance of the main line, the enemy was making a firm stand once more and the ammunition for the Spencer rifles had given out. Fortunately Colonel Edwards discovered the situation, and the Second Rhode Island, having filled their pockets with Spencer cartridges, were deployed as skirmishers and pushed across an artillery swept plain several hundred yards in breadth, bearing timely succor to the regiment still resolutely holding with empty guns its vantage ground.

Preparations were now being made for the grand charge which it was intended should close the day in triumph for the Union arms. The Eighth Corps was crumbling the Confederate left flank, and the cavalry to right and left were instructed to cooperate the moment Early's lines should yield before the blows of the infantry. The resulting charge was the most magnificent of the war. The roar of Crook's guns gave the signal for the bugles of the other corps and "Forward!" shouted general and colonel and captain and private. Everywhere the Confederate lines gave way, and as they broke the flashing sabers of the Union cavalry began to slash and hew upon the yielding flanks and toward the rear. There were earthworks near Winchester which had been constructed long before, and behind them the disorganized Southrons strove to make a stand. Vain attempt! The Union cavalry press around toward the rear, the Union infantry sweep down upon the front; there are cheers and shouts and screams of triumph from the victors, and the broken remnants of Early's army goes hurrying through Winchester and up the pike or across fields, wherever it may be possible to escape their vengeful pursuers. The Union victory was full and complete, the pursuit being continued to Kernstown, where Ramseur's division succeeded in making something of a stand, and as the Union army was hungry and tired, although boiling over with enthusiasm, it was decided that they should rest till morning.

The victory had been won at a severe cost. The loss on each side was not far from 5,000, the Federal a little greater and the Confederate something less. The latter had Generals Rodes and Godwin killed. The most notable loss on the Union side was that of General Russell, already referred to.

The Thirty-seventh had fought brilliantly from beginning to end of the battle, and had won for itself the highest praise for unwavering gallantry and well-directed effort; but it had been at a serious cost. Taking into the fight 296 muskets, it had lost 15 enlisted men killed and 7 officers and 72 men wounded—very nearly one-third of its numbers. The killed were: Company A—Corporal William Palmer, Daniel Cronin, George A. Ferrin and Edwin G. Taylor; B—Lyman Chapel, George J. Daniels and James Gendron; C—Sergeant Martin Schemmerhorn; D—John M. Worthington; G—Sergeant Vincent H. Tanner, Seth Belden and John T. Follansbee; H—Corporal Moses S. Ames and Miles H. Blood; I—Augustus E. Pease.

The wounded officers comprised Captains Mason W Tyler, neck; J. A. Loomis, thigh; and George Pierce (transferred from the Tenth), shoulder; First Lieutenants Charles S. Bardwell, abdomen, fatally;* E. W Harris, hand; Francis E. Gray, neck; and William H. Cousens, (transferred from the Tenth), thigh. The loss in non-commissioned officers was especially heavy (see Appendix for complete list), and of many of those who had fallen it might with great truth be said that "Death loves a shining mark."

---

*Lieutenant Bardwell was wounded just before the last charge by a musket bullet which passed through his body while he was bending over giving a drink of water from his canteen to a wounded comrade. He made a brave fight for life, enduring great suffering with unflinching fortitude till the morning of October 6, when he died. His last few days were encouraged by the presence of his home pastor, Rev. J. W. Lane, who after his death accompanied the body home. It is no disparagement to his comrades to say that no braver officer, no purer patriot, no truer Christian could have been found in all the army. These qualities won for him the universal regard and the warm friendship both of his fellow-officers and the men whom he commanded or with whom he came in contact. Making a formal profession of religion and uniting with the church after his enlistment, he never for a moment wavered in the cause of his espousal, and his death was a notable scene of Christian trust and triumph. During his last hours a message was sent to Colonel Montague, who had been his personal friend and on his arrival the dying man said with a smile, "Colonel, I have tried to do my duty!" "I know, and so does every member of the regiment, that you always have done your duty," was the sincere response.

CHAPTER XVIII

THE SERVICE AT WINCHESTER.

ON PROVOST DUTY.—CHANGES AND PROMOTIONS.—BATTLE OF
CEDAR CREEK.—SHERMAN'S CAMPAIGN.

The gallant service of Colonel Edwards and his command during the battle of the Opequan met prompt and hearty recognition from Generals Sheridan and Wright. No sooner did the fighting cease than Colonel Edwards was made commandant of the post at Winchester with his brigade for a garrison. Lieutenant-Colonel Montague was made Provost Marshal of the city and the Thirty-seventh regiment was detailed as Provost Guard. That night the regiment bivouacked in the yard of the Court House, but were next day assigned quarters in convenient buildings. The other regiments of the brigade were quartered at various points about the city.

The garrison found an immediate demand for their services. The dead of both armies were to be buried,* 1,200 of the Confederate wounded were left as prisoners in the hands of the victors; not less than 4,000 Union wounded required hospital accommodations and care; the spoils of the battle-field were to be gathered, assorted and taken care of, with all the other duties of a permanent post, while the rest of the army pushed on in pursuit of the retreating foe.

The best arrangements possible under the circumstances, it is needless to say, were made for the wounded. The hotels and churches, barns and sheds and many of the dwellings were

---
*One of the burial parties sent out the morning after the battle found a dead Confederate with his dog lying beside him. The poor brute made so earnest protest to their moving or touching the body of his master that they passed on and left it unburied. Next morning he was still there and had to be dragged away by a rope thrown about his body. He was afterward released, but at once returned to the grave and howled so piteously that he was again removed by the soldiers, who were much affected by the scene.

ROUTINE DUTIES AND CHANGES. 383

packed with them, Blue and Gray side by side, the Taylor House holding at least a thousand. Such as could bear transportation were sent to hospitals farther north within a few days. The Sanitary and Christian Commissions were on hand with their comforts and skilled attendants. The subsequent events in the Valley were conducted with Winchester as a center, so that the position of Colonel Edwards became one of importance from its various routine and executive duties. These were discharged with zeal and fidelity, winning the warm approval of General Sheridan, who desired to attach Colonel Edwards to his personal staff.

During the weeks passed by the regiment at Winchester very little happened requiring special narration. There were various details, expeditions from time to time into the surrounding country, occasional duty as escort for prisoners being sent north; but generally the current of life ran smoothly. Chaplain Morse, who at the time of the battle was on a furlough, returned toward the end of the month and at once fitted up a room for a chapel where services were held on Sundays as well as frequent evening meetings. The freedom of the city was practially enjoyed by the men, their fare was good, and after their terribly severe campaign of the summer they were quite content to watch the waning of the season from their comfortable quarters.

Notice must now be made of many changes which had occurred in the roster of officers and of others which were to occur while the regiment remained in the city. Second Lieutenant Robert A. Gray of Company I resigned June 26, to receive promotion in another branch of the United States service. During July following First Lieutenant Jonas A. Champney of Company E was mustered as captain of Company B, vice Pease who died of wounds May 14; Second Lieutenant Charles S. Bardwell of Company D was mustered as first lieutenant of Company E vice Champney, but continued to serve in command of Company A till his death wound was received. Major Marcus T. Moody was mustered out July 26, and First Lieutenant James C. Chalmers July 30, both on account of disability resulting from wounds. Second Lieutenant Elihu R. Rockwood was discharged

August 29 for promotion in the Fourth Heavy Artillery. The regiment having no second lieutenants for promotion, First Sergeant William A. Calhoun of Company I was commissioned first lieutenant of Company G, vice Chalmers, and mustered September 17. About the same time First Lieutenant Carlos C. Wellman of Company A was commissioned and mustered as captain, and borne on the rolls of Company K, but on account of disability he performed no duty in the new rank and was mustered out October 12. Second Lieutenant Albert C. Sparks of Company E, who had been commissioned but not mustered as first lieutenant, was discharged for disability September 20, as was Captain Joseph L. Hayden of Company H two days later.

As previously noted, the consolidation of the veterans from the Seventh and Tenth regiments in the companies of the Thirty-seventh gave the latter sufficient numbers to allow the commissioning of second lieutenants for all the companies, and October 23 the following were mustered to date from September 18 : For Company K, Sergeant Major Hubbard M. Abbott ; for A, Sergeant William C. Morrill of Company G ; for I, First Sergeant Richard H. Taylor of Company C ; for C, Sergeant John W. Stockwell of Company G ; for G, Sergeant James O'Connor of Company K ; for F, First Sergeant William A. Waterman of Company A but serving with Company E ; for H, First Sergeant Flavel K. Sheldon of Company D ; for D, First Sergeant David M. Donaldson of Company A ; for B, Private Samuel E. Nichols of Company G ; for E, Sergeant Jesse Prickett of the same company, transferred from the Tenth. Prickett being promoted vice Sparks, his muster only dated back to September 20, and Morrill and Donaldson being absent wounded were not mustered till their return, about November 1. Few of these officers served with the companies on whose rolls they were borne. Donaldson, Sheldon and Waterman continued to do duty with the companies from which they were promoted, while Nichols took the place of adjutant, temporarily vacated by Bradley, who was made assistant Provost Marshal under Montague. The promotion of Nichols from private to lieutenant was an exceptional incident in the history of the regiment. Having filled with credit various clerical positions, declining non-commissioned rank, he was serving as adjutant's clerk when his commission as second lieutenant was received, and it is pleasant to record that he took the new position with the hearty good-will of all the sergeants and corporals who had nominally been "jumped" by his promotion.

It is not amiss to say in reference to this wholesale advancement of enlisted men, that these and other like promotions were judiciously made, and that in every case officers who were raised from the ranks in recognition of fitness shown justified in the more responsible positions the confidence thus manifested in them. The discipline of the regiment in no way suffered from these promotions; the men recognized the fitness of the selections and respected the choice; while on their part the new officers understood and sympathized with those they were called to command. Thus a mutual respect and esteem deepened the tie which bound the different grades of the citizen soldiery with a common fraternity and made the whole a strong and grand organization. Nor should it be forgotten that, while no better disciplined volunteer regiment than the Thirty-seventh went into the United States service, there was none in which the bond between the officers and the enlisted men was stronger or more enduring. Twenty years have not weakened the admirations and friendships formed in those days of trial,—time nor distance can ever efface them.

A few additional changes, occurring somewhat later in the season, may be noted here. Captain J. A. Loomis of Company E resigned on account of disability November 19, and Surgeon Charles P Crehore resigned December 1. Assistant Surgeon Elisha M. White was promoted to fill the last-named vacancy. First Lieutenant Thomas G. Colt was promoted to captain and mustered November 27; First Lieutenant John S. Bradley was at the same time made nominally the regimental adjutant; Second Lieutenant H. M. Abbott was made first lieutenant of Company H but was detailed for service with Company F; while First Sergeant Edward D. Taylor of Company G was commissioned and mustered as second lieutenant of Company K, but continued in service with G.

The selection of a major to succeed Moody, resigned July 26, which had been hanging fire for some time, was completed December 2 by the commission and muster of Captain Rufus P Lincoln of Company C. First Lieutenant George H. Hyde of Company B was mustered as captain of C two weeks later, but continued to command B ; the vacant first lieutenancy was filled by the commission and muster on the same day of First Sergeant Albert H. Vincent of Company H. On the 1st of January, 1865, the vacancy in the roster of Company A caused by the promotion of Wellman to captain was filled by the commission and muster of Second Lieutenant Richard H. Taylor of Company I, First Sergeant Julius H. Reed of Company B being made second lieutenant of I.

Meantime, what had become of Early and his pursuers ? We have said that on the night of the 19th of September Ramseur made a stand at Kernstown, and the pursuit was given over at that point by the Federal cavalry. The Confederate army as such made no halt, however, till it reached Fisher's Hill, where it took up a strong defensive position. Sheridan promptly made his plans for a flank movement by the Eighth Corps while the Sixth and Nineteenth threatened the apparently impregnable front. On the 22d the movement was executed and crowned with entire success, the enemy being driven in confusion from the strong works, leaving more than a thousand prisoners in the hands of the victors, with nearly 20 pieces of artillery.

For four days Early retreated up the Valley till he reached Brown's Gap, where he expected to be joined by Kershaw's division, which had been ordered back to him in the hope of repairing the disaster of the past week. The expected reinforcements were on hand the following day, and the two armies faced each other again with something of the old determination—Early in the vicinity of the Gap and Sheridan at Harrisonburg. The latter was now 80 miles from his base of supplies at Martinsburg ; and desirable as it seemed to push the enemy through the mountains in the direction of Charlottesville or Gordonsville, it became increasingly apparent that it would be impossible to provision the army for such a move. The country itself would afford no supplies worth speaking of, but it swarmed with guerrillas and roving bands, making necessary a strong escort for every train and protection for all lines of communication. Meantime the Union cavalry were kept busy in laying waste the Valley, in accordance with the orders of General Grant, so that it should no longer be capable of affording subsistence for a Confederate army, as it had so often done in the past. Far as the swift horsemen in strong force could penetrate, they left but a smoking waste. Dwellings were spared, but mills, barns, granaries and store-houses,—everything which could give aid to the foe, was ruthlessly destroyed. The sight was a sad one, but it was a military necessity; the people of the Valley had been among the very first to lift the armed hand against the national government, and they were now feeling to the full the curse of that war into which they had been so eager to plunge, dragging so many innocent and unoffending ones.

Sheridan began to fall back October 5, and the next day Early who had been further reinforced by Rosser's cavalry brigade, moved out in pursuit. Rosser was especially anxious to redeem the reputation of the Confederate cavalry, and his operations assumed such an air of boldness that Sheridan directed Torbert to "either whip him or get whipped" himself. Custer met Rosser and Merritt encountered Lomax at Toms Brook on the 9th, and in both cases the Confederates were whipped with a vengeance and chased more than 20 miles. Sheridan's forces now retired to Cedar Creek, the Eighth Corps taking position east of the pike and the Nineteenth west of it, while preparations were made to dispatch the Sixth to Petersburg. The latter corps had in fact marched to the Shenandoah opposite Ashby's Gap, when it was hurriedly called back. Early on the 13th suddenly re-occupied his old position at Fisher's Hill, threw forward a reconnaissance within range of the Federal camps and made the latter aware of his presence by pitching some shells in upon them at dinner time. Two brigades of Thoburn's division of the Eighth Corps sallied out to meet them, but were driven back. The Thirty-fourth Massachusetts regiment in one of them lost fully a hundred men, while Colonel George D. Wells, commanding the brigade, was mortally wounded and fell into the enemy's hands. Early then retired to his old fortifications, and the Sixth Corps on returning to the scene was placed in the rear of the others.

Early could not long maintain his position in the face of the Union army, for since the vigorous treatment of the Valley by the latter it did not afford sustenance for his troops, and his supplies were fast becoming exhausted. Both armies knew that a battle or Early's retreat must soon take place, and the reports of the Union scouts indicated that the latter had really begun. That was a mistake. The daring Confederate had thoroughly reconnoitered the Union position, made his plans for a flank attack, and during the night of the 18th his army crept forward past the flank of the unsuspecting camp, and in the early gray of the foggy morning the blow, sure, swift and deadly, was struck.

Thoburn's division received the first volley It was fired by Kershaw's men as they came pouring over the intrenchments into the sleeping camp. The men rushed bewildered from their tents to find the alternative of flight or captivity only left. The gallant Thoburn received a mortal wound while attempting to rally his panic-stricken command. The other two divisions of the Eighth Corps under Generals Hayes and Kitching were hastily formed to resist Kershaw's further progress, while General Wright, in command of the army during the absence of Sheridan, sent to General Ricketts in command of the Sixth Corps to form two divisions on the pike. Kershaw was firing from the captured camp upon the rest of the Eighth Corps with the Union artillery left in his hands, when Gordon's division broke from the forest on the flank of Hayes and Kitching and the already demoralized commands gave way utterly. The position thus obtained by the Confederates commanded the Nineteenth Corps completely, and the latter was also directed to fall back.

Not far in the rear of the captured camps the Confederates encountered the Sixth Corps, a portion of which was making a stand on a wooded eminence to check the enemy till a stronger position could be taken up in the rear. Here General Ricketts was wounded and the command devolved upon General Getty of the Second Division, General Grant of the Vermont Brigade taking the division. West of Middletown this division made another stand, and when Wharton's division was thrown against it, not only were the assailants repulsed but they were driven back in disorder by a gallant counter charge. Here General Bidwell, commanding the Third Brigade of the Union division, was mortally wounded. The Confederate repulse had been so serious that Early paused to concentrate his army to attack this single sturdy division, and when he again advanced it was to find the entire Sixth Corps strongly planted across the pike north of Middletown, with the cavalry on the flanks. Before this firm front Early's demoralized troops recoiled, and he found it impossible immediately to bring them to another attack.

At this point General Sheridan rode upon the scene. On his way back from Washington he had passed the night with Colonel Edwards at Winchester. Cannonading was heard before he started for the front in the morning, but it was known that a Federal reconnaissance had been ordered for that morning, and no importance was attached to the sound. A short distance out fugitives from the battle-field began to be met and Edwards's Brigade was at once ordered out to deploy across the pike and the fields to stop them. The retreating trains were directed to park beside the turnpike and Sheridan dashed on toward the front, uttering everywhere words of assurance and confidence. The line of the Sixth Corps as General Wright had been able to establish it was corrected and strengthened, such of the Nineteenth Corps as remained serviceable was brought up from its rallying point in the rear and placed on the right of the Sixth, and when Early finally succeeded in forcing his half-hearted troops forward once more against the Federal right they were easily repulsed.

At 4 o'clock the Union advance began, and it was one invincible onward sweep, the movement being a magnificent left half wheel with Custer's cavalry on the marching flank, then the Nineteenth Corps and the Sixth, with Merritt's horsemen at the pivot. Early had taken the precaution to send his prisoners to the rear early in the day, but he saved little else. The 24 guns which he had captured in the morning were retaken with an equal number of his own, 56 of his ambulances and over 1,200 of his soldiers fell into the hands of the final victors. Never in the whole war was there a more utter rout than had now befallen the Confederates. The infantry pursuit stopped at Cedar Creek, but the cavalry kept on some miles further, riding through the mass of fugitives, capturing, burning and destroying.

Early's prestige as a commander and his military power in the Valley were now completely broken, but it had been at a cost of nearly 6,000 Union soldiers killed, wounded and missing. Among the dead was one of the Old Bay State's noblest young soldiers,—Charles Russell Lowell, Jr., whose commission as a brigadier general of cavalry had that day been signed. Colonel Kitching, commanding a division of the Eighth Corps, was also mortally wounded. Among the other wounded were General Wright, General Grover and Colonels Mackenzie and Penrose commanding brigades.

For the glorious termination of that day's adventure the country rang with the praises of General Sheridan, salutes were fired by all the Union armies, and he was commissioned a major general in the regular army on McClellan's resignation a little later. But soldiers of the Sixth Corps will never forget the credit due to that organization and its efficient commander, General Wright. Repeatedly did a fragment of that corps throw itself across the path of the demoralizing rout and the exultant pursuit, checking the tide and gaining time for the stronger line in the rear, till at the third stand it presented the complete front before which the Confederate onset broke and recoiled with no possibility of further advance.

The battle of Cedar Creek practically ended the fighting in the Valley, with the exception of some minor cavalry engagements. Early withdrew to the vicinity of New Market, where his army was somewhat reorganized, and when Sheridan on the 9th of November took up a position at Kernstown he followed and three days later made a show of offering battle. Finding that his challenge was to be accepted he withdrew next night and thenceforth remained steadily on the defensive in strong positions well up the Valley. It may be stated as disposing of General Early as a factor in the war, that after most of his valuable troops had been dispatched to the assistance of Lee the remainder took up a strong position near Waynesboro and Rockfish Gap. An attack by Custer's cavalry division on the 2d of March, 1865, carried the position, capturing most of the troops with scarcely the loss of a life, while Early and a few of his officers escaped and fled to Richmond.

During the year now drawing to a close events of great importance had transpired in other portions of the national field. General Grant on his promotion to the lieutenant generalship had given the immediate command of the Military Division of the Mississippi to General W T. Sherman, directing him to make General Johnston's army, then in camp near Dalton, Ga., his immediate objective, in connection with the simultaneous movement of all the Union armies which was planned for the early spring.

The advance began the 7th of May, 1864. Sherman's forces consisted of the Army of the Cumberland, General Thomas, composed of the Fourth Corps, General Howard, Fourteenth Corps, General Palmer, and the Twentieth Corps, made up of the old Eleventh and Twelfth consolidated under General Hooker; the Army of the Tennessee, General McPherson, consisting of the Fifteenth Corps, General Logan, the Sixteenth, General Dodge, and the Seventeenth, General Blair; the Army of the Ohio or the Twenty-third Corps, General Schofield. These organizations with a proportionate force of cavalry and about 250 pieces of artillery made up a total of nearly 100,000 efficient men, under able and trusted commanders.

Skirmishing and minor engagements immediately followed, Sherman's army forcing its way through the rocky passes and defiles of that wild region and without a severe encounter forcing Johnston to evacuate his strong camp at Dalton and hasten to Resaca, a dozen miles south, to meet the Union army which had passed around his flank. Serious fighting ensued on the 14th and 15th, and during the night of the latter Johnston, whose position had become imperiled, withdrew. Pushing steadily southward to Adairsville, the Southern commander thought to make a halt and offer battle; but after a slight engagement he again withdrew in the night, moving most of his force to Cassville, while a smaller detachment took the road to Kingston. At the former place another stand was made, but no battle resulted, for with the firing of the first Federal artillery the Confederate corps commanders, Hood, Polk and Hardee, declared their positions untenable, and again the columns moved southward. The Etowah river was crossed, and finally Johnston selected New Hope Church as the proper point for offering battle. His lines ran from a point two miles south of Dallas and extended several miles to the northeast. The position was a strong one and had been carefully intrenched.

The battle of New Hope Church was begun by Hooker's corps near night of the 25th, during a severe thunder storm, but its determined assaults were repulsed. The rest of the Union army came up as rapidly as possible and intrenched in front of the enemy's position, and through the succeeding days there was more or less fighting, with continuous sharp-shooting and skirmishing. On the afternoon of the 28th a very determined assault was made on Logan's front by Bate's rebel division, involving other troops of both armies, but the assailants were driven back with severe loss. On the 4th of June Johnston evacuated his lines at New Hope Church, Sherman having worked so far to the east as to render the position untenable, and the tide of battle surged back to the vicinity of Marietta, in front of and covering which Johnston drew his new lines.

The two armies confronted each other again on the 14th, the Confederates behind strong lines of intrenchments, and during the skirmishing the Southern General Polk was killed by a cannon-shot. A long series of engagements, charges and counter-charges had now begun, the enemy being slowly but continually pressed back toward Marietta. On the 22d Hood made a determined attack on Hooker and suffered a considerable loss; on the 27th Sherman assaulted in turn and was repulsed at all points with a loss of 3,000 men.

Sherman now decided upon another movement by the flank,

and as it progressed Johnston was obliged to quit his intrenchments before Marietta, which he did July 2, closely followed by Sherman. Two days later he crossed the Chattahooche and intrenched. On the 7th Schofield crossed at Powell's Ferry on his flank, and on the 10th Johnston took a position covering Atlanta and facing Sherman. A week later the latter began active siege operations, which were carried on till the fall of the city with great energy. A sharp sally was made by Hood on the 20th, which was easily repulsed; but on the 22d a more determined sortie was made, resulting in what is known as the battle of Atlanta. During the fight General McPherson was killed, General Logan taking temporary command of the Army of the Tennessee, to which General Howard was appointed four days later. General Hooker, feeling aggrieved at the selection, resigned his command of the Twentieth Corps and was succeeded by General Slocum, General D. S. Stanley succeeding Howard in the command of the Fourth Corps. On the Confederate side, Johnston had some days before been succeeded by Hood, who carried on a steadily losing struggle till the 1st of September, when he evacuated Atlanta and the following day General Sherman took possession.

The purpose of Sherman's campaign had thus in a great measure been attained. The most important point in Georgia was in his possession, for in a manufacturing as well as in a military sense Atlanta was the heart of the Commonwealth. Hood had moved westward into Alabama with the remnants of his army, and it was evident that he intended to harass Sherman by falling upon his communications or leading him a wild race back into the border states if the victorious general should undertake to follow him. The plan upon which Sherman decided was quite different, being to march directly through the heart of Georgia to Savannah on the sea coast, leaving General Thomas with a portion of the army to attend to Hood.

The march through Georgia was one of the remarkable and picturesque features of the war. It was decided upon October 11, and the resistless legions started southward from Atlanta on the 14th of November. Moving in parallel columns, living upon the country and leaving behind a trail of war's desolation 60 miles in width, the expedition moved unchecked and without fighting a battle worthy the name to the sea-coast, investing Savannah on the 10th of December. On the 13th a force under General Hazen captured Fort McAllister, an important work opening communication with the Union fleet off the harbor. General Hardee, who commanded the garrison of about 18,000, evacuated Savannah during the night of the 20th, retreating to Charleston, and the following day Sherman occupied the city.

The campaign between Hood and Thomas proved an exciting and an important one, but its main features may be very briefly recorded. Thomas concentrated at Nashville, which was certain to be Hood's objective point, and the first severe engagement was the battle of Franklin, which was fought November 30 between General Schofield's command, consisting of the Twenty-third and part of the Fourth Corps, and Cheatam's, Stewart's and Lee's corps of Hood's army. The latter assaulted the Union position with reckless desperation and obtained possession of an advanced work held by two brigades, but their success ended there. The assault on the main lines was repulsed with terrible slaughter. Twelve of Hood's generals were killed or wounded, 32 of his battle flags were left in Federal hands, and his entire loss can hardly have been less than 8,000 men; the Union loss was 2,326. That night Schofield retired to Nashville to join forces with Thomas, and on the 4th of December Hood formally invested the place.

The battle of Nashville, fought on the 15th and 16th of December, was one of the most disastrous to the Confederate arms in the entire course of the war. On the first day Hood's lines were by a vigorous attack of Thomas's army driven back fully two miles to a strong line of hills, to which the waning army strove desperately to cling the following day; but the resistless energy of the Union assault drove Hood's weakened battalions out in a complete rout. A broken rabble retreated to Tupelo, Miss., where Hood assembled what he could, furloughed a considerable part and then asked to be relieved of the command.

Thomas, having followed the remnants of Hood's force across the southern line of Tennessee over horrible roads, was preparing to go into winter quarters in Northern Georgia, Alabama and Mississippi when he received orders from General Grant to continue the campaign, in common with the other commanders.

While these and minor military events had been transpiring, an important presidential election had taken place. President Lincoln was renominated by the Union National Convention at Baltimore, June 7, and Andrew Johnson, then military governor of Tennessee, was named for vice-president. The platform adopted indorsed President Lincoln, promised to sustain the Government, declared against compromise with the rebels and for the sacredness of the public debt. The opposition or Democratic convention at Chicago, August 29, put General George B. McClellan in nomination for the presidency with George H. Pendleton of Ohio, a rank secession sympathizer, for the second place. The key-note of their platform declared the war a failure, and on that issue the political canvass was waged. It was a remarkably bitter one, but ended in the triumphant re-election of Mr. Lincoln, only three states—New Jersey, Delaware and Kentucky—giving their electoral votes for General McClellan.

With this expression of the unalterable determination of the loyal people of the North, with Sherman sweeping through the heart of the Confederacy, with the harbor of Mobile occupied by Farragut's fleet, with Hood's and Early's armies practically annihilated, with the grasp of Grant constantly tightening on the principal Confederate army in front of Petersburg, with universal exhaustion and loss of heart throughout the South, with only Davis's iron despotism to hold the Confederacy together, it needed no astute prophet to realize that the beginning of the end was at hand.

CHAPTER XIX

THE PETERSBURG CAMPAIGN

AGAIN IN THE TRENCHES.—DAYS OF SIEGE.—AT HATCHER'S RUN.—PREPARING TO STRIKE.—FALL OF PETERSBURG.

The Sixth Corps began to leave the Shenandoah Valley on its return to the Army of the Potomac before Petersburg early in December. The Third Division went through Winchester on the 3d, the Second following six days later. A heavy fall of snow the following night wrapped everything in its white pall— a very disagreeable one to the soldiers in their temporary camps. For a day or two alternating rain and snow rendered existence out of doors peculiarly disagreeable, and when fair weather again prevailed it brought with it such severe cold as seemed to proclaim that the reign of winter had indeed begun.

In the midst of this material chill, on the evening of December 12, just twelve weeks from the time that the regiment had been ordered into Winchester, it received orders to prepare for departure on the morrow. There was some speculation, some preparation, some words of regret were spoken; but marching orders had long since lost their novelty, a sort of involuntary philosophy had been adopted by the men, based on the old maxim that "what can't be cured must be endured," so that morning found the command refreshed by a good night's rest and prepared to accept whatever fate might have in store. Lieutenant-Colonel Montague was at this time absent, having been disabled by an accident some time previous while at home in Massachusetts on a furlough, the regiment having during his absence been commanded by Captain Donnelly, the senior officer present.

Morning brought the unavoidable bustle of preparation, the battalion line was formed, and a few parting words were spoken by Colonel Edwards, who expressed regret at the necessity for a temporary separation. Marching to Stephenson's Depot, some six miles to the northeast of Winchester, where the regiment stowed itself upon a train of freight cars, the journey was made thence by rail to Washington. It was not wholly a pleasure trip; the weather still remained sharply cold, the movements of the train were unavoidably slow, the positions of the men were cramped and uncomfortable. Yet when the latter recalled the many terrible pilgrimages made over the same region on foot, they simply drew a little closer to each other to avoid the searching winds and listened placidly to the steady rumbling of the train as it rolled on through valley and past hill.

Harper's Ferry was reached about dusk, and with but little delay the train moved on in the direction of Washington. The moon was at its full and shone with rare splendor, but its charm could be little enjoyed; there was a piercing chill in the night air and every one was glad to wrap himself up as securely as possible and doze away the long hours, if that were practicable. Soon after daylight of the 14th Washington was reached, and in pursuance of his instructions Captain Donnelly reported to General Halleck the arrival of the regiment. "You will have to wait a few days for transportation to City Point," was the apparently indifferent response; but this was not unwelcome intelligence, for the officers had many a little "errand" which it would be convenient to attend to during such a delay, and the men would be quite willing to look over the Capital if opportunity should present. But Captain Donnelly had scarcely left General Halleck's head-quarters when an orderly in haste summoned him back. An explanation was in order. Halleck had misunderstood the report; he wanted the Thirty-seventh immediately at the front; he did not understand what regiment had arrived; the command would therefore report at the wharf immediately where it would be provided with facilities for reaching its destination.

The afternoon saw the Thirty-seventh on board the transport

steamer Lizzie Baker, a neat and stanch craft on which they journeyed comfortably to City Point, which was reached the following afternoon. A military railroad ran from this point along the rear of the Union lines for the purpose of furnishing supplies to the troops with the least possible employment of wagon transportation, and on this the regiment was conveyed as far as Parke Station where the short winter's day ended and a place of bivouac was selected near by. The night was cold, the ground damp, and the contrast with the comfortable quarters for so considerable a time enjoyed at Winchester was one which the men could not banish from mind as they shivered through the long night.

A march of scarcely a mile the next morning brought the regiment to the "front," where in rear of the strong cordon of works which encompassed the Union camps it rejoined the brigade, now under command of Colonel Isaac C. Bassett of the Eighty-second Pennsylvania, who about that time was commissioned a brigadier general. The position was near the line of the Weldon railroad, in the vicinity of Fort Wadsworth—a strong work covering the railroad and the Halifax road near the intersection of the Vaughn road.

The location was far from desirable. The ground was so low as to be almost marshy, and the frequent storms which alternated with excessive cold made the entire region a sea of mud. Regardless of surroundings, or rather necessitated by the surroundings to act promptly, the men at once set to work to construct a camp on the thorough model of the two previous winters. The details were much modified, however. The regimental line had shrunk to a fraction of the former length and the ten company streets of former years now shrank to five, two companies occupying the different sides of the same avenue and each finding ample accommodation in six or seven cabins. A little distance to the rear of the streets ran the line of breastworks facing in the direction of the enemy. The line officers' tents and the cook houses were located in front of the men's quarters, while still farther out were the tents of the commanding officer and his staff. On the right of the camp, as one looked from the head-quarters, were the drum corps, hospital, commissary and similar departments, stables, and subsequently the regimental chapel. Owing to the nature of the ground, corduroy walks were a necessity, and were laid in every direction, so that it was soon practicable to go from any tent in the camp to any other without stepping upon the muddy ground. But all these "improvements" took time and a vast deal of toilsome work. While that is being carried out we will glance at the work which had been done by the army in the absence of the Sixth Corps.

During the month of July, 1864, a mine had been run from a point in the lines of the Ninth Corps under an earthwork in the enemy's fortifications known as Elliott's Salient, the explosion of which it was expected would make such a breach in the Confederate fortifications that an assaulting column could pass through, seize Cemetery Hill in the rear and force Lee out of his strong line. The explosion took place early in the morning of July 30, under especially favorable auspices. A large part of Lee's troops had been drawn north of the James a few days before by an expedition in that direction by the Second Corps and cavalry supports; the explosion itself was a complete success and a surprise to the Confederates from which they were remarkably slow to recover. The apology for an assault by the Ninth Corps, however, was one of the most disgraceful failures in the history of the war. It resulted simply in the sacrifice of many lives and in showing how utterly incompetent were some of the general officers of that corps.

Two weeks later another and more formidable move was made to the north side of the James, and considerable sharp fighting ensued; but no important results were obtained, and on the 20th of August the expedition, which had been under the command of General Hancock, returned to the old camps. While this expedition drew troops from Lee's southern lines a strong push was made on the 18th by General Warren with the Fifth Corps to extend the Union lines to the left, and this was attended with good success. The Weldon railroad, an important line of communication for the beleaguered army, was reached and held, despite frantic efforts of the enemy to drive out the men of the Maltese cross. On the scene of this triumph the Thirty-seventh were located on their return from the Valley.

General Hancock immediately on his return to camp was ordered to Reams Station, to tear up the railroad, from Warren's position to that point, and if possible to Rowanty Creek crossing, eight miles south of there. The former was done and Gibbon's Division had just started out on the morning of the 25th for the latter part of the task when A. P. Hill with a heavy Confederate force appeared on the scene and a stubborn battle ensued, the brunt of which was borne by Miles's division. Hancock withdrew at night, having lost 2,400 of the 8,000 Union troops engaged, 1,700 being prisoners, Hancock having no other intrenchments than those very hastily cast up by the Sixth Corps on the occasion of its visit the previous June. On the 28th of September a strong movement from the Army of the James to the north of the James River resulted after a severe struggle in the capture of Fort Harrison, a strong work containing 15 pieces of artillery, on the New Market road, and as the position was a somewhat important one it was retained, notwithstanding the fierce efforts of the enemy to regain it. During this engagement General Ord was severely wounded in the leg and the command of the Eighteenth Corps passed to General Weitzel. Previous to this time General Ord had succeeded General "Baldy" Smith, General Birney had succeeded General Gillmore in the command of the Tenth, and General Parke was now at the head of the Ninth.

In connection with the above movement another had been made from the left at the Weldon railroad, by two divisions each from the Fifth and Ninth Corps, and the line was by severe fighting extended some two miles on that flank. This ground was held and connected with that already secured by a strong chain of works, that at the extreme flank being known as Fort Fisher, afterward famous in the history of the Thirty-seventh regiment. The Union lines had now been extended so far in this direction that Lee's communications were restricted to the Boydtown plank road and the Southside railroad and the roads running beside it near the river. It was the earnest wish of the

Federal commanders before settling down for winter quarters that the remaining railroad might at least be broken if it could not be held, and for that purpose the available men of the three corps were concentrated late in October and a movement in force ensued. It was scarcely more than three miles from the Federal left to the Boydtown road and about the same distance from that point to the railroad; but these few miles were full of difficulties. Lee, realizing the importance to his army of the remaining avenues of communication, had extended his intrenchments southward covering the Boydtown road to Hatcher's Run, and the country, being heavily wooded and swampy, was very embarrassing to military movements.

The army moved in three parallel columns, Parke on the right feeling for the enemy's left flank, Warren to the southward to prolong the line when the position should finally be reached, and Hancock still farther to the left making his way by a more circuitous route. It will be noticed that all such movements were met by a sharp counter-stroke from the enemy, delivered if possible upon the unprepared columns, and this time the blow fell upon Hancock. Halting near Dabney's Mills to endeavor to establish connection with the other corps, he received an attack from Hill which for a moment threw the Union troops into confusion, but they rallied nobly and repelled their assailants with severe loss. The prospect of accomplishing anything more than a purposeless sacrifice of life was so faint, however, that the expedition was given up and the troops returned to their camps on the morning of October 28.

With the battle of Dabney's Mills ended the active campaigning of General Hancock, than whom none had done braver or better service. He was soon after ordered to Washington to organize what it was intended to make a new First Corps, the command of the shattered old Second Corps being given to Major General Andrew A. Humphreys.

The winter now wore away with the usual routine. Both armies were so strongly intrenched that a small part of the force could be safely left to hold the lines while the remainder in camp made themselves as comfortable as possible. The picket and artillery firing was kept up most of the time at some part of the lines, but a common code of honor was adopted, by which due notice was given to the enemy of the intended resumption of hostilities by either side when they had temporarily ceased. The long lines being in many places within the reach of the human voice, it was no unusual thing to hear some stentorian Confederate sing out: "Look out, Yanks! Creep into your holes; we are going to blaze!" or the call of caution might emanate from the Union works, when instantly the brown walls on the other side would be deserted in anticipation of the coming storm.

Not far from Fort Fisher, between the picket lines, was a piece of wood from which each army cut supplies of fuel. Blue and Gray often met in this forest in perfect fraternity. One day a Yankee having a heavy stick asked a good-natured Johnny to give him a lift and the two came into the Federal lines. "It seems pretty comfortable here," remarked the Southron, as he looked around; "I reckon I'll stay!" Another Confederate started out with a mule team for wood, but kept straight on into the Federal lines and turned his property over to the Provost Marshal, saying that he had got through soldiering for the waning cause. In fact, throughout the entire winter and till the close of the struggle desertions from the Confederate skirmish lines were very frequent. Notwithstanding every precaution, there was scarcely a night which did not leave their pickets sadly weakened from the loss of those who had crept over to the Union lines. These men had fought bravely, desperately, so long as there was a possibility of their success; but they saw plainly now that to remain would be only to risk their lives in a cause long since hopeless. On the subject of desertions the Confederate historian Pollard says: "The world will be astonished when the extent of this evil is fully and authentically known, and will obtain a new insight into that maladministration which wrecked the Confederate cause, and which is positively without parallel in any modern history of war." He declares that two thirds of the Southern armies were for the last two years in the character of deserters or absentees. Early in February General Lee was made commander-in-chief of the armies of the Confederacy, but it was then too late to institute reforms.

During December General Warren succeeded in destroying the Weldon railroad for 40 miles from Petersburg, so that it could not as before be used by the Confederates to within a few miles of the Union lines, whence supplies could be transferred by wagon; when this had been accomplished another period of watching and waiting followed.

Little snow fell during the winter, but there was an abundance of rain, and the armies literally lived in mud. Sometimes the storms would wash down the earthworks to such an extent that firing would cease by mutual consent till they could be repaired, and this work, together with continual extending and strengthening of the fortifications, filled the soldier's life with a tiresome round of fatigue duty. Much of the work done by the men of the Thirty-seventh was on Fort Fisher, the large earthwork at the angle of the Union lines, and in that vicinity were some other notable structures. Among these was the Signal Tower, 150 feet in hight, composed of timbers bolted together, from the dizzy summit of which the signal officers kept vigil over the surrounding country. In that vicinity, also, the Fiftieth New York Engineers designed and built a neat Gothic structure which they named the Poplar Grove Church, from a plain country church in the vicinity, their engineering tools and the forests of the region furnishing the means.

The Thirty-seventh in camp near Warren Station met with no experiences during the month of January demanding especial notice. Drills were resumed to some extent when the weather permitted, for no commander of the regiment was willing to see the splendid efficiency of the organization impaired by neglect. During this period the regiment was commanded by Major Lincoln, in the absence of Lieutenant-Colonel Montague, who was suffering from the injuries previously referred to. The latter returned to the command on the 30th of January, though still unable to perform much active duty.

Chaplain Morse, ever solicitous for the spiritual welfare of his charge, had succeeded in fitting up a chapel which, without formal consecration was used for the first time Sunday afternoon, February 5. Another service was intended for the evening; the chapel was warmed and lighted, the audience had assembled and the exercises were about to begin when the "long roll" broke upon the evening air, emptying the house of worship at a double-quick. Marching orders had been promulgated early that morning, and the regiment made due preparations to set forth at a moment's notice, which had been delayed till the present. A heavy cannonade was raging along the main lines, but this was only a cloak to the real movement.

In fact another expedition had set out toward the left, the familiar region about Hatcher's Run. Gregg's cavalry division had been sent to the Boydtown plank road in the hope of striking the Confederate wagon trains, which were said to be abundant on that thoroughfare. A strong infantry force from the corps of Warren and Humphreys under command of the former undertook at the same time the familiar farce of an attempt to turn the enemy's right, was itself struck in flank, the move resulting only in a sharp engagement and the return of both armies to their camps. This showed, however, that the Confederate lines had been extended and strengthened in that direction so efficiently as to preclude the hope of making any impression upon them. Warren's troops having encountered the enemy during the day, one division from the Ninth Corps and the First (Wheaton's) Division of the Sixth were called upon as reinforcements.

The division was soon on its way and till midnight the Thirty-seventh in their place in the column marched and counter-marched, though putting but a few miles between their actual position and the camp. Finally they were set to work constructing rifle-pits—which they had now acquired the faculty for doing with great rapidity. Large trees were cut down, the trunks trimmed and rolled into place, while other squads in the detail very quickly threw against them an embankment of earth sufficient to resist even cannon shot. Then a "head-log" was put in position and the work was complete. Having thus passed a very tedious night, the weather being cold and windy, the regiment remained behind the intrenchments thus thrown up till afternoon when the division was ordered forward in support of Crawford's division of the Fifth Corps which on the west side of the Run was trying to make its way toward the Boydtown road.

The scene of action was reached about sunset, and position was taken behind earthworks in reserve. The regiment had been there but a short time when the troops of the Fifth Corps, flanked and broken, came pouring to the rear in a panic, some of them dashing into the creek with the icy cold water up to their necks; but contrary to expectations the Confederates did not follow up their advantage and the Thirty-seventh were not engaged. Late in the evening the regiment moved back some two miles over the road by which it had come, and an attempt was made to obtain some rest. The effort was not very successful, as the night was cold, but the men built large fires around which they slept fitfully. A snow-storm prevailed during the latter part of the night, changing to sleet and a cold rain which increased in severity after day-break.

At 9 o'clock the regiment was again ordered to the front, but on reaching the Run halted till after dinner before crossing. Gathered in smoking groups about the great fires which were only kept ablaze through the skill acquired by long experience, the drenched soldiers presented a sorry spectacle; but the worst was still to come. Soon after noon the command crossed the Run and took position in the works facing the enemy, expecting each moment to be called into action. They were in fact under a heavy artillery fire, by which three men in the Thirty-seventh were wounded, and were obliged to lie close through the long hours while the storm constantly increased in fury, drenching everything and chilling animals and human beings exposed to it till it seemed that they must perish from cold. The sleet and rain, congealed by the intense cold, not only loaded all inanimate objects with a heavy coating of ice, but as well the clothing of the soldiers. After the cessation of firing the men collected such fuel as they could find, and under the philosophy that it was no worse to be killed by the enemy than to freeze to death built fires and warmed their benumbed limbs. The regiment had seldom been in a more disheartening situation. Around it stretched a desolate, forbidding region, every tradition of which was connected with disaster to the Union arms, and when this element was added to the storm and the exhausted condition of the soldiery it needs scarcely be said that the order received soon after midnight to return to the camp was a welcome one. Of the return march an officer who participated says:

At 1 o'clock we started on the homeward trip. The storm had now ceased, the clouds had broken away revealing the bright silvery light of the moon. The ground was now frozen firm, the atmosphere piercing cold and the trees loaded with ice which gave them a beautiful and glistening appearance when the moon shone through the parted clouds. We reached camp about 4 o'clock in the morning; and a more weary, jaded and forlorn lot of men you never saw.

Following this unsatisfactory experience another season of winter routine intervened. The little chapel proved a valuable factor in the social life of the regiment, for in addition to the direct religious interest which centered there many evening gatherings were planned which interested the men, and at no other period was the morale of the regiment better than in the closing months of its service. As the warming weather of early spring succeeded the interminable storms of the severe winter, and the hoarse voice of the frog began to resound from the surrounding marshes, games of quoits and ball became possible on the color line and mingled with the good news of the collapsing of the rebellion in other directions came persistent rumors of the early movement of the main Union army under Grant.

At his own request Colonel Edwards had been relieved from command of the post at Winchester and reporting to General Wright for duty was on the 25th of February assigned to the command of his old brigade, much to the satisfaction both of himself and his command. Frequent changes in the roster of the regiment's officers transpired, some of which should be here noted.

First Lieutenant George B. Chandley of Company K was mustered January 28 as captain of the same company, Second Lieutenant John W Stockwell of Company C being advanced vice Chandley. Captain Hugh Donnelly resigned on account of disability January 31. On the 17th of February Second Lieutenant William C. Morrill of Company A was mustered first lieutenant of Company E vice Bardwell, died of wounds; the next day First Lieutenant F. Edward Gray of Company I was mustered as captain of Company E, vice Loomis, but continued to serve with Company I. First Sergeant Joseph D. Calahan of Company C, transferred from the Seventh, was mustered the 20th as second lieutenant of Company C, vice Stockwell promoted. On the 7th of March two additional musters were made —Second Lieutenant William A. Waterman of Company F being made first lieutenant of Company I vice Gray promoted, but continuing to serve with Company E; while First Sergeant Harrie A. Cushman of Company E, transferred from the Seventh, was made second lieutenant of Company A, vice Morrill promoted, but also continued with Company E.

An especially important change occurred on the 3d of March, when to the deep regret of his command Lieutenant-Colonel Montague (with the brevet rank of colonel) felt obliged to resign on account of disability. On the Hatcher's Run expedition he had been unable to accompany his regiment and the advancing season brought him no improvement in health. From the terrible days of Spottsylvania, through a long series of the most trying experiences of the regiment, his had been the directing hand, and he had good reason to be proud of the brilliant record which had been made under his leadership. Later in the month the following promotions and musters were made on account of the vacancy thus created: Major Rufus P. Lincoln to be lieutenant-colonel, Captain Mason W Tyler of Company F to be major, and First Lieutenant George N. Jones of Company C to be captain of Company F. Both Lincoln and Jones were at this time absent on staff duty and did not afterward serve with the regiment. First Lieutenant Walter B. Smith of Company D was March 22 mustered as captain of Company I, vice Donnelly, and Second Lieutenant Flavel K. Sheldon of Company H was made first lieutenant of Company D, vice Smith. The size of the companies did not allow the promotion of officers of lower rank.

The morning of March 25 brought a genuine sensation to the

Army of the Potomac in an attack on its intrenched line by a Confederate column. It was a desperate resort, but being well planned and daringly executed it succeeded to the extent that Fort Steadman within the lines of the Ninth Corps was seized, the garrison of heavy artillerists and a brigade of General Parke's troops were captured or dispersed, but there the triumph of the enemy ceased. Return to their own lines or advance was equally out of the question; as soon as it became light a cordon of fire surrounded the intruders, they were driven within the works which they had seized, where they were presently captured in bulk by General Hartranft and his division.

The Thirty-seventh with other troops of the Sixth Corps had been called upon when it was known that a breach had been made in the Union lines, and the regiment marched some four miles toward the scene when intelligence was received that their services would not be needed. Instead of returning quietly to camp, however, the portion of the Sixth Corps which was available was massed near Fort Fisher and in the afternoon a determined charge resulted in the capture of the enemy's intrenched picket line, which was firmly held. To accomplish the latter six companies of the Thirty-seventh were detailed as skirmishers, and by a judicious use of their Spencer rifles repelled unassisted the repeated attempts of the Confederates to regain the lost picket line. During the assault Edwards's Brigade was in the second line and was not seriously engaged, the loss of the Thirty-seventh being three wounded, including Major Tyler, commanding, who was struck in the knee and disabled, the command of the regiment devolving upon Captain Archibald Hopkins,—the senior captain and the only one in the regiment serving under a commission received at Pittsfield.

Preparations for the supreme blow were now pushed with great vigor, and on the 29th the movement of troops began for another effort against the enemy's right and a more determined one than had previously been made. The movement was under the command of General Sheridan and consisted of his cavalry and the Second and Fifth Corps. The troops were in position the following morning to begin active operations, but a heavy rain-storm coming the roads were made very difficult, so that operations would have been suspended for a day or two had not the enemy, having hurried into position what troops he could gather, took the initiative by a sharp attack on the Union cavalry at Five Forks. Sheridan's troopers were forced back toward Dinwiddie Court House, where next morning (April 1) they were joined by the Fifth Corps. The battle of Five Forks followed, one of the most brilliant of the war, in which the Confederate line was flanked and taken in the rear by the Fifth Corps while the cavalry pressed its front. Five thousand prisoners were captured, while those that escaped fled toward the west, so that the entire force was practically lost to Lee's army in front of Petersburg. No sooner did the news of Sheridan's victory reach General Grant than he ordered an attack along the entire line at 4 o'clock next morning.

The position of the Union forces was now as follows: The Ninth Corps was on the right; that and the Sixth held the main line from the Appomattox to Forts Fisher and Welch. Three divisions from the Army of the James under General Ord extended diagonally from the left of the Sixth to Hatcher's Run. (The white troops of the Army of the James had been organized as the Twenty-fourth Corps under General Ord, and the colored troops with the colored division of the Ninth Corps had been constituted the Twenty-fifth Corps, General Weitzel commanding.) West of the Run the Second Corps prolonged the line in the same direction, while further away and detached were the victors at Five Forks.

Since the affair at Fort Steadman the Thirty-seventh had every morning been called up before daylight and placed under arms in the rifle-pits, and on the 30th of March orders were issued that nothing was to be unpacked. This state of constant expectancy continued till evening of the 1st of April when the corps was concentrated in front of Forts Fisher and Welch, where the ground captured on the 25th of March gave an excellent opportunity for the formation of the column of assault. Edwards's Brigade formed the right of the Sixth Corps, being in rear echelon to the Second Division, the brigade being in three lines, the Thirty-seventh with the Fifth Wisconsin in front. Captain Hopkins commanded the regiment. Captain Edwards the right wing and Captain Gray the left. The skirmish line was made up of 75 picked men and volunteers from the Thirty-seventh under command of Captain Robinson assisted by Lieutenant Cushman. Formed alternately on the same line with the skirmishers were the brigade pioneers commanded by Lieutenant Donaldson, armed only with axes with which to cut through the abatis.

In this formation the long night was passed under skirmish fire, with a single ludicrous incident to break the monotony of the oppressive hours. One of the pioneer mules, loaded with picks and shovels, was struck by a skirmisher's bullet and under the smart of the wound broke away and charged directly toward the enemy. The clatter which his armament created alarmed the Confederates, who suspected an assault and at once opened a heavy fire all along the line, which was kept up for some time. The mule was found next day inside Lee's lines, having received no additional injury.

As soon as it was light enough for the soldiers to see the ground upon which they were to step two guns from Fort Fisher boomed out the signal and in an instant the dark lines swept forward. The forlorn hope of skirmishers and pioneers reached the abatis in a few moments. It was not only firmly secured by earth thrown over the trunks, but was strengthened by a double row of sharpened stakes firmly fixed in the ground. A destructive fire was opened upon the exposed line, which the skirmishers returned with interest from their Spencer rifles while the pioneers chopped and wrenched away the obstructions with desperate energy. Captain Robinson was wounded in the arm while striving to force his way through the obstructions; Sergeant Charles H. Tracy of Company A, on duty with the pioneers, was severely wounded, and while lying on the ground encouraging his comrades received a second shot in the knee joint causing the loss of his leg. Fortunately in the gloom most of the enemy's fire went over the attacking forces and the loss was but a fraction of what it would have been a few minutes later.

Meantime the line of battle sprang forward with a rush and a cheer. It gave little heed to the pioneers or the obstructions on which they were engaged; into and through them it went somehow—no one could tell in the wild excitement just how—and straight forward to the enemy's works. A three-gun fort was the objective of the Thirty-seventh,—a strong work protected by a ditch. Company E led in the scramble up the parapet, Corporal Richard E. Welch and Private Ansel R. Cook being the first to spring inside, while the colors of the Thirty-seventh were the first to crown the rebel works. Corporal Welch knocked down the Confederate color-bearer and siezed his flag, for which he subsequently received a Medal of Honor. Lieutenant Waterman was shot through the wrist as he gained the crest of the parapet while cheering on his men, but his assailant was next moment bayoneted by Corporal Patrick Kelly. Michael Kelly of the same company was killed and Corporal Luther M. Tanner—a brave and well-beloved soldier—received a fatal wound in the knee. Then the wave of blue poured over in resistless strength, such of the defenders of the fort as could not escape surrendered, and the Confederate lines were broken. The regimental lines were reformed, Company E under Lieutenant Cushman—its only commissioned officer after the wounding of Lieutenant Waterman—was detailed to hold the fort and the guns it had done so much toward winning, and the remainder of the column pressed on.

The loss of the regiment in the assault was found to be three men killed and three officers and 29 men wounded; in addition to those already named Lieutenant F. K. Sheldon being wounded, Corporal Calixte Beauchemin of Company G and George P. Edwards of Company I killed.

The first line of the brigade now changed front to the left and moved down inside the Confederate works till it met Hyde's brigade of the Second Division; the second line faced to the right and cleared the works for some distance in that direction; while the third line pushed straight ahead to clear the ground in the rear, reaching the Southside railroad and cutting the telegraph wires. Then the entire corps pressed on toward the left for a mile, driving the enemy toward Hatcher's Run and destroying his camps and wagons. Then a grand countermarch took place and the victorious corps moved up toward the interior line of works protecting Petersburg on the west.

At one point near the close of the day the Alleghany Artillery, Captain Carpenter's battery, opened on the flank of the Thirty-seventh. The regiment was moved under cover and Captain Champney with two companies was detailed to silence the fire. This was effectually done, the horses being killed, and the Second Division soon after advancing over that part of the field captured every gun.

The Sixth Corps had won credit enough for one day, and within a few hundred yards of Petersburg the halt for the night was made. The lines ran past the fine mansion used by General Lee for headquarters, occupied that night by General Grant of the Vermont Brigade. Colonel Edwards was appointed general officer of the day and posted his skirmish line, on which were Companies E and I of the Thirty-seventh.

Meantime to the left Generals Ord and Humphreys had also broken through the Confederate intrenchments, dispersing such of the foe as were found, and then joining forces with Wright moved toward Petersburg, Ord's command capturing Fort Gregg after a stubborn resistance. On the Union right General Parke had made a lodgment in the enemy's lines, but found the works too strong to be carried, and later in the day was subjected to a sharp counter-attack by General A. P. Hill's command, in which that able leader lost his life.

Early in the morning of the 3d, before daylight, Colonel Edwards advanced his skirmishers and reserves into the outskirts of the city without opposition, and a few minutes later he received from Mayor Towne and other officials a formal surrender. Lee had completed the evacuation scarcely 15 minutes before the Union skirmishers entered. The Thirty-seventh were at once ordered into the city to preserve order, and were the only troops from the Sixth Corps to enter. There was no disturbance. "Bress de Lor' for dis day! Yesterday I was a slave now I am free!" was a frequent exclamation of the elated negroes. The white inhabitants were not so happy.

CHAPTER XX

ONE COUNTRY AND ONE FLAG

LEE'S FLIGHT AND THE PURSUIT—THE GRAPPLE AT SAILOR'S
CREEK—THE SURRENDER AT APPOMATTOX—IN SEARCH OF
JOHNSTON.

Not the Army of the Potomac alone but the whole country was electrified by the tidings which that never-to-be-forgotten 3d of April, 1865, proclaimed to the world. Not only Petersburg but Richmond had been evacuated during the night; the Confederate Government as well as Lee's army was in full flight.

General Weitzel, whose lines faced the Richmond defenses, was startled by heavy explosions and volumes of black smoke rising from the city. A cavalry vidette was pushed forward which entered unopposed the city to gain which such countless thousands of lives had been sacrificed and planted its guidons on the late Confederate Capitol. The retiring traitors in their eagerness for destruction had fired large warehouses filled with tobacco situated in the heart of the city; and though Weitzel's soldiers were at once hurried to the spot and fought the fire with all their power, it could not be checked till the business part of the city was destroyed and a vast number of people rendered homeless.

General Lee on retiring from Petersburg moved north to Chesterfield Court House, half way to Richmond, where the fragments of his army from different directions concentrated, marching thence with all speed due west. The route led across the Appomattox at Goode's Bridge to Amelia Court House on the Danville railroad, 38 miles west of Petersburg, whence Lee intended to move by the railroad to Burkesville, 20 miles to the southwest, the crossing of the Danville and Southside roads. From that point he could retreat either in the direction of Danville or Lynchburg, prolonging the struggle indefinitely; but Providence decreed that the mad folly which for four years had reigned should come to a sudden end at last. On reaching Amelia, Lee found that large quantities of supplies which had been ordered to that place had by a misunderstanding been carried on to Richmond, and they had in fact been burned there with other stores. His army was consequently without food and was obliged to remain there during the 4th and 5th while numerous foraging parties were sent out in all directions to gather such supplies as were obtainable from the surrounding country.

General Sheridan with the cavalry advance of the Union army gained the Danville railroad at Jetersville, some miles to the southwest of Lee's position, on the morning of the 4th, cutting off the intended retreat toward Danville. The Fifth, Second and Sixth Corps coming up during the following day, preparations were made to attack on the morning of the 6th.

The Thirty-seventh regiment, after a brief stop in Petersburg on the morning of the 3d, rejoined its brigade, and about noon set forth on its westward march, the soldiers of all the commands quite beside themselves with enthusiasm. The forces from the Army of the James, under General Ord, followed the Southside railroad, while Sheridan's cavalry, the Fifth, Second and Sixth Corps, in the order named, pursued the roads between the railway and the river. Some ten miles were made the first day, the march was resumed at daylight of the 4th, and continued with brief halts for breath till an hour after dark. On the morning of the 5th an order was read to each regiment asking the troops to cheerfully endure hardships and hunger if necessary in order to ensure the speedy downfall of the rebellion, which was greeted with cheers and followed by another hard day's march, the corps joining Sheridan's forces at Jetersville late in the evening.

An advance was promptly made toward Amelia at daylight of the 6th, but it was soon evident that the prey had escaped during the night. Lee had in fact moved past the Union left flank and made a strong push for Farmville, 35 miles west, where he hoped to cross to the north side of the Appomattox and still escape to Lynchburg and the mountains beyond. General Ord, whose command had reached Burkesville, was at once directed to move to Farmville, and sent on in advance of his main body a light column of some 500 men under General Theodore Read. This little force succeeded in reaching Farmville in advance of the enemy and in checking the latter till General Ord arrived; but General Read was killed and his command nearly destroyed.

Meantime the three infantry corps of the Army of the Potomac, preceded by cavalry, moved westward from Jetersville on parallel routes, the Sixth Corps on the southernmost road following General Sheridan. At Deatonsville he began to feel the Confederate rear guard, fully a third of Lee's army under General Ewell, which was making determined efforts to protect what remained of the wagon trains. Custer's cavalry division had succeeded by a detour in cutting off the train and its guards, while Sheridan pressed sharply on the rear. A running fight ensued for some distance, when the Confederates having reached favorable ground on the west side of Sailor's Creek turned upon their pursuers for a last desperate stand. The afternoon was waning, and if they could hold the Federals at bay till dusk it might be possible to save something from the surrounding and converging circle of fire.

The Thirty-seventh had already marched more than 20 miles over the sandy, rolling, pine-covered country on that warm 6th of April when the desultory artillery fire which had been heard at intervals assumed that steadiness which proclaimed to the toiling infantry that their services were to be called for. Never had so many miles been made with such heart as the 70 marched over since leaving Petersburg, and dashing the sweat from their faces the enthusiastic fellows began to fill the magazines of their rifles, to cast aside knapsacks, blankets and superfluous clothing in preparation for the anticipated struggle. The men were ready to break into a run when the order to "double-quick" was received, and for three miles they went forward at a pace which nothing but the intense excitement of the occasion could have enabled them to sustain.

Just where the road passed the crest of an elevation Generals Sheridan and Wright sat upon their horses watching on the one side the magnificent advance of the troops and on the other the scene of the coming battle. Pausing for a moment to receive a welcome and directions as to the placing of his command, General Edwards bore straight for the battle-field and his men followed with no slackening of speed. As they passed the crest the scene of strife lay spread before them like a panorama. For a mile a gentle open slope led down to the creek, a narrow, sluggish stream with marshy and bush-grown banks; on the opposite side there was a somewhat more marked ascent, broken by ravines and covered with a scattering thicket of pines and bushes. On the latter slope, protected by the contour of the ground, Ewell's lines of battle were disposed. Far beyond the smoke of burning wagons showed the presence and the work of Custer's horsemen. On the eastern side of the creek the guns of Sheridan's artillery had been holding the enemy to cover till the Union infantry could get up.

Wheaton's and Seymour's (Third) Divisions were pushed across the creek, which was waist deep and difficult to ford, while Getty's was held in reserve on the eastern bank. Once across the creek the lines were deployed, the Thirty-seventh on the left of the brigade with a detail of skirmishers covering the front, and an advance was ordered up the hill and through the thicket toward the position of the unseen enemy. "Who should appear by my side at this moment," says Captain Hopkins who commanded the regiment, "in front of the line, but the chaplain, who whenever a fight was imminent seemed to feel that he had been grievously put upon in being appointed to fill a non-combatant's role. It required a peremptory order to send him to the rear." The brave chaplain accompanied the regiment into action, however, and in ministering to the wounded rendered valuable service.

As the foot of the ascent was reached the lines were again adjusted, moved by the right flank for a short distance, and once more advanced up the slope. A scattering fire was immediately encountered from the enemy's skirmishers, and one of the first of the Thirty-seventh to fall was First Sergeant Ezra P. Cowles of Company D, which he commanded, Captain Edwards acting as major. Sergeant Cowles was mortally wounded through the body, but heroically cheered on his comrades as he fell. Shortly afterward as the regiment scrambled through the undergrowth a terrific crash of musketry burst from the Confederate lines but a few yards in front. Fortunately, owing to the position of the foe on somewhat higher ground and the impossibility of their taking proper aim through the thicket, what was intended for an annihilating volley at close range mostly went over the heads of the Thirty-seventh. The men pressed forward, holding their fire with wonderful self-control till they were in plain sight of the enemy, almost face to face.

Then the Spencer rifle did the work for which it was intended. Volley followed volley with almost the rapidity of thought, tearing the opposing line into demoralized fragments. While some surrendered and many fell, the rest broke away and ran through the forest, pursued by the elated Thirty-seventh. In the wild exultation of the moment the officers did not discover that the regiment was alone and utterly unsupported in its advance. The rest of the Union line had been broken and pushed back temporarily by the mad onset of Ewell's corps, some of them to and across the creek to the shelter of Sheridan's artillery. Of course this temporary success of the enemy would be brief, but it was sufficient to place the little more than 200 members of the Thirty-seventh in a remarkably unpleasant position.

The first realization of the true situation came from the discovery of what seemed to be a heavy column of the enemy passing the left flank of the regiment. Front was changed in that direction and a few volleys from the Spencers drove the force out of sight, but not a moment two soon. General Custis Lee, the son of the Confederate commander-in-chief, on the right of the Thirty-seventh, saw his opportunity and moved his brigade through a ravine to the rear of the isolated regiment. His command included the famous Seventh regiment of Savannah and a battalion of marines from the gun-boats which had been destroyed at the evacuation of Richmond. The latter were picked men and especially anxious to signalize their presence on the field of battle.

Captain Hopkins had barely time to face his command to the rear to meet this new danger when Lee's brigade burst from the cover of the gulch and dashed in a ferocious charge upon the thin line of the Thirty-seventh. It was the severest test to which the veteran regiment had ever been subjected, but it was most magnificently met. Lee's wave of chivalry struck the rock of Massachusetts manhood only to recoil. Both sides fought with desperate courage, hand to hand with bayonets, swords and pistols. The lines of Blue and Gray, half hidden in the veil of smoke, seemed to mingle in one mass as they swayed back and forth, and for a time the issue seemed in doubt. But the Men in Blue did not give an inch. Meeting blow with blow, loading and firing their deadly repeating rifles as rapidly as possible, they checked the onset of the enemy, held him, pushed him back, at first slowly and with obstinate resistance, then in a broken rout into the gorge from which he had emerged.

As the disorganized Confederates took shelter in the ravine a sharp fire was poured in upon them, when they made signals of surrender. Adjutant Bradley stepped forward to meet a Confederate officer who was advancing as though to give himself up, when the latter drew a pistol and wounded the adjutant, who grappled his assailant and they rolled down the bank in the struggle which followed. Bradley having been shot in the thigh by a bystanding rebel was overpowered, and his antagonist was poising his pistol to give a death-shot when his own traitorous life was extinguished by a well-directed shot from the rifle of Private Samuel E. Eddy of Company D. Simultaneously with the shot Eddy was thrust through the breast with a bayonet in the hands of a stalwart Southron. The weapon protruded from the back near the spine, and the unfortunate soldier being thrown down was literally pinned to the ground. The assailant then endeavored to wrest away Eddy's Spencer rifle, but the wounded man grasped his trusty weapon with a grip which few men in either army could equal, and notwithstanding his awful situation succeeded in throwing another cartridge into his rifle, the bullet from which was next moment sent through the heart of his antagonist. The Confederate fell across the prostrate Unionist, but the latter threw aside the body with one hand as though it were the carcass of a dog, withdrew the bayonet from his own horrible wound, rose to his feet and walked to the rear.*

After this exhibition of treachery the regiment re-opened fire with a vengeance, and it required but a few volleys to bring the Confederates to their senses and to a surrender in reality, the cavalry at the upper end of the ravine cutting off their retreat. The Thirty-seventh secured and sent to the rear over 300 prisoners, considerably in excess of the number of men it took into the fight, while from all sides captives and captures of every sort poured to the rear in bewildering numbers and quantity. No less than six Confederate generals were secured, including Ewell, Kershaw and Custis Lee, with about all that remained of Ewell's corps. There was little attempt to count, scarcely to guard the captures made; everywhere the shout was "Forward!" "Onward!" to strike the final blows and destroy everything that remained to Lee as an organized army.

In such a struggle as the Thirty-seventh had passed through, where every man had proved himself a hero and fought largely on his own responsibility, it is impossible to note more than a few of the noteworthy deeds performed, and the narration of certain incidents will only serve to show the character of many which must be passed without chronicle but which will live long about the camp fire and in the traditions of the home. General Custis Lee, who directed the charge upon the Thirty-seventh, had till shortly before filled a clerkship at Richmond, but finally laid down the pen to take up the sword, surrendering

---

* Private Eddy had received a wound at the affair in front of Fort Fisher, March 25, but had followed the fortunes of the regiment notwithstanding, and previous to the encounter just narrated several of the enemy had gone down before his careful aim. Contrary to all expectations his iron constitution enabled him to survive the terrible transfixion, and as these pages go through the press he is still living at his home in West Chesterfield.

The records of the Thirty-seventh present several cases of remarkable recovery from supposed fatal wounds through the chest. Of these especial note may be made of the cases of Lieutenant Albert C. Sparks, already referred to; of William J. Simmons of Company E, shot through the lungs in such a manner that the breath passed out through the orifice in his back; and of several others nearly as severe, in one of which the breast bone was shattered and split by a ball which passed through the body. In all these cases the recovery was considered, even by the medical faculty, little less than miraculous.

the latter at the muzzle of the Spencer rifle to Corporal David White of Company E. First Sergeant Almon M. Warner of the same company attempted to capture a battle-flag, but was severely wounded, when Private Charles A. Taggart of Company B sprang forward and secured the colors, for which act of bravery he received a medal.*

One brave corporal becoming somewhat separated from his comrades encountered a Confederate officer whose surrender he demanded and on receiving a refusal shot him, inflicting a fatal wound. As the wounded man fell the corporal bent over him, saying: "I am sorry that I had to shoot you! I am a Christian, and if you wish I will pray with you; it is all I can do for you now." The offer was thankfully accepted, and while the tempest of battle raged near them the earnest voice of prayer rose in behalf of the departing spirit. At its close the dying officer joined in the "Amen," gave his sword to the young soldier with a message for his wife, when the latter, who had been fired at on the supposition that he was committing a robbery, resumed his rifle and continued the battle. For gallant conduct at the storming of the works before Petersburg Captain Hopkins received the brevet of major, to which in recognition of Sailor's Creek was added that of lieutenant-colonel. After the wounding of Adjutant Bradley, Lieutenant S. E. Nichols was detailed as adjutant, serving most creditably till the muster out.

The Thirty-seventh regiment had fought its last battle—in some respects its most brilliant. Its fair record, never tarnished, was nobly closed and crowned by this desperate encounter. Meeting superior numbers, cut off from all support and almost surrounded, receiving in hastily prepared formation without intrenchment or cover of any nature the charge of a select brigade led by an ambitious young officer,—with never the yielding of an inch or a backward step, the regiment had nobly shown the superb quality of its composition.

* These medals had been authorized by a resolution of Congress approved July 12, 1862, "to provide for the presentation of Medals of Honor to the enlisted men of the army and volunteer forces who have distinguished, or may distinguish, themselves in battle during the present rebellion." On the back of the Medal was engraved, " The Congress, to Private Charles A. Taggart, Co. B, 37th Mass. Vols." That these Medals were not promiscuously distributed is sufficiently attested by the fact that but 18 were bestowed on Massachusetts soldiers, of which two—those of Taggart and of Corporal Welch, were received by members of the Thirty-seventh.

Though the loss was severe, it was found to be far less than might have been expected from the ferocity of the conflict. Nine had been killed and 31 wounded, several of the latter fatally and nearly all seriously. The killed were: Company B—Corporal Henry L. Messinger and Edgar N. Phelps. C—Sergeant Samuel M. Bolton and Charles Blakesley. D—Corporal Timothy D. Smith. E—William H. Henderson. F—William F. Leggett. H—Sergeant David B. Miller. K—Timothy Mullin. Captain Walter B. Smith and Lieutenant Harrie A. Cushman were severely wounded in the early part of the engagement— the former by a charge of "buck and ball" in the thigh received at short range. The loss in non-commissioned officers was especially severe. Four first sergeants were wounded—Warner of E, Cowles of D, Freeman of B and Partridge of H, the three latter fatally. Sergeant Bolton of Company C, who was killed, was one of the transfers from the Tenth, a fine soldier, who in the closing battle of the rebellion crowned nearly four years of faithful service by the supreme sacrifice.

That night the regiment camped near the battle-field, and the succeeding two days were occupied in following up the retreating fragments of the Confederate army. On the night of the 6th Lee had retired across the Appomattox at High Bridge with what was left to him of the hungry, broken, dispirited army, but before the bridges behind him could be destroyed the Second Corps was rushing across and the pursuit was unbroken. The 8th found his forces hopelessly hemmed in at Appomattox Court House, the Federal troops closing in resistlessly and General Grant demanding his surrender to save the further waste of life. There was one more desperate attempt on the morning of the 9th to force the thin lines through the cavalry environment which Sheridan had placed between the Confederates and further retreat, but the pushing back of the dismounted horsemen only disclosed the advancing bayonets of the Army of the James, and the white flag which preceded formal surrender took the place of the Stars and Bars.

As the fact of Lee's surrender became generally known through the Union army that afternoon there was joy too wild, too deep, too sincere for utterance in formal words. Cannon thundered, men shouted themselves hoarse, then pitched their shelter tents for the first time since leaving winter quarters and lay within them with the strange realization that there was no longer an opposing army to be watched and feared.

The Thirty-seventh enjoyed a night and a day of unbroken rest and were then ordered to report back to Burkesville, for which place they started on the morning of the 11th in a drizzling rain, marching 20 miles toward Farmville over the road by which they had moved toward Appomattox. Both the rain and the march continued for two days longer, camp being pitched near Burkesville on the afternoon of the 13th in a beautiful pine grove. There the regiment remained for ten days, during which time every heart was inexpressibly saddened by the news of the assassination of President Lincoln.

During this time occurred the last muster of officers—Doctor Charles E. Inches of Boston on the 13th as assistant surgeon and on the 15th Second Lieutenant James O'Connor of Company G as first lieutenant of Company C, vice Jones promoted. Surgeon Inches was a young man enthusiastic and ambitious in his profession, with a heart overflowing with kindness for his fellow-beings; and brief as was his service and happily free from the ravages of battle, his tender humanity won prompt and heart-felt appreciation from every member of the regiment.

Meantime in every direction the end of the armed rebellion was approaching. General Sherman after tarrying at Savannah for some weeks had moved forward in resistless force to Columbia, S. C., whence he swept straight through the Carolinas toward Richmond, driving before him the remnants of the Confederate forces which General Johnston was striving to gather somewhere for a determined stand. Fort Fisher, guarding the harbor of Wilmington, N. C., having fallen before the determined assault of General Terry and Wilmington itself before General Schofield's Twenty-third Corps, which had been brought to the Carolina coast by way of Washington, these forces were transferred to Newbern, and moved—though not without opposition and some sharp fighting—toward the center of the state to intersect the line of Sherman's march. Hardee had evacuated Charleston on hearing of Sherman's movement, lighting fires which burned most of the city and killed 200 of the inhabitants by an explosion, and at Averasboro had a sharp engagement with some of Sherman's forces on the 16th of March. This was followed by the more determined battle of Bentonville, three days later, in which Johnston succeeded in checking the column under General Slocum from the 19th to the 21st, when Sherman having concentrated an enveloping force the Confederate commander retired during the night and the march of the Union army was resumed.

At Goldsboro Sherman formed a connection with Schofield and halted to rest his exhausted troops, communication being opened by rail with Newbern, but on the 10th of April the campaign was resumed. Next day the tidings of Lee's surrender were received, and Raleigh was occupied on the 13th; the day following Johnston sent in a flag of truce and from the armistice which resulted his surrender ensued on the 26th. In his case as in that of Lee, the hungry Confederate soldiers were supplied with rations by the government they had so long fought against, and at once started for their homes to resume the pursuits of peace and begin the great task of repairing the ravages of war.

Meantime the Sixth Corps had been ordered from Burkesville to Danville, on the North Carolina border, 100 miles away, and on the morning of the 23d set forth. The roads, following the general direction of the railroad, were good and the weather was quite favorable, which with the encouragement received from recent events gave the troops great heart and strength for whatever trials might be deemed necessary. Twenty-five miles were made the first day and 20 the next, bringing the corps to bivouac on the banks of the Staunton river. Soon after dark of the 27th the regiment as rear guard of the corps passed through Danville and a mile beyond went into camp.

As the corps approached the city, which is situated on the south bank of the Dan river, an attempt was made by some of the bitter inhabitants to burn the bridge, but the mayor and the more sensible citizens protested so vigorously that the purpose was abandoned. To the right on an elevation a fort with six guns commanding the bridge looked grimly down, but it had no garrison and was simply a reminder of the days which had passed. The city had also been a depot for Union prisoners, but such as were there had been released and with joy had hurried to the now all-potent protection of the triumphant Stars and Stripes.

Reliable intelligence of Johnston's surrender, which had been prematurely rumored, was received on the following day, and then it was even more vividly realized that with the dispersion of the last formidable armed force the existence of the rebellion practically ceased, that the long looked for day had come when there was in reality but one Country beneath one Flag.

CHAPTER XXI.

THE CLOSING SCENES.

FACING NORTHWARD.—REVIEWS AT RICHMOND AND WASHINGTON.—THE FINAL ROSTER.—MUSTERED OUT.—THE WELCOME HOME.

The Thirty-seventh remained quietly in camp at Danville till the morning of May 3, when cars were taken for Wilson's Station on the Southside railroad, 28 miles west of Petersburg. The journey was very slowly made, lasting, including a stop of a few hours at Burkesville, till late in the afternoon of the following day, when the regiment went into camp in a beautiful grove near the Station. There two weeks passed very pleasantly, the brigade nominally guarding the railroad to Nottaway Court House, 14 miles distant; but as there was no enemy save an occasional roving band of marauders who took good care not to come within the reach of Union troops, the duty was very light.

News of the capture of Jefferson Davis, the president of the late Confederacy, reached camp on the 15th, and two days later came an order to march next morning. The soldiers now realized that they were indeed on the homeward route, but there were just murmurs that the journey of the 18th was made to cover 25 miles of hot and dusty road when there was no exigency requiring such exertion. The halt for the night was made within four miles of Petersburg. At 3 o'clock next morning the reveille sounded, and soon after daylight the march was resumed. Petersburg was passed through early in the forenoon, and it was gratifying to note the signs of renewed life which were already being manifested. Passing on toward Richmond, about half the distance between the two cities was covered by easy stages during the day, the intense heat culminating in a thunder shower during the afternoon. The following forenoon brought the corps within sight of Richmond, and the camps were pitched near Manchester, in the midst of the elaborate fortifications protecting that suburb, where the regiment remained till the 24th, many of the command going over into the late rebel Capital to view the various objects of interest, bathing in the waters of the historic James River, or lying idly in camp dreaming of the speedy reunion with loved ones at home and the return to the duties and pleasures of civil life.

The grand review of the united armies of Generals Meade and Sherman took place at Washington on the 23d and 24th of May, the 23d being devoted to the Army of the Potomac, composed of the cavalry corps, and the Second, Fifth and Ninth Corps of infantry; while on the 24th the Armies of the Tennessee and of Georgia passed before the enthusiastic throngs. As the Sixth Corps could not take part in the pageant it was arranged to have it reviewed in Richmond on the 24th by Generals Halleck, Ord, and others. Reveille accordingly sounded at 3 o'clock and at 5 the column moved through Manchester, across the river into Richmond, passing the reviewing stand by company front, the streets everywhere lined by an interested throng, of which the enthusiastic blacks formed the most interesting element.

The review proved but the beginning of a trying day's experience. Straight on the column moved, out through the abandoned fortifications, past fields and scenes of historic interest without number, till at 9 o'clock at night, with 25 miles of distance covered, the halt was made at Hanover Court House. The Pamunkey was crossed next day on a ponton bridge, the march of the 26th being accompanied by a heavy rain which made the mud almost impassable. The 27th and 28th were given to rest, and the following day a march of 20 miles brought the corps to Fredericksburg, "on our annual May visit," as some of the soldiers humorously suggested.

Four days more of continuous plodding, crossing Occoquan Creek at Wolf Run Shoals and moving by Fairfax Station and Court House, brought the Thirty-seventh on the 2d of June to

Bailey's Cross Roads, five miles from Washington on the Arlington side of the Potomac. There the regiment encamped during the remainder of its stay in the United States service, and the days which followed had but little more than routine interest. On the 6th the brigade turned out to speed with military honors the One Hundred and Nineteenth Pennsylvania, which set out for home, and on the 8th occurred the review of the corps in Washington by President Johnson, his Cabinet, Generals Grant. Meade, and a large body of prominent officers.

For this event the command was roused very early in the morning, crossing Long Bridge to the vicinity of the Capitol, where the corps was massed. At 9.30 the advance guard, the First Connecticut cavalry, cleared the way, and at 10 the column began to move. The brigades and divisions proceeded in numerical order, the artillery following the Third Division and the rear being composed of 200 New York Engineers with a ponton train. The Third Brigade, First Division, General Edwards, moved in the following order : Eighty-second Pennsylvania Veterans, 960 men, Brevet Brigadier General Bassett : Second Rhode Island Veterans, 450 men, Lieutenant-Colonel Rhodes ; Forty-ninth Pennsylvania Veterans, 305 men, Colonel Hickman ; Thirty-seventh Massachusetts, 300 men, Major Tyler : Fifth Wisconsin, 400 men, Colonel Allen. As the Thirty-seventh passed the reviewing stand by company front, fewer in numbers than any of its sister organizations, the waste of the terrible campaigns it had passed through was vividly realized. Company K, the color company, proudly bore the tattered standards before the cheering multitudes with scarcely eight files to guard the priceless treasures.

It was an especially glorious day for the Sixth Corps, for apart from the noble record which it had made from the day of its organization, the people of Washington had not forgotten that it came to their assistance the previous summer when Early was thundering at the northern gates of the city, and their enthusiasm was loud and earnest. But notwithstanding all the ardor of the populace, the day was a very trying one to the soldiers, as it was terribly hot, and the sun beat down into the crowded streets with a ferocity which prostrated many with sun-stroke and obliged the great majority of the corps to fall from the ranks before their camps were regained.

General Edwards, commanding the brigade, who had received the brevet of brigadier general for gallant conduct at the battle of the Opequan, had for his part in the fall of Petersburg received a commission as brigadier general of volunteers from May 19, with the brevet of major general in recognition of his services at Sailor's Creek. Other brevets will be noted as the recipients are mentioned. While the regiment was awaiting its turn for muster out, the officers absent from their commands on account of wounds were being honorably discharged the service. On the 15th of May Captain (brevet Major) John C. Robinson, Adjutant (brevet Captain) John S. Bradley and Second Lieutenant Harrie A. Cushman thus left the service: Second Lieutenant Jesse Prickett resigned on the 21st, and Captain (brevet Major) Thomas G. Colt* on the 23. First Lieutenants William A. Waterman and Flavel K. Sheldon were mustered out June 17.

A busy scene was the camp of the regiment on the 21st of June, 1865. On that day the Thirty-seventh was mustered out of the Government service as an organization, the recruits of the Thirty-seventh proper with the transfers from the Tenth and Seventh regiments being transferred to the Twentieth Massachusetts. The roster of the regimental officers was as follows, a star designating those transferred to the Twentieth:

Field and Staff—Lieutenant Colonel Rufus P Lincoln,* Major Mason W Tyler.* Surgeon Elisha M. White,* Assistant Surgeon Charles E. Inches,* Chaplain Frank C. Morse,† Quartermaster Edward Bridgman.

---

*Captain Colt was one of the most popular officers in the regiment on account of his unwavering courage, quick military genius, warm social nature and untiring interest in the welfare of all with whom he came in contact. Returning to his home in Pittsfield, he retained ever a keen interest in all that pertained to his much-loved regiment. His early death, which occurred from pneumonia on the 10th of May, 1883, at the age of 41, was deeply mourned by a wide circle of comrades and friends in all walks of life.

†Chaplain Morse, whose character as a noble Christian and a devoted patriot has been so fully illustrated heretofore as to need no further portrayal here, left the service with health irreparably injured. Returning to the ministry which he had left to become a private soldier, he was settled over the Methodist church at Leyden till the spring of 1868, when he went to Kansas and bought a farm near Reno which he occupied for a year, in the vain hope of regaining his health. Afterward he took a position as express and station agent at Ladore, which he held till his health utterly gave way. January 14, 1871, at the early age of 36, he laid down a life which, though brief, had not been lived in vain, and whose influence for good still lives in many a human heart.

Company A—Captain Walter B. Smith,* First Lieutenant Richard H. Taylor. B—Captain George H. Hyde, First Lieutenant Albert Vincent, Second Lieutenant Samuel E. Nichols, acting adjutant. C—Captain Archibald Hopkins, First Lieutenant James O'Conner,* Second Lieutenant Joseph D. Calahan. D—Captain Charles L. Edwards, Second Lieutenant David M. Donaldson. E—First Lieutenant (brevet Captain) William C. Morrill. F—Captain George N. Jones,* First Lieutenant Erastus W Harris. G—First Lieutenant William H. Calhoun. H—Captain (brevet Major) Jonas A. Champney, First Lieutenant Hubbard M. Abbott. I—Captain F. Edward Gray, Second Lieutenant Julius H Reed. K—Captain George B. Chandley, First Lieutenant John W Stockwell, Second Lieutenant Edward D. Taylor.

Preparations for the homeward journey, so far as preparations were needed, now occupied the thoughts of all. The Sanitary Commission had since the arrival of the troops from the field spared no pains to provide them with delicacies, comforts and luxuries and after the muster out rations were drawn in profusion, so that the supplies received by the men were only limited by their disposition to accept.

Reveille sounded next morning at half-past 3 and at 5 camp was broken, the regiment under the lead of General Edwards marching through Georgetown to Washington where at 11 o'clock cars were taken. Baltimore was reached at half-past 3 in the afternoon, dinner was eaten, cars changed, and at 5 the homeward route was resumed. Arriving at Philadelphia some time past midnight, the never-failing hospitality of the Quaker City was enjoyed in a bountiful breakfast at the Cooper Shop of blessed memory ; at daylight cars were taken to Amboy, whence the journey to New York was made by the steamer Transport, reaching the Metropolis at noon. After a most excellent dinner, the regiment marched up Broadway once more and at 6 o'clock took the steamer Traveler for Hudson. That city was reached about daylight of the 24th, and at half-past 5 the citizens provided a generous breakfast, welcoming the return as they had speeded the departure of the Thirty-seventh.

Pittsfield was reached at 10 o'clock, and at this first stopping place on Massachusetts soil, the point of the regiment's formation and departure. it was received with hearty demonstrations. Yet sadness had a share, for it could not escape notice that while 27 cars had been required to take the command away, it was comfortably returned in six. At the depot the regiment was met by an escort of firemen and conducted to the park, where a bountiful collation was served and the veterans were eloquently welcomed by Hon. H. L. Dawes and E. H. Kellogg. General Edwards responded briefly, with a touching allusion to those who had fallen, the regiment gave a brief exhibition of the manual of arms and then continued the journey.

Springfield was entered at half-past 2, and the reception there was of the most enthusiastic nature. Many of the relatives and near friends of the members were in waiting at the depot, and as the command left the cars the greetings were rapturous and affecting. Presently the line of marched was formed and the regiment, escorted by the fire department, led by the Railroad band, marched to the City Hall. The streets were filled with enthusiastic people waving handkerchiefs and cheering the veterans, to whom a more familiar sound was the thunder of the Union Battery, whose rapid discharges emphasized the welcome. The national colors were everywhere displayed and many of the buildings and banners bore appropriate mottoes. In the City Hall a bounteous repast had been prepared, and when the soldiers were seated an appropriate address of welcome was made by N. A. Leonard, Esq., in the absence of the mayor. General Edwards responded in behalf of the regiment, after which his command did ample justice to the tempting viands; another period of hand-shaking followed, the column returned to the depot, and the Thirty-seventh that evening reached their last camp at Readville.

While the regiment remained there waiting for the final settlement of its affairs and formal disbanding, Governor Andrew issued the following commissions. which gave the regiment a nominally complete roster of officers, but the promoted were of course never mustered in the new rank:—

DISBANDING OF THE REGIMENT. 431

Lieutenant-Colonel Rufus P. Lincoln as colonel; Major Mason W Tyler as lieutenant-colonel and colonel; Captain Archibald Hopkins as major and lieutenant-colonel; Captain Charles L. Edwards as major; First Lieutenants Hubbard M. Abbott, Edward Bridgman, Albert H. Vincent and William A. Calhoun as captains; Second Lieutenants Samuel E. Nichols, David M. Donaldson, Edward D. Taylor and Julius H. Reed as first lieutenants; First Sergeant Michael Casey of Company K as second lieutenant and first lieutenant; and as second lieutenants Commissary Sergeant Dwight H. Parsons, First Sergeants William A. Shaw of Company D, Edward E. Stannard of C, Joseph F Bartlett of I, Almon M. Warner of H and William E. Lewis of F, Sergeants Charles H. Tracy of A, Frederick A. Farley of F and Color Sergeant Edward D. Hooker of D.

On the 26th of June the colors of the Thirty-seventh were sent to Boston, where on the 22d of December following they were in common with those of the other Massachusetts commands which had served the Union placed in appropriate receptacles in Doric Hall at the State House, where they still remain, silent yet eloquent witnesses to the patriotism of the citizen soldiers of the old Bay State. They are torn and rent by bullets and deadly missiles; they are stained with the life-blood of her sons, but never with dishonor.

For a few days the members of the regiment remained at the camp, with frequent excursions to Boston and the neighboring objects of interest; but on Sunday, July 2, the last of them were paid for their services and discharged, and the Thirty-seventh Massachusetts Regiment ceased to exist save in the deeds it had done and the fraternal associations of its surviving members. For the former no words of praise need be spoken here; for the fallen, while we drop a tear, we will extend the patriot's chaplet, the victor's wreath, the martyr's crown.

APPENDIX.

THE ROLL OF HONOR.

KILLED IN ACTION.

Company A.
Sergt. Sylvanus Muller, May 6, 1864.
Corp. Levi Davis, Aug. 21, 1864.
Corp. Wm. A. Palmer, Sept. 19, '64.
Edward Bergley, May 12, 1864.
Florence Burke, June 18, 1864.
Daniel Cronin, Sept. 19, 1864.
George A. Ferrin, Sept. 19, 1864.
Oliver C. Hooker, May 6, 1864.
Edwin G. Taylor, Sept. 19, 1864.
Ithamer Woodin, Aug. 21, 1864.

Company B.
Corp. H. L. Messinger, Apr. 6, '65.
George N. Barnes, May 10, 1864.
Lyman Chapel, Sept. 19, 1864.
Edward W Coope, May 6, 1864.
George J. Daniels, Sept. 19, 1864.
Gordon Dunn, May 6, 1864.
James Gendron, Sept. 19, 1864.
Michael Keys, June 19, 1864.
George King, May 6, 1864.
John McNerny, May 12, 1864.
Silas Miller, Aug. 21, 1864.
Harrison Mills, June 3, 1864.
Eugene Murphy, May 6, 1864.
Edgar N. Phelps, Apr. 6, 1865.
George F. Phinney, May 6, 1864.
James B. Rudd, May 6, 1864.

Company C.
Sergt. Sam'l M. Bolton, Apr. 6, 1865.
Sergt. Geo. D. Chapin, May 12, 1864.
Sergt. Martin Schemmerhorn, Sept. 19, 1864.
Corp. Michael Moren, May 12, 1864.
Charles Blakesley, Apr. 6, 1865.
Thomas McCabe, 2d, May 12, 1864.
James Moran, May 21, 1864.
John W. Newton, May 6, 1864.
Egbert Pexley, May 6, 1864.
John Walcott, May 6, 1864.

Company D.
Corp. Wm. M. Kingsley, May 12, '64.
Corp. Timothy D. Smith, Apr. 6, '65.
George C. Clark, May 6, 1864.
John S. Hyde, May 6, 1864.
John D. Smith, May 6, 1864.
John M. Worthington, Sept. 19, '64.
George M. Wolcott, May 6, 1864.

Company E.
Sergt. John M. Partridge, May 6, '64.
Urbane H. Crittenden, May 6, 1864.
Richard Fulton, May 6, 1864.
Colonel D. Halsey, May 12, 1864.
William H. Henderson, Apr. 6, 1865.
Michael Kelly, Apr. 2, 1865.
Joel J. Lobdell, June 4, 1864.
James H. Perkins, July 3, 1863.
Joseph Rivet, May 6, 1864.
Francis Sherman, May 6, 1864.

Company F.
Sergt. John W. Field, May 6, 1864.
Corp. John M. Dunbar, May 6, 1864.
Orange Bardwell, May 6, 1864.

iv   THE ROLL OF HONOR.

Frederick B. Crocker, June 21, '64.
Martin S. Hubbard, May 12, 1864.
William F. Leggett, Apr. 6, 1865.
Joseph J. Rogers, May 6, 1864.

Company G.
Sergt. Wm. M. Knapp, May 6, 1864.
Sergt. V H. Tanner, Sept. 19, 1864.
Corp. John E. Banks, Aug. 21, 1864.
Corp. C. Beauchmin, Apr. 2, 1865.
Corp. Theo. A. Church, May 5, '64.
Seth Belden, Sept. 19, 1864.
Joseph Bushman, May 6, 1864.
John T. Follansbee, Sept. 19, 1864.
Paschal Janes, June 18, 1864.
Maurice Moore, May 6, 1864.
Henry D. Temple, May 6, 1864.
William Whitney, May 6, 1864.

Company H.
Sergt. Ira Larkins, May 18, 1864.
Sergt. David B. Miller, Apr. 6, 1865.
Corp. Moses S. Ames, Sept. 19, 1864.
Corp. Thos. J. Crandall, June 1, '64.
Lyman C. Bartlett, May 12, 1864.
Miles H. Blood, Sept. 19, 1864.
Robert Elder, June 5, 1864.
Arthur T. Merritt, May 6, 1864.
Edmund H. Sears, May 11, 1864.

Stephen G. Warner, Dec. 13, 1862.
Sumner Warner, May 6, 1864.
Charles T. Wing, May 18, 1864.
Sydney P. Wood, May 6, 1864.

Company I.
Corp. Josiah B. Hawks, May 12, '64.
Corp. W. C. Stockwell, June 18, '64.
Albert R. Clark, May 9, 1864.
Clarkson H. Decker, June 5, 1864.
George P Edwards, Apr. 2, 1865.
Edward S. King, May 21, 1864.
Augustus E. Pease, Sept. 19, 1864.
Erastus B. Pease, June 3, 1864.
Edwin O. Wentworth, May 12, 1864.
John Wilcox, May 6, 1864.

Company K.
Michael Freeman, May 12, 1864.
Patrick Hussey, July 3, 1863.
John Maloney, June 11, 1864.
Timothy McNamara, May 6, 1864.
Timothy Mullin, Apr. 6, 1865.

Unassigned Recruits.
Christopher Harding, June 16, '64.
Patrick Lovett, July 12, 1864.
Robert Rhinehart, Aug. 21, 1864.

DIED OF WOUNDS.

Officers.
Capt. F. W. Pease, May 14, 1864.
1st Lieut. C. S. Bardwell, Oct. 6, '64.
2d Lieut. Geo. S. Cooke, May 12, '64.
2d Lieut. J. Follansbee, May 28, '64.

Company A.
John D. Day, Apr. 29, 1865.
Henry E. Eddy, May 14, 1864.
Charles A. Grostick, Aug. 14, 1864.
Michael Holohan, Aug. 7, 1864.
Seth P. Lanfair, May 27, 1864.
Edward M. Morley, Apr. 22, 1865.
Elmer M. Sprout, May 7, 1864.

Company B.
1st Sergt. Charles W Freeman, Apr. 18, 1865.
Corp. Wm. H. Mausir, May 22, '64.
Corp. George Prindle, May 29, 1864.
Enos Besoncon, July 27, 1863.
Jules Besoncon, May 29, 1864.
James Brown, May 29, 1864.
Alexander Deforest, May 24, 1864.
Elijah L. Flint, July 1, 1864.
Charles Russell, Oct. 7, 1864.

Company C.
Corp. Geo. L. Shook, Oct. 18, '64.

DIED OF WOUNDS.

John W Cooney, May 26, 1865.
Buel Gleason, May 17, 1864.
Lewis M. Mosier, June 19, 1864.
Demas Mozier, May 18, 1864.
Josiah O. Ostrom, June 23, 1864.

Company D.

1st Sergt. E. P. Cowles, Apr. 9, '65.
Corp. Wm. J. Nichols, May 30, '64.
Corp. J. C. Walker, May 30, 1865.
Sylvanus C. Bryant, May 19, 1864.
Edward Burt, June 2, 1864.
Daniel D. Currie, May 16, 1864.
John Shea, Apr. 7, 1865.

Company E.

Corp. L. M. Tanner, May 18, 1865.
James Davis, June 18, 1864.
Charles Gurney, July 10, 1863.

Company F.

1st Sergt. E. Graves, May 21, '64.

DIED OF DISEASE.

1st Sergt. J. K. Taylor, Aug. 30, '64.
Elihu Coville, July 22, 1863.
Edgar H. Field, May 10, 1864.
Neville Preston, May 27, 1864.
James K. Sanderson, May 12, 1864.
John H. Vining, June 12, 1864.
Chauncey Waite, June 27, 1864.
George D. Whitmore, Apr. 13, 65.

Company H.

1st Sergt. Thomas J. Partridge, Apr. 12, 1864.

Company I.

Shubael Winslow, Jr., Apr. 24, '64.

Company K.

Corp. D. Driscoll, May 29, 1863.
James Casey, July 5, 1864.
Michael Conway, May 5, 1863.
James Crampton, July 13, 1863.
James N. Perry, July 25, 1864.

DIED OF DISEASE.

Company A.

Joel Briggs, June 19, 1864.
Edmund M. C. Fuller, Jan. 13, '64.
Samuel J. Hillman, Dec. 4, 1862.
Orlo Hunt, Feb. 15, 1863.
Lyman Matthews, June 14, 1864.
Addison H. Mosely, Oct. 12, 1862.
Ezra J. Tripp, July 1, 1864.
William A. Williams, Feb. 12, 1863.

Company B.

1st Sergt. Wm. E. Pease, July 1,'63.
Corp. Chas. N. Snow, June 6, 1864.
Corp. L. W Spofford, March 3, '63.
Quinton F. Bliss, Feb. 28, 1865.
Charles J. Kelsey, Aug. 17, 1864.
Stephen Kirby, Dec. 17, 1864.
Albert Noble, Jan. 20, 1863.
William H. Sheffield, April 6, 1863.
Philo N. Snow, July 28, 1864.

Company C.

Peter Durant, April 11, 1863.
Elijah P. Hatch, Oct. 18, 1863.
Nathan J. Hedger, Aug. 11, 1864.
Frederick Mills, Apr. 21, 1863.
Russel M. Purvere, April 13, 1865.
John Smith, April 12, 1863.

Company D.

Darius Collier, Oct. 21, 1862.
Horace Collier, Feb. 9, 1864.
James Dorgan, June 18, 1864.
Alfred Hitchcock, Aug. 7, 1864.
Robert Parsons, Nov. 18, 1862.
George Pease, March 29, 1864.
Jonathan W Phelps, April 3, '64.
Fred'k D. Simpson, June 22, 1864.
Myron D. Taylor, March 18, 1864.

Company E.

Geo. E. Cline, Convalescent Camp.

Thomas B. Edwards, Jan. 12, 1863.
Lewis Leonard, April 11, 1863.
William O'Brien, Nov. 16, 1862.
William O'Connell, Feb. 17, 1863.
Jacob Van Bramer, Feb. 18, 1863.
Henry Van Tassel, Sept. 13, 1863.
Francis H. Wright, Feb. 18, 1863.

Company F.

John J. Beals, Feb. 22, 1863.
Otis Cummings, Dec. 11, 1862.
Henry J. Fales, April 1, 1863.
Albert A. Pratt, Sept. 5, 1864.
Ethan A. Taft, Feb. 3, 1863.
Charles P. Waite, Feb. 13, 1863.

Company G.

William Ackors, Oct. 8, 1863.
Legar R. Harris, May 1, 1864.
Miles Holmes, Aug. 9, 1864.
Louis Lanier, Feb. 5, 1863.
Alpheus D. Lathrop, Jan. 28, 1863.
Henry Leonard, April 1, 1864.

Company H.

Sergt. R. M. Porter, Aug. 29, 1864.
Hiram Blackmer, June 15, 1863.

William H. Averill, Jan. 10, 1865.
Hiram Blackmer, June 15, 1863.
Freeman Brackett, July 12, 1864.
Raymond C. Flowers, Jan. 5, 1863.
Emulus B. Gillett, Dec. 15, 1862.
Daniel W. Kane, Dec. 16, 1862.
Caspar Lilly, April 23, 1863.
Urbane Sears, Nov. 12, 1862.
Frederick E. Smith, April 14, 1863.
Jonas H. Thayer, May 4, 1863.

Company I.

Sergt. Martin Luther, May 11, '64.
Corp. Albert F. Brown, Oct. 29, '62.
Giles A. Bailey, Dec. 20, 1863.
James W. Burns, March 8, 1864.
William Daley, Jan. 8, 1864.
Edward Dunn, July 30, 1864.
James O. Lee, Sept. 9, 1863.
Chas. E. Stockwell, Feb. — 1864.

Company K.

Chas. H. R. Ball, Jan. 26, 1863.
Samuel Beals, Feb. 3, 1863.
Scott Brown, March 23, 1863.
Albert E. Pelton, April 20, 1865.
Nathaniel J. Tilden, Dec. 28, 1862.

DIED IN SOUTHERN PRISONS.

At Andersonville, Ga., unless other locality is given.

Company A.

Mus. O. W Kelly, Nov. 1864,
   Salisbury, N. C.
Patrick Hayes, Sept. 2, 1864.

Company B.

Charles B. Dole, Sept. 14, 1864.

Company D.

Sumner P. Fuller, Aug. 10, 1864.
N. P. Taylor, Aug. 15, 1864.

Company E.

P. H. Sherman, June 22, 1864.

Company H.

E. T. Blood, Sept. 10, 1864.
W. H. Cook, Sept. 2, 1864.
H. C. Ramsdell, Oct. 1, 1864.

Company I.

John G. Bean, Dec. 29, 1864,
   Danville, Va.

Company K.

John O'Brien, June 26, 1864.

MISCELLANEOUS.

Company A.
Henry H. Clark, Missing May 6, '64.

Company B.
G. F. Hubbard, Prisoner May 19, '64.

Company H.
Louis Ligard, Missing May 6, '64.

Company K.
J. E. Bliss, Murdered Dec. 8, '62.

WOUNDED

[Fatal wounds are indicated by a star (*).]

FIELD AND STAFF.

Maj. Marcus T. Moody, head, May 6, 1864.
Maj. Marcus T. Moody, thigh, May 12, 1864.
Lt. Col. G. L. Montague, foot and arm, May 12, 1864.
Sergt. Maj. H. M. Abbott, hand, May 18, 1864.
Maj. Mason W. Tyler, knee, March 25, 1865.
Adjt. John S. Bradley, thigh and shoulder, April 6, 1865.

LINE OFFICERS.

2d Lt. A. L. Bush, thigh, July 3, '63.
Capt. Joseph L. Hayden, thigh, May 5, 1864.
Capt. R. P. Lincoln, side, May 6, '64.
1st Lt. James G. Chalmers, hand, May 6, 1864.
Capt. F. W. Pease,* arm, May 12, 1864.
Capt. Rufus P. Lincoln, chest, May 12, 1864.
1st Lt. J. A. Champney, leg, May 12, 1864.
1st Lt. C. C. Wellman, May 12, '64.
2d Lt. A. C. Sparks, side, May 12, 1864.
2d Lt. Geo. S. Cooke,* back, May 12, 1864.
2d Lt. J. Folansbee,* back, May 12, 1864.
Capt. Hugh Donnelly, head, June 5, 1864.
1st Lt. Geo. N. Jones, arm, June 5, 1864.
Capt. J. A. Loomis, thigh, Sept. 19, 1864.
1st Lt. Charles S. Bardwell,* abdomen, Sept. 19, 1864.
Capt. Geo. Pierce, shoulder, Sept. 19, 1864.
Capt. Mason W. Tyler, neck, Sept. 19, 1864.
1st Lt. Erastus W Harris, hand, Sept. 19, 1864.
1st Lt. Francis E. Gray, neck, Sept. 19, 1864.
1st Lt. William H. Cousins, thigh, Sept. 19, 1864.
Capt. John C. Robinson, arm, Apr. 2, 1865.
1st Lt. F. K. Sheldon, Apr. 2, 1865.
1st Lt. Wm. A. Waterman, wrist, Apr. 2, 1865.
Capt. Walter B. Smith, thigh, Apr. 6, 1865.
2d Lt. Harrie A. Cushman, thigh, Apr. 6, 1865.

ENLISTED MEN.

Company A.

Thomas Caffrey, hand, May 3, '63.
Thomas B. Jenks, July 3, '63.
Josiah T. Hunt, July 3, '63.
George W Truell, July 3, '63.
George H. Oakes, hand, May 6, '64.
Geo. H. Spencer, hand, May 6, '64.
Nicholas Reed, knee, May 6, '64.
Sergt. Wm. Shepardson, May 6, '64.
Corp. John Plass, hand, May 6,'64.
Elmer M. Sprout,* thigh, May 6,'64.
Seth P. Lanfair,* knee, May 6, '64.
Ezra J. Trippe, leg, May 6, '64.
Corp. F. R. Bell, foot, May 6, '64.
M. Hollohan,* ankle, May 6, '64.
Andrew J. Mason, leg, May 6, '64.
T. D. Richardson, hand, May 12, '64.
Henry E. Eddy, chest, May 12, '64.
John D. Strong,* hand, June 3, '64.
Corp. Levi Davis, hip, June 3, '64.
Chas. A. Grostick,* shoulder, June 3, '64.
G. M. Dutcher, head, June 3, '64.
Sergt. George S. Chapin, shoulder, June 18, 1864.
Michael Ploss, arm, July 12, '64.
F. V Oviatt, feet, Aug. 21, '64.
1st Sergt. D. M. Donaldson, thigh, Sept. 19, '64.
Edward Deady, thigh, Sept. 19, '64.
Julius Strong, arm, Sept. 19, '64.
Reuben Chace, head, Feb. 5, '65.
Sergt. Charles H. Tracy, lost leg, Apr. 2, '65.
L. E. Searles, breast, Apr. 2, '65.
John D. Day,* leg, Apr. 2, '65.
Corp. F. R. Bell, leg, Apr. 2, '65.
E. M. Morley,* thigh, Apr. 6, '65.

Company B.

Corp. G. Prindle, finger, May 3, '63.
George L. Hill, finger, May 3, '63.
Walter J. Lester, breast, May 3, '63.

Enos Besoncon,* July 3, '63.
Almon S. Cadwell, July 3, '63.
Charles A. Taggart, July 3, '63.
George T. Carter, July 3, '63.
Calvin Goodbo, July 3, '63.
Winfield S. Tyrrell, side, May 5, '64.
Corp. C. Ingham, thigh, May 6, '64.
Corp. Wm. H. Mansir,* arm, May 6, 1864.
Corp. G. Prindle,* thigh, May 6, '64.
Alexis Baron, hand, May 6, '64.
Jules Besoncon,* thigh, May 6, '64.
Geo. F. Bidwell, face, May 6, '64.
Henry Bretcher, hand, May 6, '64.
Wm. B. Church, hand, May 6, '64.
Alex. Deforest,* side, May 6, '64.
John A. Durant, hand, May 6, '64.
Elijah L. Flint,* face, May 6, '64.
George L. Hill, finger, May 6, '64.
Asa L. Landon, wrist, May 6, '64.
Herbert Morin, ankle, May 6, '64.
William Smith, hand, May 6,'64.
Philo N. Snow, arm, May 6, '64.
1st Sergt. Chas. W. Freeman, arm, May 12, '64.
Corp. Watson F. Bentley, jaw, May 12, '64.
D. P. Bradley, arm, May 12, '64.
Egbert J. Olds, leg, May 18, '64.
Noah M. Freeman, leg, May 18, '64.
Alex. Deforest, legs, May 21, '64.
Alfred D. Jones, hand, May 21, '64.
Corp. Henry L. Messinger, arm, June 4, '64.
S. Van Dusen, leg, Aug. 21, '64,
Corp. L. Huntley, side, Sept. 19, '64.
Alfred D. Jones, side, Sept. 19, '64.
G. H. Whittaker, foot, Sept. 19, '64.
Herbert Morin, neck, Sept, 19, '64.
Geo. L. Hill, foot, Sept. 19, '64.
Charles Russell,* Sept. 19, '64.
Sergt. Gilbert G. Bentley, breast, Apr. 2, '65.

1st Sergt. C. W Freeman,* thigh, Apr. 6, '65.
H. C. Clark, shoulder, Apr. 6, '65.

Company C.

Corp. John Alvin Hall, July 3, '63.
John Kelly, July 3, '63.
Frederick S. Shephard, July 3, '63.
James Ferry, July 3, '63.
John M. Taylor, July 3, '63.
Thomas Burns, thigh May 6, '64.
Andrew J. Knight, arm, May 6, '64.
Wm. H. Barnes, legs, May 6, '64.
Corp. George J. Pineo, May 6, '64.
Corp. Albert L. Strong, thigh, May 6, '64.
Edgar Barnum, chest, May 6, '64.
John W. Cooney,* arm, May 6, '64.
James Ferry, foot, May 6, '64.
Corp. W. H. Dunbar, leg, May 6, '64.
Buel Gleason,* breast, May 6, '64.
Nathan W Halsey, hip, May 6, '64.
George W. Jones, leg, May 6, '64.
George A. Palmer, arm, May 6, '64.
A. Stanward, wrist, May 6, '64.
Oscar Sweet, hand, May 6, '64.
R. Decker, hand, May 6, '64.
T. Fitzerald, breast, May 6, '64.
Sergt. L. M. Stannard, cheek, May 12, '64.
Sergt. M. Schemmerhorn, hand, May 12, '64.
N. J. Hedger, hand, May 12, '64.
Demas Mozier,* neck, May 12, '64.
L. M. Mosier, arm,* May 21, '64.
Sergt. R. O'Brien, side, June 3, '04.
J. O. Ostrom,* knee, June 3, '04.
H. W. Sikes, lost right arm, June 3, '64.
Sergt. Robert O'Brien, thigh, Sept. 19, '64.
Corp. O. E. Cutting, breast, Sept. 19, '64.
Corp. G. L. Shook,* foot, Sept. 19, '64.

Judson Bradley, side, Sept. 19, '64.
Corp. H. J. Deming, Sept. 19, '64.
M. P. Gleason, thighs, Sept. 19, '64.
Richard Holmes, arm, Sept. 19, '64.
T. Hamilton, shoulder, Sept. 19, '64.
T. Sackett, foot, Sept. 19, '64.
Peter Smith, hand, Sept. 19, '64.
Corp. E. Strickland, leg, Sept. 19, '64.
Jas. McCormick, scalp, Feb. 5, '65.
Corp. J. A. Hall, face, Feb. 5, '65.
James Ferry, hand, Apr. 2, '65.
Andrew J. Knight, knee, Apr. 2, '65.
Wm. H. L'Hommedieu, hip, Apr. 2, '65.
J. H. Wagner, shoulder, Apr. 2, '65.
A. G. Williams, side, Apr. 6, '65.
W. H. Jackson, thigh, Apr. 6, '65.
James McCormick, leg, Apr. 6, '65.
Sergt. George A. Seelye, head, Apr. 6, '65.

Company D.

Corp. J. H. Bissell, face, May 3, '63.
George Pease, face, May 3, '63.
E. P. Hadley, head, May 5, '64.
Sumner L. Niles, arm, May, 5, '64.
Charles W Nash, jaw, May 6, '64.
James F. Ross, shoulder, May 6, '64.
Francis Brooks, hand, May 6, '64.
Corp. John H. Bissell, back, May 6, '64.
Corp. Chester D. Holbrook, shoulder, May 6, '64.
Corp. William J. Nichols,* arm, May 6, '64.
Edward Burt,* thigh, May 6, '64.
George W. Gray, lost left arm, May 6, '64.
John F. Keyes, leg, May 6, '64.
Edward Law, arm, May 6, '64.
Michael Munsing, hand, May 6, '64.
Corp. John C. Rockwood, shoulder, May 6, '64.
1st Sergt. William H. Shaw, lost hand, May 6, '64.

Daniel D. Currie,* May 6, '64.
Sylvanus C. Bryant,* hip, May 9, '64.
William W. Hitchcock, hand, May 9, '64.
Sumner P. Fuller, May 9, '64.
Corp. Jefferson C. Walker,* thigh, May 12, '64.
Corp. George L. Streeter, foot, May 12, '64.
Corp. Chester D. Holbrook, arm, May 18, '64.
Corp. George A. Bisbee, back, May 18, '64.
Walter G. Brewer, arm, June 3, '64.
Paul Trotier, hip, Sept. 19, '64.
Wm. M. Clement, leg, Sept. 19, '64.
John Shea, leg, Sept. 19, '64.
James W. Wetherbee, foot, Sept. 19, '64.
Paul Trotier, chest, Mar. 25, '65.
Samuel E. Eddy, knee, Mar. 25, '65.
James W Wetherbee, knee, Apr. 2, '65.
1st Sergt. Ezra P Cowles,* groin, Apr. 6, '65.
Samuel E. Eddy, bayonet through chest, Apr. 6, '65.
John Shea,* thigh and hand, Apr. 6, '65.

Company E.

Sergt. D. R. Fields, leg, July 3, '63.
James L. Bowen, legs, July 3, '63.
J. M. Fletcher, head, July 3, '63.
Charles Gurney,* legs, July 3, '63.
Edwin E. Phelps, hip, July 3, '63.
Daniel Lewis, July 3, '63.
Corp. Daniel O'Neil, arm, May 6, '64.
George Haley, arm, May 6, '64.
W. J. Simmons, breast, May 6, '64.
Corp. A. M. Cane, arm, May 6, '64.
Milton Brooks, leg, May 6, '64.
Edward Gregson, leg, May 6, '64.
William J. Pettitt, leg, May 6, '64.

Corp. R. Welch, shoulder, May 12, '64.
Chas. M. Babbitt, head, May 12, '64.
M. V B. Dingman, face, May 18, '64.
James H. Olds, breast, June 1, '64.
John Stickney, mouth, June 1, '64.
James Davis,* arm, June 11, '64.
S. M. Hogle, hand, June 18, '64.
Dennis McGrah, thigh, Aug. 21, '64.
Corp. W H. Couch, thigh, Sept. 19, '64.
Corp. Arthur M. Cane, neck, Sept. 19, '64.
Ansel R. Cook, thigh, Sept. 19, '64.
F. W. Crossett, thigh, Sept. 19, '64.
William Elston, leg, Sept. 19, '64.
John Kelly, thigh, Sept. 19, '64.
Edw. R. Lobdell, leg, Sept. 19, '64.
Charles H. Loomis, Sept. 19, '64.
Henry Slater, breast, Sept. 19, '64.
N. E. Walden, shoulder, Sept. 19, '64.
Edwin R. White, Sept. 19, '64.
Corp. R. Welch, neck, Sept. 19, '64.
Hiram Caswell, leg, Apr. 2, '65.
Corp. L. M. Tanner,* knee, Apr. 2, '65.
1st Sergt. A. M. Warner, arm, Apr. 6, '65.
H. L. Luce, leg and thigh, Apr. 6,'65

Company F.

Elihu Coville,* hip, July 3, '63.
Corp. M. Thesier, hand, May 5, '64.
Edgar H. Field,* May 5, '64.
C. H. Russell, head, May 5, '64.
J. K. Sanderson,* leg, May 5, '64.
William J. Smith, hand, May 5, '64.
Charles O. Squires, foot, May 5, '64.
F. P. Wheeler, hand, May 5, '64.
1st Sergt. Edwin Graves,* knee, May 6, '64.
Corp. E. L. Covill, shoulder, May 6, '64.
Robert Brown, foot, May 6, '64.
Sergt. E. C. Hanks, head, May 6, '64.

WOUNDED.

David P. Lamb, arm, May 6, '64.
Levi J. Pratt, leg, May 6, '64.
Joseph F. Smith, arm, May 6, '64.
William J. Smith, side, May 6, '64.
Chauncey Waite,* May 6, '64.
1st Sergt. William E. Lewis, leg, May 12, '64.
William Fahay, ear, May 12, '64.
E. R. Pearson, ear, May 18, '64.
John F. Pease, leg, May 18, '64.
Neville Preston,* foot, May 21, '64.
John A. Glazier, head, May 21, '64.
William Fuller, foot, June 3, '64.
George W Nash, face, June 5, '64.
John H. Vining,* neck, June 8, '64.
Sergt. Fred A. Farley, head, Aug. 21, '64.
Sergt. Joseph K. Taylor,* groin, Aug. 21, '64.
Sergt. John Beston, leg, hand and wrist, Aug. 21, '64.
Sergt. Ebenezer F. Wiley, head, Aug. 21, '64.
Patrick Beston, hand, Aug. 21, '64.
Geo. F. Enderton, leg, Aug. 21, '64.
Corp. J. W. Foster, side, Sept. 19, '64
William Fuller, side, Sept. 19, '64.
Jas. W Horton, arm, Sept. 19, '64.
J. A. Leggett, hand, Sept. 19, '64.
John A. Pease, leg, Sept. 19, '64.
Edward E. Sanderson, shoulder and ankle, Sept. 19, '64.
Timothy Spellman, leg, Sept. 19,'64.
Stephen G. Stearns, leg, Sept. 19,'64.
Jas. W. Horton, thigh, Apr. 2, '65.
G. D. Whitmore,* temple, Apr. 2,'65
Oliver Warner, hand, Apr. 2, '65.
Corp. J. W. Foster, arm and hand, Apr. 6, '65.
James L. Dunbar, arm and hand, Apr. 6, '65.

Company G.

Albert C. Kinney, arm, May 3, '63.
Francis A. Gouch, leg, May 3, '63.

W. H. Bigelow, breast, May 6, '64.
C. C. Colson, head, May 6, '64.
Edward W Colson, leg, May 6, '64.
J. Marey, arm and breast, May 6, '64.
Nepthali Parent, arm, May 6, '64.
Chas. W Phelps, arm, May 12, '64.
Sergt. W. Ludden, leg, May 12, '64.
Wm. C. Birge, hand, June 5, '64.
J. Burnhardt, shoulder, June 18,'64.
Orson E. Train, foot, June 18, '64.
O. M. Bird, shoulder, June 19, '64.
Dolphus Halbert, hand, Aug. 21,'64.
Corp. H. P. Pratt, knee, Aug. 21,'64.
Samuel Parent, leg, Aug. 21, '64.
Sergt. William. C. Morrill, face, Sept. 19, '64.
Sergt. Wm. F. Abbott, arm and side, Sept. 19, '64.
Ernst Q. Pfiel, thigh, Sept. 19, '64.
G. C. Clapp, shoulder, Sept. 19, '64.
Thos. Dumphries, hands and arms, Sept. 19, '64.
L. F. Stockwell, arm, Sept. 19, '64.
Alexander Leon, leg, Sept. 19, '64.
C. S. Edwards, hand, Sept. 19, '64.
E. B. Ockington, head, Sept. 19, '64.
John Burnhardt, arm, April 2, '65.
O. C. Powell, arm, April 2, '65.
Simon Birge, leg, April 2, '65.
Corp. Jay Leonard, thigh, April 6, '65.
Ozro M. Bird, back, April 6, '65.

Company H.

David B. Dwight, Dec. 13, '62.
Horace C. Ramsdell, July 3, '63.
Alonzo F. Turner, July 3, '63.
Charles N. Clark, July 3, '63.
N. Chamberlin, foot, May 5, '64.
Clark G. Rice, hand, May 6, '64.
Lyman A. Shaw, leg, May 6, '64.
Monroe Snow, finger, May 6, '64.
Lorenzo Leech, finger, May 6, '64.
Wm. G. Phillips, neck, May 6, '64.
William Wright, fingers, May 8, '64.

M. Londergon, hand, May 8, '64.
Andrew B. Owen, May 8, '64.
William H. Averill, May 10, '64.
1st Sergt. Albert H. Vincent, head, May 12, '64.
Corp. Patrick Dunnivan, head, May 12, '64.
Thomas Bragel, leg, May 12, '64.
Sergt. A. P. Cook, head, June 3,'64.
J. Sandling, abdomen, July 12, '64.
Sergt. D. B. Miller, leg, Sept. 19,'64.
Sergt. A. J. Ferrill, leg, Sept. 19, '64.
1st Sergt. Thomas J. Partridge, leg and arm, Sept. 19, '64.
Color Sergt. P Dunnivan, shoulder, Sept. 19, '64.
Corp. Thomas Maginley, shoulder, Sept. 19, '64.
H. Graves, Jr., head, Sept. 19, '64.
Simon Fontine, leg, Sept. 19, '64.
John Dorsey, thigh, Sept. 19, '64.
A. F. Tafts, thigh, April 2, '65.
Joel Lilly, thigh, April 2, '65.
1st Sergt. Thomas J. Partridge,* breast, April 6, '65.
John H. Walker, face, April 6, '65.
Francis Walker, thigh, April 6, '65.
J. Leving, shoulder, April 6, '65.

Company I.

Willard Armstrong, July 3, '63.
John Mayan, hand, May 6, '64.
John Tewhill, fingers, May 6, '64.
1st Sergt. W. A. Calhoun, arm, May 12, '64.
Sergt. E. B. Hovey, head, May 12,'64.
L. P. Shaw, leg and hand, May 12, '64.
Alfred Lepine, arm, May 12, '64.
E. B. Pease, head, May 12, '64.
Lyman Jones, shoulder, June 1,'64.
A. H. Carpenter, June 1, '64.
Corp. W. C. Stockwell, June 3, '64.
John Morris, head, June 5, '64.
Heber Blake, foot, June 11, '64.
Peter Plant, groin, June 11, '64.

Corp. Samuel E. Trask, shoulder, June 18, '64.
Allen F. Parker, ankle, June 19, '64.
John Norris, knee, Aug. 21, '64.
Sergt. J. Johnson, head, Sept. 19, '64.
Corp. L. Strong, face, Sept. 19, '64.
Cornwell Baker, side, Sept. 19, '64.
Cyrus Cole, leg, Sept. 19, '64.
Geo. C. Hosmer, leg, Sept. 19, '64.
F. D. Hickox, knee, Sept, 19, '64.
Thos. Moran, hand, Sept. 19, '64.
John L. Knight, arm, Sept. 19, '64.
Corp. W. J. Hildreth, leg, Apr. 2, '65.
A. H. Carpenter, leg, Apr. 2, '65.
S. Winslow, Jr.,* leg, Apr. 2, '65.

Company K.

Corp. D. Driscoll,* breast, May 3,'63.
Michael Conway,* chest, May 3, '63.
James Crampton,* July 3, '63.
E. Duggan, shoulder, May 5, '64.
John Kenady, leg, May 5, '64.
T. T. Manning, hip, May 6, '64.
John Andrews, wrist, May 6, '64.
Michael Kilkelly, thigh, May 12, '64.
Corp. M. Rowe, hand, May 12, '64.
Thos. F. Rowe, hand and side, May 18, '64.
John McLaughlin, leg, May 18, '64.
Patrick Dalton, leg, May 18, '64.
James Casey,* May 18, '64.
Patrick J. Fallon, head, May 21, '64.
John Manning, hip, June, 3, '64.
Sergt. W. Hamilton, knee, Apr. 2,'65.
Corp. J. Welch, ankle, Apr. 2, '65.
M. Kilkelly, shoulder, Apr. 2, '65.
Geo. Richardson, thigh, Apr. 2, '65.
I. H. Burrows, hand, Apr. 2, '65.
Tim. Moriarty, hand, Apr. 2, '65.
Corp. T. Ellsworth, back, Apr. 6,'65.
Corp. M. Rowe, side, Apr. 6, '65.
C. C. Spellman, abdomen, Apr. 6,'65.
A. E. Pelton, shoulder, Apr. 6, '65.
John Murphy, arm, Apr. 6, '65.
John Morrisey, arm, Apr. 6, '65.

DESERTION IN THE 37TH MASS. VOLUNTEERS.

CLASSIFIED IN PERIODS.

(Enlisted men only.)

COMPANY.	From Enlistment to Oct. 5, 1862. That is, previous to joining Army at the Front.	From Oct. 5, 1862, to Jan. 26, 1863, or from time of joining Army of Potomac till Hooker assumed command.	From Jan. 26, 1863, to July 30, 1863. The Chancellorsville and Gettysburg campaigns, and till departure for New York.	From July 30, 1863, to Oct. 16, 1863. Being the time absent from Army of Potomac, on special duty in New York.	Balance of Service.	Aggregate.
A	0	0	3	7	1	11
B	0	1	1	5	0	7
C	1	0	1	4	1	7
D	0	2	1	1	1	5
E	4	0	2	7	1	14
F	0	0	0	0	0	0
G	0	0	1	5	0	6
H	1	1	3	2	2	9
I	1	0	0	4	2	7
K	5	0	4	11	0	20
Unassig'd	0	0	0	1	0	1
Total,	12	4	16	47	8	87

ROSTER OF 37TH REGIMENT, MASS. VOLS.

[Cause of termination of service is thus indicated:—*a*, killed in action; *b*, died of wounds; *c*, died of disease; *d*, died in southern prisons; *e*, commissioned; *f*, transferred to 20th regiment; *g*, transferred to Veteran Reserve Corps; *h*, transferred to Navy; *i*, expiration of service; *j*, disability; *k*, deserted; *l*, dishonorable discharge; *m*, missing in action; *n*, prisoner, fate unknown; *o*, discharged by order of War Department; *p*, resigned. Transfers from the 10th Regiment are shown by a *, from the 7th by a †.]

Name and Rank.	Date of Com.	Age		Term. Service.
Oliver Edwards, Col.	Aug. 27, '62	27	Springfield	{ Brig. Gen. May 19, '65 }
Rufus P. Lincoln, Col.	May 19, '65	24	Amherst	f As Lt. Col.
Mason W. Tyler, Col.	June 26, '65	24	Amherst	f As Major
Alonzo E. Goodrich, Lt. Col.	Aug. 27, '62	45	Pittsfield	p Jan. 16, '63
Geo. L. Montague, Lt. Col.	Jan. 17, '63	29	S. Hadley	j Mar. 3, '65
Rufus P. Lincoln, Lt. Col.	Mar. 4, '65	24	Amherst	e Col.
Mason W. Tyler, Lt. Col.	May 19, '65	24	Amherst	e Col.
Arch. Hopkins, Lt. Col.	June 26, '65	23	W'mstown	i June 24, '65
Oliver Edwards, Maj.	Aug. 9, '62	27	Springfield	e Col.
George L. Montague, Maj.	Aug. 27, '62	28	S. Hadley	e Lt. Col.
Eugene A. Allen, Maj.	Jan. 27, '63	26	Springfield	j Nov. 25, '63
Marcus T. Moody, Maj.	Dec. 5, '63		N'thamp'n	j July 26, '64
Rufus P. Lincoln, Maj.	July 27, '64	24	Amherst	e Lt. Col.
Mason W. Tyler, Maj.	Mar. 4, '65	24	Amherst	e Lt. Col.
Archibald Hopkins, Maj.	May 19, '65	22	W'mstown	e Lt. Col.
Charles L. Edwards, Maj.	June 26, '65	35	S'thamp'n	i June 21, '65
Charles P Crehore, Surg.	Aug. 7, '62	34	Boston	p Dec. 1, '64
Elisha M. White, Surg.	Dec. 21, '64	24	Boston	f June 19, '65
Thos. C. Lawton, Asst. Surg.	Aug. 15, '62	28	Sheffield	p Feb. 23, '64
Joshua J. Ellis, Asst. Surg.	Aug. 18, '62	37	Marshfield	Mar. 27, '63
A. L. Mitchell, Asst. Surg.	Mar. 27, '63	23	Boston	Dec. 26, '63
Elisha M. White, Asst. Surg.	Mar. 29, '64	23	Boston	e Surgeon
C. E. Inches, Asst. Surg.	April 7, '65	24	Boston	f
Frank C. Morse, Chap.	Aug. 27, '62	24	Blandford	i June 21, '65
Edwin Hurlburt, Capt.	Aug. 11, '62	44	Gt. Bar't'n	p Oct. 14, '62
George L. Montague, Capt.	Aug. 13, '62	28	S. Hadley	e Major
Hugh Donnelly, Capt.	Aug. 27, '62	22	Springfield	j Jan. 31, '65
Jarvis P Kelley, Capt.	Aug. 27, '62	29	Chicopee	p June 3, '63
Franklin W. Pease, Capt.	Aug. 27, '62	40	Lee	b May 14, '64
Algernon S. Flagg, Capt.	Aug. 27, '62	39	Wilbraham	May 14, '64
Archibald Hopkins, Capt.	Aug. 27, '62	19	W'mstown	e Major
Eugene A. Allen, Capt.	Aug. 27, '62	26	Springfield	e Major
Marcus T. Moody, Capt.	Aug. 27, '62		N'thamp'n	e Major
Joseph L. Hayden, Capt.	Aug. 27, '62	33	W'msburg	j Sept. 22, '64
Peter Dooley, Capt.	Aug. 27, '62	40	Cheshire	j Mar. 9, '63
Rufus P. Lincoln, Capt.	Oct. 15, '62	23	Amherst	e Major
Mason W. Tyler, Capt.	Jan. 17, '63	23	Amherst	e Major
John B. Mulloy, Capt.	Mar. 10, '63	24	Springfield	o April 4, '64
Joshua A. Loomis, Capt.	June 4, '63	25	N'thamp'n	j Nov. 19, '64

ROSTER.   xv

Name and Rank.	Date of Com.	Age	Residence.	Term. Serv:ce.
William Bliss, Capt.	Dec. 5, '63		N'thamp'n	p Dec. 23, '63
John C. Robinson, Capt.	Dec. 24, '63	25	Adams	May 15, '65
William M. Hale, Capt.†	April 1, '64	43	Taunton	July 1, '64
George Pierce, Capt.*	April 3, '64	31	Greenfield	Nov. 13, '64
Charles L. Edwards, Capt.	April 5, '64	34	S'thamp'n	e Major
Jonas A. Champney, Capt.	May 15, '64	32	Adams	i June 21, '65
Carlos C. Wellman, Capt.	May 15, '64	22	Chicopee	j Oct. 12, '64
George H. Hyde, Capt.	July 27, '64	23	Lee	i June 21, '65
Thomas G. Colt, Capt.	Sept. 23, '64	22	Pittsfield	May 23, '65
George B. Chandley, Capt.	Oct. 13, '64	24	Springfield	i June 21, '65
Francis E. Gray, Capt.	Nov. 20, '64	21	Springfield	i June 21, '65
George N. Jones, Capt.	Feb. 1, '65	29	Hadley	f
Walter B. Smith, Capt.	Mar. 4, '65	33	Pittsfield	f
Edward Bridgman, Capt.	May 16, '65	46	N'thamp'n	i 1st Lieut.
Hubbard M. Abbott, Capt.	May 24, '65	24	N'thamp'n	i 1st Lieut.
Albert H. Vincent, Capt.	May 24, '65	22	Hawley	i 1st Lieut.
William A. Calhoun, Capt.	June 26, '65	22	Springfield	i 1st Lieut.
Thomas G. Colt, 1st Lieut.	Aug. 5, '62	20	Pittsfield	e Captain
Daniel J. Dodge, 1st Lieut.	Aug. 5, '62	42	Pittsfield	p Jan. 28, '63
Mason W Tyler, 1st Lieut.	Aug. 13, '62	22	Amherst	e Captain
Eli T. Blackmer, 1st Lieut.	Aug. 27, '62	31	Chicopee	p Nov. 17, '62
T. F. Plunkett, jr., 1st Lieut.	Aug. 27, '62	19	Pittsfield	June 2, '63
John C. Robinson, 1st Lieut.	Aug. 27, '62	24	Adams	e Captain
Chas. L. Edwards, 1st Lieut.	Aug. 27, '62	33	S'thamp'n	e Captain
Jonas A. Champney, 1st. Lt.	Aug. 27, '62	30	Adams	e Captain
William Bliss, 1st Lieut.	Aug. 27, '62		N'thamp'n	e Captain
Joshua A. Loomis, 1st Lieut.	Aug. 27, '62	24	N'thamp'n	e Captain
J. Milton Fuller, 1st Lieut.	Aug. 27, '62	20	Springfield	p Dec. 29, '62
John B. Malloy, 1st Lieut.	Aug. 27, '62	23	Springfield	e Captain
Carlos C. Wellman, 1st Lt.	Nov. 20, '62	22	Chicopee	e Captain
Charles Phelps, 1st Lieut.	Dec. 30, '62	19	Springfield	p Nov. 17, '63
George H. Hyde, 1st Lieut.	Jan. 17, '63	23	Lee	e Captain
Edward Bridgman, 1st Lt.	Jan. 29, '63	46	N'thamp'n	e Captain
George B. Chandley, 1st Lt.	Mar. 10, '63	23	Springfield	e Captain
Erastus W. Harris, 1st Lt.	June 3, '63	30	N'thamp'n	i June 19, '65
Andrew L. Bush, 1st Lt.	June 4, '63	20	Westfield	j Feb. 5, '64
Francis E. Gray, 1st Lt.	Nov. 18, '63	20	Springfield	e Captain
James G. Chalmers, 1st Lt.	Dec. 5, '63	23	Pittsfield	j July 30, '64
George N. Jones, 1st Lieut.	Dec. 24, '63	28	Hadley	e Captain
John S. Bradley, 1st Lieut.	Feb. 9, '64	22	Lee	May 15, '65
Walter B. Smith, 1st Lieut.	April 5, '64	32	Pittsfield	e Captain
Charles S. Bardwell, 1st Lt.	May 15, '64	27	Whately	b Oct. 6, '64
Albert C. Sparks, 1st Lieut.	May 15, '64	23	Lee	j Sept. 20, '64
William B. Allen, 1st Lt.*	May 19, '64	35	N'thamp'n	Oct. 8, '64
William H. Cousens, 1st Lt*	May 22, '64	27	Adams	Nov. 26, '64
William A. Calhoun, 1st Lt.	May 31, '64	21	Springfield	e Captain
Albert H. Vincent, 1st Lt.	July 31, '64	21	Hawley	e Captain
Hubbard M. Abbott, 1st Lt.	Sept. 23, '64	24	N'thamp'n	e Captain
William C. Morrill, 1st Lt.	Oct. 7, '64	23	N'thamp'n	i June 21, '65
Richard H. Taylor, 1st Lt.	Oct. 13, '64	29	Gt. Bar't'n	i June 21, '65
John W Stockwell, 1st Lt.	Oct. 13, '64	24	N'thamp'n	i June 21, '65

Name and Rank.	Date of Com.	Age	Residence.	Term. Service.
Wm. A. Waterman, 1st Lt.	Nov. 20, '64	25	Blandford	June 17, '65
James O'Connor, 1st Lt.	Feb. 1, '65	29	Springfield	∫
Flavel K. Sheldon, 1st Lt.	Mar. 4, '65	33	S'thamp'n	June 7, '65
Samuel E. Nichols, 1st Lt.	May 15, '65	23	N'thamp'n	i June 21, '65
David M. Donaldson, 1st Lt.	May 16, '65	28	Chicopee	i June 21, '65
Edward D. Taylor, 1st Lt.	May 24, '65	29	Agawam	i June 21, '65
Julius H. Reed, 1st Lieut.	May 24, '65	23	Lee	i June 21, '65
Michael Casey, 1st Lieut.	June 26, '65	21	Pittsfield	i June 21, '65
Peter Dooley, 2d Lieut.	July 30, '62	40	Cheshire	e Captain
Thos. F. Plunkett, jr., 2d Lt.	Aug. 14, '62	19	Pittsfield	e 1st Lieut.
Carlos C. Wellman, 2d Lt.	Aug. 27, '62	21	Chicopee	e 1st Lieut.
P. Woodb'ge Morgan, 2d Lt.	Aug. 27, '62	20	Lee	p June 19, '63
Rufus P. Lincoln, 2d Lt.	Aug. 27, '62	22	Amherst	e Captain
George H. Hyde, 2d Lieut.	Aug. 27, '62	22	Lee	e 1st Lieut.
Walter B. Smith, 2d Lieut.	Aug. 27, '62	31	Pittsfield	e 1st Lieut.
Elihu R. Rockwood, 2d Lt.	Aug. 27, '62	19	Greenfield	Aug. 29,'64
Edward Bridgman, 2d Lt.	Aug. 27, '62	45	N'thamp'n	e 1st Lieut.
Andrew L. Bush, 2d Lt.	Aug. 27, '62	19	Westfield	e 1st Lieut.
Charles Phelps, 2d Lieut.	Aug. 27, '62	18	Springfield	e 1st Lieut.
George B. Chandley, 2d Lt.	Aug. 27, '62	23	Springfield	e 1st Lieut.
Erastus W. Harris, 2d Lt.	Oct. 15, '62	29	N'thamp'n	e 1st Lieut.
James C. Chalmers, 2d Lt.	Nov. 20, '62	22	Pittsfield	e 1st Lieut.
David M. Moore, 2d Lt.*	Nov. 27, '62	24	Spencer	July 1, '64
Francis E. Gray, 2d Lt.	Dec. 30, '62	19	Springfield	e 1st Lieut.
George N. Jones, 2d Lieut.	Jan. 17, '63	27	Hadley	e 1st Lieut.
John S. Bradley, 2d Lieut.	Jan. 29, '63	21	Lee	e 1st Lieut.
Michael Harrigan, 2d Lt.	Mar. 10, '63	27	Springfield	p Oct. 30, '63
William J. Fisher, 2d Lt.†	May 4, '63	31	Milton	Sept. 16, '64
Albert C. Sparks, 2d Lieut.	June 3, '63	22	Lee	e 1st Lieut.
Robert A. Gray, 2d Lt.	June 4, '63	23	Springfield	p June 26, '64
Charles S. Bardwell, 2d Lt.	June 20, '63	27	Whately	e 1st Lieut.
Hubbard M. Abbott, 2d Lt.	Oct. 31, '63	23	N'thamp'n	e 1st Lieut.
Richard H. Taylor, 2d Lt.	Nov. 18, '63	29	Gt. Bar't'n	e 1st Lieut.
William C. Morrill, 2d Lt.	Dec. 5, '63	22	N'thamp'n	e 1st Lieut.
George E. Cooke, 2d Lt.	Dec. 25, '63	23	Amherst	b May 12, '64
Joseph Follansbee, 2d Lt.	Feb. 10, '64	27	Springfield	b May 23, '64
John W. Stockwell, 2d Lt.	April 5, '64	24	N'thamp'n	e 1st Lieut.
Wm. A. Waterman, 2d Lt.	May 15, '64	24	Blandford	e 1st Lieut.
David M. Donaldson, 2d Lt.	May 15, '64	27	Chicopee	e 1st Lieut.
Jesse Prickett, 2d Lieut.	May 15, '64	23	Springfield	p May 21, '65
James O'Connor, 2d Lt.	May 24, '64	28	Springfield	e 1st Lieut.
Flavel K. Sheldon, 2d Lt.	June 27, '64	32	S'thamp'n	e 1st Lieut.
Samuel E. Nichols, 2d Lt.	Aug. 30, '64	22	N'thamp'n	e 1st Lieut.
Edward D. Taylor, 2d Lt.	Sept. 23, '64	29	Agawam	e 1st Lieut.
Julius H. Reed, 2d Lieut.	Oct. 13, '64	22	Lee	e 1st Lieut.
Joseph D. Calahan, 2d Lt.	Oct. 13, '64	27	Taunton	i June 21, '65
Harrie A. Cushman, 2d Lt.	Oct. 13, '64	19	Boston	j May 15, '65
Michael Casey, 2d Lieut.	Mar. 2, '65	20	Pittsfield	e 1st Lieut.
William H. Shaw, 2d Lieut.	Mar. 4, '65	29	Cu'm'ng'n	i June 21, '65
Dwight H. Parsons, 2d Lt.	Mar. 4, '65	21	L'meadow	i June 21, '65
Edward E. Stannard, 2d Lt.	Mar. 15, '65	22	N. M'boro	i June 21, '65

ROSTER. xvii

Name and Rank.	Date of Com.	Age	Residence.	Term. Service.
Charles H. Tracy, 2d Lieut.	Mar. 16, '65	29	Chicopee	i June 21, '65
Frederick A. Farley, 2d Lt.	May 21, '65	30	Coleraine	i June 21, '65
Joseph F. Bartlett, 2d Lt.	May 24, '65	21	Pelham	f
Edward D. Hooker, 2d Lt.	May 24, '65	23	W'hamp'n	i June 21, '65
Almon M. Warner, 2d Lt.	June 7, '65	19	Plainfield	i June 21, '65
William E. Lewis, 2d Lt.	June 26, '65	23	Ware	i June 21, '65

NON-COMMISSIONED STAFF.

Name and Rank.	Residence.	Age	Date of Muster	Term. Service.
Robert A. Gray, Sergt. Maj.	Springfield	22	Sept. 4, '62	e 2d Lieut.
H. M. Abbott, Sergt. Maj.	N'thamp'n	25	Aug. 30, '62	e 2d Lieut.
John W. Nye, Sergt. Maj.*	Lee	24	Dec. 21, '63	f June 21, '65
John E. Banks, Q. M. Sgt.	N'thamp'n	23	Aug. 30, '62	Ret. Co. G
Thos. Porter, jr., Q. M. Sgt.	Chesterfi'd	29	Sept. 4, '62	i June 21, '65
Edward S. Sears, Q. M. Sgt.	Springfield	21	Sept. 2, '62	i June 21, '65
Jas. C. Chalmers, Com. Sgt.	Pittsfield	25	Sept. 4, '62	e 2d Lieut.
D. H. Parsons, Com Sergt.	L'meadow	24	Aug. 30, '62	e 2d Lieut.
W. A. Champney, Hos. Stwd.	Hatfield	22	Aug. 1, '62	i June 21, '65
R. E. Morgan, Hosp. Stwd.	Pittsfield	22	Sept. 4, '62	Ret. Co. E
J. D. Warner, Hos. Stwd.*	Hatfield	46	Dec. 21, '63	
John L. Gaffney, Prin. Mus.	Chicopee	40	Aug. 30, '62	i June 21, '65

ENLISTED MEN.

Company A.

Name and Rank.	Residence.	Age	Date of Muster	Term. Service.
Ballard, Chester H., 1st Sgt.	Chicopee	19	Sept. 2, '62	i June 21, '65
Donaldson, D. M., 1st Sgt.	Chicopee	25		e 2d Lieut.
Waterman, Wm. A., 1st Sgt.	Blandford	22		e 2d Lieut.
Ballard, George L., Sergt.	Chicopee	23		i June 21, '65
Bonney, Henry B., Sergt.†	Marshfield	33	Dec. 26, '63	f June 21, '65
Chapin, George S., Sergt.	Greenwich	28	Sept. 2, '62	j April 4, '65
Hadfield, Joseph, Sergt.	Chicopee	23		k Sep. 28, '63
Muller, Sylvanus, Sergt.	Chicopee	24		a May 6, '64
Reed, Stephen W., Sergt.*	Holyoke	18	Dec. 21, '63	f June 21, '65
Shepardson, Wm., Sergt.	Chicopee	40	Sept. 2, '62	i " 21, '65
Tracy, Charles H., Sergt.	Chicopee	29		e 2d Lieut.
Bell, Frederick R., Corp.	Greenwich	21		i June 21, '65
Cahoon, William C., Corp.†	Taunton	18	Jan. 21, '64	f " 21, '65
Cowles, Edwin M., Corp.	Chicopee	27	Sept. 2, '62	i " 21, '65
Davis, Levi, Corp.	Sheffield	22		a Aug. 21, '64
Palmer, William A., Corp.	Chicopee	38		a Sep. 19, '64
Plass, John, Corp.	Richmond	26		i June 21, '65

ROSTER.

Name and Rank.	Residence.	Age	Date of Muster	Term. Service.
Kelly, Ormand W., Mus.	Chicopee	16	Sept. 2, '62	d Nov. 18,'64
Kelly, Samuel W., Mus.	Chicopee	40		j Aug. 7, 64
Reynolds, Ewd. M., Wag.	Lenox	25		j May 18. '65
Ariel, Isaac	Taunton	22	June 15, '61	i June 15, '65
Bartlett, Alonzo F.	Sandisfield	18	Sept. 2, '65	
Barry, George H.†	D'chester	24	Jan. 20, '64	f June 21. '65
Bergley, Edward	Chicopee	25	Sept. 2, '62	a May 12, '65
Boucock, William	Webster	43	Jan. 27, '65	f June 21.'65
Bradley, James F.†	Abington	24	Feb. 6, '62	l May 12, '65
Briggs, George T.†	Taunton	21	Jan. 20, '64	f June 21,'65
Briggs, Joel†	Berkley	26	June 15, '61	c " 19, '64
Brokaw, Abram†	Fall River	20	Dec. 26, '63	f " 21, '65
Brown, William O.†	Dighton	25	Feb. 19, '62	i Feb. 19. '65
Bryant, John	Dalton	31	Sept. 2, '62	k Ap. 12. '63
Burzitt, Charles P.	Gt. Bar't'n	42		
Burns, James†	Taunton	25	Feb. 19, '64	k Sep. 10, '64
Burke, Florence	W S'field	35	Jan. 5, '64	a June 18,'64
Burke, Richard	N'thamp'n	22	Jan. 26, '65	f " 21, '65
Caffrey, James	S'kbridge	22	Sept. 2, '62	i " 21, '65
Caffrey, Philip	S'kbridge	18		i " 21. '65
Caffrey, Thomas	S'kbridge	20		g Mar. 13, '65
Chace, Reuben†	Swanzey	21	Dec. 26, '63	f June 21,'65
Clark, Henry H.	Springfield	27	Sept. 2, '62	m May 6. '64
Clary, James	Sund'land	40	Sept. 2, '62	i June 21. '65
Clough, Francis W.	Pittsfield	21		k Aug. 26. '63
Cochrane, Charles W.*	Holyoke	34	Dec. 21, '63	o June 17.'65
Cochrane, Hugh D.		38	Nov. 11, '64	f June 21,'65
Cronin, Daniel*		20	Jan. 11, '64	a Sep. 19. '64
Cunningham, John†	Taunton	27	Feb. 27, '79	f June 21,'65
Day, John D.	N'thamp'n	18	Dec. 23, '64	b Ap. 29, '65
Deady. Edward*	Worcester	35	Dec. 10, '63	f June 21. '65
Daley, Patrick	Chicopee	18	Sept. 2, '62	i " 21, '65
Donahue, William†	Fall River	37	Jan. 20, '64	f " 21. '65
Dutcher, Gideon M.	S'kbridge	36	Sept. 2, '62	i " 21, '65
Eddy, Henry E.	Greenfield	20		b May 14. '64
Ferrin, George A.	Chicopee	18		a Sep. 19, '64
Fettlear, Joseph	Washing'n	44		i June 21,'65
Fisk, Edmund D.	Chicopee	24		i " 21, '65
Flaherty, John†	Fall River	30	Jan. 20, '64	f " 21, '65
Ford, John M.†	Marshfield	18	Feb. 12, '62	i Feb. 10, '65
Fowler, Thomas W	Chicopee	21	Sept. 2. '62	j Mar. 10, '63
Fuller. Edmund M. C.	Sandisfield	37		c Jan. 13, '64
Gallagan, Bartholomew	Chicopee	36		i June 21,'65
Grostick, Charles A.	Greenfield	20		b Aug. 14,'64
Harrin, William	Chicopee	19	Sept. 2, '62	j Feb. 15, '64
Hathaway, Isaac T.†	Dighton	18	Jan. 20, '64	j Jan. 12. '65
Hathaway, Warner A.	Savoy	36	Sept. 2, '62	j Mar. 31. '63
Hayes, James*	Agawam	19	Dec. 21. '63	f June 21,'65
Hayes, Patrick	Greenfield	19	Sept. 2. '62	d Sep. 2, '64
Hayes, Philip	Leyden	32	Dec. 24, '64	f June 21,'15
Hillman, Samuel J.	Cum'ing'n	28	Sept. 2, '62	c Dec. 4. '62

ROSTER.   xix

Name and Rank.	Residence.	Age	Date of Muster	Term. Service.
Holohan, Michael	Chicopee	18	Sept. 2, '62	b Aug. 7, '64
Hooker, Oliver C.	Pittsfield	18		a May 6, '64
Howard, Everett F.†	N. B'water	31	March 4, '62	i Mar. 4, '65
Huot, Peter*	Holyoke	34	Dec. 10, '63	f June 21, '65
Hunt, Josiah T.	Cum'ing'n	19	Sept. 2, '62	j Aug. 12, '64
Hunt, Nathaniel N.		22		June 9, '65
Hunt, Orlo		21		c Feb. 15, '63
Ingles, Thomas†	Pembroke	36	Dec. 29, '64	f June 21, '65
Ireal, Henry	Sheffield	23	Sept. 2, '62	j Jan. 10, '64
Janes, Galitzine A.	W'hamp'n	19		j Mar. 10, '63
Jenks, Thomas B.	Cheshire	44		j Jan 20, '64
Johnson, John†	Easton	37	Jan. 4, '64	f June 21, '65
Kearsley, John	Lenox	34	Sept. 2, '62	k Sep. 17, '63
Lanfair, Seth P.	Deerfield	37		b May 27 '64
Madison, Francis	Richmond	25		k July 3, '63
Mahoney, John	Lenox	37	Sept. 2, '02	i June 21, '65
Mallison, Dwight	Chester	23		i " 21, '65
Mason, Andrew J.		33		g Jan. 18, '64
Matthews, Lyman	Shut'bury	40		c June 14, '64
Mayhew, William H.	Sheffield	27		i " 21, '64
McClester, John N.	Chicopee	20		i " 21, '64
McKibbon, John S.	Lenox	28		i " 21, '64
Morley, Edward M.*	Springfield	18	Jan. 21, '64	h Ap. 22, '65
Morse, Frank C.	Blandford	27	Sept. 2, '62	e Chap.
Morton, Lyman	Springfield	34		i June 21, '65
Morrison, William	Chicopee	28		k Sep. 26, '63
Morrison, William H.	Barrington	37		g Ap. 17, '64
Mosely, Addison H.	Wilbrah'm	18		c Oct. 12, '62
Myers, Samuel H.	Lenox	25		i June 21, '65
Oakes, George H.	Chicopee	21		i " 21, '65
O'Shaunsy, William		21		g Aug. 16, '64
O'Shea, John		21		g Jan. 10, '65
Oviatt, Franklin V		38		o Aug. 21, '64
Peck, William A.	Mid'lefield	40		k May 17, '63
Ploss, Michael	Richmond	18	Jan. 5, '64	f June 21, '65
Quigley, Michael	Washing'n	19	Sept. 2, '62	k Sep. 17, '63
Ransom, Charles F.	L' meadow	37		k Oct. 1, '63
Reed, Nicholas	Chicopee	26		i June 21, '65
Richardson, Timothy D.	Cum'ing'n	41		j May 18, '65
Rice, William A.	Springfield	25		i June 21, '65
Riley, Edwin	N'thamp'n	18	Jan. 10, '65	f " 21, '65
Scott, George M.*	Agawam	31	Dec. 21, '63	j May 26, '65
Searles, Lyman E.	Otis	41	Sept. 2, '62	o June 16, '65
Shaw, Theodore D.	Ware	35		j Ap. 15, '63
Shannon, Thomas	Belchert'n	27		k Sep. 26, '63
Smith, Luther J.	Greenfield	19	Sept. 7, '62	i Sep. 17, '64
Snow, John A.	Chicopee	32	Sept. 2, '62	g Aug. 8, '63
Snow, Nathan C.	S. Hadley	30		j Mar. 10, '63
Spencer, George H.	Sheffield	21		i June 21, '65
Sprout, Elmer M.	Greenwich	22		b May 7, '64
Stalker, Peter	Chicopee	34		i June 21, '65

Name and Rank.	Residence.	Age	Date of Muster	Term. Service.
Statker, Peter	Alford	21	Feb. 6, '65	f June 19, '65
Streeter, Homer O.	Greenfield	19	Sept. 2, '62	j Mar. 18, '63
Strong, George D.	N'thamp'n	22		j May 16, '65
Strong, Julius		36	Dec. 24, '63	j June 3, '65
Stumph, Joseph	Lenox	19	Sept. 2, '62	i " 21, '65
Taylor, Edward H.	N'thamp'n	36	Dec. 17, '63	f " 21, '65
Taylor, Edwin G.	Otis	25	Sept. 2, '62	a Sep. 19, '64
Tripp, Ezra J.	Chicopee	32		c July 1, '64
Truell, George W.	Chester	30	Sept. 2, '62	i June 21, '65
Ungerer, Jacob	W. Sp'field	32		h April 4, '64
Upham, Albert B.	Buck'y, Vt	18		i June 21, '65
Vetter, Joseph	Washing'n	44		
Wade, Charles C.	Springfield	22	Aug. 16, '62	
Wade, George	Springfield	22	Sept. 2, '62	
Walker, William E.†	Dighton	18	Jan. 20, '64	f June 21, '65
Vemeyx, David	Gt. Bar't'n	34	Jan. 27, '65	f " 21, '65
Williams, William A.	Cum'ing'n	40	Sept. 2, '62	c Feb. 12, '63
Winter, Andrew	Sheffield	30	Sept. 2, '62	i June 21, '65
Woodin, Ithamer	Sheffield	28	Sept. 2, '62	a Aug. 21, '64

Company B.

Name and Rank.	Residence.	Age	Date of Muster	Term. Service.
Bradley, John S., 1st Sergt.	Lee	20	Aug. 30, '62	e 2d Lieut.
Freeman, C. W., 1st Sergt.		20		b Ap. 18, '65
Pease, William E., 1st Sgt.	Blandford	31		c July 1, '63
Reed, Julius H., 1st. Sergt.	Lee	20		e 2d Lieut.
Wood, Otis B., 1st Sergt.*	Hawley	21	Dec. 21, '63	f June 19, '65
Bentley, Gilbert J., Sergt	Monterey	28	Aug. 30, '62	j " 3, '65
Murphy, Michael, Sergt.*	Buckland	22	Feb. 21, '64	f " 19, '65
Sparks, Albert C., Sergt.	Lee	21	Aug. 30, '62	e 2d Lieut.
Vincent, Micajah H., Sergt.*	Ashfield	32	Dec. 21, '63	f June 20, '65
Allbee, George, Corp.	Lee	20	Aug. 30, '62	g Ap. 10, '64
Allen, James F., Corp.		21		o May 18, '65
Bentley, Watson S., Corp.	Monterey	22		j Feb. 1, '65
Bliss, Jay S., Corp.	Lee	23		i June 21, 65
Bliss, Martin H., Corp.		20		j Ap. 15, '63
Brauning, Edward L., Corp.	Otis	25		j Jan. 4, '65
Butler, Charles H., Corp.	Monterey	19		i June 21, 65
Conners, Martin, Corp.	Lee	18		i " 21, '65
Drake, Clement F., Corp.*	Holland	20	Feb. 20, '64	f " 21, 65
Freeman, Noah M., Corp.	Lee	24	Aug. 30, 62	i " 21, '65
Harding, Berton C., Corp.	Sandisfield	18		t " 21, '65
Hinckley, William H., Corp.	Lee	19		j Dec. 8, '62
Huntley, Levi, Corp.	Becket	27		i June 21, '65
Ingham, Charles, Corp.		23		j Jan. 19, '65
Kelly, David, Corp.	Washing'n	18		i June 21, '65
Mansir, William H., Corp.	Monterey	19		b May 22, '64

ROSTER.   xxi

Name and Rank	Residence	Age	Date of Muster	Term. Service
Messinger, Henry L., Corp.	Becket	32	Aug. 30, '62	a April 6, '65
Prindle, George, Corp.	Alford	20		b May 29, '64
Snow, Charles N., Corp.	Sandisfield	27		c June 6, '64
Spofford, Lewis W., Corp.	Lee	18		c Mar. 3, '63
Pelton, Timothy, Mus.	Gt. Bar't'n	18		f April 2, '63
McCann, John, Wag.	Lee	29		i June 21, '65
Allen, George A.	Becket	19		i " 21, '65
Austin, Chauncey L.*	Buckland	19	Jan. 5, '64	f " 19, '65
Baron, Alexis	Becket	24	Dec. 8, '63	j Jan. 4, '65
Barnes, George N.	Agawam	18	Feb. 25, '64	a May 10, '64
Beers, Samuel P.	Lanesboro	22	Aug. 30, '62	i June 21, '65
Besoncon, Enos	Sandisfield	29		b July 27, '63
Besoncon, Jules	Becket	28		b May 29, '64
Bidwell, George F.	Lee	18		o May 21, '65
Bliss, George C.	Lee	18		i June 21, '65
Bliss, Quinton F.	Lee	18	Sept. 2, '64	c Feb. 28, '65
Bradley, Dwight P.	Lee	19	Aug. 30, '62	i June 21, '65
Bretcher, Henry	Lanesboro	38	Aug. 30, '62	May 16, '65
Brown, James	Becket	26		b May 29, '64
Cadwell, Almon	N. M'boro	21		j May 19, '64
Carter, George T.	P.Val'y, Ct	18		g Mar. 2, '64
Carpenter, William T.	Lanesboro	29		j Jan. 2, '64
Chapel, Lyman	Becket	26		a Sep. 19, '64
Chapman, William C.	W. S'brid'e	47		j Mar. 15, '63
Church, William B. Jr.	Springfield	32	Dec. 29, '63	
Clark, Holly C.*	Becket	18	Nov. 5, '63	j Oct. 5, '64
Cole, John	Springfield	31	Dec. 29, '63	f June 19, '65
Coope, Edward W	Lee	19	Aug. 30, '62	a May 6, '64
Daniels, George J.	Becket	23		a Sep. 19, '64
Deforest, Alexander	Sandisfield	35		b May 24, '64
Dole, Charles B.*	Shelburne	19	Dec. 21, '63	d Sep. 14, '64
Dowd, Chandler T.	Monterey	36	Aug. 30, '62	k Ap. 28, '63
Dresser, William O.*	W. S'field	28	Jan. 9, '64	f June 19, '65
Dunn, Gordon	Sandisfield	18	Aug. 30, '62	a May 6, '64
Durant, John A.	Lee	28		i June 21, '65
Flint, Elijah L.	Otis	38		h July 1, '64
Fuller, Benjamin F.*	F'ming'm	30	Dec. 21, '63	f June 19, '65
Gendron, James	W S'field	36	Jan. 21, '64	a Sep. 19, '64
Goodbo, Calvin	Becket	34	Aug. 30, '62	i June 21, '65
Guilford, Murray J.*	Ashfield	20	Sept. 12, '61	i Feb. 1. '65
Granger, Paul L.	Becket	31	Aug. 30, '62	j Oct. 16, '62
Gibbons, John L.	Sandisfield	43		k Dec. 4, '62
Gilbert, John	Washing'n	24		k Aug. 1, '63
Hargis, Jacob*	Shelburne	25	Feb. 20, '64	o June 21, '65
Haskell, George W.	Otis	23	Aug. 30, '62	i " 21, '65
Hersey, John W.*	Springfield	21	Feb. 20, '64	g Jan. 9, '65
Hill, George L.	Otis	19	Aug. 30, '62	j May 22, '65
Hollenbeck, Duane	Egremont	18		i June 21, '65
Hubbard, Francis A.	Otis	39		j Jan. 7, '63
Hubbard, George F.*	N'thamp'n	25	Dec. 31, '63	n May 19, '64
Humphrey, Loyal S.	Sandisfield	20	Aug. 30, '62	i June 21, '65

Name and Rank.	Residence.	Age	Date of Muster	Term. Service.
Johnson, Gilbert S.	Monterey	22	Aug. 30, '62	j May 20, '63
Johnson, William I.	Lee	18		j Nov. 20, '63
Jones, Alfred D.	Otis	33		June 29, '65
Keene, Briggs O.†	Kingston	34	Feb. 12, '62	i Feb. 9, '65
Kelsey, Charles J.	Egremont	19	Jan. 4, '64	c Aug. 17, '64
Kelly, Thomas	W. S'brid'e	21	Aug. 30, '62	k Sep. 13, '63
Keyes, Michael	Lee	33		a June 19, '64
Keyes, William	Lee	28		j Jan. 16, '63
King, George	Becket	25		a May 6, '64
Kerby, Stephen	S'kbridge	22		c Dec. 17, '64
Landon, Asa L.	W. S'brid'e	25		i June 21, '65
Lester, Walter J.	Becket	18		g Sep. 24, '63
Martin, George	Becket	26	Aug. 30, '62	k Oct. 14, '63
McNerny, John	Becket	18	Dec. 23, '63	a May 12, '64
Messenger, Adelbert W.	Becket	18	Feb. 6, '64	f June 19, '65
Miller, Charles H.	S'kbridge	18	Aug. 30, '62	i " 21, '65
Miller, Silas	Egremont	18		a Aug. 21, '64
Millerd, John	Lee	20		i June 21, '65
Mills, Harrison	Becket	26		a June 3, '64
Morey, Charles E.	Lee	18	Sept. 2, '04	i " 21, '65
Morin, Herbert	Becket	30	Dec. 8, '63	f " 19, '65
Moshier, Lewis	W. S'brid'e	45	Aug. 30, '62	k Oct. 8, '63
Murphy, Eugene	Norfolk, Ct	18		a May 6, '64
Noble, Albert	W. S'brid'e	33		c Jan. 20, '63
Olds, Egbert J.	Monterey	20		j May 5, '65
Pecoy, James	Becket	33		i June 21, '65
Phelps, Edgar N.	Sandisfield	19		a April 6, '65
Phinney, George F.	Lee	19		a May 6, '64
Randall, Eathan A.†	Marshfield	37	Dec. 26, '63	f June 19, '65
Rudd, James B.	Becket	18	Aug. 30, '62	a May 6, '64
Russell, Charles*	Shelburne	21	Feb. 20, '64	b Oct. 7, '64
Sheehan, John*	Buckland	28	Feb. 29, '64	f June 19, '65
Sheehan, Robert††	Taunton	27	Feb. 25, '64	f June 19, '65
Sheffield, William H.	Lenox	22	Aug. 30, '62	c April 6, '63
Smith, William	Lee	32		i June 21, '65
Snow, Philo N.	Otis	18		c July 28, '64
Squire, Dwight M.	Washing'n	22		i June 21, '65
Soules, Frederick	Egremont	26		j Mar. 15, '63
Taggart, Charles A.	Otis	19		i June 21, '65
Taylor, Charles M.	Lee	23		j Oct. 16, '63
Taylor, Merritt D.	W. S'brid'e	42		j Mar. 16, '63
Tierney, John	Lee	24		k Oct. 14, '63
Twining, William B.	Otis	31		i June 21, '65
Tyrrell, Winfield S.	Monterey	31		i " 21, '65
Van Dusen, Sylvester	Lee	21		i " 21, '65
Whittaker, Garrett H.	Lenox	36		i " 21, '65
Willis, Frederick A.	Becket	22		i " 21, '65
Wilcox, James	W. S'brid'e	31		i " 21, '65

Company C.

Name and Rank.	Residence.	Age	Date of Muster	Term. Service.
Adams, Edwin S., 1st Sgt.	N. Marlb'o	21	Aug. 30, '62	j Mar. 16. '63
Calahan, J. D., 1st Sgt.†	Taunton	24	Feb. 10, '64	e 2d Lieut.
Pierce, Orlando W., 1st Sgt.*	Windsor	21	Dec. 21, '63	g Jan. 10, '65
Stannard, Edw. E., 1st Sgt.	N. Marlb'o	22	Aug. 30, '62	e 2d Lieut.
Taylor, Richard H., 1st Sgt.	Gt. Bar't'n	28		e 2d Lieut.
Bolton, Samuel M., Sgt.*	Heath	19	Dec. 21, '63	a April 6, '65
Chapin, George D., Sgt.	Sheffield	28	Aug. 30, '62	a May 12. '64
Cutting, Orville E., Sgt.*	Lee	19	Dec. 21, '63	f June 21, '65
Dunning, William H., Sgt.	Gt. Bar't'n	26	Aug. 30, '62	k Oct. 2, '62
O'Brien, Robert, Sergt.	Sheffield	28		i June 21, '65
Schemmerhorn, Martin, Sgt.	Gt. Bar't'n	21		a Sep. 19, '64
Seeley, George A., Sergt.	Gt. Bar't'n	18		i June 21, '65
Stannard, Levi M., Sergt.	Sheffield	23		i " 21, '65
Bailey, William H., Corp.	W.S'brid'e	36		i " 21, '65
Deming, Henry J., Corp.	Sheffield	18	Aug. 8, '62	i " 21, '65
Dunbar, William H., Corp.	N. Marlb'o	21	Aug. 30, '62	i " 21, '65
Hall, John Alvin, Corp.	" "	26		i " 21, '65
Moren, Michael, Corp.	" "	21		a May 12. '64
Pineo, George J., Corp.	Gt. Bar't'n	28		i June 21, '65
Shook, George L., Corp.	W.S'brid'e	23		h Oct. 18. '64
Stannard, Valentine, Corp.	N. Marlb'o	21		i June 21, '65
Strong, Albert L., Corp.	Sheffield	21		g
Strickland, Erastus, Corp.	Gt. Bar't'n	23		j May 3, '65
Warner, George, Wag.*	Hatfield	32	Jan. 20, '64	f June 21, '65
Barnam, Edgar	Sheffield	18	Dec. 27, '63	f " 21, '65
Barnes, William H.	W.S'brid'e	24	Aug. 30, '62	g Ap. 25, '65
Beckwith, Alexander	Alford	29	Dec. 25, '63	j May 16, '65
Blakesley, Charles*	Agawam	24	Dec. 21, '63	a April 6, '65
Blodget, Martin	Sheffield	28	Aug. 30, '62	i June 21, '65
Brazee, Benson	Alford	34		k July 3, '63
Bradley, Judson	W.S'brid'e	27		j May 3, '65
Brewer, Henry	Gt. Bar't'n	22		
Burns, Thomas	" "	18		i June 21, '65
Chapin, George S.	Alford	26		j Ap. 15, '65
Collar, Stephen H.	Sheffield	24		i June 21, '65
Cooney, John W.	S'kbridge	19		b May 26, '65
Darby, Thomas	Sheffield	36		i June 25, '65
Decker, Jacob	N. Marlb'o	18		f Mar. 17, '63
Decker, Rodolphus	Sheffield	18	Aug. 30, '62	i June 21, '65
Durant, Peter	N. Marlb'o	45	Aug. 30, '62	c Ap. 11, '63
Estes, Enos	Alford	48		j Jan. 7, '63
Ferry, James	Sheffield	23		June 27, '65
Fitzgerald, Timothy	N. Marlb'o	26	Jan. 25, '64	k July 12. '64
Ford, Rufus M.	W.S'brid'e	26	Aug. 30, '62	i June 21, '65
French, Albert B.	" "	20	Aug. 30, '62	g Jan. 27, '64
Fuarey, Charles H.		22		i June 21, '65
Fuarey, James M.	" "	43		j Mar. 21, '63
Gleason, Buel	Gt. Bar't'n	20		b May 17, '64
Gleason, Edwin P.		22		g Ap. 26, '65

Name and Rank.	Residence.	Age	Date of Muster	Term. Service.
Gleason, Miles P.		18	Aug. 30, '62	i June 21, '65
Gorham, Grove	Sheffield	19		i " 21, '65
Halsey, Nathan W.	Gt. Bar't'n	22		g
Hamilton, Trafton*	Greenfield	18	Feb. 22, '62	i Feb. 23, '65
Harper, Edward	Sheffield	21	Aug. 30, '62	j Oct. 30, '62
Hart, George L.*	Egremont	24	Dec. 21, '63	f June 21, '65
Hart, Hiram	Sheffield	45	Aug. 30, '62	" 13, '65
Hatch, Elijah P.	Gt. Bar't'n	50		c Oct. 18, '63
Hayes, Wilson	Sheffield	28		i June 21, '65
Hecox, James*	N. Marlb'o	21	Dec. 21, '63	f " 21, '65
Hedger, Nathan J.	Sheffield	28	Aug. 30, '62	c Aug. 11, '64
Holmes, Morrison A.	S'kbridge	27		i June 21, '65
Holmes, Richard A.	Alford	45		i " 21, '65
Jacote, Jules A.	N. Marlb'o	21		k Oct. 14, '63
Jackson, William H.		23		May 30, '65
Jones, George W.	S'kbridge	22		May 25, '65
Kelly, John	Sheffield	18		k Oct. 14, '63
Knight, Andrew J.		23		j Sept. 4, '65
L'Hommedieu, William H.	Gt. Bar't'n	20		June 17, '65
Manvil, John M.	Sheffield	27		g Jan. 6, '64
Martin, Charles C.	Gt. Bar't'n	19		i June 21, '65
Markham, Lafayette*	" "	21	Mar. 24, '64	f " 21, '65
McCabe, Thomas, 2d	S'kbridge	30	Aug. 30, '62	a May 12, '64
McConnell, Arthur	Gt. Bar't'n	35		Ap. 23, '63
McCormick, James	N. Marlb'o	30		i June 21, '65
Miller, Christopher	Gt. Bar't'n	18		i " 21, '65
Miller, Cornelius	S'kbridge	44		Feb. 13, '63
Mills, Frederick	"	44		c Ap. 21, '63
Moran, James	Greenfield	19	Jan. 25, '64	a May 21, '64
Moore, John	Gt. Bar't'n	38	Aug. 30, '62	o June 13, '65
Mosier, Lewis M.	W. S'brid'e	22		b June 19, '64
Mozier Demas		18	Jan. 10, '64	b May 18, '64
Murphy, Edward	Becket	18	Jan. 8, '63	o June 13, '65
Newton, John W	S'kbridge	19	Aug. 30, '62	a May 6, '64
Newton, Solomon D.*	Greenfield	23	Sept. 1), '61	i Jan. 9, '65
O'Brien, Alonzo	Sheffield	24	Aug. 30, '62	k Oct. 6, '63
Ostrom, Josiah. O.	N. Marlb'o	21		b June 23, '64
Orcutt, George W	Gt. Bar't'n	28	Aug. 30, '62	j Ap. 15, '63
Packard, Henry	Alford	21		i June 21, '65
Palmer, George A.	"	21		i " 21, '65
Pease, George	Sheffield	23		i " 21, '65
Pepoon, Louis	S'kbridge	45		j Ap. 11, '63
Pexley, Egbert	Gt. Bar't'n	36		a May 6, '64
Phelps, William H.	Belchert'n	19	Oct. 15, '62	July 2, '65
Prime, John H.	Gt. Bar't'n	22	Aug. 30, '62	j Mar. 19, '63
Purvere, Russell M.*	Agawam	25	Dec. 21, '63	c Ap. 13, '65
Purvere, Rufus*	Greenfield	21	Sept. 10, '61	i June 21, '65
Riley, William	Seekonk	18	Aug. 19, '64	f " 21, '65
Ring, Joseph*	Springfield	21	Dec. 21, '63	f " 21, '65
Russell, Abram	S'kbridge	33	Aug. 30, '62	Jan. 15, '63
Sacket, Trelewney	N. Marlb'o	19		i June 21, '65

Name and Rank.	Residence.	Age	Date of Muster	Term. Service.
Selmier, George	S'kbridge	45	Aug. 30, '62	May 30, '65
Shephard, Frederick S.	Sheffield	18		i June 21, '65
Sherman, George W	Gt. Bar't'n	43		k Oct. 4, '63
Shelley, John		19		i June 21, '65
Shea, Richard		39		Jan. 25, '65
Sikes, Henry	Sheffield	23		j June 17, '65
Slocum, William E.	S'kbridge	18		" 6, '65
Smith, John	Gt. Bar't'n	27		c Ap. 12, '63
Smith, Peter*	Sheffield	32	Dec. 21, '63	f June 21, '65
Stanward, Arlington		26	Aug. 30, '62	i " 21, '65
Sweet, Oscar	S'kbridge	25		o " 5, '65
Tarpy, Daniel	Sheffield	22		i " 21, '65
Taylor, John M.	Alford	32		q
Turner, Egbert	Gt. Bar't'n	22		i " 21, '65
Wagner, James H.	Alford	21		o " 9, '65
Wolcott, John	Gt. Bar't'n	18		a May 6, '64
Webster, Charles	Sheffield	40	Dec. 12, '63	f June 21, '65
Wheelock, William L.	N. Marlb'o	30	Aug. 30, '62	g Ap. 16, '64
William, Austin G.*	Agawam	27	Dec. 21, '63	f June 21, '65
Wright, Luther S.		45	Aug. 30, '63	July 10, '65

Company D.

Name and Rank.	Residence.	Age	Date of Muster	Term. Service.
Bridge, Watson W., 1st Sgt.	W'braham	26	Aug. 30, '62	e Feb. 19, '63
Cowles, Ezra P., 1st Sergt.	W'rthing'n	20		b April 9, '65
Shaw, William H., 1st Sgt.	Cum'ing'n	29		e 2d Lieut.
Sheldon, Flavel K., 1st Sgt.	S'thamp'n	30		e 2d Lieut.
Brines, John H., Sergt.	Ludlow	33		i June 21, '65
Hooker, Edward, D., Sergt.	W'thamp'n	21		e 2d Lieut.
Pepper, Bennett H., Sergt.	L'meadow	19		i June 21, '65
Moody, Frederick A., Sergt.		25		i " 21, '65
Bancroft, Talcott, Corp.	Ch'terfield	40		i " 21, '65
Bisbee, George A., Corp.		22		i " 21, '65
Bissell, John H., Corp.	Goshen	20		i " 21, '65
Chapman, Dwight M., Corp.	L'meadow	19		i " 21, '65
Hamill, David S., Corp.*	Windsor	18	Jan. 20, '64	g Jan. 10, '65
Holbrook, Chester D., Corp.	L'meadow	30	Aug. 30, '62	j Nov. 22, '64
Jones, John, Corp.*	W. S'field	18	Mar. 23, '64	f June 21, '65
Kingsley, William M., Corp.	S'thamp'n	29	Aug. 30, '62	a May 12, '64
Nichols, William J., Corp.	Ch'terfield	20		b May 30, '64
Orr, Samuel, Corp.	L'meadow	28		j May 20, '63
Parsons, William E., Corp.		20		i June 21, '65
Rockwood, John C., Corp.		18		i " 21, '65
Smith, Timothy, D., Corp.	W'braham	24		a April 6, '65
Streeter, George L., Corp.	Ludlow	24		i June 21, '65
Stratton, Albert O., Corp.	W'braham	23		May 30, '65
Walker, Jefferson C., Corp.	L'minister	28		b May 30, '65

Name and Rank.	Residence.	Age	Date of Muster	Term. Service.
Gaffney, John L., Mus.	Chicopee	40	Aug. 30, '62	Prin. Mus.
Sager, George, Mus.†	Taunton	18	Feb. 18, '64	f June 21,'65
Allen, Sylvester W.*	Hinsdale	25	Jan. 21, '64	f " 21, '65
Ashman, John*	Agawam	26	Dec. 21, '63	f " 21, '65
Bartlett, William A.	W'hamp'n	31	Aug. 30, '62	g Dec. 15, '63
Bates, Augustus P.	S'thamp'n	20		i June 21,'65
Bly, Charles H.		19		i " 21, '65
Bramble, Henry	Ludlow	32		k Oct. 16, '62
Brewer, Walter G.	W'braham	19		i June 21,'65
Brookings, David I.	Boston	21	April 20, '64	j " 20, '65
Brooks, Francis	W'braham	18	Aug. 30, '62	k Feb. 8, '65
Bryant, Sylvanus C.	Ch'terfield	22		b May 19, '64
Burcham, Amaziah E.	Ludlow	21		i June 21,'65
Burt, Edward	L'meadow	22		b " 2, '64
Calkins, Horatio R.	W'braham	30		i " 21, '65
Chapin, Henry G.	Springfield	20	Sept. 6, '62	i " 21, '65
Chapin, John C.	Greenfield	18	Aug. 5. '62	i " 21, '65
Clark, George C.	S'thamp'n	21	Aug. 30, '62	a May 6, '64
Clapp, William H.*	Agawam	30	Dec. 21, '63	k Feb. 10, '65
Clement, William M.	Ludlow	23	Aug. 30, '62	o June 7, '65
Collier, Daniel G.	Ch'terfield	26		j Sept. 2, '64
Collier, Darius	W'rthing'n	24		e Oct. 21, '62
Collier, Horace	Ch'terfield	24		c Feb. 9, '64
Collier, Thomas W		20		j Jan. 23. '63
Cooley, Clavin S.	Ludlow	31		i June 21,'65
Cross, Cyrus W	W'braham	20		i " 21. '65
Cummings, Lee*	Sheffield	27	Dec. 21, '63	f " 21, '65
Currie, Daniel D.	Ludlow	25	Aug. 30, '62	b May 16, '64
Daggett, George C.	L'meadow	30		g Sep. 16, '63
Dorgan, James	Cum'ing'n	19		c June 18, '64
Dwight, Wilbur F.	Cheshire	18		k Oct. 9, '63
Eddy, Samuel E.	Ch'terfield	40		June 9, '65
Fuller, Sumner P.	W'braham	35	Sept. 2, '62	d Aug.10, '64
Gray, George W		19	Aug. 30, '62	j Oct. 15, '64
Green, Daniel	L'meadow	35		i June 21, '65
Hadley, Edmund P.	Lunenbu'g	18	Dec. 19, '63	j " 20, '65
Hale, Albro C.	Westfield	19	Sept. 2, '64	i " 21, '65
Hall, Henry	L'meadow	36	Aug. 30, '62	i " 21, '65
Hannum, Frederick M.	S'thampt'n	19		i " 21, '65
Hitchcock, Alfred	L'meadow	19		c Aug. 7, '64
Hitchcock, William W	Agawam	29	Feb. 25, '64	j Sep. 29, '64
Hoag, Timothy W	M'gomery	21	Aug. 30, '62	i June 21, '65
Hyde, John S.	S'thampt'n	21		a May 6, '64
James, Justin E.	W'hamp'n	25		j Mar. 29, '63
Keyes, John F	W'braham	18		June 28,'65
Knox, Barnabas C.	L'meadow	45		j Mar. 6, '63
Knowlton, Charles B.	Springfield	19		i June 21, '65
Knowlton, Daniel		30		h Ap. 13, '64
Law, Edward	Lanesboro	19	Jan. 16, '64	f June 21, '65
Lemon, Francis O.	W'braham	44	Aug. 30, '62	j Jan. 8, '63
Mansfield, Charles W	L'minster	21		i June 21,'65

ROSTER. xxvii

Name and Rank.	Residence.	Age	Date of Muster	Term. Service.
McCray, Benjamin F.	W'braham	32	Aug. 30, '62	j May 16,'65
McGee, Hugh	W'msburg'	26	Feb. 20, '64	j Feb. 14, '65
Meyer, Carl	Cambridge	29	Jan. 25, '64	f June 21,'65
Mills, Thomas J.	W'braham	20	Aug. 30, '62	g Nov. 18, '63
Mokler, Thomas	Ludlow	25		k Oct. 16, '62
Munsell, Enos W.	W'braham	18		j Dec. 21, '62
Munsing, Michael	Ludlow	43		g Oct. 4, '64
Murphy, Patrick	Springfield	19	Jan. 20, '64	f June 21, '65
Nash, Charles W	Ludlow	28	Aug. 30, '62	i " 21, '65
Neff, Jacob	W'braham	25		g Dec. 15, '63
Niles, Sumner L.	W'thamp'n	22		i June 21,'65
Orr, John	L'meadow	33		k " 18, '63
Packard, Charles*	Pittsfield	22	Dec. 21, '63	f " 21, '65
Parker, Joseph A.	W'braham	18	Jan. 4, '64	f " 21, '65
Parsons, Dwight H.	L'meadow	21	Aug. 30, '62	Com. Sgt.
Parsons, Robert	Ludlow	25		c Nov.18, '62
Pease, George	W'braham	18		c Mar. 29, '64
Phelps, Jonathan W.	W'thamp'n	19	Feb. 20, '64	c April 3, '64
Pittsinger, Ephraim W.	Ch'terfield	30	Aug. 30, '62	i June 21,'65
Porter, Hiland	L'meadow	21		i " 21, 65
Porter, Thomas, jr.	Ch'terfield	26		Q. M. Sgt.
Robbins, Darwin C.	Cum'ing'n	22		j Jan. 16, '63
Robbins, William W		22		g Aug.16, '64
Ross, James F.	L'meadow	38		g
Searle, Henry A.	S'thampt'n	20		g Sep. 16, '63
Searle, Reuben S.		18		i June 21,'65
Shaftoe, William, jr.*	Adams	18	Dec. 21, '63	f " 21, '65
Shea, John	L'meadow	21	Aug. 30, '62	b April 7, '65
Sheen, William	Springfield	32		j April 9, '65
Simpson, Frederick Dwight	S'thampt'n	18		c June 22,'64
Smith, John D.	Ch'terfield	20		a May 6, '64
Speight, John,	W'braham	21		i June 21.'65
Staples, Charles E.†	Taunton	24	Jan. 20, '64	f " 21, '65
Stacy, James A.	W'braham	18	Aug. 30, '62	h Ap. 10, '64
Taylor, Myron D.	L'meadow	19		c Mar. 18, '64
Taylor, Nathaniel P.	—		Jan. 4, '64	d Aug. 15,'64
Thompson, William		29	Aug. 30, '62	i June 21.'65
Trotier, Paul	S'thampt'n	22		j May 25, '65
Wetherbee, James W.*	Agawam	35	Dec. 21, '63	f June 21,'65
Winica, Elbridge G.	W'braham	43	Aug. 30, '62	g Nov. 6, '63
Worthington, John M.*	Westfield	24	Dec. 21, '63	a Sep. 19, '64
Wolcott, George M.	S'thampt'n	21	Aug. 30, '62	a May 6, '64
Wood, Spencer H.	L'meadow	18		g Oct. 4, '64

Company E.

Name and Rank.	Residence.	Age	Date of Muster	Term. Service.
Cushman, H. A., 1st Sgt.†	Taunton	16	Dec. 26, '63	e 2d Lieut.
Nye, John W., 1st Sergt.*	Lee	22	Dec. 21, '63	e 2d L'eut.

ROSTER.

Name and Rank.	Residence.	Age	Date of Muster	Term. Service.
Prickett, Jesse, 1st Sergt.*	Springfield	20	Dec. 21, '63	e 2d Lieut.
Fields, Darwin R., Sergt.	Adams	34	Sept. 2, '62	June 9, '65
Hadlock, Harvey L., Sergt.	Ashfield	18		i June 21,'65
Partridge, John M., Sergt.	Adams	20		a May 6, '64
Sherman, Thomas B., Sgt.†	Abington	29	Dec. 26, '63	f June 21,'65
Wheelock, F. L., Sergt.	Adams	21	Sept. 2, '62	i " 21, '65
Cane, Arthur M., Corp.	Savoy	20		i " 21, '65
Couch, Willet H., Corp.	Cheshire	22		i " 21, '65
Davis, Theodore, Corp.		21	Aug. 30, '62	i " 21, '65
Dean, Samuel J., Corp.	W'mstown	18		i " 21, '65
Kelly, Patrick, Corp.		36	Dec. 9, '63	f " 21, '65
O'Neal, Daniel, Corp.	Adams	25	Sept. 2, '62	i " 21, '65
Rouse, John B., Corp.		34		h Ap. 21, '64
Tanner, Luther M., Corp.		22		b May 18, '65
Welch, Richard, Corp.	W'mstown	37		i June 21, '65
White, David D., Corp.	Cheshire	18		i " 21, '65
Peters, Charles A., Mus.*	Springfield	23	Mar. 20, '64	j May 16, '65
Babbitt, Charles M.	Adams	33	Sept. 2, '62	i June 21, '65
Baldwin, William W	W'mstown	24		i " 21, '65
Boss, Adam	Windsor	22		k Aug. 28, '62
Boss, John		29		k Oct. 2, '62
Billings, Stephen H.	Gt. Bar't'n	31		f June 21,'65
Bowen, James L.	Adams	20		j Ap. 21, '64
Brown, Jay	Cheshire	19		i June 21, '65
Brooks, Milton	Adams	22		i " 21, '65
Bryant, Walter B.	W'mstown	19	Dec. 15, '63	f " 21, '65
Bulman, William	Adams	34	Sept. 2, '62	k Oct. 2, '63
Caswell, Hiram K.*	Westfield	28	Dec. 21, '63	f June 21,'65
Clancy, Patrick	Cheshire	20	Sept. 2, '62	k Aug. 26, '63
Cleary, Patrick	Gt. Bar't'n	34		i June 25, '65
Cline, George E.	W'mstown	40		c
Collins, Patrick		31		
Conklin, Ebenezer		18	Dec. 14, '63	f June 21,'65
Cook, Albert H.*	Westfield	22	Dec. 21, '63	f " 21,'65
Cook, Ansel R.	Adams	18	Sept. 2, '62	i " 21,'65
Cook, Dwight	Northfield	17	Dec. 7, '63	f " 21,'65
Crittenden, Urbane H.	Adams	27	Sept. 2, '62	a May 6, '64
Crossett, Frederick W		22		o May 22, '65
Daniels, Francis	W'mstown	18	Aug. 30, '62	j Feb. 5, '63
Davis, James	Adams	18	Sept. 2, '62	b June 18, '64
Dempsey, Philip		25		k Aug. 26,'63
Dingman, Martin V. B.	W.S'bridge	30	Dec. 23, '63	f June 21,'65
Eddy, Benjamin F.	Cheshire	19	Sept. 2, '62	i " 21, '65
Edwards, Thomas B.	Savoy	18		c Jan. 12, '63
Elston, William	W'mstown	40		i June 21,'65
Fletcher, James M.		18		i " 21,'65
Fletcher, Lucius D.		32		j Dec. 6, '63
Fulton, Richard	Adams	30		a May 6, '64
Furron, George F.*	Westfield	18	Dec. 21, '63	i Dec. 6, '64
Ginn, John N.*	Pittsfield	18	Mar. 17, '62	i Mar. 18, '65
Grace, John	Cheshire	22	Sept. 2, '62	i June 21,'65

ROSTER.

Name and Rank.	Residence.	Age	Date of Muster	Term. Service.
Gregson, Edward	Adams	26	Sept. 2, '62	i June 21,'65
Gurney, Charles	Cum'ing'n	23		b July 10, '63
Halsey, Colonel D.	Gt. Bar't'n	18		a May 18, '64
Haley, George	W'mstown	34		i June 21,'65
Harrington, Alonzo	Cheshire	19		i " 21, '65
Hathaway, John W.	Savoy	26		j Mar. 31, '63
Hathaway, William R.	Cheshire	32		j " 28, '63
Henderson, William H.	Lee	23	Jan. 5, '64	a April 6, '65
Hogle, Samuel W	Adams	40	Sept. 2. '62	j Sep. 8, '64
Horn, Hiram	W'mstown	43		i June 21,'65
Jeffers, Joel J.	Clarksbu'g	40		k
Kelly, John	Adams	21		i " 21. '65
Kelly, Michael	W'mstown	24	Dec. 12, '63	a Ap. 2, '65
Kidder, George		44	Sept. 2. '62	g Jan. 15. '64
Lawloa, James J.	W'msburg	18	Dec. 16. '63	g
Leonard, Lewis	W'mstown	44	Sept. 2. '62	c Ap. 11, '63
Lewis, Daniel	Adams	24		g Jan. 15, '64
Lobdell, Edward R.		21		i June 21,'65
Lobdell, Joel J.		23		a June 4. '64
Loomis, Charles H.	Gt. Bar't'n	35		i June 21,'65
Lovell, Osmand H.	Adams	19		j Mar. 30, '63
Luce, Henry L.	Ashfield	24		j July 1, '65
McCormick, Michael	Adams	22		i June 21,'65
McGrah, Dennis		21		j June 24,'65
McMahon, John	W'mstown	21		i June 21,'65
Mead, Michael		21		k Oct. 14, '63
Mead, Thomas W		22		k Oct. 2, '63
Meany, Patrick†	Fall River	19	Dec. 21, '63	f June 21,'65
Meacham, James	Cum'ing'n	34	Sept. 2, '62	k Oct. 2. '62
Morgan, Leonard	Adams	19		i June 21,'65
Morgan, Richard E.	Gt. Bar't'n	22		j Nov. 13, '63
Mulcare, Patrick	Adams	23		k Oct. 14, '63
O'Brien, William	W'mstown	21		c Nov. 16, '62
O'Conner, Patrick†	Dorchester	21	Dec. 26, '63	f June 21,'65
O'Connell, Stephen	Adams	22	Sept. 2, '62	k Oct. 14. '63
O'Connell, William		27		c Feb. 17, '63
Olds, James H.	Gt. Bar't'n	18		g Oct. 17. '64
Osborne, Hubert P.*	Russell	20	Nov. 30, '63	June 15,'65
Parsons, Warner	Clarksbu'g	22	Sept. 2, '62	i " 21, '65
Perkins, Henry E.*	Westfield	24	Dec. 21, '63	f " 21, '65
Perkins, James H.	Adams	21	Sept 2. '62	a July 3, '63
Pettit, William J.		20		g
Phelps, Edwin E.		28		j May 15, '65
Phillips, Howard W.†	Easton	25	Jan. 20, '64	f June 21,'65
Pucell, William†	Fall River	32	Dec. 26. '63	f " 21, '65
Regan, David		25	Mar. 8, '65	f " 21, '65
Rice, Levi A.	Adams	24	Sept. 2, '62	i June 21,'65
Riley, Patrick		18		i " 21,'65
Rivet, Joseph		20		a May 6, '64
Roberts, George		23		o July 1, '65
Rowell, Daniel M.*	Westfield	20	Dec. 21, '63	f June 21,'65

Name and Rank.	Residence.	Age	Date of Muster	Term. Service.
Sargent, Theodore*	Westfield	20	Dec. 21, '63	f June 21, '65
Sears, George H.	Adams	18	Sept. 2, '62	j May 24, '63
Sherman, Francis		25		a May 6, '64
Sherman, Philip H.	Savoy	33		d June 22, '64
Simmons, William J.	Cheshire	23		j Jan. 18, '65
Slater, Henry	Adams	33		i June 21,'65
Stickney, John	W'mstown	21		j May 16, '65
Stowell, John W.†	Westford	19	Nov. 27, '63	i June 21,'65
Stone, William	Adams	32	Sept. 2, '62	" 15, '65
Sullivan, Bartholomew	B'nardston	33	Dec. 22, '64	f " 21, '65
Taylor, Darius W	Ashfield	32	Sept. 2, '62	j Jan. 8, '64
Temple, Henry R.	Cheshire	23		k July 3, '63
Thompson, George W.*	Greenfield	24	Jan. 13, '64	Feb. 11, '65
Van Bramer, Jacob	Gt. Bar't'n	28	Sept. 2, '62	i Feb. 18, '63
Van Tassell, Henry	Adams	44		c Sep. 13, '63
Walden, Nelson E.		21		i June 21, '65
Wallace, Thomas*	Westfield	35	Dec. 23, '63	j Mar. 3, '65
White, Edwin R.	W'mstown	19	Sept. 2, '62	i June 21,'65
Wilcox, Giles D.	Clarksbu'g	21		i " 21, '65
Wolf, Henry E.	B'nardston	36	Dec. 22, '64	f " 21, '65
Wright, Allen†	Marshfield	18	Dec. 26, '63	f " 21, '65
Wright, Francis H.	W'thamp'n	22	Sept. 2, '62	c Feb. 18, '63
Wright, Orsemus H.	W'mstown	23		k June 18,'63

Company F.

Name and Rank	Residence.	Age	Date of Muster	Term. Service.
Cooke, George E., 1st Sergt.	Amherst	22	Aug. 30, '62	e 2d Lieut.
Graves, Edwin, 1st Sergt.	Hatfield	38		b May 21, '64
Jones, George N., 1st Sgt.	Hadley	26		c 2d Lieut.
Lewis, William E., 1st Sgt.	Ware	23		e 2d Lieut.
Taylor, Joseph K., 1st Sgt.	Granby	21		b Aug. 30, '64
Bardwell, Charles S., Sergt.	Whately	26		e 2d Lieut.
Beston, John, Sergt.	Amherst	20		i June 21,'65
Coville, Emerson L., Sergt.	Hatfield	25		j Jan. 7, '65
Farley, Frederick A., Sgt.	Coleraine	30		e 2d Lieut.
Field, John W., Sergt.	Hatfield	27		a May 6, '64
Hanks, Edwin C., Sergt.	Amherst	20		i June 21,'65
Lyman, Warren J., Sergt.	Hadley	31		j May 28, '63
Wiley, Ebenezer F., Sergt.	Sund'rland	22		g
Dunbar, John M., Corp.	Ware	19		a May 6, '64
Fish, Francis W., Corp.	Amherst	31		i June 21,'65
Foster, Joseph W., Corp.	Ware	20		j Oct. 14, '65
Hodge, Samuel, Corp.	Hadley	26		i June 21,'65
Mahogany, Edw. A., Corp.	Sund'rland	20		i " 21, '65
Pooley, John, Corp.*	Chicopee	40	Dec. 21, '63	f " 21, '65
Stockbridge, S. L., Corp.	Hadley	21	Aug. 30, '62	j Feb. 22, '63
Thessier, Moses, Corp.		19		i June 21,'65

Name and Rank.	Residence.	Age	Date of Muster	Term. Service.
Tisdale, Estes F., Corp.	Ware	28	Aug. 30, '62	i June 21, '65
Turner, Charles F., Corp.	Amherst	25		i " 21, '65
Kellogg, Albert H., Mus.		18		i " 21, '65
Chaffin, Lysander, Wag.	Worcester	21		i " 21, '65
Allis, Earnest A.	Whately	19		j Mar. 10, '63
Baggs, Frederick L.	Bernards'n	27		i June 21,'65
Ball, Nelson O.*	Amherst	22	Dec. 21, '63	g Feb. 2, '65
Barry, James	N'thamp'n	18	Feb. 7, '65	f June 21,'65
Bardwell, Orange	Whately	19	Aug. 30, '62	a May 6, '64
Bartlett, Reuben E.	Shutesb'y	19		i June 21,'65
Bartlett, William	Ware	44		g May 6, '63
Beaman, Edwin D.	Hadley	19		j Mar. 16, '64
Beals, John J.		21		c Feb. 22, '63
Beston, Dennis,	Amherst	18	July 2, '64	i June 21,'65
Beston, Patrick		18	Aug. 30, '62	j May 16, '65
Brown, Robert	Whately	18	Nov. 10, '63	f June 21,'65
Champney, William A.	Hatfield	19	Aug. 1, '62	Hos. Stew.
Connor, John	Amherst	21	July 26, '64	i June 21,'65
Cooley, George L.	Sund'rland	22	Aug. 30, '62	i " 21, '65
Cooke, Willard S.	Amherst	23		i " 21, '65
Coville, Clavin N.	Hatfield	27		i " 21, '65
Coville, Elihu		18		b July 22, '63
Crandall, Joel	Shutesb'y	31		i June 21,'65
Crocker, Frederick B.	Sund'rland	26		a " 21, '64
Cummings, Otis	Ware	21		c Dec. 11, '62
Curtis, David B.	Hatfield	30		i June 21,'65
Cutter, Consul B.	Leverett	44	Dec. 25, '63	j " 13, '65
Dickinson, Levi P.	Amherst	20	Aug. 30, '62	j Jan. 17, '64
Dodge, Philip M.	Leverett	23	Dec. 21, '63	f June 21,'65
Doebrick, Henry	S. Hadley	41	Aug. 30, '62	i " 21, '65
Dunbar, James L.	Ware	21		i " 21, '65
Enderton, George F.	S. Hadley	18		i " 21, '65
Fahay, William	Amherst	25		i " 21, '65
Fales, Henry J.	Hadley	29		c April 1, '63
Field, Edgar H.	Whately	18		b May 10, '64
Foster, William A. P.*		24	Sept. 1, '61	i Dec. 6, '64
Franklin, Benjamin R.	Amherst	19	Aug. 30, '62	i June 21,'65
Fuller, William	Pittsfield	21		i " 21, '65
Glazier, Henry B.	Leverett	18	Dec. 11, '63	f " 21, '65
Glazier, John A.	Amherst	22	Aug. 30, '62	j May 17, '63
Glazier, William R.	Leverett	19	Dec. 11, '63	f June 21,'65
Graves, William O.	Amherst	36	Aug. 30, '62	i " 21, '65
Gushee, Samuel M.	Taunton	20	Feb. 12, '65	j " 21, '65
Hartwell, Francis E.*	Montague	19	Jan. 20, '64	f " 21, '65
Hemenway, John*	Greenfield	18	Dec. 21, '63	f " 21, '65
Hodge, Charles D.	Hadley	35	Aug. 30, '62	i " 21, '65
Horton, James W	Montague	32		j May 23, '65
Hubbard, Charles E.	Hatfield	22		j Ap. 18, '63
Hubbard, Martin S.	Sund'rland	21		a May 12, '64
Johnson, Eben M.*	N thamp'n	24	Jan. 20, '64	f June 21,'65
King, Jerome E.	Hatfield	26	Aug. 30, '62	i " 21, '65

Name and Rank.	Residence.	Age	Date of Muster	Term. Service.
Lamb, David P.	Ware	19	Aug. 30, '62	j Feb. 8, '65
Leggett, John A.	W. H'n, Ct	21		g Jan. 18, '65
Leggett, William F.		19		a April 6, '65
McDonald, James*	Medford	27	Dec. 21, '63	f June 21,'65
McGrath, John	N'thamp'n	21	Feb. 9, '64	f " 21, '65
McGlinn, Thomas	Springfield	18	Feb. 2, '62	f " 21, '65
Mell, Henry A.	Whately	23	Aug. 30, '62	i " 21, '65
Meservey, William D.	S. Hadley	30		i " 21, '65
Miller, John D.	Hadley	28		j Mar. 1, '64
Morse, Richard D.	Charlest'n	40	Jan. 14, '64	f June 21,'64
Munsel, Charles C.	Amherst	30	Aug. 30, '62	Feb. 23, '63
Nash, George W.	Hadley	17		j Ap. 13, '65
Pearson, Edmund R.	S. Hadley	19		i June 21,'65
Pease, John F.	Whately	21		i " 21, '65
Post, Flavius A.	S. Hadley	37		o May 22, '65
Pratt, Albert A.	Shutesb'y	32	Feb. 16, '64	c Sep. 4, '64
Pratt, Levi J.	Leverett	18	Dec. 14, '63	June 20,'65
Preston, Neville	S. Hadley	21	Aug. 30, '62	b May 27, '64
Robbins, Reuben S.*	Belchert'n	32	Dec. 21, '63	j June 7, '65
Rogers, Joseph J.	Ware	24	Aug. 30, '62	a May 6, '64
Russell, Clement H.	Hadley	18		June 12,'65
Sanderson, Edward E.	Whately	24		o " 9, '65
Sanderson, James K.	Amherst	18		b May 12, '64
Sanderson, Samuel E.	Whately	18		i June 21,'65
Shipple, Melzarl	Fitchburg	18	Aug. 1, '64	j May 23,'65
Sietz, Lorenz	Hatfield	30	Aug. 30, '62	i June 21,'65
Smith, Joseph F.	Hadley	19		i " 21, '65
Smith Samuel D.		26		i " 21, '65
Smith, William J.	Amherst	40		i " 21, '65
Spellman, Timothy		18		j Jan. 17, '6–
Squires, Charles O.	Hadley	20		j Nov. 10, '64
Stearns, Luther G.	Whately	28		i June 21,'65
Stearns, Stephen G.		21		i " 21, '65
Stockbridge, Francis J.	Hadley	18		i " 21, '65
Taft, Eathan A.	Amherst	21		c Feb. 3, '63
Thayer, Samuel M.		31		j Mar. 30, '63
Tisdale, James W.	Ware	44		j July 12, '63
Vining, John H.	Hatfield	37		b June 12,'64
Vining, Oliver S.		33		j Ap. 16, '63
Waite, Austin A.	Whately	19		i June 21,'65
Waite, Charles P.	Hatfield	24		c Feb. 13, '63
Waite, Chauncey	Whately	33		b June 27,'64
Wait, Marshall M.	Greenfield	19	Dec. 21, '63	f " 21, '65
Warner, Oliver	Hatfield	31	Aug. 30, '62	i " 21, '65
Wetmore, Davis L.	S. Hadley	18		i " 21, '65
Wheeler, Francis P.	Hadley	21		j May 6, '65
Whitmore, George D.	Sund'rland	22		b Ap. 13, '65
Wood, Edwin E.	Roxbury	22	Jan. 20, '64	f June 21,'65

Company G.

Name and Rank.	Residence.	Age	Date of Muster	Term. Service.
Harris, Erastus W., 1st Sgt.	N'thamp'n	29	Aug. 30, '62	e 2d Lieut.
Taylor. Albert G., 1st Sgt.		21		i June 21,'65
Taylor, Edward D., 1st Sgt.	Agawam	27		e 2d Lieut.
Abbott, William F., Sergt.	S. Hadley	25		i June 22, '65
Abbott, Hubbard M., Sergt.	N'thamp'n	23		Sgt. Maj.
Bartlett, Levi H., Sergt.	N'thamp'n	21		i " 21. '65
Follansbee, Joseph, Sergt.	Springfield	25		e 2d Lieut.
Knapp, William M., Sergt.	N'thamp'n	19		a May 6, '64
Ludden, Waldo, Sergt.		34		i June 21, '65
Morrill, William C., Sergt.		21		e 2d Lieut.
Parent, Oniseme A., Sergt.		23		i June 21, '65
Stockwell, J. Wesley, Sgt.		22		e 2d Lieut.
Tanner, Vincent H., Sgt.	Springfield	25		a Sep. 19, '64
Banks, John E., Corp.	N'thamp'n	23		a Aug. 21,'64
Bartlett, Edmund M., Corp.		44		June 5, '65
Beauchmin, Calixte, Corp.		23		a April 2. '65
Church, Theodore, Corp.	S. Hadley	28		a May 5, '64
Dayton, Franklin O., Corp.	Springfield	28		i June 21, '65
Dunnakin, Henry A., Corp.*	Hadley	25	Dec. 21, '63	f " 21, '65
Hutchins. Osborn C., Corp.	N'thamp'n	34	Aug. 30. '62	i " 21. '65
Houghton, Richard, Corp.		22		i " 21, '65
McKnight, Thomas, Corp.		32		k Oct. 14, '63
Nichols, Samuel E., Corp.		20		e 2d Lieut.
Pratt. Horatio P., Corp.		30		i June 21, '65
Todd, Ira, Mus.		24		i July 2. '65
Stowell, Edward C., Wag.		28		i June 21, '65
Abbott, George B.	N. Andov'r	19		j Feb. 12, '63
Ackors, William	N'thamp'n	32		c Oct. 8, '63
Aldrich, Ira		33		i June 21, '65
Aldrich, Jonathan J.		37		i " 21. '65
Allis, Austin J.		26		i " 21. '65
Ames, George N.		23		i " 21, '65
Belden, Henry		26		i " 21, '65
Belden, James	Deerfield	19	Nov. 9, '63	o May 23. '65
Belden, Seth	N'thamp'n	22	Aug. 30, '62	a Sep. 19, '64
Bigelow, Charles H.*		36	Dec. 21, '63	f June 21. '65
Bigelow, William H.		19	Aug. 30, '62	o " 12, '65
Bird, Ozro M.		18		i " 21. '65
Birge, Simon		39		i " 21. '65
Birge, William C.		36		j Feb. 24, '65
Bishop, Charles	S. Hadley	25		i June 21. '65
Brew, Michael*		18	Dec. 21, '63	f " 21, '65
Bridgman, Edmund P.	N'thamp'n	28	Aug. 30, '62	i " 21, '65
Brooks, Samuel		33		i " 21, '65
Buckman, Ofden D.		33		i " 21, '65
Burnhardt, John		30		j May 30, '63
Bushman, Joseph		24		a May 6, '65
Carter, John W.		28		i June 21, '65
Clapp, George C.		29		j Ap. 13, '65
Clark, Horace P.		19		i June 21. '65

Name and Rank.	Residence.	Age	Date of Muster	Term. Service.
Colson, Christopher C.	N'thamp'n	22	Aug. 30, '62	o June 12,'65
Colson, Edward W.		18	Oct. 28, '63	
Congdon, David		38	Aug. 30, '62	g
Cornwell, Norman S.*		25	Dec. 21, '62	j Jan. 6, '65
Cunningham, Joseph		34	Dec. 9, '63	f " 21, '65
Damon, William H.		21	Aug. 30, '62	j Feb. 25, '63
Dawes, Lander J.		18		i June 21, '65
Dayton, Henry E.	Springfield	24		k Oct. 14, '63
Day, Luke	N'thamp'n	22		i June 21, '65
Dickinson, Ashley W		22		i " 21, '65
Doane, Henry R.		29		o " 9, '65
Dumphries, Thomas		18		i " 21, '65
Edwards, Charles S.*		25	Dec. 21, '63	f " 21, '65
Edwards, George W.		38	Aug. 30, '62	i " 21, '65
Ely, William A.		19		i " 21, '65
Evans, Charles W.*	Hatfield	20	Jan. 20, '64	f " 21, '65
Farrall, William	N'thamp'n	19	Aug. 30, '62	k Oct. 14, '63
Follansbee, John T.	Groveland	19	Nov. 11, '63	a Sep. 19, '64
Frost, Augustus S.	Springfield	36	Aug. 30, '62	j May 1, '63
Gouch, Francis A.	N'thamp'n	34		j Nov. 17, '63
Graves, Elisha, jr.		29		o June 6, '65
Halbert, Dolphus		37		j Ap. 19, '65
Harris, Legar R.		19		c May 1, '64
Holmes, Miles		33		c Aug. 9, '63
Janes, Pascal		19		a June 18, '64
Kellogg, Charles A.		19		k July 1, '63
Kinney, Albert C.		18		j Aug. 21, '63
King, Otto	Greenfield	22	Nov. 18, '63	f June 21, '65
Kingsley, Theodore P.	N'thamp'n	21	Aug. 30, '62	i " 21, '65
Lanier, Louis		23		c Feb. 5, '63
Lathrop, Adelphus D.	Springfield	26		c Jan. 28, '63
Leon, Alexander	N'thamp'n	22	Nov. 22, '63	f June 21, '65
Leonard, Henry		18	Aug. 30, '62	c April 1, '64
Leouard, Jay	Agawam	26		i June 21, '65
Lucore, Solomon D.	N'thamp'n	30		i " 21, '65
Marcy, John		23		i " 21, '65
May, Joshua		42		i " 21, '65
Mitchel, James		33		i June 8, '65
Moody, Lucian	S. Hadley	18		i " 21, '65
Moore, Maurice	N'thamp'n	24		a May 6, '64
Munyan, Alfred J.		23		o Aug. 1, '65
O'Brien, John		18		i June 21, '65
Ockington, Edwin B.	Deerfield	24		o May 24, '64
Parent, Nepthali	Springfield	19	Jan. 26, '64	g Oct. 15, '64
Parent, Samuel	N'thamp'n	19	Aug. 30, '62	i June 21, '65
Pfiel, Ernst Q.		34		i " 21, '65
Phelps, Charles W.		21		i " 21, '65
Powell, Oscar C.		30		o " 15, '65
Pratt, Henry L.		25		k Oct. 14, '63
Royce, Charles H.	Pittsfield	18		e 57th Regt.
Rushford, Mitchell	N'thamp'n	26		k Sep. 12, '63

Name and Rank.	Residence.	Age	Date of Muster	Term. Service.
Smith, Charles W	N'thamp'n	23	Aug. 30, '62	i June 21, '65
Stikes, Jerome B.		25		i " 21, '65
Stockwell, Austin H.		22		j Feb. 28, '63
Stockwell, Lewis F.		42		i June 21, '65
Temple, Henry D.		31		a May 6, '64
Train, Orson E.		41		i June 21, '65
Whitney, John		30	Dec. 23, '63	f " 21, '65
Whitney, William	Springfield	22	Aug. 30, '62	a May 6, '64

Company H.

Name and Rank.	Residence	Age	Date of Muster	Term. Service.
Partridge, Thos. J., 1st Sgt.	W'msburg	25	Aug. 30, '62	b Ap. 12, '65
Ferrell, Andrew J., 1st Sgt.	E'hampton	24		i June 21, '65
Vincent, Albert H., 1st Sgt.	Hawley	21		e 1st Lieut.
Warner, Almon M., 1st Sgt.	Plainfield	19		e 2d Lieut.
Cook, Alexander P., Sgt.	Granby	19		i June 21, '65
Cook, Edson A., Sergt.	R'tland, Vt	28		j May 12, '64
Dunnivan, Patrick. Sergt.	W'msburg	19		j June 15, '65
Johnson, George C., Sgt.	Conway	20		i " 21, '65
Larkins, Ira, Sergt.	Hawley	25		a May 18, '64
Miller, David B., Sergt.	W'msburg	31		a April 6, '65
Parsons, Alpheus W., Sgt.	E'thamp'n	21		j Ap. 14, '63
Porter, Richard M., Sergt.	W'msburg	27		c Aug. 29, '64
Ames, Moses S., Corp.		34		a Sep. 19, '64
Cobb, Freeman L., Corp.	Hawley	24		i June 21, '65
Crandall, Thomas J., Corp.	Adams	18		a " 1, '64
Field, Henry H., Corp.	Hatfield	19		i " 21, '65
Hill, Andrew J., Corp.	E'thamp'n	20		i " 21, '65
Sandford, Merritt S., Corp.	L'meadow	20	Dec. 21, '63	f " 21, '65
McCaffrey, Edward, Corp.	W'msburg	21	Aug. 30, '62	o " 9, '65
McDowell, William, Corp.	Belchert'n	23		j Dec. 27. '62
Phillips, William G., Corp.	W'msburg	25		i June 21, 65
Streeter, Lorenzo, Corp.	Plainfield	30		j Nov. 21, '63
Allen, Albert C.	Belchert'n	23		j Jan. 12, '64
Ames, Myron	W'msburg	30		g Feb. 11, '64
Averill, William H.	Conway	40		c Jan. 10, '65
Bartlett, Lyman C.	W'msburg	22		a May 12, '64
Beals, Leander J.	Hunting'n	28		j Ap. 27, '63
Bell, William	Belcher'tn	32		k June 20, '63
Blossom, James W *	L'meadow	21	Dec. 21, '63	f " 21, 65
Bigelow, Samuel	Conway	43	Aug. 30, '62	j Dec. 31, '63
Bishop, Francis	Belchert'n	41		k Oct. 13. '63
Blackmer, Hiram		40		c June 15, '63
Blood, Ebenezer T.	Conway	31		d Sep. 19, '64
Blood, Miles H.	Pittsfield	18		a " 19, '64
Blythe, Marshall	E'thamp'n	18		i June 21, '65
Brackett, Freeman	Hawley	28		c July 12, '64
Bradford, Lyman A.	Conway	19		j Ap. 20, '63

Name and Rank	Residence.	Age	Date of Muster	Term. Service.
Bragel, Thomas	W'msburg	21	Nov. 30, '63	i June 21, '65
Carpenter, George	Savoy	21	Aug. 29, '62	Aug. 23, '64
Carle, Thomas	Buckland	24	Dec. 21, '63	f June 21, '65
Chamberlin, Dwight B.	Belchert'n	31	Aug. 30, '62	j Sep. 22, '63
Chamberlin, Norris		29		j Feb. 25, '65
Chapman, Henry B.	E'thamp'n	21		j " 7, '63
Childs, Otis	Conway	19		j " 23, '63
Clark, Charles H.	E'thamp'n	20		g Ap. 15, '64
Clark, Charles N.	M'tgomery	21		g Oct. 15, '64
Cook, Nelson M.	Plainfield	22		j Aug. 18, '63
Cook, William H.	W'msburg	27		d Sep. 2, '64
Cowan, Emery E.	"	21		g July 2, '63
Davis, Henry G. W	W'mstown	18	Dec. 12, '63	j May 19, '64
Dix, E. Stillman	Charlem't	42	June 27, '64	j Ap. 18, '65
Dole, Augustus O.	Buckland	18	Aug. 30, '62	f June 21, '65
Dorsey, John	Cum'iug'n	39		i " 21, '65
Dwight, David B.	Belchert'n	34		g Mar. 3, '64
Elder, Robert	W'msburg	20		a June 5, '64
Fahey, David	E'thamp'n	18		i " 21, '65
Flowers, Raymond C.	Belchert'n	23		c Jan. 5, '63
Fontine, Simon	Greenfield	19	Nov. 19, '63	f June 21, '65
Gaffuey, John*	N. Adams	21	Dec. 21, '63	f " 21, '65
Galligan, Peter*		25		f " 21, '65
Garry, John	N'thamp'n	35	Aug. 11, '64	f " 21, '65
Gillett, Emulus B.	Belchert'n	43	Aug. 30, '62	c Dec. 15, '62
Graves, Henry, jr.	E'thamp'u	20		i June 21, '65
Green, Levi R.*	N. Adams	26	Dec. 21, '63	f " 21, '65
Harrington, William H.*	Adams	28	Jan. 20, '64	f " 21, '65
Hathaway, William E.†	Taunton	25		f " 21, '65
Herman, John*	Adams	28		j Dec. 8, '64
Hillman, James W.	W'msburg	21	Aug. 30, '62	i June 21, '65
Hillman, Jerome E.		28	Dec. 15, '63	f " 21, '65
Hitchcock, Henry H.	Cum'ingt'n	21	Aug. 30, '62	i " 21, '65
Hogeucy, Philo	Belchert'n	33		i " 21, '65
Houghtling, Christopher*	Coleraine	24	Dec. 23, '63	f " 21, '65
Jenkius, Rosser*	Agawam	30	Dec. 21, '63	f " 21, '65
Johnsou, William	N'thamp'n	18	Nov. 10, '63	f " 21, '65
Joslyn, Lorenzo	Belchert'u	20	Aug. 30, '62	k Sep. 30, '64
Kane, Daniel W.	E'thamp'n	18		c Dec. 16, '62
Kel'ogg, Frank H.	W'msburg	18		j Ap. 20, '63
Keplinger, John S.		18		i June 21, '65
Kittridge, Henry G. W.†	Newtou	20	Dec. 26, '63	f " 21, '65
Leech, Lorenzo	Belchert'n	21	Aug. 30, '62	i " 21, '65
Lemau, David		24		k Dec. 28, '62
Leving, John	N'thamp'n	19	Nov. 22, '63	f June 21, '65
Ligard, Louis	Hadley	18	Nov. 25, '63	m May 6, '64
Lilly, Casper	Ashfield	28	Aug. 30, '62	c Ap. 23, '63
Lilly, Joel		35		o June 27, '65
Lombard, Napoleon	Greenfield	21	Nov. 18, '63	f " 21, '65
Londergon, Michael	W'msburg	21	Dec. 17, '63	k Sep. 28, '64
Lord, James F.	Dorchester	22	Dec. 26, '63	f June 21, '65

Name and Rank.	Residence.	Age	Date of Muster	Term. Service.
Madden, William	W'msburg	28	Aug. 30, '62	j Feb. 19, '64
Maginly, Thomas*	Coleraine	24	Dec. 21, '63	g
McArthur, James*	Adams	18	Jan. 4, '64	f June 21, '65
Merritt, Arthur T.	W'msburg	22	Aug. 30, '62	a May 6, '64
Merrifield, Lucius W.	Conway	18		i June 21, '65
Nichols, Edward P.	N'thamp'n	36		j Jan. 5, '64
Owen, Andrew B.	Belchert'n	18		i June 21, '65
Parsons, Lyman W.	Goshen	24		i " 21, '65
Peck, Edward	Hawley	44		j Mar. 17, '63
Perkins, Calvin N.	Buckland	35		i June 21, '65
Pettit, Robert C.*	Agawam	21	Dec. 21, '63	f " 21, '65
Peters, William L.	Pittsfield	26	Aug. 30, '62	k Feb. 19, '63
Ramsdell, Horace C.	Belchert'n	25		d Oct. 1, '64
Rice, Clark G.	W'msburg	20		i June 21, '65
Rouse, Ashbell W.*	Adams	34	Dec. 21, '63	f " 21, '65
Rowe, Frederick E.	Conway	18	Aug. 30, '63	j " 29, '63
Ryan, Thomas	W'msburg	31		k " 20, '63
Sandling, John	Amherst	21	Nov. 10, '63	j May 16, '65
Scars, Edmund H.	Hawley	21	Aug. 30, '62	a " 11, '64
Sears, Urbane	Savoy	26		c Nov. 12, '62
Shaw, Lyman A.	Belchert'n	19		i June 21, '65
Shelden, James W.*	Adams	21	Jan. 20, '64	f " 21, '65
Smith, Frederick E.	Belchert'n	19	Aug. 30, '62	c Ap. 14, '63
Smith, John H.		21		g Mar. 15, '64
Smith, Warren M.*	Adams	21	Jan. 20, '64	f June 21, '65
Snow, Monroe	Belchert'n	23	Aug. 30, '62	i " 21, '65
Squires, Jerry W		24		i " 21, '65
Stockwell, David	N'thamp'n	33		j May 20, '65
Tafts, Anthony F.	W'msburg	19	Nov. 30, '63	f June 21, '65
Thayer, Jonas H.	Belchert'n	40	Aug. 30, '62	c May 4, '63
Towle, William L.	Savoy	23		i June 21, '65
Turner, Alonzo F.	Hawley	28		g
Vining, Rodolphus	W'msburg	28		g
Von Volkenburg, Charles*	Adams	22	Dec. 21, '63	f June 21, '65
Walker, Charles H.	Whately	18	Nov. 23, '63	j May 2, '65
Walker, Francis	L'meadow	28	Dec. 21, '63	f June 21, '65
Walker, John H.		27		f " 21, '65
Warner, James P.	W'msburg	37	Dec. 16, '62	f " 21, '65
Warner, Stephen G.		40	Aug. 30, '62	a Dec. 13, '63
Warner, Sumner	Conway	22	Jan. 4, '64	a May 6, '64
Whalen, Thomas	Lee	21	Aug. 30, '62	k Oct. 8, '63
Williams, Samuel W.	W'msburg	21		i June 21, '65
Wing, Charles T.	Buckland	22		a May 18, '64
Wood, Sydney P.	Hawley	20		a " 6, '64
Wood, William B.	Leyden	19	Aug. 13, '64	j " 16, '65
Wright, William	W'msburg	28	Aug. 30, '62	g Dec. 19, '04
Wrisley, William M.		23	Dec. 31, '63	f June 21, '64

Company I.

Name and Rank.	Residence.	Age	Date of Muster	Term. Service.
Bartlett, J. F., 1st Sgt.*	Pelham	20	Dec. 21, '63	e 2d Lieut.
Gray, Francis E., 1st Sgt.	Springfield	18	Sept. 2, '62	e 2d Lieut.
Burke, Michael, Sergt.		35		k Sep. 15, '63
Calhoun, William A., Sgt.		21		e 1st Lieut.
Chapman, Henry W., Sgt.		18		i June 21,'65
Cooley, Orrin B., Sergt.*	L'meadow	36	Feb. 20. '64	e 17th Regt.
Hovey, Eugene B., Sergt.	Springfield	24	Sept. 2, '62	i June 21,'65
Johnson, James, Sergt.		38		i " 21, '65
Leonard, Edwin, Sergt.	Agawam	39		i " 21, '65
Luther, Martin, Sergt.	Springfield	18		c May 11, '64
Brown, Albert F., Corp.		19		c Oct. 29, '62
Coomes, Isaac W., Corp.		28		i June 21,'65
Hawks, Josiah B., Corp.		18		a May 12, '64
Hildreth, Watson J., Corp.		19		o May 31, '65
Scott, James L., Corp.*		20	Dec. 21, '63	f June 21,'65
Shaw, Alvin D., Corp,*		23		f " 21, '65
Shaw, Leander R., Corp.		28	Sept. 2, '62	i " 21, '65
Strong, Leander, Corp.		22		i " 21, '65
Stockwell, Wm. C., Corp.		20		a " 18, '64
Trask, Samuel E., Corp.		20		i " 21, '65
Hyde, William, Mus.		23		i " 21, '65
Murphy, John, Wag.*	Buckland	39	Jan. 20, '64	f " 21, '65
Angeline, Michael	Springfield	30	Sept. 2, '62	g Sep. 13, '63
Armstrong, Jeremiah		18		g Mar. 16, '64
Armstrong, Willard		22		g Mar. 2, '64
Bailey, Giles A.	Agawam	18		c Dec. 20, '63
Baker, Cornwall	Springfield	33		i June 21. '65
Barnes, Daniel G.	Agawam	24		j Sep. 30, '64
Barrett. Horace J.	Springfield	34		i June 21,'65
Blake, Heber	S. Hadley	36	Feb. 29, '64	j Dec. 16, '64
Bean, John G.	Auburn	18	Sept. 2, '62	d Dec. 29, '64
Brannon, John	Springfield	30		k Oct. 3, '63
Bragel, Thomas	W'msburg	21	Nov. 30, '63	i June 21,'65
Bresnahan, Patrick	Springfield	21	Sept. 2, '62	k Aug. 15,'63
Brett, Patrick*	Montague	37	Dec. 21, '63	f June 21,'65
Burton, Henry B.	Ware	23		f " 21, '65
Burns, James W	Agawam	18	Sept. 2, '62	c Mar. 8, '64
Carpenter, Albert H.	Springfield	21		j May 16, '65
Chilson, Frank		34		j Feb. 24, '63
Clark, Albert R.	Agawam	21		a May 9, '64
Clynes, Peter	Springfield	26	Sept. 2, '62	k Oct. 25, '63
Cole, Cyrus*		44	Jan. 5, '64	f June 21,'65
Cook, Henry		18	Sept. 2, '62	i " 21, '65
Daley, William		35		c Jan. 8, '64
Decker, Clarkson H.		21		a June 5, '64
Deverereaux, George L. A.		25		o May 1, '65
Devlin, Mark		36		i June 21,'65
Dunn, Edward		38		c July 30,'64
Edwards, George P.		27		a Ap. 2, '65
Gibbons, William V.		23		i June 21,'65
Gifford, Martin S.		27		i " 21, '65

Name and Rank.	Residence.	Age	Date of Muster	Term. Service.
Giline, Francois	Springfield	23	Sept. 2, '62	j Feb. 8, '63
Gilligan, Oscar J.	W'braham	27	Nov. 20, '64	f June 21,'65
Green, Henry J.	Buckland	38	Sept. 2, '62	i " 21,'65
Hanaford, Charles H.	Auburn	20		i " 21, '65
Hartwell, George B.	Springfield	18		i " 21, '65
Hetherston, Martin C.†	Quincy	22	Dec. 26, '63	f " 21, '65
Hickox, Fred D.	Springfield	18	Sept. 2, '62	o May 28, '65
Hosmer, George C.		21		o Ap. 26, '65
Jones, Lyman		43		i June 21,'65
Kenny, John		21		i " 21, '65
Kenny, Patrick M.		30		g Sep. 13, '6-
Keogh, Henry		26		i June 21,'65
King, Edward S.		34		a May 21, '64
Knight, John L.*		25	Dec. 21, '63	f June 21,'65
Lashaway, John	S. Hadley	41	Feb. 27, '64	f " 21, '65
Lee, James O.	Springfield	32	Sept. 2, '62	c Sep, 9, '63
Lenox, Lewis	S'kbridge	23	Aug. 27, '64	j Dec. 7, '64
Leonard, Francis	Agawam	18	Sept. 2, '62	i June 21,'65
LePine, Alfred		20		j Jan. 25, '65
Walker, James	Springfield	28		Dec. 31, '64
McGrath, James		23		j Ap. 4, '64
Millard, Rufus W.*		38	Dec. 21, '63	f June 21,'65
Moran, Thomas		24	Sept. 2, '62	i " 21, '65
Moulton, Albert S.		21		i " 22, '65
Mullin, Patrick*	Greenfield	23	Dec. 21, '63	f " 21, '65
Norris, John	Holyoke	32	Sept. 2, '62	i " 21, '65
O'Brien, Patrick	Agawam	21		l Jan. 18, '64
O'Brien, Patrick H.†	Fall River	32	Feb. 27, '64	f June 21,'65
O'Neal, Michael	Granby	44	Jan. 4, '64	f " 21, '65
Oliver, William	Springfield	29	Sept. 2, '62	i " 21, '65
Packer, Edward H.	Agawam	22		i " 21, '65
Parker, Allen F.	Springfield	18		i " 21, '65
Parent, Louis	Chicopee	21		g July 18, '63
Pease, Augustus E.	Springfield	24		a Sep. 19, '64
Pease, Erastus B.		21		a June 3, '64
Peck, Charles H.†	Taunton	20	Dec. 20, '63	f " 21, '65
Phelps, Harlin S.	Springfield	25	Sept. 2, '62	i " 21, '65
Pike, George H.		22		j Nov. 11,'62
Plant, John M.		35		j Feb. 3, '65
Plant, Peter		25		j Mar. 14, '64
Quivillon, Joseph B.	Ware	20	June 27, '62	June 27, '65
Ramsdell, Samuel D.†	Hanson	43	Jan. 17, '62	j Jan. 27, '65
Randall, Edward E.†	Easton	18	Jan. 31, '62	i Jan. 30, '65
Reed, Joseph	Keene, N.H	21	Sept. 16, '62	Aug. 7, '63
Remington, Benjamin F.*	Egremont	24	Dec. 21, '63	f June 21,'65
Rogers, Hiram†	Taunton	38	Dec. 26, '63	f June 21,'65
Rowley, Charles S.	Springfield	23	Sept. 2, '62	j Dec. 8, '62
Sears, Edward S.		18		i June 21,'65
Seel, Charles		28		k Aug. 5, '63
Shay, Daniel		21		k Oct. 25, '63
Shannon, Philip		26		k Aug. —,'62

Name and Rank.	Residence.	Age	Date of Muster	Term. Service.
Smeddy, Morris†	A'hburn'm	27	Jan. 18, '64	f June 21,'65
Smithe, Robert†	Fall River	21	Dec. 26, '63	f " 21, '65
Sullivan, Dennis		41	Sept. 2, '62	Feb. 28,'65
Stockwell, Charles E.		18		c Feb. —, '64
Tewhill, John	Holyoke	26		i June 21,'65
Thayer, Edwin S.†	Hanson	25	Jan. 30, '62	i Jan. 27, '65
Tilson, Ichabod A.†	Carver	22	Feb. 19, '62	i Feb. 14, '65
Trafton, George R.†	Dighton	19	Jan. 6, '62	j Jan. 20, '65
Ufford, Charles D.*	Holyoke	27	Dec. 21, '62	f June 21,'65
Ufford, Edwin M.	Springfield	19	Sept. 2, '62	i " 21, '65
Wadsworth, Samuel		17		i " 21, '65
Ward, Patrick C.		31		o May 30,'65
Wentworth, Edwin O.		29		a May 12, '64
Winslow, Henry L.		34		i June 21,'65
Wilbur, Levi S.		22		g Aug. 10,'63
Wilcox, John	N. Adams	23		a May 6, '64
Williams, Thomas	Agawam	24		Feb. 28,'65
Winslow, Shubael M., jr.*	Springfield	23	Dec. 21, '63	h Ap. 24, '64
Withington, Henry†	Canton	31	Feb. 7, '62	i Feb. 12, '65

Company K.

Name and Rank.	Residence.	Age	Date of Muster	Term. Service.
Casey, Michael, 1st Sergt.	Pittsfield	19	Sept. 2, '62	e 2d Lieut.
Harrigan, Michael, 1st Sgt.	Springfield	26	Sept. 4, '62	e 2d Lieut.
Shay, John C., 1st Sergt.		22		k June 7, '63
Hamilton, William, Sergt.	W'msburg	21		i June 21,'65
O'Connor, James, Sergt.	Springfield	26		e 2d Lieut.
Driscoll, Dennis, Corp.		25	Sept. 2, '62	b May 29, '63
Ellsworth, Thomas, Corp.	W'msburg	22		o May 25, '65
Fallon, Thomas, Corp.	Pittsfield	44		j Feb. 28, '63
Howe, Robert, Corp.		44	Sept. 4, '62	y Nov. 28, '63
Lane, William, Corp.	Springfield	27	Sept. 2, '62	k Oct. 13, '63
Rowe, Michael, Corp.	N'thamp'n	22	Sept. 4, '62	o June 9, '65
Welch, James, Corp.*		22	Dec. 21, '63	f June 21, '65
Dolan, Thomas, Mus.†	Taunton	26	Feb. 24, '64	f " 21, '65
Adams, Charles E.*	Agawam	21	Dec. 21, '63	" 21, '65
Anderson, Dennis	Ludlow	18	Sept. 2, '62	i " 21, '65
Andrews, John	N. L., N.J.	19		o May 25, '65
Ball, Charles H. R.	Ware	19		c Jan 26, '63
Ball, John D.*	Amherst	44	Dec. 21, '63	f June 21,'65
Beals, Samuel	Savoy	35	Sept. 2, '62	c Feb. 3, '63
Black, Lewis T.*	W'msburg	23	Dec. 21, '63	f June 21, '65
Bliss, James E.	L'meadow	21	Sept. 2, '62	m'dDec.8,'62
Brown, Scott	Cheshire	43		c Mar. 23, '63
Buckley, Dennis G.	Springfield	19		k Oct. 9, '63
Burrows, Isaac H.†	Fall River	22	Dec. 26, '63	f June 21,'65
Cahill, Michael	Springfield	24	Sept. 2, '62	k Oct. 15, '63

ROSTER. xli

Name and Rank.	Residence.	Age	Date of Muster	Term. Service.
Carroll, John	Florida	25	Sept. 2, '62	i June 21, '65
Casey, James	Gt. Bar't'n	18		b July 5, '64
Chalmers, John	Pittsfield	22		
Clary, Michael	Springfield	28		i June 21, '65
Clough, Edgar*	Chicopee	24	Dec. 21, '63	j Oct. 1, '64
Conn, Charles H.	Springfield	18	Sept. 2, '62	i June 21, '65
Conway, Michael	Chelsea	19		b May 5, '63
Cowden, James C.	Adams	39		j May 16, '65
Crampton, James	N'thamp'n	35		b July 13, '63
Crawford, Samuel*	Springfield	26	Sept. 6, '61	i Sep. 5, '64
Cronin, Timothy J.	Chicopee	24	Sept. 2, '62	g Ap. 15, '64
Cummings, John	Lanesboro	22		j Mar. 7, '64
Dalton, Patrick	Cheshire	21		i June 21, '65
Day, John S.*	Springfield	22	Dec. 21, '63	f June 21, '65
Donlan, Andrew	Pittsfield	26	Sept. 2, '62	k July 1, '63
Donnely, William	Athol	43	July 27, '64	o May 19, '65
Duggan, Edmund	W'msburg	18	Dec. 17, '63	f June 21, '65
Evans, George*	Palmer	26	Dec. 21, '63	f June 21, '65
Evens, John	Chicopee	28	Sept. 2, '62	i June 21, '65
Fallon, Patrick J.	Pittsfield	18		o June 3, '65
Farrell, Christopher		44		g Ap. 15, '64
Foley, William	Lee	44		j May 16, '65
Fortune, John	N'thamp'n	18		i June 21, '65
Frazier, William H.	D'chester	44	July 21, '64	f June 21, '65
Freeman, Michael	Springfield	21	Sept. 2, '62	a May 12, '04
Garvey, John		21		k Sep. 13, '63
Gunn, Charles S.	Amherst	18		i June 21, '65
Hake, Eber	W'msburg	24	Sept. 4, '62	i " 21, '65
Harrington, Jeremiah	Springfield	27		k Sep. 27, '63
Hayes, William	Chicopee	26		k Oct. 13, '63
Healey, Michael F.	Needham	21	Dec. 14, '64	f June 21, '65
Hickey, Charles*	N'thamp'n	21	Dec. 21, '63	g
Higgins, John	Sheffield	30	Sept. 4, '62	g Oct. 29, '63
Hopkins, Andrew	Chicopee	35		j Dec. 6, '63
Hussey, Patrick	Pittsfield	21		a July 3, '63
Jones, Ira L.*	Enfield	23	Dec. 21, '63	f June 21, '65
Kelly, John	Hadley	25	Jan. 26, '65	f " 21, '65
Kenady, John	Springfield	21	Sept. 2, '62	f " 21, '65
Kennedy, Martin*	Boston	22	Dec. 8, '63	f " 21, '65
Kilroy, James*	Leverett	20	Dec. 21, '63	f " 21, '65
Kilkelly, Michael	Springfield	21	Sept. 2, '62	i June 21, '65
Loftes, Nicholas†	Fall River	41	Feb. 18, '64	j Ap. 24, '65
Lombard, Dexter W.	Springfield	18	Sept. 2, '62	i June 21, '65
Londergan, James*	N'thamp'n	20	Feb. 29, '64	o June 9, '65
Madden, Patrick	Springfield	40	Sept. 4, '62	k July 7, '63
Maloney, John	W.S'brid'e	18		a June 11, '64
Maloney, John, 2d	Springfield	24		i June 21, '65
Maloney, William	W.S'brid'e	43		j June 4, '63
Manning, John	Springfield	22		
Manning, Timothy T.	Chicopee	28		o Mar. 7, '65
McCarthy, John D.	Springfield	22		i June 21, '65

ROSTER.

Name and Rank.	Residence.	Age	Date of Muster	Term. Service.
McCormick, James	Ashfield	20	Dec. 24, '64	f June 21, '65
McGechin, John	Pittsfield	33	Sept. 4, '62	i June 21, '65
McGregory, Albert B.	Wilbrah'm	19	Dec. 26, '63	f June 21, '65
McLaughlin, John	B'chert'wn	18	Sept. 4, '62	o May 26, '65
McNamara, Timothy	Springfield	21		a May 6, '64
Meehan, Michael	N'thamp'n	32		l July 28, '63
Miner, Charles T.	Conway	43	Aug. 2, '62	f June 21, '65
Moffit, William	E'thamp'n	18	Dec. 24, '63	f " 21, '65
Mohan, Patrick	Lee	18	Sept. 4, '62	i " 21, '65
Monahan, Patrick	Springfield	18		j Dec. 29, '62
Morrisey, Edward*	Agawam	24	Dec. 21, '63	i June 21, '65
Morrisey, John*	Springfield	23	Jan. 20, '64	f June 21, '65
Morin, Joseph	Springfield	28	Sept. 4, '62	k Mar. 28, '63
Moriarty, Timothy	Chicopee	22		i June 21, '65
Mulligan, James A.		24		j Feb. 7, '63
Mulloy, Michael	Boston	29		g Nov. 18, '63
Mullin, Timothy	L'meadow	18	Jan. 4, '64	a April 6, '65
Murphy, James	Springfield	21	Sept. 4, '62	i June 21, '65
Murphy, John		18		j July 10, '65
Norton, James		20		k Oct. 13, '63
O'Brien, John	S'kbridge	44		d June 26, '64
O'Brien, John, 2d.*	N'thamp'n	22	Feb. 29, '64	f June 21, '65
Paddock, Ichabod S.*	Windsor	24	Dec. 21, '63	f " 21, '65
Pelton, Albert E.*	Agawam	23		c April 20, '65
Perry, James N.†	Fall River	22	Jan. 21, '64	b July 25, '64
Pierce, Patrick	Springfield	23	Sept. 4, '62	k Sep. 30, '63
Potter, Edward T.*	W'msburg	21	Dec. 21, '63	f June 21, '65
Preston, Robert*	Grafton	23	May 18, '64	o July 2, '65
Richardson, George	Springfield	39	Sept. 4, '62	o June 9, '65
Rice, Sylvanus N.*	Agawam	26	Dec. 21, '63	f June 21, '65
Rodgers, James	Pittsfield	26	Sept. 4, '62	k Oct. 4, '63
Rowe, Thomas F.	N'thamp'n	18	Dec. 21, '63	f June 21, '65
Ryan, Edward	W'msburg	30	Dec. 29, '63	j Dec. 29, '64
Scully, Michael	Springfield	22	Sept. 4, '62	k Oct. 13, '63
Shannon, Thomas	Pittsfield	21	Feb. 24, '62	f June 21, '65
Shanley, William F.		41	Sept. 4, '62	j Aug. 24, '63
Smith, Henry*	Barre	22	Dec. 21, '63	f June 21, '65
Squires, John E.*	S. Hadley	25		f " 21, '65
Spellman, Charles E.*	L'meadow	20		f " 21, '65
Staples, Edward E.†	Taunton	23	Jan. 20, '64	f " 21, '65
Thompson, George W.*	Springfield	20	Jan. 13, '64	f " 21, '64
Tilden, Nathaniel J.	Whately	42	Sept. 4, '62	c Dec. 28, '62
Tootles, Edward†	Fall River	32	June 15, '61	f June 21, '65
Turner, Charles R.*	Becket	19	Nov. 13, '63	f " 21, '65
Wademan, Peter	Pittsfield	20	Sept. 4, '62	j Ap. 15, '63
Walsh, Patrick J.	Springfield	27		k Sep. 19, '63
Warrilton, William*	L'meadow	20	Dec. 21, '63	f June 21, '65
Welsh, John	Pittsfield	22	Sept. 4, '62	i June 21, '65
Whittaker, James	B'chert'n	18		o July 26, '65
Wiggins, Henry A.*	Springfield	23	Dec. 21 '63	f June 21, '65
Willis, George E.†	Easton	26	Feb. 26, '62	i Jan. 27, '65

Name and Rank.	Residence	Age	Date of Muster	Term. Service.
Wilbur, Lloyd†	Fall River	20	Dec. 26, '63	f June 21, '65
Winters, Philip	Sheffield	52	Sept. 4, '62	j Feb. 25, '63
Witherell, Albert*	N'thamp'n	25	Dec. 21, '63	f June 21, '65

UNASSIGNED RECRUITS.

Name and Rank.	Residence.	Age	Date of Muster	Term. Service.
Benton, Henry S., 1st Sgt†	Taunton	20	Dec. 26, '63	b July 10, '65
Chace, Joseph A.†	Fall River	21	June 15, '61	f June 21, '64
Crossley, George E.†	Marshfield	30	Dec. 26, '63	f " 21, '65
Eldridge, Jeremiah C.†	Taunton	30	Jan. 20, '64	f " 21, '65
Harding, Christopher†	Fall River	40	Dec. 26, '63	a June 16, '64
Lovett, Patrick*	N'thamp'n	40	Dec. 21, '63	a July 12, '64
Reinhart, Robert*	Pittsfield	21	April 1, '62	a Aug. 21, '64

☞ In the columns of "Residence" and "Date of Muster" blanks signify the date or name above them.

[The above Roster is compiled from the records of the Adjutant General of Massachusetts. A multitude of errors have been corrected, but it cannot be hoped that the list is perfect. The roster of officers is especially misleading in its dates unless reference is made to the explanations in the body of the book.]

INDEX

A.

Abbott, Sgt. Major, H. M., 201, 318; Lieut., 384–5.
Alarms, 117, 229, 295, 372, 404.
Allen, Capt. E. A., 64; Major, 125, 244.
Andrew, Gov. John A., 42 et seq., 48, 58, 221.
Angle, battle of the, 292; second battle, 317.
Antietam, battle of, 38; battle-field, 80.
Army of the James, 327, 400, 409, 414.
Army of the Potomac, changes in, 30, 36, 82, 104, 135, 168, 267.
Atlanta, siege and capture of, 393.

B.

Bailey's Cross Roads, camp at, 427.
Ball's Bluff, battle of, 26.
Baltimore, 22, 71, 213, 223.
Banks, Gen. N. P., 29, 34, 133, 204, 256.
Bardwell, Color Sergt. C. S., 65, 188; Lieut., 201, 266, 381, 393.
Barlow, Mrs. Gen., 308.
Bassett, Gen. I. C., 398.
Battle-field scenes, 152, 190, 382.
Battle-flags captured, 295, 377, 411, 420.
Berlin, Md., 89, 198.
Berryville, camp at, 374.
Big Bethel, battle of, 24.
Blackmer, Lieut. E. T., 103.
Bliss, Capt. William, 244.

Bolton, Sergt. S. M., 421.
Bradley, Lieut. J. S., 125, 266, 385, 418, 423.
Brandy Station, camp at, 235, 243 257.
Bridgman, Lieut. Edward Q. M., 125, 358.
Brigade, in 2d Div., 267; in 1st Div., 346.
Briggs, Gen. H. S., 49, 59, 73, 75 et seq., 197.
Bristoe Station, battle of, 227.
Brooks, Gen., 135, 151, 168, 328.
Browne, Col. W. H., 83, 136, 140, 150.
Buchanan, President, 17, 19.
Buell, Gen., 127.
Bullock, Gov. A. H., 57.
Bull Run, battle of, 25; second battle, 35; the field, 229.
Burnside, Gen. 28, 82, 95, 106, 114, 117, 134, 245, 252, 271.
Burkesville, camp at, 422.
Bush, Lieut. A. L., 187, 201, 265.
Butler, Gen. B. F., 20, 22, 24, 28, 49, 133, 340.

C.

Calahan, Lieut. J. D., 407.
Calhoun, Lieut. W. A., 384.
Camp Briggs, 59, 68.
Camp Canby, 220, 223.
Camp Chase, 74.
Camp Crehore, 78.
Camp Dodge, 81.
Camp Edwards, 124, 155.

Camp Sedgwick, 257.
"Carleton," quotations from, 305, 309.
Catoctin Mts., 77, 194, 361, 368.
Cedar Creek, 371, 387; battle of, 388 et seq.
Cedar Mountain, battle of, 34.
Chalmers, Lieut. J. C., 103, 244, 281, 383.
Chambersburg, burning of, 366.
Champney, Lieut. J. A., 297; Capt., 377, 383, 412.
Chancellorsville, battle of, 141 et seq.
Chandley, Lieut. G. B., 126; Capt., 406.
Chantilly, battle of, 36; the field, 105, 224.
Chapin, Sergt. G. D., 216.
Charlestown, Va., 370; skirmish at, 372.
Cherry Run, march to, 86.
Chickahominy, crossing the, 338.
Chickamauga, battle of, 247.
Christian Commission, 56, 122, 258, 305, 345, 383.
Cochrane, Gen. J., 83.
Cold Harbor, 326; march to, 329; battle of, 328 et seq.
Colored regiments, 54.
Colt, Adjt. T. G., 64, 166; Capt., 351, 385, 428.
Company A, 63, 196.
Company B, 61, 63.
Company C, 61, 63, 218, 371.
Company D, 61, 63, 122, 153, 156, 221.
Company E, 63, 86, 125, 216, 363, 411, 412.
Company F, 61, 63, 65, 86, 153, 221, 228.
Company G, 61, 63, 65, 196, 218, 221, 228, 363, 371.
Company H, 61, 63, 154.

Company I, 63, 196, 412,
Company K, 62, 63, 427
Confederacy organized, 18.
Cook, Ansel R., 411.
Cooke, Lieut. Geo. E., 266, 297.
Corinth, battle of, 128.
Corps badges and flags, 136.
Couch, Gen. D. N., 83, 104, 135, 168.
Cowles, Sergt. E. P., 417.
Crehore, Surg. C. P., 385.
Crook, Gen., 270, 347, 362.
Crumps Mills, 325.
Cushman, Lieut. H. A., 407, 410, 411, 421, 428.

D.

Dabney's Mills, battle at, 401.
Danville, camp at, 423.
Davis, Jefferson, made president, 18; captured, 425.
Declaration of war, 22.
Desertions, 116, 134, 222, 361. Confederate, 402,
Devens, Gen. Charles, 26, 50, 83, 108, 113, 136, 139, 143, 328, 331.
Dix, Gen. John A., 211.
Dodge, Q. M. Daniel J., 60, 64, 125.
Donaldson, Lieut. D. M., 384, 410.
Donnelly, Capt. Hugh, 66, 267, 334, 380, 396-7, 406.
Dooley, Capt. Peter, 125.
Downsville, camp near, 81, 88.
Draft riot in Boston, 56; in New York, 208.
Dress parade in New York, 218.
Drewry's Bluff, battle of, 328.

E.

Early, Gen. J. A., raid of, 346; threatens Washington, 350; final defeat of, 391.
Eddy, Samuel E., 418.
Edwards, Lieut. C. L., 64, 259; Capt., 266, 410, 417.

Edwards, Major Oliver, 60; Col.,
64, 71, 93, 114, 150, 186, 214, 217,
220; commands brigade, 290, 352,
357, 376; at Winchester, 382, 397;
rejoins brigade, 406; 412, 416;
Gen., 428.
Eighth Mass., 20, 49.
Ellsworth, Col., 24.
Emancipation proclamation, 116.
Eustis, Col. H. L., 83, 150; Gen.,
268, 290.

F.

Fair Oaks, battle of, 31.
Fair View, Md., 85.
Falmouth, camp near, 115.
Field, Color Sergt. J. W., 279.
Fifth Wis., 212, 220, 410.
Final Petersburg, battle of, 410.
Fisher's Hill, battle of, 386.
Five Forks, battle of, 409.
Flagg, Capt. A. S., 122, 154, 266.
Follansbee, Lieut. J., 266, 297.
Fort Fisher, 400, battle of, 408.
Fort Hamilton, camp at, 215.
Fort Steadman, capture of, 408.
Fort Stevens, battle of, 351.
Fort Wadsworth, camp near, 398.
Forty-second Mass., 131.
Forty-sixth Mass., 197.
Fourth Mass., 20, 49.
Franklin, battle of, 394.
Franklin, Gen. W. B., 30, 40, 83, 104,
110, 350.
Frederick, Md., 76.
Fredericksburg, field at, 105; battle
of, 110; scenes in, 146, 303; hospitals at, 304 et seq.
Fuller, Lieut. J. M., 125.
Funkstown, skirmish at, 195.

G.

Gaffney, Prin. Mus. John, 64, 218.
Gaines Mills, battle of, 32.
Gainesville, battle of, 35.

Georgia, march through, 393.
Getty, Gen. George W., 82, 268,
274.
Gettysburg, march to, 171 et seq.;
battle of, 177 et seq.
Goodrich, Lieut. A. E., 60; Lieut.
Col., 64, 125.
Grant, Gen. U. S., 127, 131, 249;
Lieut. Gen., 265.
Gray, Lieut. F. E., 125, 244, 381;
Capt., 407, 410.
Gray, Lieut. R. A., 201, 383.

H.

Halleck, Gen., 33, 36, 127, 168, 223,
397.
Halltown, Va., 367, 373.
Hancock, Gen. W S., 82, 111, 168,
179, 190, 267, 273, 344, 401.
Hancock, Md., march to, 84.
Hanover Court House, 31.
Harlow, Lieut. Col. F. P., 148, 316,
386.
Harper's Ferry, 20, 37, 168, 367, 370,
397.
Harrigan, Lieut. M., 126, 244.
Harris, Lieut. E. W., 103, 201, 381.
Hatcher's Run, affair at, 404 et seq.
Hayden, Capt. J. L., 71, 224, 275,
384.
Hooker, Gen. Joseph, 29, 31, 35, 40,
82, 104, 111, 134 et seq., 168, 226,
252, 303.
Hooker, Sergt. E. D., 378.
Hopkins, Capt. A., 76, 378, 498, 410,
418, 420.
Hospital scenes, 299 et seq.
Howard, Gen. O. O., 135, 178.
Howe, Gen. A. P., 83, 104.
Hudson, N. Y., reception at, 69,
429.
Hunter, Gen. David, 348, 368.
Hurlburt, Captain E., 103.
Hyde, Lieut. G. H., 125; Capt. 386.

I.

Inches, Dr. Charles E., 422.
Incidents and anecdotes, 78, 85, 87, 91, 100, 145, 157, 170, 226, 234, 402.
Iuka, battle of, 128.

J.

Jackson, "Stonewall," 31, 34, 36, 142.
James River, crossing the, 339.
Jerusalem road, 345.
Jetersville, 414.
Johns, Col. T. D., 136, 147.
Johnston, surrender of, 423.
Jones, Lieut. George N., 125, 244, 334; Capt. 407.

K.

Kelley, Capt. J. P., 201.
Kelly's Ford, 234.
Kentucky, events in, 20.
Killed and wounded, 112, 154, 187, 275, 280, 287, 318, 320, 330, 334, 343, 373, 381, 410-11, 421.
Kilpatrick, Gen., raid of, 262.

L.

Lawton, Dr. T. C., 266.
Lee, Col. W. R., 60.
Lee, Gen. Custis, brigade of, 417; captured, 419.
Lee, Gen. R. E., 31; invades Maryland, 37, 41; retreats from Petersburg, 413; surrenders, 421.
Leonard, Sergt. Edwin, 342.
Lincoln, Abraham, election of, 17; inaugurated, 18; official acts, 19, 33, 51, 58, 206, 369; review by, 138; incidents of, 351-2, 356; re-elected, 395; assassinated, 422.
Lincoln, Capt. R. P., 103, 279, 281, 297; Major, 386, 403; Lieut. Col., 407.
Lookout Mountain, battle of, 253.

Loomis, Lieut. J. A., 64, 125, 151, 161, 201, 216; Capt., 320, 363, 378, 385.
Lowell, Gen. C. R., Jr., 390.

M.

Madison Court House, march to, 263.
Malvern Hill, battle of, 31.
Manchester, Md., bivouac at, 130.
Manchester, Va., camp at, 426.
Marye's Hights, 105, 110; battle of, 140 et seq.
Massachusetts Congressmen, 47; ministers abroad, 47.
Massachusetts soldiers, 51 et seq.
McClellan, Gen. G. B., 24, 26, 28 et seq., 36, 94, 395.
Meade, Gen. George G., 82, 110, 135, 168, 177, 315.
Mechanicsville, battle of, 32.
Medals of Honor, 411, 420.
Merrimac, the, 21, 28, 30.
Militia of Massachusetts, 48.
Mine Run campaign, 236.
Missionary Ridge, battle of, 254.
Missouri, events in, 130.
Monocacy, battle of the, 350; camp on the, 369.
Montague, Capt. George L., 65; Major, 64; Lieut. Col., 125, 150, 212; commands regiment, 290; brevet Col., 296; wounded, 297; return of, 336; 358, 363, 371, 376, 379, 382, 396; resigns, 407.
Moody, Capt. M. T., 66; Major, 244, 280, 297, 383.
Morewood, Mrs., presents a flag, 66.
Morgan, Lieut. P. W., 201.
Morrill, Lieut. W C., 384, 407.
Morse, Chaplain F. C., 66, 80, 93, 123, 242, 261, 302, 369, 383, 403, 416, 428.
Mud March, the, 118 et seq.

INDEX.   xlix

Mulloy, Lieut. J. B., 66; Capt., 126, 220, 266.
Murder of J. E. Bliss, 102.
Musketry fire at Angle, 296.
Muster in, 62.

N.

Nashville, battle of, 394.
Naval operations, 27, 28.
Neill, Gen. T. H., 268, 277.
New Baltimore, 93, 229.
New Hope Church, battle of, 392.
Newton, Gen. John, 104, 136, 181.
New York, journey to, 212; service in, 217.
Nichols, Lieut. S. E., 384, 420.
Night marches, 85, 86, 141, 171, 193, 314, 316, 320, 324, 338, 347, 364.
Norfolk navy-yard, 21.
North Anna, affair at, 321 et seq.

O.

O'Connor, Lieut. James, 384, 422.
Opequan Creek, 370; battle of, 375 et seq.
Ord, Gen., 27, 128, 409, 415.

P.

Pamunkey, crossing the, 325, 426.
Parsons, Sergt. D. H., 103.
Paymaster, visits of, 100, 235, 370.
Peake's Station, skirmish at, 325.
Pease, Capt. F. W., 297, 383.
Peninsula, battles on, 31 et seq.; Grant crosses the, 337.
Perryville, battle of, 128.
Petersburg, 339; battle of, 342; surrender, 412.
Phelps, Lieut. Charles, 125, 244.
Philadelphia, 70, 214, 223, 429.
Pittsfield, departure from, 69; return to, 430.
Plunkett, Lieut. T. F., Jr., 125.
Political events, 206, 256.

Ponton bridges, laying of, 106, 140.
Pope, Gen., 33-36, 127.
Port Hudson, 131, 204.
Potomac River, crossing the, 167, 361, 365, 367, 368, 370.
Prickett, Lieut. Jesse, 384, 428.
Promotions after muster out, 431.
Property of U. S. seized, 18.

R.

Railroad accident, 70.
Rapidan, crossing the, 236, 271.
Rappahannock, camp on, 100, 115; crossing, 108, 140, 154, 159.
Rappahannock Station, battle of, 233.
Rations, 96, 170, 228, 321, 324, 344, 429.
Readville, final camp at, 430.
Reams Station, 345, 400.
Reed, Lieut. J. H., 386.
Religious services, etc., 79, 122, 200, 258, 271, 315, 318, 362, 404.
Reviews, 138, 230, 235, 426; at Richmond, 426; at Washington, 427.
Reynolds, Gen. J. F., 104, 135, 178.
Richmond, evacuation of, 413.
Ricketts, Gen. J. B., 82, 349, 363, 388.
Rifle-pits, constructing, 160, 191, 404.
Robinson, Capt. J. C., 244, 410, 428.
Rockwood, Lieut. E. R., 383.
Rosecrans, Gen., 128, 205, 245.
Roster of officers, 62; changes in, 103, 125, 201, 244, 265, 383, 422; the final, 428.
Russell, Col. D. A., 83; Gen., 135, 232, 290, 352; killed, 378.

S.

Sailor's Creek, battle of, 416, et seq.
Salem Church, battle of, 150.
Sanitary Commission, 56, 305, 311, 345, 383, 429.

Savannah, capture of, 394.
Sears, E. S., Q. M. S., 358.
Secession of states, 17, 19.
Second R. I., 83, 87, 108, 334, 380, 427.
Sedgwick, Gen. John, wounded, 40; 82, 135, 145, 152, 155, 176, 230, 239, 262, 267, 273, 276, 283, 287; death of, 288.
Seventh Mass., 83, 147, 339.
Shenandoah river, crossing the, 363.
Shenandoah Valley, 31, 86, 362, 366, 386; farewell to, 396.
Shepardson, Corp. William. 260,
Sheridan, Gen. P. H., 255, 268; cavalry raid, 326; takes command in Valley, 369; at Cedar Creek, 389; at Five Forks, 408; at Sailor's Creek, 416.
Sherman, Gen. W T., 132, 204, 252, 269, 391, 422.
Sickles, Gen. D. E., 135, 143, 182.
Sickness and death, 103, 116, 121, 123.
Sigel, Gen. Franz, 270, 347.
Signal tower, 403.
Sixth Corps organized, 30.
Sixth Mass., 20, 49.
Slocum, General H. W., 83, 135.
Smith, Gen. W. F., 83, 104, 135, 328, 340.
Smith, Lieut. W B., 64, 266, 354; Capt., 407, 421.
Smoky Hill, 101.
Snicker's Gap, 362.
South Mountain, battle of, 38; crossing, 77, 80.
Sparks, Lieut. A. C., 201, 207, 384.
Spencer Rifle, the, 354 et seq., 363, 372, 408, 417.
Sports and pastimes, 61, 260, 406.
Spottsylvania, march to, 285; battle of, 287.

Springfield, reception at, 430.
Stafford Court House, 99.
Statistics of Mass., 55.
Stockwell, Lieut. J. W., 384, 406.
Stone River, battle of, 129.
Stuart, Gen. J. E. B., 84.
Sumter, fall of Fort, 19.
Sumner, Gen. E. V., 20, 40, 82, 104.
Sumner, Senator Charles, 45.
Surgeons' work, 301, 304.

T.

Taggart, Charles A., 420.
Taylor, Lieut. E. D., 385.
Taylor, Lieut. R. H., 384, 386.
Taylor, Sergt. J. K., 373.
Telegrams, seizure of, 23.
Tennessee, events in, 20, 127.
Tenth Mass., 80, 83, 343, 352.
Tents furnished, 117.
Texas, events in, 20, 130.
Thanksgiving day, 90, 236.
Third Mass., 20, 49.
Thirty-fourth Mass., 50, 363, 387.
Thirty-sixth N. Y., 83, 147, 151, 165.
Thomas, Gen., 130, 247, 394.
Tracy, Sergt., C. H., 41).
Trent affair, the, 27.
Troops, calls for, 19, 23, 48, 51, 58.
Truce at Cold Harbor, 334.
Twenty-fifth Mass., 331.
Twenty-seventh Mass., 331.
Twenty-third Mass., 331.
Tyler, Capt. M. W., 125, 297, 336, 365, 381; Major, 407-8.

U.

Underwood, Gen. A. B., 251.
Upton, Col. Emory, 232, 268; Gen., 352, 378-9.

V.

Vallandigham, C. L., 207, 256.
Vermont Brigade, 29, 152, 330, 341, 343.

Veterans consolidated with 37th, 374.
Vicksburg, 131, 202.
Vincent, Lieut. A. H., 386.
Virginia, movements into, 24, 28, 88, 90, 199.

W.

Wadsworth, Gen. J. S., 267, 276, 278.
Wagon trains, 357 et seq.
Warner, Sergt. A. M., 216, 260, 420.
Warren, Gen. G. K., 182, 267, 273, 286.
Warren Station, camp near, 403.
Warrenton, camp near, 200, 230; the town, 231.
Washington, scenes in and about, 23, 26, 72, 75, 351; return to, 365, 397; review at, 427.
Waterman, Lieut. W. A., 384, 407, 428.
Wauhatchie, battle of, 251.
Weldon Railroad, capture of, 399, 403.
Wellman, Lieut. C. C., 103, 279, 384.

Wells, Col. G. D., 387.
West Virginia, events in, 20, 24.
Wheaton, Col. Frank, 83; Gen., 136, 268.
White, Corp. David, 420.
White Plains, 92.
White, Surg. E. M., 266, 385.
Wilderness, battle of, 272.
Willcox, Gen. O. B., 82, 104.
Williamsburg, battle of, 29.
Williamsport, 88, 196.
Wilson, Senator Henry, 46.
Wilson's Station, camp at, 425.
Winchester, 371.
Winter quarters, 115, 121, 243, 308.
Woman's work, incidents of, 57.
Wool, Gen. J. E., 21.
Worcester, camp at, 59.
Wright, Gen. H. G., 168, 232, 267; commands corps, 290, 319, 352; at Cedar Creek, 388.

Y.

Yellow Tavern, battle of, 327.
Yorktown, siege of, 29.

www.ingramcontent.com/pod-product-compliance
Lightning Source LLC
Chambersburg PA
CBHW030321020526
44117CB00030B/279